3/10/17

NOTTINGHAMSHIRE AVIATION DIARY

Aviation Incidents 1930 -1945

A P and R M Glover

TO MARK (LEADER)
'THE MAN'
NOT A MYTH
BUT A LEGEND!
Best Wishes Dave.

Horsburgh Publishing

Nottinghamshire Aviation Diary:
Aviation Incidents from 1930 to 1945

ISBN 978-0-9566159-0-9

First edition published 2010

Published by Horsburgh Publishing,
E-mail: horsburghpublishing@ntlworld.com

Design by A P and R M Glover
Layout by Russell Strong

Printed and bound in England

Contents

Introduction

This book has been compiled after many years of research. The interest began during investigation into our father's service in No.504 (County of Nottingham) Squadron, Auxiliary Air Force during World War Two. We had a general interest in WWII airfields but mainly in those located in the counties of Nottinghamshire, Lincolnshire and Norfolk. Whilst visiting many of these airfields we also discovered local memorials to lost aircrew which then initiated the interest in wanting to know how and why the airmen had died. Rather than spread our investigations and research too wide, as residents of Nottinghamshire, we decided to investigate aircraft accidents and incidents occurring during WWII in and around the boundaries of the county. This was then expanded to include incidents from 1930 to 1945 and other activities associated with aviation.

The book is effectively an aviation diary of Nottinghamshire with the most emphasis placed on the years 1939 to 1945. Within the scope of the book importance is placed on information about the high number of air force personnel lost during this time despite the airfields of the County of Nottinghamshire being mainly used for training purposes, with few operational stations. The losses can be attributable to many things: aircraft engine/structural failure, crew error, crew inexperience especially when the four engine bomber was introduced, enemy aircraft intrusion, inclement weather etc. It was noticeable during the research that a number of aircrew that perished had completed a tour of operations but had been still actively involved in training aircrews in Operational Training Unit's.

The incidents recorded range from aircraft having relatively minor mishaps to those lost during training or operations.

The book documents incidents with relevance occurring in Nottinghamshire; involving aircraft and aircrew flying from local and other airfields; providing a source of local history in memory of those aircrew members who tragically died in such incidents; promoting interest and awareness of local history during World War Two.

Some other significant dates affecting the role of the Air Force have also been chronicled.

The book may well help and inspire other researchers in much the same way as we were by Mr W R Chorley's Bomber Command Losses series of books and the Air-Britain series of books depicting aircraft serial numbers compiled by James J Halley.

Much of the information contained within the book has been obtained from the Air Ministry Aircraft Accident Record Card, AM Form 1180, which was designed to record accidents involving RAF aircraft so that the causes could be analysed and any resulting data could be used in accident prevention (for an example see 8th April 1942). The card was in a form layout and completed by hand, the information being written in the various pre-printed boxes on the cards. Not all copies of these cards are easily read as the hand writing on them can be poor, leading to limited detail and in some cases misleading information. Some of the cards are also difficult to read due to illegibility.

The form contained increasingly more information as time passed by and more experience was gained by the incident investigators.

Bomber Command created a similar card to register the loss of aircraft on operational sorties. These cards were also a pre-printed form which was filled in whenever an aircraft was lost. The data recorded on the cards was then used to try and identify ways of reducing aircraft and aircrew losses.

It was noticeable during the writing of this book that a great number of airmen who were involved in relatively minor incidents in Nottinghamshire were subsequently killed at a later date beyond the Nottinghamshire boundaries and these are chronicled where known.

In the context of the incidents recorded in this book the following grim statistics should be noted. For any given hundred aircrew flying with Bomber Command during World War Two: 51 were killed on operations,

9 killed in crashes in England, 3 seriously injured, 12 were made Prisoners of War, 1 evaded capture and 24 survived unarmed. A total of 55,500 Bomber Command aircrew lost their lives during World War Two. (an extract from 'Aircrew' by Bruce Lewis).

The detailed information contained within the book has been written in good faith and any inaccuracies are the responsibility of the authors.

Finally a poignant quote from English Heritage: 'crash sites have significance for remembrance, commemoration, their cultural value as historic artefacts and the information they contain about both the circumstances of the loss and of the aircraft itself. Crash sites may on occasion also contain human remains, giving them additional value and status as sacred sites and war graves.

...all crash sites should be considered of historic significance and the information they contain should not be needlessly destroyed or removed without adequate record.'

Acknowledgements

The authors would especially like to thank the following for their direct or indirect assistance in compiling some aspects of this book.

Commonwealth War Graves Commission
Department of Research and Information Services, Royal Air Force Museum, Hendon.
Mr M Brooke (49 Squadron Association)
Mr W R Chorley in the production of his series of books 'RAF Bomber Command Losses'
Mr J B Cynk
Mr D Fell and the RAF Elsham Wolds Association
Mr J J Halley and Air-Britain (Historians) Ltd for the production of the Royal Air Force series of books listing aircraft serial numbers and fates.
Mr T Handley 504 Squadron Historian
Mr A Harvell, Photographic services
Mr D Homewood
Mr M J Ingham
Mr Mikkel Plannthin (Denmark)
Ms L Russell, IT services
Mr W Taylor, north Nottinghamshire RAF Historian
Mr A Thomas, Air Historical Branch (AHB) RAF
Mr K Youngs (Aircrew Remembrance Society)
The National Archives Public Record Office, Kew

Sources and Bibliography

Air Historical Branch (RAF)
Auckland Museum, New Zealand
Commonwealth War Graves Commission
Nottingham Evening Post
National Archives of Australia
Public Records Office, Nottingham
Royal Air Force Museum, Hendon; Aircraft Accident Cards
The National Archives Public Record Office, Kew; Operational Record Books (ORB)

The London Gazettes
USAAF/USAF Aircraft Accidents in the United Kingdom and Ireland
Veterans Affairs Canada

Air-Britain (Historians) Ltd:
Broken Wings, Post-War Royal Air Force Accidents, James J Halley
The K File, the RAF of the 1930s, J J Halley
RAF Aircraft, J J Halley, various volumes: L1000-N9999; P1000-R9999; T1000-V9999; W1000-Z9999; AA100-AZ999; BA100-BZ999; DA100-DZ999; EA100-EZ999; FA100-FZ999; HA100-HZ999; JA100-KZ999; KA100-KZ999; LA100-LZ999; MA100-MZ999; NA100-NZ999; PA100-RZ999
RAF Aircraft Flying Training and Support Units, R Sturtivant, J Hamlin, J J Halley
The Halifax File, R N Roberts
The Harvard File, J F Hamlin
The Oxford, Consul & Envoy File, John F Hamlin
The Whitley File, R N Roberts

Aircraft Crash Log: Lancaster, N Roberts
Aircraft Crash Log: Halifax, N Roberts
DH Mosquito Crash Log, David J Smith
Handley Page Hampden & Hereford Crash Log, Nicholas Roberts
The Battle File, Sydney Shail
Vickers Wellington Crash Log, Volume 1 1937-1942, David J Smith

50 Squadron Profiles, Chris Ward
57 Squadron Profiles, Chris Ward
207 Squadron RAF Langar 1942-1943, B Goodwin & R Glynne-Owen
408 (Goose) Squadron Profiles, Chris Ward
Action Stations, Vols 2 and 4, B B Halpenny
Airfield Focus No.28 Swinderby, S Scott
Attack Warning Red, The Royal Observer Corps and the Defence of Britain 1925-1975, D Wood
Aviation in Leicestershire and Rutland, Roy Bonser
Avro Lancaster, The Definitive Record, Harry Holmes, 1997
Avro Manchester, The Legend Behind the Lancaster, Roberty Kirby
Bomber Squadrons of the RAF, P J R Moyes
'But all are Losers', The Air Raids on Nottinghamshire 1940-1944, John Hook
For Your Tomorrow, Vols 1-2, E W Martyn
Netherthorpe at War, Roger North
Northumberland Aviation Diary, Aviation Incidents from 1790-1999, Derek Walton
Nottingham at War, Clive Hardy, N Arthur
Nottingham's War (Evening Post), I Manning
Nottinghamshire & Derbyshire Airfields in the Second World War, Robin J Brooks
Nottinghamshire Evening Post
On the Wings of the Morning, RAF Bottesford 1941-1945, Vincent Holyoak
Polish War Graves, Newark-on-Trent Cemetery, B Clements and R L Grasse
RAF Bomber Command Losses, Vols 1-9, W R Chorley
RAF Fighter Command Losses of the Second World War, Vols 1-3, N Franks
RAF Flying Training and Support Units, R Sturtivant, J Hamlin, J J Halley
RAF Winthorpe, 1940-1945, W Taylor
The Bomber Command War Diaries: An Operational Reference Book 1939-1945, Martin Middlebrook and Chris Everitt
The History of RAF Stations Ossington and Gamston, World War Two, W Taylor
The Polish Air Force at War, The Official History, 1939-1943, Jerzy B Cynk
The Polish Air Force at War, The Official History, 1943-1945, Jerzy B Cynk
They Shall Not Grow Old, L Allison, H Hayward; Commonwealth Air Training Plan Museum
Twelve Days in May, Brian Cull and Bruce Lander with Heinrich Weiss.
White Rose Base, Brian J Rapier
Yorkshire Airfields in WWII, P Otter

Glossary of Terms

AA	Anti-aircraft
AACU	Anti-aircraft Co-operation Unit
AA School	Air Armament School
A&AEE	Aeroplane and Armament Experimental Establishment
AAS	Air Armament School
AC1	Aircraftman First Class
AC2	Aircraftman Second Class
AFM	Air Force Medal
AFS	Advanced Flying School
Air Gnr	Air Gunner
ANS	Air Navigation School
A/P/O	Acting Pilot Officer
A/Sgt	Acting Sergeant
ARP	Air Raid Precautions
AS	Armament School
ASI	Air Speed Indicator
A/S/L	Acting Squadron Leader
ATC	Air Training Corps
Aux	Auxiliary
BAT Flt	Blind Approach Training Flight
BCIS	Bomber Command Instructors School
BDT	Bomber Defence Training
BDTF	Bomber Defence Training Flight
BEM	British Empire Medal
Capt	Captain
CFS	Central Flying School
CGS	Central Gunnery School
Chance Light	Similar to a small searchlight
CO	Commanding Officer
Cpl	Corporal
CSU	Constant Speed Unit
CU	Conversion Unit
CWGC	Commonwealth War Graves Commission
DFC	Distinguished Flying Cross
DFM	Distinguished Flying Medal
DSO	Distinguished Service Order
E&W	Electrical and Wireless
EFTS	Elementary Flying Training School
ERFTS	Elementary and Reserve Flying Training School
Flt	Flight
F/Eng	Flight Engineer
F.F.I.	French Forces of the Interior
F/L	Flight Lieutenant
F/O	Flying Officer
Flak	Anti-aircraft fire
FP	Ferry Pool
FPP	Ferry Pilots Pool
FRS	Flying Refresher School
F/S	Flight Sergeant
FTC	Flying Training Control
FTS	Flying training school
G/C	Group Captain
GCF	Group Communication Flight
GPEU	Glider Pilot Exercise Unit
GSU	Group Servicing Unit
(H)	Hellenic
HCU	Heavy Conversion Unit
HE	High explosive
HF	High Frequency
Hrs	Hours
I/C	Intercommunication
K	Day decoy airfield
LAC	Leading Aircraftman
LF	Low Frequency
LFS	Lancaster Finishing School
Lt	Lieutenant
MCU	Mosquito Conversion Unit
MD	Doctor of Medicine
Mph	Miles per hour
MU	Maintenance Unit
MUAG	Mid-upper Air Gunner
Nav	Navigator
Navex	Navigation exercise
O/C	Officer Commanding
Op	Operation
ORB	Operational Record Book
OS	Ordnance Survey
OTU	Operational Training Unit
PAF	Polish Air Force
(P)AFU	(Pilots) Advanced Flying Unit
(P)FTS	Polish Flying Training School
P/O	Pilot Officer
POW	Prisoner of War
PRFU	Pilots Refresher Flying Unit
PRO	Public Records Office
(P)SFTS	(Polish) Service Flying Training School
Q	Lighting decoy for airfields
QDM	International Q-code Signal for Magnetic course to Steer

QF	Small fire decoy	SFTS	Service Flying Training School
QL	Lighting decoy	Sgt	Sergeant
RAAF	Royal Australian Air Force	S/L	Squadron Leader
RAE	Royal Aircraft Establishment	Sqn	Squadron
RAF	Royal Air Force	TI	Target Indicator
RAFC	Royal Air Force College	TSTU	Transport Support Training Unit
RAFVR	Royal Air Force Voluntary Reserve	UAS	University Air Squadron
RAOC	Royal Army Ordnance Corps	USA	United States of America
RCAF	Royal Canadian Air Force	USAAF	United States Army Air Force
RFC	Royal Flying Corps	u/s	unserviceable
RLG	Relief Landing Ground	u/t	under training
RN	Royal Navy	VC	Victoria Cross
RNZAF	Royal New Zealand Air Force	WAAF	Women's Auxiliary Air Force
RPM	Revolutions Per Minute	W/C	Wing Commander
RT	Radio Telephone	W/O	Warrant Officer
SF	Starfish	W.Op	Wireless Operator

Aircraft Types

The following data identifies the aircraft involved in incidents in Nottinghamshire. Numbers in () indicate volumes produced.

Airspeed Envoy
Twin engine civilian light transport.

Airspeed Horsa (3655)
A WWII troop carrying glider used for air assault by Allied forces. Named after Horsa, the legendary 5th Century conqueror of Southern Britain.

Airspeed Oxford (4000)
Twin engine advanced trainer.

Armstrong Whitworth Whitley (1814)
Twin engine front line medium bomber.

Avro Anson (8000)
Twin engined multi-role aircraft mainly used as an aircrew trainer.

Avro Manchester (209)
Twin engined heavy bomber.

Avro Lancaster (7000)
Four engine heavy bomber.

Avro Tutor (795)
A two seat single engine training bi-plane.

B-17 Flying Fortress (12731)
American four engine heavy bomber.

B-25 Mitchell (9984)
American twin engine medium bomber.

Bristol Beaufighter (5928)
Long range heavy fighter.

Bristol Blenheim (4400)
Twin engined high speed light bomber.

Curtiss P-40 Tomahawk (13738)
Single engine single seater fighter.

De Havilland Dominie
Radio and navigation training aircraft.

De Havilland Mosquito (7781)
Twin engined multi-role combat aircraft

De Havilland Tiger Moth (8868)
Two seat 1930s biplane operated as a primary trainer.

Douglas Boston (7385)
American twin engine bomber.

Fairy Battle (2200)
Single engined light bomber.

Fairy Barracuda (2607)
Three seater torpedo, bomber, reconnaissance aircraft.

Fairy Swordfish (2400)
Torpedo bomber.

Handley Page Halifax (6000)
Four engine heavy bomber.

Handley Page Hampden (1400)
Twin engined medium bomber.

Hawker Audax (700)
Two seat single engine biplane light bomber.

Hawker Hind (528)
Two seat single engine biplane used as a light bomber.

Hawker Hurricane (14000)
Single seat interceptor fighter.

Hawker Henley (200)
Two seat single engine target tug.

Heinkel He 111 (6508)
German twin engine fast medium bomber.

Lockheed P-38 Lightning (10037)
Twin engine American heavy fighter.

Miles Magister (1300)
Single engine two seat monoplane basic trainer, being the first monoplane designed specifically as a trainer for the Royal Air Force.

Miles Martinet (1724)
Target tug aircraft for towing targets

Miles Master (3250)
Single engine two seat monoplane advanced trainer.

North American Harvard (15500)
Single engine advanced trainer.

P-51 Mustang (16766)
American long range single engine single seat fighter.

Short Stirling (2883)
Four engine heavy bomber.

Supermarine Spitfire (20000)
Single seater interceptor fighter.

Taylorcraft Auster (1630)
Military liaison and observation aircraft.

Vickers Wellesley
Two seat single engine light bomber.

Vickers Wellington (11000)
Twin engined medium bomber.

Westland Lysander (1786)
Single engined British Army Co-operation and liaison aircraft.

Westland Wallace (104)
Two seat general purpose bi-plane.

Aircraft Incidents

The purpose of this section of the book is to identify the aircraft incidents occurring in the County of Nottinghamshire between the years 1930 and 1945. The losses include some of those aircraft having incidents within the local airfield boundaries, and also aircraft having incidents on, or just outside, the County boundary. In many cases insufficient evidence is available to determine exact crash locations.

The sequence of reporting is: date of incident; time of incident using the 24 hour clock system; type of activity the crew were performing; aircraft type and identity; squadron number/identity; operating airfield and/or incident location. This is followed by a description of the incident, list of the crew members and some personal details, if known, and their final resting places where appropriate. A high number of aircrew who were involved in incidents incurred slight or no injury but subsequently lost their lives and this has been recorded where known.

The National Grid reference of the position of the incidents shown have been 'converted' from those found in the incident reports, where positions are recorded using the wartime 'Cassini' grid, a system which differs in orientation, origin and geometry from that applied to modern maps.

The authors are indebted to many people for providing photographs but in some cases it has not been possible to identify the original source and so credits are given where known. If any photographs have not been correctly credited the authors' apologise.

'Hymn for the RAF' by Patience Strong

1930

SUNDAY 9th NOVEMBER 1930

1600 hrs

DH.60X Moth G-AAMT from Tollerton owned by the Nottingham Aero Club was taken up in the air by Ronald Leslie Wing age 20, a qualified pilot who had been granted his aviators' certificate by the Royal Aero Club of the United Kingdom on 5th September. He flew the aircraft at a fairly low altitude over the Cotgrave district and made a sharp left hand turn and in doing so seemed to lose flying speed. The aircraft rolled over twice, nose dived, and went into a spin at about 1,000 feet. After 4 complete turns it came out of the spin started to climb but fell over to the left and nose dived into a ploughed field at Cotgrave, turned a couple of somersaults and was wrecked. Ronald Wing was killed instantly and his body was taken by ambulance to the Manvers Arms, Cotgrave.

He was the only child of Mr and Mrs A Leslie Wing of Coldwell Road, Sheffield, and a nephew of Mr Ronald Shipstone. He was staying during the weekend at Reigate House, Cyprus road, Mapperley Park.

1931

FRIDAY 30th OCTOBER 1931

Daytime | Training

Tutor K2498 of 3 FTS from Grantham was practicing manoeuvres when it did not complete a spin and crashed on the 14th tee of Bulwell Hall Golf Course. The aircraft had arrived at Hucknall only five minutes earlier, flown by F/O W Stevenson and a pupil pilot. It was thought that the aircrew, F/O Louis McHardy age 27 and F/O Jack Eugene Markby age 25, both New Zealanders, had taken the aircraft to practice aerobatics. They were both stationed at Grantham Flying Training School and were attached to 504 (County of Nottingham) Bomber Squadron at Hucknall aerodrome. It was not known who was piloting the aircraft at the time.

The coffins were taken to Hucknall Parish Church on 2nd November, an hour before the service, which was attended by a large number of personnel from various RAF stations. After the service, the two coffins were carried to Hucknall Cemetery for burial.

F/O McHardy was a single man, F/O Markby had only been married for two months and lived on the aerodrome with his wife and both were the first fatal accidents to 504 Squadron personnel.

As can be seen from the photograph the headstones are badly in need of repair.

The graves of F/O Markby and F/O McHardy at Hucknall Cemetary

1932

TUESDAY 23rd FEBRUARY 1932

1800 hrs

DH.60X Moth G-AAPM took off from Tollerton airfield with E F Winser at the controls. The aircraft had been flying at normal cruising speed at 500 feet a few miles from Tollerton when the engine suddenly started to run irregularly and made an unusual noise or clatter. The pilot then opened the engine to full throttle resulting in a loud report and the engine ceased to function. He attempted to execute a sharp turn towards a grass meadow on his right, the aircraft stalled and fell into a spiral dive/spin. The spin was corrected and the pilot gained a measure of control but was unable to pull out of the dive before the aircraft struck the ground. The cause of the crash was valve rocker studs appearing to have failed resulting in engine failure. E F Winser was slightly injured.

1934

SATURDAY 3rd NOVEMBER 1934

1205 hrs

DH.60X Gipsy Moth G-EBXG from Tollerton crashed near Chilwell Manor golf course and caught fire killing both occupants. Two Nottingham Flying Officers, who both lived at 20 Lucknow Avenue, Nottingham, had chartered the private aeroplane to use for showering confetti at a reception after the marriage of one of their friends. It seems that after looping the loop one of the wings broke loose and the plane fell to the ground but the cause of the crash was not known. A joint funeral was held at West Hallam Church for the airmen, F/O Philip S Rook, age 24, and P/O Alan Cuyler Grant-Dalton, also age 24, both Special Reserve Officers of 504 (County of Nottingham) Bomber Squadron based at Hucknall. They are both buried in the same grave in West Hallam Churchyard Cemetery. The Rook family home was West Hallam Hall, adjacent to the church, which was demolished after the war.

At the inquest on the two pilots, among a number of comments made by the district coroner, was the observation that if the men had had parachutes they would have been alive today. In the RAF at this time it was compulsory to have parachutes.

Grave of F/O Rook and P/O Grant-Dalton.

1936

WEDNESDAY 22nd JANUARY 1936

Daytime

DH.60M Moth K1892 of 24 Sqn crashed in making a forced landing at Hucknall and a miraculous escape from injury was experienced by a RAF pilot who was the only occupant of the orange coloured plane. Hucknall residents had noticed the aircraft flying at low altitude shortly after 1 pm and fears that the pilot had lost his bearings were confirmed when the aircraft flew over Wood Lane and Park Drive trying to locate the aerodrome less than a mile away. It was very low above the houses for around five minutes, then the pilot set a westerly course in the direction of the aerodrome.

At Hazel Grove and the residential part of Watnall Road on the Hucknall side of No.2 Colliery people rushed from their houses. The pilot could be seen distinctly, and many on the ground pointed in the direction of the aerodrome. There was considerable mist at 500 feet however and it was hopeless to give any help in this way.

After the plane had circled a grass field at the east of the colliery at least half a dozen times the pilot prepared to land at least half a dozen times and a hundred people watching below held their breath as he manoeuvred to face the wind.

When within a few yards of the ground, however, with no chance of landing safely, owing to restricted space, the pilot rose again over the high tension wires running along the edge of the field and landed in a ploughed field owned by Mr Harry Raynor.

The ground was soggy and uneven but the nose of the machine was well into the wind and kept upright for 40 yards ploughing a trench in the land. Losing speed it turned on its nose and the propeller and undercarriage smashed. A hundred people who were on the spot in less than a minute saw the pilot step down from the plane unhurt except for a shaking. Among those present was Dr R H Vartan, one of the officers of the 504 (County of Nottingham) Bomber Squadron, who spoke to the pilot who was then taken on to the Aerodrome by road, and air force men were later sent to dismantle the aircraft. (Extract from the Hucknall Despatch).

TUESDAY 22nd SEPTEMBER 1936

Hawker Hind K5368 of 98 Sqn from Hucknall approached landing at Hucknall aerodrome too fast, bounced and the pilot A/Sgt G R Watkins found that he was likely to overshoot. The aircraft ran through a hedge onto the main road and the brakes were applied too hard causing the aircraft to turn completely over onto its back.

THURSDAY 24th SEPTEMBER 1936

Night

Moth Major DH.60G a two seater aircraft of the Nottingham Flying Club was being flown solo by Wilfred Clarke, age 25, of 840 Westville Estate, Hucknall, when it crashed in a field, adjoining Glebe Farm, between Tollerton and Edwalton whilst doing aerobatics. Apparently the aircraft made a turn, climbed to gain height, stalled and dropped into a spin. The nose of the aeroplane was partly buried in the ground, the wings were damaged, and the cockpit a crumpled wreck.

Mr Clarke was taken to Nottingham General Hospital with concussion and injuries to his back.

WEDNESDAY 2nd DECEMBER 1936

Hawker Hind K5514 of 104 Sqn from Hucknall had its engine cut on take-off and immediately crash landed.

The pilot, Sgt 43142 William Alfred Shillitto, was unhurt but was killed seven years later on 20th October 1943 having been promoted to the rank of F/L and during this time awarded the DFC. He was the pilot of Blenheim IV Z7960 of 527 Calibration Sqn, tasked with calibration of radar stations in southern England and East Anglia, which had taken off from Castle Camps, Cambridge, on an air test and was seen to be doing steep turns at a very low altitude. It crashed onto the Felixstowe Road, Ipswich, having had insufficient height to recover, preparatory to landing. He is buried in Felixstowe New Cemetery.

His citation for the award of the DFC reads: 'This officer has carried out many flights of a technical nature in which he has shown great devotion to duty. The majority of flights, undertaken in all forms of weather conditions, have been over the English Channel and towards enemy-occupied territory. On one occasion his aircraft was repeatedly attacked by a Messerschmitt Me 109F. After taking successful avoiding action Flight Lieutenant Shillitto succeeded in firing a long burst which damaged the Messerschmitt and the engagement was broken off.'

1937

FRIDAY 9th APRIL 1937

Hawker Hind K5514 of 104 Sqn from Hucknall was taking off in formation when the pilot, A/P/O H P Powell, allowed the aircraft to swing into the leader's slipstream. In attempting to land and pull up when a few feet off the ground the pilot throttled down but applied the brakes too coarsely and the aircraft overturned but he escaped without injury. This aircraft had also been involved in an incident on 2nd December 1936.

TUESDAY 1st JUNE 1937

Hawker Hind K4641 of 104 Sqn from Hucknall whilst landing in a formation of five aircraft the pilot, P/O 37834 Norman John Starr RAF, touched down at the same moment as the leader with the tail of his aircraft just above horizontal. The airscrew tips hit the ground and the aircraft turned over onto its back but P/O Starr escaped injury.

P/O Starr was a very experienced pilot when he was killed eight years later on 8th January 1945. By now he had risen to the rank of Wing Commander and also been awarded the DFC and Bar. He was the pilot of Anson MG552 of 276 Sqn Air Sea Rescue of B.83 aerodrome, Knocke-le-Zoute, Belgium, care of the British Liberation Army. He took off from B.83 aerodrome to fly to the UK and was reported missing. He and the bodies of the other crew members, the Commanding Officer of 157 Wing, W/C 33258 James Heathcote Humphries RAF, S/L 43885 Henry Crawford Haley RAF age 49 and F/O131734 Rowland Baber Moore RAFVR were recovered and are buried in Dunkirk Town Cemetery. S/L Haley had 3 times been mentioned in despatches.

W/C Starr received the award of the DFC when serving with 23 Sqn and the citation read: 'This officer has completed 36 sorties, involving attacks on airfields, factories and marshalling yards, achieving much success. He has made persistent attacks on railways in Sicily and Tunis. One night in January, 1943, he destroyed an enemy aircraft over its airfield and, on 3 other such sorties, he has damaged 4 more. Squadron Leader Starr, who has displayed great courage and determination, is an outstanding pilot.' He received the Bar to the DFC on 21st November 1944 when serving with 605 Sqn.

THURSDAY 10th JUNE 1937

2300 hrs — Training

Avro Anson K6249 of 48 Sqn from RAF Manston took off on a navigation training flight with Sgt A F Underhill at the controls. The aircraft made a forced landing in a field of barley at West View Farm, Papplewick near the Griffins Head public house, at the height of a storm after the crew had used a powerful searchlight to get the lie of the land. The aircraft skimmed a thorn hedge, ripping the underside off the fuselage putting the rudder out of commission and ran on about 300 yards into the field. The pilot and crew of three were not injured. The aircraft was dismantled and carried to Hucknall Aerodrome.

TUESDAY 15th JUNE 1937

Morning — Training

Hawker Hind K4648 of 104 Sqn from Hucknall took off in a massed take off with P/O D C Smythe at the controls. Almost immediately the engine cut and the aircraft made a forced landing, hit a hedge and overturned at Sunnydale, between Long Hill and Misk, near Whyburn Lane, Hucknall and was badly damaged. The wings were buckled and broken and half the propeller was lost. Later that day the aircraft was towed from the field and taken back to the aerodrome by lorry. The pilot was unhurt.

FRIDAY 25th JUNE 1937

Hawker Audax I K3078 of 26 Sqn bounced on landing and overturned at Hucknall aerodrome and was written off damaged beyond repair. The pilot was F/O H L Maxwell.

An aeroplane, probably from Tollerton airfield, landed in a cornfield at West Bridgford, piloted by Mrs Pyddoke of Pleasley, a member of Nottingham Flying Club. The propeller of the aircraft was damaged.

The demise of the aeroplane of Mrs Pyddoke (inset).
Courtesy Nottingham Guardian

FRIDAY 2nd JULY 1937 Training

Hawker Hind K5380 of 98 Sqn from Hucknall bounced on landing at Hucknall and hit trees on overshoot. The pilot, P/O 39199 Brian Rutter Kerridge RAF, was practicing landings and it was his first flight on this type of aircraft.

P/O Kerridge, by now an experienced pilot, was killed in May 1940 flying with 226 Sqn having attained the rank of Flight Lieutenant.

On 2nd September 1939, 16 Battles of 226 Sqn, including F/L Kerridge, landed at Rheims, France, as part of No.72 Wing of the Advanced Striking Force. During the German invasion

Hawker Hind of 98 Squadron similar to K5380

of Belgium and France the squadron fought hard, bombing motor transport columns and motor transport and other tactical targets in an attempt to delay the enemies advance. On 10th May 1940 the overall British Commander, Air Marshall Barratt, acting on his own initiative, ordered 32 Battles from Nos 12, 103,105, 142, 150, 218 and 226 Squadrons to attack German troops advancing through Luxembourg at noon. As it was impossible to provide fighter escort the bombers were briefed to make a very low approach to target and attack from as little as 250 feet using bombs with a delayed fuse. Intense small arms fire was encountered and three

Battles of the first wave were shot down. A similar fate befell the second wave during the afternoon. Of the 32 Battles that took part that day, 13 were lost and all the rest damaged. F/L Kerridge was the pilot of Battle L5247 MQ- of 226 Sqn which took off at 1700 hrs on 10th May from Rheims, France and was shot down in flames by ground fire over enemy lines whilst dive-bombing troop columns between Wallendorf and Diekirch and crashed near Faubourg de Luxembourg. He was captured, badly wounded, and his death is recorded as 15th May and he is buried in Luxembourg (Hollerich) Communal Cemetery. His two fellow crew members, Sgt D I Anthony and Cpl G H Dixon who was badly burned, survived and were made POWs.

F/L Kerridge is commemorated on the Thorpe Green War Memorial shown.

TUESDAY 20th JULY 1937 **Training**

Wellesley I K7731 of 76 (B) Sqn from Finningley piloted by A/P/O J S Sherwood was held off too high when coming in to land at Finningley, the aircraft stalled and hit the ground heavily with the port wing down causing the port chassis to collapse.

Wellesley I of 76 Squadron similar to K7731

MONDAY 9th AUGUST 1937

Night Training

Hawker Hind K6722 of 104 Sqn from Hucknall when coming into land on the flare path the pilot, Sgt 562560 E E B Le Voi, misjudged his height, made a heavy landing and the undercarriage collapsed.

Sgt Voi was made a POW on 11th May 1940. He was the pilot of Blenheim IV L9255 of 18 Sqn which took off from Meharicourt on a reconnaissance flight and the fate of his aircraft is not known. However his W/Op, LAC 539392 Ronald C Davies age 21, was killed and is buried in Reichswald Forest War Cemetery. Sgt Voi and the other crew member, Sgt J C Sands, were both made POWs.

SATURDAY 21st AUGUST 1937

1940 hrs

Moth Major GACZX from Tollerton had been borrowed by club member Mr James Daniel Bradbury age 35, the pilot, for a flight. He had been conducting stunts over the Huthwaite Carnival ground for a few minutes when he crashed the aeroplane into a nearby cornfield killing its two occupants, Mr Bradbury and Mr Roy Houbart Crossland age 21 both residents of Sutton.

The 'Free Press' report stated that the pilot began a series of stunts which included the falling leaf, looping the loop, and an exhibition of crazy flying, which were given with considerable skill. Apparently as a grand finale to the display, the machine began climbing preparatory to going into a spiral dive. It climbed until it was just entering the clouds, and then the engine was switched off and the dive commenced. The plane failed to flatten out and nose dived into the ground.

SUNDAY 12th SEPTEMBER 1937

1600 hrs Training

Hawker Hind K6789 of 504 Sqn from Hucknall with F/O 90060 James Boyd Parnall at the controls practicing aerobatics when the engine cut in a spin and the aircraft made a forced landing on a farm owned by Mr O Hollingworth, hit a ditch and overturned at Blidworth, near Hucknall. F/O Parnall was unhurt. It was due to running into dense fog at an altitude of 400 feet that he decided to land.

A guard was mounted on the aeroplane during the night which was flown back to Hucknall the next day by F/L Griffiths.

F/L Parnall was subsequently killed on 15th May 1940 whilst still serving with 504 Sqn, who were temporary based in France, having previously been promoted to Squadron Leader. He was on patrol in his Hurricane I L1639 when he was shot down in combat with He 111s near Louvignies at 1230 hrs. He was the unit CO and is buried in Chaussee-Notre-Dame-Louvignies Communal Cemetery.

Extract from 'Twelve days in May': '...on 14.5.40 in air operations over the Louvain-Tirlemont area a section of 504 Squadron Hurricanes, S/L Parnell in L1639, F/O M E A Royce (L1950) and P/O B Van Mentz attacked a Ju 88 from 3(F)/122 on a reconnaissance from astern. It fell in flames and Brian Van Mentz followed it down, seeing it crash near the Albert Canal.'

Also; '...on the afternoon of 14.5.40 S/L Parnall led a section of 4 aircraft on a patrol in the Louvain area. They came across 6 He 111Hs from III/LG/1 and a number of Bf 109s from II and III/JG26. They attacked the bombers and S/L Parnall was seen (by F/O M E A Royce) to badly damage a He 111 but was then shot down himself. His aircraft (L1639) crashed at Hameau du Caillou and he was killed.'

S/L Parnall's brother Stuart Boyd Parnall also died serving with the RAF, on 9th September 1940 flying with 607 Sqn. He was on patrol in his Hurricane P3574 when he crashed after combat with bombers and fighters at 1730 hrs over Goudhurst, Kent. He was cremated at Golders Green Crematorium.

S/L Parnall's Hurricane I L1639 of 504 Squadron. Via P R Rogers

No.504 (City of Nottingham) Squadron groundcrew work on 'Scruffy' Royce's Hurricane

FRIDAY 24th SEPTEMBER 1937 Training

Hawker Hind K6719 of 98 Sqn from Hucknall developed engine trouble and nose dived into a field at Gunthorpe. Both occupants escaped with slight cuts.

MONDAY 4th OCTOBER 1937

Night Training

Wellesley K7741 of 76 (B) Sqn from Finningley was held off slightly too high by the pilot F/O L R Stewart when landing and stalled onto the ground, hit heavily on the starboard undercarriage, which collapsed. F/O Stewart was unhurt.

TUESDAY 14th DECEMBER 1937 Training

Hawker Hind K6744 of 50 (B) Sqn was on instrument flying practice in poor visibility when the pilot, A/P/O 39576 Ronald Edward Smissen, decided to return to the aerodrome but flew west instead of north and got lost. He circled a field, lost height and approached his landing too fast so he went around again and the aircraft slipped inwards on a turn at 70mph and went down in a spiral at New Ollerton. There were two injuries.

FRIDAY 17th DECEMBER 1937 Training

Wellesley K7746 of 76 (B) Sqn from Finningley took off for low level bombing practice when engine failure occurred and the aircraft landed and struck a hedge. The pilot was P/O J M Warren.

1938

TUESDAY 4th JANUARY 1938

Night Taxiing

Wellesley K8527 of 76 (B) Sqn from Finningley piloted by P/O 37825 George Kenneth Peacock RAF taxied out too fast and ran into the tail of Wellesley K7726 which was waiting to take off. P/O Peacock was killed on 12th July 1941 in a flying accident at Mount Gambier, Australia as a result of an air collision between his and another aircraft, during a heavy rain squall at 0850 hrs. His burial took place on 14th July in Mount Gambier Cemetery.

Wellesleys taking off from Finningley. Courtesy 'Flightglobal'

THURSDAY 27th JANUARY 1938

Night | Training

Wellesley K7744 of 76 (B) Sqn from Finningley overshot the flarepath on landing and the pilot, F/O 39372 Royston Henry Bullard-Davies RAF, mis-judged his height and dropped his aircraft from eight feet and the under carriage collapsed.

F/O Bullard-Davies was killed on 20th March 1940 when his aircraft, Hampden L4137 of 144 Sqn, crashed at Scunthorpe on a training exercise. He is buried in Harpswell (St Chad) Churchyard.

TUESDAY 1st MARCH 1938

Night | Training

Wellesley K7767 of 76 Sqn from Finningley undercarriage collapsed in a heavy landing after the pilot P/O 39127 James Eric Riepenhausen mis-judged his height.

P/O Riepenhausen, now a F/L, was killed on 11th October 1940 when as pilot of Whitley N1526 of 10 OTU he crashed on a training flight. He is buried in Birkenhead (Flaybrick Hill) Cemetery.

TUESDAY 3rd MAY 1938

Night | Training

Wellesley K2687 of 76 Sqn from Finningley was taking off when the pilot, P/O B P Jones, was momentarily unsighted by the reflection of a rotating beacon off his windscreen and subconsciously mishandled the aircraft causing it to skid and stall.

TUESDAY 10th MAY 1938 | Training

Wellesley I K7725 of 76 Sqn from Finningley during landing the pilot P/O W D Corr misjudged his height and landed rather heavily and the undercarriage collapsed.

FRIDAY 13th MAY 1938 | Taxiing

Wellesley K7719 of 76 Sqn from Finningley made a normal landing and was taxiing towards the hangar when the undercarriage collapsed. The pilot was P/O J S Sherwood.

MONDAY 13th JUNE 1938

Night | Training

Wellesley K7941 of 76 Sqn from Finningley port tyre burst during take-off causing both undercarriages to collapse. The pilot was Sgt W G Redding.

THURSDAY 16th JUNE 1938

Wellesley K7741 of 76 Sqn swung on landing at Finningley aerodrome and the undercarriage collapsed. This aircraft was also involved in an incident on 4th October 1937.

This photograph was taken circa 1938 and of the sixteen No.76 Squadron pilots shown nine were involved in incidents recorded in this book. P/O Sherwood, Sgt Jenkins, P/O Riepenhausen and P/O Peacock did not survive the war. Courtesy of 'Flightglobal'

WEDNESDAY 22nd JUNE 1938 Training

Tutor K3199 of RAF College Cranwell stalled in a forced landing while lost and crashed in-field at Castle Donington aerodrome. The pilot was Flying Cadet 33493 Peter William Vaughan RAF who was killed on 13th May 1940 with the rank of P/O. He was the pilot of Lysander P9063 of 4 Sqn supporting the British Expeditionary Force when he and his crew member AC2 Edin Mold, his air gunner, were initially listed as 'Missing, believed killed in action, death presumed 13.5.40'. It was later noted that they had been buried in Gutgaarden Communal Cemetery.

Tutor K3199 in a sorry state in-field at Castle Donington aerodrome

FRIDAY 1st JULY 1938

Wellesley K8528 of 76 (B) Sqn from Finningley undercarriage collapsed on landing after the pilot F/S 561090 E G Couch failed to hold off correctly. F/S Couch was also involved in an incident on 22nd August.

SATURDAY 20th AUGUST 1938

Battle I K9212 of 98 Sqn from Hucknall engine cut on take off and the aircraft belly landed. The pilot was P/O M J B Young.

MONDAY 22nd AUGUST 1938

Night Training

Wellesley K2690 of 76 (B) Sqn from Finningley overshot the flarepath and jumped a small ditch on the boundary and damaged the tail. The cause was attributed to sudden fog. The pilot, F/S E G Couch, was also involved in an incident on 1st July.

MONDAY 5th SEPTEMBER 1938

Day

Gloster Gauntlet K5314 of 19 (F) Sqn from Duxford was on a flight from Montrose to Hucknall when the pilot A/P/O Bernard G Piddocke landed in a field near Ollerton Railway Station (South), on the Rufford side of the railway bridge which goes over the A614 road, to ask for directions. On take-off the aircraft hit an obstruction and crashed upside down two miles south of Ollerton at Rufford. A/P/O Piddocke went on to join 41 Sqn.

Gauntlet K5314 upside down at Rufford. Courtesy of W Taylor

MONDAY 3rd OCTOBER 1938 Training

Battle I K9206 of 98 (B) Sqn from Hucknall engine cut during flight and the aircraft belly landed and crashed through fences into a field at Beeston. The pilot F/O 37838 Eric Richard Dennis Vaughan RAF survived but was a member of 12 Sqn when he was killed on 14th May 1940. 12 Squadron moved to France on the first day of the war to begin operations and F/O Vaughan was the pilot of Battle L4950 which crashed whilst on a raid to Sedan. He is buried in Choloy War Cemetery.

Battle I K9210 of 98 (B) Sqn from Hucknall had a wing drop on touching down due to undercarriage failure and became bent. The pilot, P/O 36112 Guy de Laval Harvie RAF, who was unhurt, subsequently had a very eventful, if short, life.

He was born in Cambridge, New Zealand, to the Reverend Frank Graham Harvie and Laura Kathleen Harvie, who had been in charge of parishes in New Plymouth and Auckland, and was the middle brother of three. The Harvie household was a prominent aviation family in New Zealand where the other brothers, Ted Harvie and Monty Harvie, were both Cambridge airmen, Ted achieving the rank of Wing Commander and Monty rising to Squadron Leader. Guy attended Auckland University and in 1934 went to Oxford University, England, to continue his education. There he joined the Oxford University Air Squadron, became a Pilot Officer on 22nd September 1936 and began pilot training on Hart and Audax aircraft in 1937. He also graduated from the University in 1937.

He passed his training on 15th February 1938 and was promoted to Flying Officer on 25th April. He completed his Service Flying Training on 1st June and then joined the RAF the same month with a permanent commission and on 13th June commenced a course at the School of Air Navigation at RAF Manston. This was completed on 20th August. He was then posted to 98 (B) Sqn based at Hucknall flying Battle aircraft and was promoted to Acting Flight Lieutenant on 3rd March 1939.

On 14th September he was transferred to 207 Sqn based at Cranfield flying Anson bombers and on April 1940 moved to 12 OTU at RAF Benson as an instructor, was made an Acting Squadron Leader on 15th May and then in December moved on to Wellington aircraft.

He also got married in 1940, to Isolda Kingsley Harvie of Clevedon, Somerset, daughter of Air Marshall C E Havers.

In Jack West's book on past pupils of New Plymouth Boys' High School he wrote 'It is evident from a close reading of the message between the lines of Guy Harvie's record sheet that his knowledge and practical expertise not only in navigation but also in the general handling of twin-engine light bombers, was such that he was used extensively as an instructor during the first year of the war. It is fairly clear also, that by December 1940 "enough was enough" and he had to get into a Squadron actively taking the war to the enemy. But it appears that during 1941that ambition had to be postponed yet again. The simple fact was that he was far too valuable an asset in the training establishment of the RAF to be spared without very good reason'.

Throughout the most of 1941 he was the Chief Ground Instructor at Benson. On 14th February he was posted to 57 Sqn at RAF Feltwell on Wellingtons and completed 6 Operations, to Essen, Lubeck, Hanau, the Renault Works at Paris, St Nazaire and Le Havre.

The authors are indebted to Dave Homewood for the above information.

Vickers Hart trainers. Courtesy of W J Wilson

Guy de Laval Harvie was killed on 2nd April 1942, age 28, when he took off from Feltwell, Norfolk, at 2120 hours as the pilot of Wellington X3410 of 57 Sqn. He was making low level attacks on railway targets at Hanau and Lohr and his aircraft was brought down over Frettenheim, Germany killing all 6 crew members. 13 of the 49 aircraft on this operation were lost. He is buried in Rheinberg War Cemetery, Germany, having completed 680 flying hours. At the time of his death his parents were back in their home country of England, living at Milton Rectory, Berkshire.

Guy de Laval Harvie.
Courtesy of Dave Homewood

Rheinberg War Cemetery

FRIDAY 21st OCTOBER 1938 Training

Whitley I K7241 of 7 Sqn from Finningley undershot landing at Finningley aerodrome in fog and hit a house 15 yards from the boundary, caused by a false reading on the altimeter. The pilot, P/O Patrick Wilfred Villiers 'Pat' Massy, and crew were un-injured.

Pat Massy had a short but interesting and eventful life. He was born in London in 1916 and joined the RAF in September 1936 training at 2 FTS. He was posted to 7 Sqn on 22nd May 1937 and confirmed as a Pilot Officer on 13th July.

On 13th February 1939 he was promoted to Flying Officer but on the same day he was commissioned into the Fleet Air Arm as an Acting Lieutenant, transferring to that service on its removal from the RAF to the RN.

A Whitley Bomber similar to K7241

He served on HMS *Eagle* as a Lieutenant with 813 Sqn in the Eastern Mediterranean in 1940 and was stationed as a member of the Air Staff aboard HMS *Eagle* at the time of the outbreak of war with Italy. He was one of two Swordfish pilots (the other Lt K Keith) to be trained by Commander Charles Keighly-Peach in the use of one of the 4 Gloster Sea Gladiators which Commander Keighly-Peach collected on Malta and these three provided the early fighter defence of the Mediterranean Fleet and claimed 8 aircraft shot down.

On 29th July Lt Massy attacked one aircraft of two flights of three S.79s at 15,000 feet and shot it down but low on fuel he ditched his aircraft near HMAS Stuart, an escorting destroyer, and was picked up unhurt. He was Mentioned in Despatches on 11th September. In 1941 Lt Massy served in 806 Squadron on HMS *Formidable* flying Fulmars.

On 25th May a formation of Ju87s was seen approaching from the North African coast and attacked the ships and Lt Massy claimed one shot down and two damaged and was again Mentioned in Despatches on 14th June. On 2nd December he was gazetted with the DSC.

He returned to the UK in April 1942 as an instructor with 760 Sqn at Yeovilton but was then assigned to HMS *Avenger's* 883 Sqn, became Commanding Officer on 10th April and on HMS *Avenger* acted as aerial escort for a convoy to North USSR.

On 15th November 1942, west of Gibralter en route from Africa to the UK, the ship was torpedoed and sunk by U-boat U-155 and Lt Massy was lost with the ship age only 26 years of age.

He was awarded a DSO for his leadership during Convoy duties, gazetted posthumously on 1st December. The citation read: 'THE KING has been graciously pleased to approve the following awards... For gallantry, skill and resolve in H M Ships escorting an important convoy to North Russia in the face of relentless attack by enemy aircraft and submarines.'

THURSDAY 3rd NOVEMBER 1938 — Training

Tutor K3284 of RAF College Cranwell overturned in a forced landing at Toton while lost, an inauspicious start for the pilot, Flying Cadet M M Stephens, a future flying ace.

Maurice Michael Stephens DFC and two Bars, DSO became a RAF flying ace of WWII. He scored 17 kills, three shared kills, one probable kill and five damaged. He was born in India on 20th October 1919, the son of a British Army Officer. He joined the RAF at Cranwell in 1938 and was awarded his wings on 19th January 1940. His first posting was to 3 Sqn at Hawkinge where he fought during the Battle of France, becoming Flight Commander of B flight. He was awarded the DFC and Bar on his return from France both gazetted at the same time.

The citations for the DFC read: 'This officer has destroyed four enemy aircraft in May 1940 and led his flight with courage and skill.'

The citation for the Bar to the DFC read: 'This officer has contined to lead his flight against formations of enemy aircraft of much superior numbers with such good leadership that he rarely lost any members of his formation. In addition Pilot Officer Stephens brought down four more enemy aircraft recently, bringing his total to eight.'

F/O M M Stephens

In fact P/O Stephens shot down 3 aircraft over Sedan on one day, 14th May, a Bf109E, a Ju87 and a Hs126 taking his tally at that time to six. His tally had risen to 11 destroyed by the time his unit evacuated France on 20th May 1940. Also on 15th May he had to force land his Hurricane N2546 when returning from a patrol but was unhurt.

After his return from France 'B' Flt was posted to Scotland and reformed as 232 Sqn and he became the CO. He was promoted to Flying Officer on 20th August 1940 and whilst flying with 80 Sqn was awarded the DSO in January 1942. The citation read: 'In December 1941 this officer led a bombing and machine-gun attack on enemy mechanical transport in the Acrome area. Following the attack, Squadron Leader Stephens observed the fighter escort in combat with a force of enemy fighters, but whilst attemting to participate in the engagement, his aircraft was severely damaged by an enemy fighter pilot whose cannon fire exploded the starboard petrol tank which, with the oil tank burst into flames. The same burst of fire wounded Squadron Leader Stephens in both feet and blew out the starboard side of the aircraft's cockpit. Squadron Leader Stephen's then prepared to abandon the aircraft but, when halfway out of the cockpit, he observed an enemy aircraft fly past him. He immediately regained his seat and shot down the enemy aircraft. Squadron Leader Stephens finally left his crippled aircraft by parachute and landed safely on the ground where he beat out the flames from his burning clothing. Although he had landed within 300 yards of the enemy's lines, Squadron Leader Stephens succeeded in regaining our own territory within three-quarters of an hour. Throughout, this officer displayed great courage and devotion to duty. Previously, Squadron Leader Stephens led his squadron on operations which were of the greatest value during the battle for Tobruk. His leadership and example proved an inspiration.'

Whilst flying with 229 Sqn in Malta he was awarded the 2nd Bar to his DFC. The citation read: 'This officer has greatly enhanced the gallant reputation he so worthily holds.'

S/L Stephens rose to the rank of Group Captain and continued in the RAF until 1960 and retired in 1980. He died age 84 in 2004.

FRIDAY 18th NOVEMBER 1938 — Training

Wellesley K8527 of 76 Sqn from Finningley was near the end of its landing run when the pilot Sgt 580289 Stanley William Jenkins RAF turned the aircraft to avoid an obstruction and the undercarriage collapsed.

Sgt Jenkins was the pilot of Hampden L4055 of 83 Sqn from Scampton which was detailed to attack a bridge and roads. On returning to base all aircraft were diverted because of bad visibility at Scampton and L4055 flew into high ground at Holmfirth when proceeding to Ringway on 23rd May 1940, and was killed along with his crew. He was age 23 and is buried in Nettleham (All Saints) Old Churchyard.

SUNDAY 20th NOVEMBER 1938

1130 hrs

Hawker Hind L7199 AW of 504 Sqn from Hucknall piloted by F/O Anthony (Tony) Hartwell Rook crashed as he was attempting to make a forced landing in fog. The aircraft stalled at low level trying to avoid trees and crashed on the farm of Messrs Cumberland Brothers, at Pleasley. He was taken to Mansfield General Hospital Nursing home with slight concussion, an injury to his nose and a lacerated leg.

A flight of three Hinds had taken off from Hucknall, but the weather deteriorated rapidly and a heavy fog developed so two of the pilots decided to land. F/O Rook crash landed and F/L Watson flying K6794 got down safely on the farm belonging to Mr V Brown.

Tony Rook was nephew of Colonel W R Rook of Edwalton and cousin of S/L Michael Rook.

He was awarded the DFC on 3rd March 1942, AFC on 8th June 1944 and Mentioned in Despatches on 14th June 1945.

Tony Rook and Micky were part of 151 Wing, a little known RAF group who fought against the Germans along side Soviet pilots for four months in the winter of 1941. When Germany invaded Russia Stalin asked Winston Churchill to send him some Spitfires. This was refused but Churchill agreed to send Hurricanes, 40 of them to begin with. 151 Wing was made up of two squadrons, No.81 and 134, and their orders were to defend the naval base of Murmansk and train Russian pilots to fly the Hurricane and when that was accomplished return to Britain.

Before leaving for Britain S/L Tony Rook, with W/C Ramsbottom-Isherwood, S/L A G Miller and F/S Haw were awarded the Order of Lenin, the only four British serviceman to receive the honour in WWII. The Order of Victory is the only higher Russian honour which has been awarded to only one Britain, Viscount Montgomery. They received their medals at the Soviet Embassy in March 1942. He also received the Soviet Order of Lenin medal on 31st March 1942.

Hawker Hind K6794 of 504 Sqn from Hucknall piloted by F/L Rupert Hartley Watson force landed at Pleasley near Mansfield (see above).

SUNDAY 27th NOVEMBER 1938 Training

Magister I L8175 of 27 EFTS from Tollerton took off with pilot Sgt 741954 Edward Watkin-Thomas age 22 at the controls. He was on solo circuit, landing and side slip practice, his tenth solo flight. He began left hand side slips and recovered then dropped his right wing and recovered, commenced a spin recovered and then stalled and dived into the Old Rectory field near Holme Pierrepont at high speed. The cause of the crash was unknown.

Sgt Watkin-Thomas, who had been flying solo for a month, was killed and lived in Zulla Road, Mapperley Park, Nottingham. He was a civilian trainee at the RAF Elementary Training School based at Tollerton.

SATURDAY 17th DECEMBER 1938

Night Training

Hawker Hind K6785 of 504 Sqn from Hucknall engine cut on take-off at about 30 feet and there was insufficient distance in which to bring the aircraft to rest on the wet surface and the aircraft skidded into the boundary fence.

The pilot, F/O 90066 John Michael Godfree Browne RAF Aux. Air Force, was unhurt but died on 9th September 1939 still flying with 504 Sqn. He was flying Hurricane L1954 at night which lost height on approach to Metheringham airfield and crashed three miles from the aerodrome and died instantly. He is buried in Southwell Minster Burial Ground. F/O Browne was the eldest son of Mr Harold Browne and lived with his wife Monica Browne at Calverton House, Calverton. In July 1936 he was commissioned as a pilot officer in the Auxiliary Air Force and was promoted to flying officer from 25th January 1938.

Grave of F/O Browne

1939

TUESDAY 3rd JANUARY 1939

Magister I L8329 of 30 ERFTS from Burnaston, Rolls-Royce, Derby, crashed at Hucknall with the cause unknown. The pilot Sgt 74420 George Anthony Bell RAFVR was killed.

Sgt Pilot Bell was born on 20th May 1917 and attended Loretto, Edinburgh, Scotland's original independent boarding school, from January1928 to April 1934, where he held a scholarship. On leaving school he trained as an engineer at the Rolls-Royce Works at Derby and after finishing his apprenticeship was appointed to a position in the experimental department which would give him full scope for developing his talent. In 1938 he joined the RAFVR and learnt to fly at Nottingham. He is listed on the Roll of Honour of Loretto School.

TUESDAY 17th JANUARY 1939 Development

Hampden I L4047 XU- of 49 Sqn from Scampton was on a development flight when it force-landed ten miles north of Nottingham, in a hollow in bad visibility and rain and was destroyed by fire. The pilot was P/O B A Mitchell.

The crash of Hampden I L4047. Courtesy Malcolm Brooke 49 Squadron

FRIDAY 10th FEBRUARY 1939 Training

Battle I K9216 of 98 Sqn from Hucknall on take off engine cut at 150 feet and the aircraft flew into a small wood and dived into the ground. The pilot, P/O J R Taylor, on his first solo flight in a Battle aircraft, was injured.

THURSDAY 23rd MARCH 1939

Night Training

Whitley III K8968 of 7 Sqn from Finningley during second approach to land in blackout conditions and a slight mist the pilot P/O T E Sanders mistook obstruction lights for red light on floodlights, undershot and crashed. The safety pilot was Sgt 514839 R C Harbourne. There were no injuries.

FRIDAY 19th MAY 1939

1615 hrs

He70 Merlin Centaur from Hucknall, a two seater experimental aircraft, crashed on the main Nottingham-Alfreton road at Watnall, 30 yards from the Queens Head Inn shortly after take off.

Eye witnesses stated that the engine was shut off in the air and the aircraft came down over a field next to the Inn. It bumped along the field for a short distance, crashed into the hedge, was spun round into the road and struck the high stone wall of the Watnall Hall home of Sir Lancelot and Lady Maud Rolleston. The propeller and both wings were damaged. There were no vehicles travelling along the road at that precise time because, as the Hucknall Despatch reported, a number of cows had just been driven out of a field nearby slowing down the traffic.

Neither the pilot Capt R T Shepherd, Rolls-Royce Test Pilot, nor his passenger, a mechanic, was injured. Shortly after the accident a lorry load of RAF personnel arrived from Hucknall Aerodrome and dragged the aircraft into the field.

Capt Shepherd, who was chief test pilot to Rolls-Royce for 16 years, died on 1st March 1955 age 58 years after a short illness.

His career began with Vickers-Armstrongs in the gun manufacturing industry, and on the outbreak of the 1914-1918 war he joined the Honourable Artillery Company, transferring to the RFC in 1916. Among the Squadrons with which he served were No.102 and No.37, and he flew on night operations against Zeppelins. He left the Service in 1918 but rejoined it 1921, serving in England and in Egypt until 1929, when he was placed on the Reserve. Thereafter he worked at Phillips and Powis, Reading, and was subsequently with National Flying Services and managed the Nottingham Flying Club.

In October 1931, Capt Shepherd made his first flight for Rolls-Royce testing a Fairy IIIF with a Kestrel engine. During the next three years he flew regularly for the company, and when they started their own flight establishment at Hucknall in 1934, he was appointed chief test pilot, a post which he held continuously until 1951. During the post-war years he was mainly concerned with gas-turbine flying. He was the first man to fly on Nene and Avon engines, in the Lancastrian flying test-bed; he flew this aircraft at the 1946 Air Show. In 1951, in which year he had a serious illness and two major operations- he relinquished full-time test flying and was appointed flying consultant to the Rolls-Royce management.

However when the Rolls-Royce 'Flying Bedstead' was ready for testing he made a special request that he should be allowed to conduct the initial work. He made the first untethered flight on 3rd August 1954. The 'Flying Bedstead' progressed to the first vertical take off and landing (VTOL) aircraft. In 35 years of flying, he handled 77 different types of aircraft and logged over 8,000 hours. He was appointed the OBE.

Crash of the He 70 Merlin Centaur. Courtesy of Hucknall Despatch

MONDAY 22nd MAY 1939 Training

Tiger Moth II N6625 of 30 ERFTS took off for forced landing practice, undershot landing, the engine failed to respond and the aircraft hit a hedge at Princes Farm, Selston. The pilot P/O 70882 C P L Wilcock was on solo flying practice. It was reported in 'Flight Global' in March 1940 that P/O Wilcock had been wounded in action. No further information is available.

THURSDAY 15th JUNE 1939

1900 hrs

Avro Cadet G-ACX Bi-plane from the Notts Aero Club crash landed on a field in Dunkirk. The plane apparently overshot the field, crashed through a hedge and overturned. The pilot, Ernest Gudgeon, 41, of Lilac Crescent, Beeston, who either jumped out or was thrown out, was taken to Nottingham General Hospital with facial cuts. The following is an extract from the Nottingham Guardian.

Mr Ernest Benjamin Gudgeon, 41, of 73 Lilac Crescent, Beeston had a remarkable escape when he made a forced landing in a field adjacent to the farm at Dunkirk formerly occupied by the Duke of Windsor when Prince of Wales. He was treated at the Nottingham General hospital for facial abrasions. The spot where the machine landed is only about 100 tards from the pylons carrying high tension cables. The machine, an Avro Cadet biplane, belongs to the Nottingham Flying Club, and the pilot actually brought it down in a field of mowing grass belonging to Mr H Farnsworth, of Trentside Farm. The plane apparently overshot the field and crashed through the hedge, overturning in the process. The pilot either jumped or was thrown out as the machine overturned, but sustained a severe cut in the region of the eye. He was treated at the Nottingham General hospital but was not detained.

Two witnesses stated that both heard the engine making an unusual noise, and then the pilot cut out the engine and glided down. He skimmed some trees and then crashed through a hedge. When enquiries were made at Tollerton aerodrome it was learned that Mr Gudgeon was an experienced pilot and the holder of an A licence. He went up about 1830 hrs and had been in the air about 30 minutes.

The overturned Avro Cadet G-ACX

FRIDAY 23rd JUNE 1939 Air Test

Hurricane I L1573 OP- of 73 Sqn (F) from RAF Digby took off at 1355 hrs with P/O Lamarque at the controls for a machine test, an exercise he had done before. At about 1430 hrs F/L F M Thomas from RAF Digby, who had authorised P/O Lamarque's flight, was also flying a Hurricane north east of Newark and L1573 formed up with his machine at which point P/O Lamarque waved. L1573 then broke away from the formation at about 1500 feet, and according to a witness banked to its left and swerved in a semi-circle round the east side of the Territorial Army camp near the Beckingham-Stapleford Road, losing height all the time. The engine was misfiring and the propeller was varying in speed. When the aircraft came down to about 500 feet the engine appeared to pick up and the nose of the plane rose and as the machine tried to climb the engine cut out altogether. The right hand wing dropped, the aircraft side-slipped and then nose dived. As it gathered speed there appeared to be an attempt to level out at about 30 feet but then it hit the ground, did a cartwheel and turned over completely in a ploughed field off the Beckingham-Stapleford Road, near Brant Broughton Lane. The witness, 14½ year old John Reckless, reached the wreckage and P/O Lamarque groaned but then lost consciousness. He tried to pull him out of the cockpit but was unable to do so as he was strapped in but he was eventually released when further help arrived. He was given first aid by men from the Royal Engineers who had arrived from the army camp and then placed on a makeshift stretcher made from part of the aircraft wing. He was taken to Newark hospital and treated for his wounds but over the next two hours his condition deteriorated and he died at 1815 hrs, probably from his severe head injuries. P/O Anthony D'Orton Lamarque had 150 flying hours experience flying Hurricanes.

MONDAY 26th JUNE 1939

Night Air Test

Battle I K9213 of 98 Sqn from Hucknall was on a flying test when a tyre burst on landing, probably due to rough ground, and a undercarriage leg collapsed. The pilot, P/O 39495 G D Clancey, subsequently joined 12 Sqn and was posted to France during the German invasion.

12 Sqn suffered horrendous casualties in a short space of time. They took part in the first attack on the German forces on 10th May 1940 when 4 out of the 4 aircraft were lost although one crew returned to the allied position. Worse was to follow on 12th May when, with the German forces threatening to break out, the order went out to destroy the Maastricht bridges. Despite the amount of defence known to be at the bridges the whole squadron volunteered for the mission, one had to turn back early due to technical problems, but the other 5 were lost. G D Clancey, now a F/L, was the pilot of one of the 5 aircraft, Battle L4952, which was shot down while on that mission. He survived and was taken prisoner but both his crew members, Sgt 563545 Kenneth Alderson (W.Op) and Sgt 551745 Ronald Theodore Ainsworth (W.Op/Air Gnr) were killed and are buried in Pouru-St Remy Communal Cemetery.

TUESDAY 4th JULY 1939 Training

Anson I N5025 of 7 Sqn from Finningley completed circuits and landings practice and during approach to land struck a floodlight. The pilot was F/O F A Willan.

On 8th September 1940 F/O Willan, now a S/L, was a member of the crew of Hampden P4287 of 50 Sqn from Lindholme which took off for a raid on Hamburg with 48 other Hampdens. Just before mid-night a communiqué was received indicating that the crew; S/L Willan, Sgt K W Wright, Sgt A B Cox and Sgt F G Brook had baled out. They were all made POWs.

WEDNESDAY 5th JULY 1939 Training

Battle I K9210 of 98 Sqn from Hucknall was approaching to land over trees after low level bombing practice, the pilot P/O J R Taylor, opened up the engines to avoid an obstruction, lost flying speed, stalled and struck a building. P/O Taylor was not injured.

THURSDAY 6th JULY 1939 Training

Magister I L8066 of 27 ERFTS from Tollerton engine cut and the aircraft hit a hedge in a forced landing near Hucknall. A strong wind and low height prevented landing in a suitable field. The pilot instructor was F/S R Kirlew and the pupil F/O Everett.

FRIDAY 21st JULY 1939 Training

Magister I L5959 of 27 ERFTS from Tollerton took off to carry out 'Precise Landings' and 'Landings with Engine'. However the aircraft landed heavily, undershot the airfield as the engine failed to open up soon enough for the aircraft to recover and ran into a hedge.

The instructor pilot, Sgt 740208 John Horner Hargreaves RAFVR, was un-injured but was killed 11 weeks later on 8th October age 27, reasons unknown, and is buried in Grindleton (St Ambrose) Churchyard. The official announcement given on 2.11.39: 'The Air Ministry regrets to announce the following casualties on various dates; killed on Active Service... Sgt J H Hargreaves.'

THURSDAY 3rd AUGUST 1939

Night Training

Hampden I L4162 of 7 Sqn from Finningley took off for local circuits and landings and immediately had engine failure and crash landed. The pilot was P/O G T Rhodes and there were no injuries. P/O Rhodes was court martialled and dismissed the service on 26th September 1939.

SUNDAY 6th AUGUST 1939

1540 hrs Training

Battle I K9263 GV-B of 103 Sqn from Benson collided with Battle K9373 over Nottingham. The observer Sgt Ronald Jefferies Williams, a passenger in K9263, was struck by the airscrew of K9373 and killed. S/L J Coverdale and AC2 541182 Peter Ivo Bligh were un-injured but both were subsequently killed during the war.

W/C 27048 John Coverdale, aged 37, was the pilot of 431 Sqn Wellington HF518 SE-J on a raid on Krefield on 22nd June 1943 and was lost without trace. He is commemorated on the Runnymede Memorial.

W/C Coverdale flew 103 Sqn's first operation on the 17th September 1939 when based in France. His was the lead aircraft of 3 which carried out a daylight reconnaissance along the Franco-German border, between Bouzonville and Lauterbourg with no opposition.

AC2 Peter Ivo Bligh, age 20, by now a Sgt, of 103 Sqn based in France, was a W.Op/ Air Gnr in Battle P2328 PM- which made a morning attack on bridges and columns in the area of Vernon. The aircraft crashed on 10th June 1940 near Gasny, possibly shot down by a Bf 109 seen chasing a Battle north of the target. He was killed and is buried in Gasny Communal Cemetery.

W/C J Coverdale (centre) seen with fellow pilots S/L W E Mulford and S/L T B Marshall

1540 hrs Training

Battle I K9373 of 103 Sqn from Benson was one of three aircraft which took off from their base at Benson, Oxfordshire and using RAF Hucknall as a refuelling and servicing point carried out low level simulated strafing attacks on main roads in the South Notts area. During the afternoon, the three aircraft, after refuelling at Hucknall, were returning to their target, the A46 road, in a V formation over The Meadows area of Nottingham. Battle K9373 drifted over the top of Battle K9263, lost sight of him and lowered its wing onto the aeroplane below. The cockpit canopy of K9263 was shattered and Observer Sgt Ronald Jefferies Williams was killed. The pilot, S/L John Coverdale, battled with the controls and managed to nurse his aircraft to Tollerton Aerodrome where he landed safely. The third member of the crew, AC Peter Ivor Bligh, the Air Gunner, was uninjured. K9373 made an emergency landing in a field on the farm of Mr Allsop at Holme Lane, near Holme Pierrepont. None of this aircraft's crew suffered injury but the aeroplanes underside and propeller was damaged. Pieces of the airman's body were found in the streets of The Meadows, as well as pieces of wreckage. The pilot of K9373 was F/O 39191 Arthur Lushington Vipan. (Courtesy of the Nottingham Evening Post.)

A L Vipan, now a S/L, was killed on 16th October 1944, age 38 years. He was piloting Wellington LN536 of 12 OTU on a training flight from Chipping Warden when it caught fire in the air and crashed near Sywell. He is buried in Cambridge City Cemetery.

F/O Vipan was involved in the first 103 Sqn combat with German fighters on 27th September 1939. He took off in Battle K9271 PM- with observer Sgt 516606 John Henry Vickers, gunner AC1 J E Summers and two other Battle aircraft for another reconnaissance flight between Bouzonville and the Rhine. While flying at 3000 feet the Battles were attacked by 3 French Curtis Hawks but after firing off recognition flares the French aircraft broke off their attack. Soon after the Battles were attacked by 3 German Bf 109s and F/O Vipan's aircraft was damaged and Sgt Vickers seriously wounded. AC1 Summers shot down one of the Bf 109s and the other German aircraft left the scene. Because Sgt Vickers was in pain and the aircraft was damaged F/O Vipan decided to crash land his Battle in a field close to French troop positions on the Maginot Line. Sgt Vickers was taken to hospital where he died on 7th October. The aircraft was struck off charge on 9th October. Sgt Vickers was awarded the Medaille Militaire by the French authorities just before he died and AC1 Summers received the DFM. Special mention of F/O Vipan was made after the success of the evacuation from France.

The Medaille Militaire is one of the rarest decorations for bravery that France can bestow on a foreign serviceman.

The results of the inquest of the above tragedy is as follows: the Coroner said that there had been large scale manoeuvres all over the country and the accident apparently happened during

A Battle aircraft similar to K9373

one of them. A flight of three planes from Benson, near Oxford, were to 'bomb' a target south of the city. For that purpose they would have to fly fairly low. Having completed the exercise they were under instructions to swing right to get away. Unfortunately, for some reason or other, one of the machines came into contact with the leading plane and the three steel propeller blades cut the head of the observer right off. In each plane was a pilot, observer and gunner. 'By some extra ordinary means and very clever piloting,' observed the coroner, 'both machines were able to land, one at Tollerton and the other one at the side of the Trent at Adbolton'.

S/L Coverdale said that 'about 3.40 pm a collision took place between the machine I was flying and the one on my right, which was piloted by F/O Vipan. After the collision we were able to land at Tollerton Aerodrome. It was then found that Williams had been practically decapitated. Considerable damage had been done to my machine.'

S/L Coverdale stated that they were engaged on home defence air exercises. The flight consisted of three machines, of which he was the leader. Part of the exercise was the bombing of a target south of Nottingham, and they were ordered to bomb it at a height of 250ft. Afterwards they were to take avoiding action against imaginary ground gunfire and then get away. After bombing they climbed, and then made a climbing turn to the right. No signal was given at the time of the turn.

P/O R Max, who was flying the third machine, said he looked down as they passed over the target and then dropped behind. 'About ten minutes before, the leader had warned us he would do unexpected turns, and we were to watch him closely.'

Accidental death was recorded.

MONDAY 7th AUGUST 1939 Training

Hawker Hind K6682 of 27 ERFTS from Tollerton propeller hit the ground on take-off for solo aerobatics and the aircraft cart wheeled and overturned due to the tail wheel being too high. The pilot Sgt E A Ireland RAFVR was un-injured.

MONDAY 14th AUGUST 1939 Training

Magister I N3797 of 27 ERFTS from Tollerton was damaged on landing heavily on the aerodrome and the port oleo leg sheared. The pilot, Sgt 745292 Stephen Austin Levenson, was also involved in an incident on 27th April 1940.

Sgt Levenson joined 611 Sqn and flew in the Battle of Britain. His record was: 21.8.40 one Do 17 probable, 11.9.40 one Ju88 destroyed, 15.9.40 one Do215 destroyed and one probable.

He was obviously very versatile and was killed on 17th September 1942 flying with 214 Sqn flying bomber aircraft. He was the pilot of Stirling I R9350 BU-T which took off from Stradishall for a raid on Essen and was shot down by a night fighter. He was on his 14th operation as captain and is buried in Heverlee War Cemetery.

SATURDAY 19th AUGUST 1939 Training

Tutor K6094 of 500 Sqn from Warmwell was on a cross country flight to Hucknall when engine cut on approach to landing, undershot and hit a boundary fence at Hucknall aerodrome. The pilot was P/O J S P Phillips.

TUESDAY 22nd AUGUST 1939 Training

Anson I N5018 of 7 Sqn from Finningley undershot landing during landing practice, opened up again but the engine did not respond and the aircraft struck a tree on the edge of the aerodrome. The pilot was F/O D L England.

SATURDAY 26th AUGUST 1939

The 504 (County of Nottingham) Squadron was embodied into the RAF.

SATURDAY 2nd SEPTEMBER 1939

Night Training

Anson I N5184 of 83 Sqn from Scampton hit high tension cables when attempting a forced landing in bad weather on a night navigation exercise and crashed at Beeston. The pilot was P/O W J (Tommy) Thompson. There was one injury.

The following account is taken courtesy of the Nottingham Evening Post: 'Tommy Thompson's war almost ended before it had begun, in a muddy field between Beeston and Long Eaton. That was where Londoner Thompson crash-landed his Avro Anson and, miraculously, walked away with hardly a scratch. The date was 2nd September 1939, just a few hours before Britain would declare war on Germany. "I was with 83 Squadron at Scampton, flying Hampdens at the time war was declared. Just before war broke out they introduced a scatter programme, sending aircraft to different stations, and I had to fly some mechanics to a partially built field at Newton in an Anson. Then, on 2nd September, the signal came through to return to base immediately." Thompson lifted the bulky twin-engined aircraft into the dark sky over Notts and flew straight into a violent weather front. The storm threw the Anson around and, alone in the cockpit with little idea of where he was, Tommy decided he should return to Newton. But there were no lights below to guide him. By the glare of the repeated lightning, he searched for some flat land for a "pancake landing". It looked as if he might pull off the dangerous manoeuvre as he slid across an open meadow, but then ran into big trouble. "I hit some high tension wires and then collided with an electricity pylon. Suddenly, there was an unholy flashing and static as I hit the wires and then I saw the pylon. I just thought in that split second I am finished."

When I came to, it was pouring with rain. I was sitting in my seat with the controls in front of me and nothing else around me. The fuselage had gone. "I thought I must be smashed up, but I gingerly got out of the wreckage and the worst I suffered from was concussion."

Anson aircraft in flight similar to N5184

He walked slowly away but believes he lost consciousness again. "I came to in the middle of a field, and heard a voice shout 'there's the pilot'. The emergency services had arrived."

Months of hospital treatment and light duties were to pass before Tommy was allowed to return to operational duties, this time flying Spitfires and Hurricanes with No.3 Squadron. "I was the wingman to the CO on the Dieppe raid. It was our job to fire at the shore guns which were firing on our troops, but we got bounced by some Focke-Wulf Fw 190s. I saw the CO go up in flames and fly straight into cliffs."

Tommy's war ended in Germany where he met an interpreter, Maria, married her and settled in Dusseldorf where he still lives, now aged 87. But he has never forgotten that dark and stormy night in 1939 when he almost died somewhere in Notts. I know it was in the Trent Valley, south of Beeston. "I would really like to find the spot and go back and visit it." '

SUNDAY 3rd SEPTEMBER 1939

1100 hrs 'I have to tell you ... this country is at war with Germany.'
Prime Minister Neville Chamberlain, in a broadcast to the nation on this day.

TUESDAY 5th SEPTEMBER 1939 Training

Hampden I L4161 of 7 Sqn from Finningley control was lost during single engine flying practice and the aircraft dived into the ground during a turn two miles north of Finningley. The pilot P/O 39679 Anthony Richard Playfair RAF age 26, a Canadian, was the only crewman killed and is buried in Finningley (Holy Trinity and St Oswald) Churchyard. P/O Playfair came from a theatrical family, his father, Alan, was a cousin of Sir Nigel Playfair. He was granted a short service commission as acting pilot officer on 9th May 1937. Six months later he joined a bomber squadron, and was promoted to pilot officer from 8th March 1938.

WEDNESDAY 4th OCTOBER 1939

1115 hrs Training

Anson I N5096 EA- of 49 Sqn from Scampton took off for West Raynham on a wireless operational training flight with W/c Chick as pilot and G/C Emmett and Capt Barrell as passengers. On arriving at West Raynham they all disembarked. N5096 then took off to RAF Newton with P/O Harker and AC2 McGurk as crew. On reaching Newton there was a strong wind and the air was bumpy and witnesses saw the aircraft approaching at low altitude from the east, circle the airfield at about 150 feet doing steep turns and finally headed west at high speed. It was then seen to do a steep left hand turn, lose height and crash about 2 miles

Grave of P/O Harker

Grave of AC2 McGurk

from the airfield, in the grounds of a mental hospital at Ratcliffe-on-Trent. It was found that the aircraft had approached the leeward side of a hill and had hit the brow whilst level fore and aft, but slightly banked to the left. The Court of Enquiry considered that the primary cause of the accident was the pilot executing low flying, and the secondary cause due to the gusty wind conditions. P/O 40620 Brian Leslie Gordon Harker RNZAF age 22 (Pilot) and AC2 546733 Francis Leo McGurk, W.Op age 22 were killed and are buried in Lincoln (Newport) Cemetery.

TUESDAY 10th OCTOBER 1939

Battle I K9437of 98 Sqn from Hucknall overshot landing and struck an ARP shelter. The pilot was P/O J C F Hayter. There were no injuries. P/O Hayter had a very eventful war.

James Chilton Francis Hayter was born in Timaru, New Zealand on 18th October 1917 and attended Nelson College from 1928 to 1934. He worked on farms and in 1936 took private flying lessons at the Marlborough Aero Club.

In November 1938 he joined the RNZAF on a short service commission and was awarded his wings on 19th April 1939. On 8th May Hayter was flying as observer in a Vildebeeste, which, flying too low, struck a beach at North Kaikoura, wiping off the undercarriage and damaging the propeller. The pilot made a crash landing at Wigram, without injury either to himself or Hayter. A month later he was again flying as observer in a vildebeeste over Lake Ellesmere and on a swan –strafing run, the aircraft struck the water and went in. Hayter and the other two aboard came close to drowning but all escaped with minor injuries.

Hayter then sailed for the UK on 4th July 1939 in the SS *Tamaroa* from Auckland. After arrival, he was posted to 98 Squadron at Hucknall, which was equipped with Fairey Battles. On 12th November, flying low, he hit an air raid shelter and wrote off the aircraft but escaped with minor injuries. Soon afterwards he was posted to 103 Squadron at Plivot in France. On 12th May 1940 he was flying one of three Battles attacking roads and bridges near Sedan. Although attacked by Me 110s, they bombed a pontoon bridge from a height of 20 feet and succeeded in holding up German tanks for some hours. On 12th June Hayter's gunner shot down a Hs 126. On 16th June Hayter was shot down by a Me 109 as he was about to land but he was unhurt. Later that day the squadron was withdrawn to Honington, Suffolk.

Hayter volunteered for Fighter Command and joined 615 Squadron at Prestwick on 4th September but moved to 605 Squadron at Croydon on the 18th. On 15th October he damaged a Me 109 and on the 26th, after damaging a Me 109, he was himself shot down by another. Hayter baled out at 25,000 feet and landed in the grounds of Great Swifts, home of Major Victor Cazalet, where a cocktail party was in progress and to which he was invited. His Hurricane, V6943, crashed at Staplehurst.

On 1st December Hayter destroyed a Me 109. He was made a Flight commander on 20th February 1941 and was posted away on 1st May to 52 OTU at Debden as an instructor. After crashing twice with the same pupil, on 17th and 19th June, Hayter returned to operations in early July 1941, when he joined 611 Squadron at Hornchurch. On 10th July he destroyed a Me 109 but crash-landed near Southend on the return from the sweep after his aircraft was badly damaged by flak. He destroyed Me 109s on 14th July, 29th August and damaged another on 17th September. He was awarded the DFC which was gazetted on 17th October 1941.

On 1st March 1942 Hayter was given command of 274 Squadron at Landing Ground 92 in North Africa. He probably destroyed a Me 109 on the 18th. At the end of September he was posted to Turkey to instruct Turkish pilots on Hurricanes. He went to Iran and took command of 74 Squadron at Mehrabad on 1st April 1943.

In May the squadron moved to Egypt, where it began convoy patrols and took part in wing sweeps over Crete. In late September Hayter took nine squadron Spitfires to Antimachi airfield on Kos Island, in the Dodacanese. On the 29th Ju 88s put the airfield out of action and on 3rd October the Germans invaded Kos and overran the airfield. Hayter and four others took to

P/O J C F Hayter. Courtesy of 74 (F) Tiger Squadron Association

the hills. After evading enemy patrols for several days, they met some men of the Special Boat Service and were taken off by boat on 8th October and put ashore on the Turkish coast. They reached Cyprus in a fishing boat on the 14th and Hayter flew back to Edku ten days later.

The squadron came together again on Christmas Day 1943 at Edku and began convoy patrols in January 1944. Hayter received a Mention in Despatches which was gazetted on 14th January 1944. 74 Squadron sailed from Port Said on 7th April for the UK and went to North Weald. Hayter received a second Mention in Despatches, gazetted on 8th June 1944, took the squadron to France on 19th August and led 74 until 30th December, when he was posted to Milfield for a course at the Fighter Leaders' School. He was awarded a Bar to the DFC, gazetted on 26th January 1945.

In mid-August 1945 Hayter sailed for New Zealand. He went on to the Reserve on 28th December.

MONDAY 23rd OCTOBER 1939 — Training

Hampden I L4077 of 50 Sqn piloted by Sgt 580291 Gerald Marsden Wild was on a low flying attack on a gun position in co-operation with AA crews at Tollerton. The aircraft flew in too low and struck a dummy gun killing Sgt 4963932 Charles Fretwell age 39 of the 28th Light Anti-Aircraft Regiment and injuring Gunner 1474701 G Wardle of the 53rd Light Anti-Aircraft Battery. Sgt Fretwell is buried in Ilkeston (Park) Cemetery.

Six months later Sgt Wild was killed, on 12th April 1940, when flying with 50 Sqn on a raid on Kristiansand. He was the pilot of Hampden L4073 which took off from Waddington and was shot down by flak and fighters. His aircraft was one of three aircraft which did not return from this operation. All the crew are commemorated on the Runnymede Memorial.

Hampdens in formation

TUESDAY 24th OCTOBER 1939

Night — Training

Hampden I L4175 of 106 Sqn from Finningley took off with P/O 40090 Alan Claude Dier at the controls on circuits and landings practice when it undershot approach, hit trees near the aitfield boundary, crash landed and hit a hut. The aircraft was a write off and P/O Dier received a broken leg.

He was promoted to F/L and was killed on 7th July 1941. He was the pilot of Magister L5984 of 24 EFTS, RAF Luton which took off at 0700 hrs and was in collision with a Tiger Moth and crashed 1½ miles north west of the RLG at Barton-in-the-Clay. He and his crew member, LAC1380334 Herbert Royson B Hearne age 21 RAFVR, were taken to Dunstable Mortuary. He is buried in Luton Church Burial Ground.

TUESDAY 11th NOVEMBER 1939

Hampden I L4084 of 50 Sqn overshot on landing at Tollerton and ran through a hedge probably due to the bad visibility. The pilot was P/O G R Taylor.

TUESDAY 28th NOVEMBER 1939 — Training

Hawker Audax I K5166 of 7 FTS(I) was on a solo cross country flight when it landed into the wind, down a slope and hit a hedge in forced landing in bad weather at Bingham. The pilot Sgt 748214 John Drummond Stein RAFVR was unhurt but was subsequently killed on 6th April 1940 flying with 35 Sqn. His Blenheim IV P6918 crashed on take-off on a training flight from Upwood Huntingdonshire. He is buried in Ramsey Cemetery.

Hawker Audax similar to K5166

WEDNESDAY 6TH DECEMBER 1939 — Training

Magister I L8291 of 30 EFTS was landed in a furrowed field at Weston-on-Trent by the pilot Sgt 754101 E A Percival due to being lost on a solo flight.

1940

SATURDAY 13th JANUARY 1940

1135 hrs — Training

Oxford II N6380 of 3 FTS (I) was on a solo cross country flight to Grantham and back in slight foggy conditions. A witness stated that at around 1130 hrs he heard the aircraft circling around near Plungar but could not see it as there was dense mist with visibility down to 50 yards. The engine sounded alright but the aircraft seemed low and then there was a crash. On inspecting the wreckage it transpired that the aircraft had at first struck a hedge with the starboard wing down and then a canal bank about 75 yards further on. The RAF pilot, P/O 42778 Stanley Mornington West age 24, was killed and is buried in Grantham Cemetery.

TUESDAY 16th JANUARY 1940 — Ferrying

Spitfire I K9893 UM- of 152 Sqn from Acklington was piloted by Sgt 566251 John Keel Barker age 23 and being ferried from Hornchurch to Acklington. He became lost in a snow blizzard and was about to land when he saw a row of houses ahead, barely visible in the snowstorm. He manoevered the aircraft to avoid them, also avoiding wooden huts, hit the ground and went through a hedge into a haystack at Boughton near Ollerton but was not injured.

Sgt Barker served as a ground wireless operator in the pre-war RAF before being trained as a pilot and was with 152 Sqn at the start of the Battle of Britain. On 18th August 1940 he claimed a Ju 87 destroyed and on 25th a Bf 109. On 4th September, while still serving with 152 Sqn, he was on patrol in his Spitfire when he was shot down by a Do 17 enemy aircraft at 1340 hours off Bognor Regis, he baled out but he was not recovered and his body was eventually washed up on the French coast. He is buried in Etaples Military Cemetery, Pas de Calais, France.

Sgt Barker

Etaples Military Cemetery

THURSDAY 25th JANUARY 1940

Hawker Henley I L3269 of No.1 AA School from Manby flew into the ground in bad visibilty at Gringley-on-the-Hill, between Bawtry and Gainsborough, whilst returning to Manby. The pilot, P/O 76592 Raymond John Shellard, RAFVR 24 years old was killed and is buried in Barry (Methyr Dyfan) burial ground. The cause of the crash was uncertain.

SATURDAY 16th MARCH 1940

1145 hrs — Training

Magister I N3794 of 30 EFTS from Burnaston piloted by Sgt 754445 Henry James Clarke age 19 RAFVR who was on a solo map reading flight when the aircraft stalled or slipped into the ground, near Kneesall, when turning to land at Ossington. The official crash report stated that he should have landed normally into the wind. No injuries were reported to him or the instructor pilot Sgt A J Samson.

Sgt Clarke and two crew members were killed on 16th December whilst serving with 101 Sqn and he is commemorated on the Runnymede Memorial. He took off from West Raynham piloting Blenheim IV T2039 SR- on a raid on Mannheim, codenamed 'Abigail Rachel' when the aircraft was presumed lost over the sea. Of around 100 various aircraft on the raid T2039 was the only Blenheim lost.

'Abigail' was the codename for a series of what turned out to be abortive major RAF bombing raids against designated German cities, in response to the German bomber attack on Coventry.

'Rachel' was the codename for Mannheim.

MONDAY 1st APRIL 1940

2115 hrs — Ferrying

Wallace II K6014 of Signal Sqn 1 E & W School from Cranwell was lost in the dark when flown by inexperienced pilot P/O T F O'Byrne, struck telephone wires on attempting a forced landing, and crashed in a field, one mile west of Tuxford. He was not injured. The pilot had been tasked to collect another aircraft from Aldergrove.

Westland Wallace II similar to K6014

SATURDAY 27th APRIL 1940

2224 hrs — Training

Spitfire I N3063 FY- of 611 Sqn from Digby was abandoned whilst in a spin, at Kilvington, north of Bottesford after the pilot Sgt 745292 S A Levenson was blinded by searchlights. He was not injured (see previous entry for 14th August 1939).

SUNDAY 5th MAY 1940 Training

Battle I K9474 of 18 OTU from Hucknall took off for forced landing practice with P/O M Rusiecki at the controls and subsequently landed back on the aerodrome with its undercarriage retracted.

FRIDAY 10th MAY 1940

Winston Churchill became Prime Minister.

SUNDAY 12th MAY 1940

504 Sqn fights in France as part of the British Expeditionary Force.

MONDAY 13th MAY 1940

Transcript of a speech given by Winston Churchill to the House of Commons on this day.
'We are in the preliminary stage of one of the greatest battles in history. That we are in action at many points – in Norway and in Holland – that we have to be prepared in the Mediterrean. That the air battle is continuous, and that many preparations have to be made here at home! I would say to the House as I said to those who have joined this government: I have nothing to offer but blood, toil, tears and sweat. We have before us an ordeal of the most grievous kind. We have before us many, many long months of struggle and of suffering.You ask, what is our aim? I can answer in one word. Victory. Victory at all costs – Victory in spite of all terror – Victory, however long and hard the road may be, for without victory there is no survival'.

SATURDAY 18th MAY 1940

1100 hrs Training

Hampden I L4059 OL- of 83 Sqn from Scampton was flying to Newton when it overshot landing and insufficient speed was gained before turning to go round again. A wing dropped and the aircraft stalled, crashed and burnt out ¾ mile south west of Newton aerodrome injuring the crew of four including the pilot Sgt 519023 W F Pritchard. The enquiry suggested that the stall may have been accentuated by opening both throttles too quickly.

FRIDAY 31st MAY 1940

2345 hrs Training

Hampden I L4174 ZN- of 106 Sqn from Finningley took off and control was lost at 1,000 feet, the aircraft went into a spin but failed to recover and struck the ground bursting into flames, two miles west of Finningley. The pilot, Sgt 590761 F M Wilkes, who had reported a similar experience when flying the previous night, and the crew which included AC1 Everson escaped from the burning wreck unhurt.

Sgt Wilkes took off as pilot of Hampden P2077 from Waddington on 14th August for a raid on Bernburg and the aircraft was hit by flak and crashed near Oosthuizen, Holland. All 4 crew members survived and were made POWs.

TUESDAY 4th JUNE 1940

'We shall fight on the beaches' speech delivered by Winston Churchill to the House of Commons.
'I have, myself, full confidence that if all do their duty, if nothing is neglected, and if the best arrangements are made, as they are being made, we shall prove ourselves once more able to defend our Island home, to ride out the storm of war, and to outlive the menace of tyranny, if necessary for years, if necessary alone.

Even though large parts of Europe and many old and famous States have fallen or may fall into the grip of the Gestapo and all the odious apparatus of Nazi rule, we shall not flag or fail. We shall go on to the end, we shall fight in France, we shall fight on the sea and oceans, we shall fight with growing confidence and growing strength in the air, we shall defend our Island, whatever the cost may be, we shall fight on the beaches, we shall fight on the landing grounds, fight in the fields and in the streets, we shall fight in the hills; we shall never surrender, and even if, which I do not for a moment believe, this Island or a large part of it were subjugated and starving, then our Empire beyond the seas, armed and guarded by the British Fleet, would carry on the struggle, until, in God's good time, the New World, with all its power and might, steps forth to the rescue and the liberation of the Old.'

FRIDAY 7th JUNE 1940

1100 hrs — Engine Test

Oxford I V4173 of 1524 BAT Flt from Newton swung on take off and the pilot, Sgt 495352 Forsyth, was unable to correct owing to the passenger's feet jamming the rudder, and the undercarriage collapsed.

FRIDAY 14th JUNE 1940

1855 hrs — Training

Battle I N2189 of 18 OTU from Hucknall overshot landing and hit a hedge because the pilot, Sgt P780128 Henryk Szwedowski, failed to go around again when the hydraulic system failed. There were no injuries and the other crew members were AC1 653448 Johnson and AC2 615070 Cooper.

Sgt Szwedowski ultimately achieved the rank of Warrant Officer. He became a pilot of long experience serving with 300 Sqn and Air Gunnery Schools and survived the war but died on 26th July 1946 at the controls of Wellington BJ884 of CGS in a mid-air collision with Spitfire SL676 during a practice 'attack' and crashed at Appleton-le-Moors, Yorkshire. He is buried in Newark-upon-Trent Cemetery.

TUESDAY 18th JUNE 1940

Winston Churchill, the Prime Minister, made the following declaration on this day.
'What General Weygand has called the Battle of France is over. I expect that the Battle of Britain is about to begin. Upon this battle depends the survival of Christian civilisation. Upon it depends our own British life, and the long continuity of our institutions and our Empire. The whole fury and might of the enemy must very soon be turned on us. Hitler knows that he will have to break us in this Island or lose the war. If we can stand up to him, all Europe may be freed and the life of the world may move forward into broad, sunlit uplands. But if we fail, then the whole world, including the United States, including all that we have known and cared for, will sink into the abyss of a new Dark Age made more sinister, and perhaps more protracted, by the lights of perverted science. Let us therefore brace ourselves to our duties, and so bear ourselves, that if the British Empire and its Commonwealth last for a thousand years, men will say, "This was their finest hour". '

THURSDAY 20th JUNE 1940

Bombs were dropped in the early hours at Owston Ferry, Q site for Finningley.

WEDNESDAY 26th JUNE 1940

0001 hrs

Air raid warning red was given at Hucknall aerodrome. All personnel took cover but the German aircraft passed overhead without bombs being dropped.

SUNDAY 30th JUNE 1940

Night | Flying Test

Hampden I P4337 of 61 Sqn from Hemswell crashed near Torksey whilst on a night flying test. The pilot, F/O 41678 Peter Morrice De Mestre, started to pull out of a dive at 500 feet and the aircraft hit high tension cables. The official crash report states that the cause could have been the pilot's lack of appreciation of the vertical space required to pull a Hampden out of a dive. Despite the inference that F/O De Mestre may have been inexperienced flying a Hampden he did receive the award of the DFC only 7 weeks later.

He took off on 19th August 1940 the pilot of Hampden P2089 of 61 Sqn from Hemswell which, after an attack on Ambes, force landed in Lyme Regis, Dorset, after running out of fuel, with all the crew escaping unhurt resulting in his DFC. The citation read: 'This officer was captain of an aircraft detailed to attack the oil tanks of Bordeaux one night in August 1940. On his first run over the target at 2,000 feet his aircraft and one engine were severely damaged by anti-aircraft fire, and the glare from search lights prevented his bombs being dropped with accuracy. In spite of the serious condition of his aircraft, and the continuous gun fire, he made a second attack and dropped his bombs with success. On the return flight with his wireless smashed, the damaged engine failed whilst over France, but with splendid determination he managed to cross the sea and made a forced landing on the English coast without causing injury to his crew. Pilot Officer De Mestre has many times pressed home his attacks on the enemy with equal courage and determination'.

He was awarded the DSO in May 1942 for numerous attacks with 49 Sqn on enemy targets varying from factories in Germany to supply ships. Unfortunately Peter de Mestre, who was an accomplished rugby union player with London Irish, lost his life on 7th June 1942. He was the pilot of Manchester L7469 of 49 Sqn on a raid on Emden which was shot down by a night fighter and crashed into the North Sea. He is commemorated on the Runnymede Memorial.

F/O P M de Mestre.
Courtesy Malcolm Brooke 49 Sqn

Runnymede Memorial, Surrey

SATURDAY 6th JULY 1940

1230 hrs Training

Hawker Hind K5413 of RAF College Cranwell on air to air RT practice flew into the ground when the pilot, Flying Cadet LAC 905524 Ronald Halford Walker Parker RAFVR age 19, mis-judged the height during unauthorised low flying, made a stalled turn, failed to recover the aircraft and crashed one mile south of South Clifton. LAC Parker and his crew member P/O 42379 Jack Clarence Burraston age 22, RAAF were both killed and were given a funeral with full military honours on 10th July and are buried in St Andrew's Church, Cranwell.

P/O Burraston was born in Glen Innes, NSW, in July 1917. He joined the Royal Australian Artillery in 1937 and was posted to Darwin in May 1938. Returning to Malbourne in January 1939 he successfully applied for a flying course at Point Cook. Opportunities to join the RAAF were limited pre-war and he successfully answered an advertisement from the RAF seeking Australians for officer and pilot training. He left for England with 21 other Australians accepted for the scheme on 13th August 1939 and undertook officer, basic and advanced training at Cambridge, Ansty and Cranwell. He was the first of 12 men among the 22 Australians to lose their lives in the Second World War.

P/O Burraston.
Courtesy L Grimmond

Graves of LAC Parker and P/O Burraston

2325 hrs Training

Hampden I L4181 ZN- of 50 Sqn from Finningley overshot the flarepath landing at night, ran into the dispersal field, and struck a tent occupied by the airfield defence gun crew. Two members of the gun crew were killed one of which was AC2 573507 Patrick Joseph Curry age 19 who is buried in Finningley (Holy Trinity and St Oswald) Churchyard, and two injured. The pilot P/O G A C Potts and his crew were un-injured.

WEDNESDAY 10th JULY 1940

The Battle of Britain begins.

THURSDAY 11th JULY 1940 Ferrying

Envoy III L7270 of 24 Sqn was being ferried from Hendon to Finningley and when landing at Finningley a wheel came off due to the pilot W/C 19108 Anthony Caron Evans-Evans landing the aircraft with drift.

W/C Evans-Evans, by now a Group Captain, was the Station Commander of Coningsby when he was killed on 21st February 1945 age 43 on operations. He was the pilot of Lancaster NE165 OL-Y of 83 Sqn (a Pathfinder Force Squadron) which took off from Coningsby at 1707 hrs to mark the Mittelland Canal. The aircraft was shot down by a night fighter and crashed in Holland killing all seven crew members. This was a very experienced crew, four of whom were decorated. G/C Evans-evans was awarded the DFC, which was announced on 16th February, five days previously.

He is buried in Mierlo War Cemetery and commemorated on the Peterborough War Memorial. G/C Evans-Evans's brother Roland Gwynne Evans-Evans, who was a F/L in the RAF with 2804 Sqn RAF Regiment was also killed in WWII. He was killed on 2nd October 1944 and is buried in Leopoldsburg War Cemetery.

THURSDAY 25th JULY 1940

Night

Hampden I P1253 of 106 Sqn from Finningley overshot the flarepath into rough ground in poor visibility with ground mist. Neither the pilot P/O G O R Kilner nor crew were injured.

FRIDAY 26th JULY 1940

2300 hrs Training

Hampden I L4139 VN- of 50 Sqn from Finningley landed and the undercarriage, which was not locked down, collapsed. The pilot, P/O 41877 Kenneth Richard Killey Smettem, and his crew were unhurt but he was killed just five weeks later. On 30th August he was piloting Hampden L4079 of 50 Sqn which took off from Lindholme for a raid on Monchengladbach, nine miles east of Arnhem, and was shot down at 0032 hrs by Oberleutant Werner Streib, his 2nd victory of the night. He and his crew: Sgt A A Horsfall, Sgt H H Best and Sgt E W J Skinner are buried in Groesbeek Canadian War Cemetery.

SATURDAY 27th JULY 1940

1535 hrs Training

Battle I N2187 of 18 OTU from Hucknall hit a brick structure whilst landing at Hucknall in poor visibility. The pilot, Cpl P/780034 R Bonkowski PAF, tried to land to one side of a formation of three aircraft and in trying to sandwich himself his starboard wing collided with the brickwork of a defence post. There were no injuries.

R Bonkowski, now a Sergeant, was killed on 19th June 1941when he was the 2nd pilot of Wellington R1365 GR- which took off from RAF Swinderby at 2224 hours on 18th June 1941. His aircraft was one of a force of one hundred aircraft sent to bomb Bremen, of which six failed to return to base. R1365 was shot down by a night-fighter piloted by Oberfeldwebel Paul Gildner of 4./NJG1, Night-fighter Squadron, and crashed at 0234 hours on 19th June into the sea off Terschelling with the loss of all six members of the crew aboard.

1600 hrs Ground

Battle I L5528 JN- of 150 Sqn from Newton was being prepared as a standby for operations when a parachute flare fell to the ground from the aircraft and ignited. Despite an effort by those inside the aircraft to put out the flames, assisted by a number of ground crew and headquarters staff, an explosion occurred and six RAF personnel were killed and five injured.

Those who died were: F/L 40041 Walter Michael Blom, DFC age 23, buried in East Bridgford Cemetery, Sgt 522061 William Henry James Franklin, BEM age 28, buried East Bridgford Cemetery, AC1 638353 Frederick Stewart age 22, buried East Bridgford Cemetery,

Cpl 619842 Dennis Harold Sharp buried Birmingham Cemetery, LAC 619068 George Arthur Hall age 20 buried St Pancras Cemetery, LAC 638518 Walter Ypres Cann age 19 buried Woolwich Cemetery,

One of those injured, Sgt 524674 Albert Edward Frank Gould age 23, died the next day and he is buried in Romsey Cemetery.

AC2 R Haywood was one of the personnel injured and Sgt Franklin was awarded the British Empire Medal for making safe bombs on the burning aircraft.

F/L Blom, who appears on the Peterborough War Memorial, was awarded the DFC on 31st May 1940. The citation read: 'During May 1940, this officer was detailed to lead a half section of aircraft in a low level bombing attack against an enemy motorised column of all arms advancing on a road in Luxemburg. Before reaching his objective a petrol tank was pierced by machine-gun fire and, although unable to locate his allotted target through being drenched and almost blinded by the escaping petrol, he pressed home his attack on another enemy column with considerable success. During this time the aircraft was subjected to very heavy fire from the ground and was repeatedly hit, receiving such damage as to render it beyond repair, but this did not prevent Flying Officer Blom from flying back to the base, a distance of 90 miles. He displayed outstanding courage and tenacity'.

F/O Blom and his crew had a narrow escape on 10th May. He was the pilot of Battle K9369 of 150 Sqn which had taken off from Ecury-sur-Coole to attack troop columns and their aircraft was badly shot up but they managed to return to base.

Graves of F/L Blom, Sgt Franklin and AC1 Stewart

MONDAY 29th JULY 1940 Taxiing

Battle I L5273 of 18 OTU from Hucknall was taxiing with LAC Bowakowski at the controls when a collision occurred due to negligence.

TUESDAY 30th JULY 1940

1800 hrs Training

Battle I P6719 of 18 OTU from Hucknall piloted by LAC Bukowiecki force landed with one wheel down onto the aerodrome. This resulted in all Battle aircraft being grounded for inspection.

MONDAY 5th AUGUST 1940

At 0040 hrs a high explosive bomb fell near the Costock to Wysall road, 1 mile from Costock village and 2 were dropped on Bar Lane, Normanton-on-the-Wold.

WEDNESDAY 7th AUGUST 1940

2350 hrs Training

Hampden I L4187 of 106 Sqn from Finningley dived into the ground at a very steep angle at Owston Ferry whilst on a night navigation exercise. The aircraft had been held by a searchlight for a considerable period although recognition signals were given and the pilot was possibly dazzled by the beam and lost control. The four crewmen were killed: Sgt 742697 Arthur

Stuart Dalgress age 23 RAFVR (Pilot) buried Nottingham Southern Cemetery, Sgt 755653 Roy Fleming Wilson age 19 RAFVR (W.Op/Air Gnr) buried Dundee (Balgay) Cemetery, Sgt 648512 William Claude Goldsmith age 18 RAF (W.Op) buried Morden Cemetery, Sgt 525767 David Kinnaird Mills age 24 RAF buried Finningley Churchyard Extension.

THURSDAY 8th AUGUST 1940

The Clifton Pastures bombing range was opened.

MONDAY 19th AUGUST 1940

0105 hrs

Bombs were dropped at Apley Head Farm on the Clumber Estate with little damage caused.

TUESDAY 20th AUGUST 1940

Speech given by Winston Churchill this day.
'Rather more than a quarter of a year has passed since the new Government came into power in this country. What a cataract of disaster has poured out upon us since then!... Meanwhile, we have not only fortified our hearts but our Island. We have rearmed and rebuilt our armies in a degree which would have been deemed impossible a few months ago... The whole Island bristles against invaders, from the sea or from the air... the stronger our Army at home, the larger must the invading expedition be, and the larger the invading expedition, the less difficult will be the task of the Navy in detecting its assembly and in intercepting and destroying it in passage; and the greater also would be the difficulty of feeding and supplying the invaders if ever they landed... Our Navy is far stronger than it was at the beginning of the war. The great flow of new construction set on foot at the outbreak is now beginning to come in.

Why do I say this? Not, assuredly, to boast, not, assuredly, to give the slightest countenance to complacency. The dangers we face are still enormous, but so are our advantages and resources. I recount them because the people have a right to know that there are solid grounds for the confidence which we feel, and that we have good reason to believe ourselves capable, as I said in a very dark hour two months ago, of continuing the war "if necessary alone, if necessary for years"...

The great air battle which has been in progress over this Island for the last few weeks has recently attained a high intensity. It is too soon to attempt to assign limits either to its scale or to its duration. We must certainly expect that greater efforts will be made by the enemy than any he has so far put forth... It is quite plain that Herr Hitler could not admit defeat in his air attack on Great Britain without sustaining most serious injury. If after all his boastings and bloodcurdling threats and lurid accounts trumpeted round the world of the damage he has inflicted, of the vast numbers of our Air Force he has shot down, so he says, with so little loss to himself... if after all this whole air onslaught were forced after a while tamely To peter out, the Fuhrer's reputation for veracity of statement might be seriously impunged. We may be sure, that he will continue as long as he has the strength to do so... It must also be remembered that all the enemy machines and pilots which are shot down over our Island, or over the seas which surround it, are either destroyed or captured; whereas a considerable proportion of our machines, and also of our pilots, are saved, and as soon again in many cases come into action... We believe that we shall be able to continue the air struggle indefinitely and as long as the enemy pleases, and the longer it continues the more rapid will be our approach, first towards the parity, and then into that superiority, in the air upon which in a large measure the decision of the war depends.

The gratitude of every home in our Island, in our Empire, and indeed throughout the world, except in the abodes of the guilty, goes out to the British airmen who, undaunted by odds, unwaried in their constant challenge and mortal danger, are turning the tide of the World War by their prowess and by their devotion. Never in the field of human conflict was so much owed by so many to so few. All hearts go out the fighter pilots, whose brilliant actions we se with our own eyes day after day...

A good many people have written to me to ask me to make on this occasion a fuller statement of our war aims, and of the kind of peace we wish to make after the war, than is contained in the very considerable declaration which was made early in the autumn... I do not think it would be wise at this moment, while the battle rages and the war is still perhaps only in its earlier stage, to embark upon elaborate speculations about the future shape which should be given to Europe.... Bur before we can undertake the task of rebuilding we have not only to be convinced ourselves, but we have to convince all other countries that the Nazi tyranny is going to be finally broken. The right to guide the course of world history is the noblest prize of victory. We are still toiling up the hill; we have not yet reached the crest-line of it; we cannot survey the landscape or even imagine what its condition will be when that longed-for morning comes. The task which lies before us immediately is at once more practical, more simple and more stern.... For the rest, we have to gain the victory. That is our task.

...Some months ago we came to the conclusion that the interests of the United States and of the British Empire both required that the United States should have facilities for the naval and air defence of the Western Hemisphere against the attack of a Nazi power... We had therefore decided spontaneously, and without being asked or offered any inducement, to inform the Government of the United States that we would be glad to place such defence facilities at their disposal by leasing suitable sites in our Transatlantic possessions for their greater security against the unmeasured dangers of the future... His Majesty's Government are entirely willing to accord defence facilities to the United States on a 99 year's leasehold basis... Undoubtably this process means that these two great organisations of the English-speaking democracies, the British Empire and the United States, will have to be somewhat mixed up together in some of their affairs for the mutual and general advantage. For my own part, looking out upon the future, I do not view the process with any misgivings. I could not stop it if I wished; no one can stop it. Like the Mississippi, it just keeps rolling along. Let it roll. Let it roll on full flood, enexorable, irresistible, benignant, to broader lands and better days.'

SUNDAY 25th AUGUST 1940

301 Sqn suffered its first operational loss. P/O Woronski crashed at Honington.

WEDNESDAY 28th AUGUST 1940

A man was fatally injured in an air raid on Sneinton Vale, Nottingham, and died the next day. At 2225 hrs bombs were dropped at Laxton. An ambulance from Southwell had just unloaded some First Aid trainees who had attended a lecture at Southwell and among them was a lady who was killed, Miss Willis, who lived alone at the Old School House. Miss Willis was apparently in the act of opening the door of her house when the bomb struck a small out-house about 15-20 feet away. There is a plaque mounted on the wall of Laxton church commemorating Miss Willis and all those servicemen and women from the village who lost their lives in World War Two.

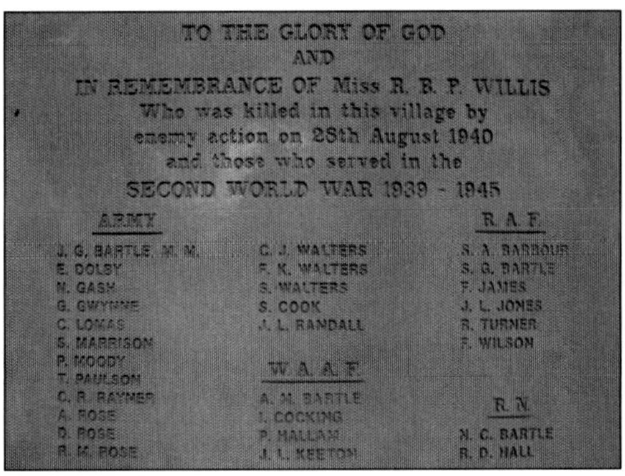

Laxton Church commemorative plaque

FRIDAY 30th AUGUST 1940

1600 hrs

Battle I P2309 of 300 Sqn from Swinderby piloted by F/L P/76611 Stefan Krynski PAF landed with one wheel retracted. No-one was injured.

F/L Krynski was subsequently killed on 28th December when as pilot of Wellington P1035, also of 300 Sqn, he was returning from a raid on Antwerpen when his aircraft crashed one mile west south west of Swinderby, at 2124 hrs. He is buried in Newark-upon-Trent Cemetery.

2230 hrs

First bombs of the war fell on, and around, Nottingham and a total of seven people were killed including an eighteen month old baby.

Judges bakery in Mapperley was damaged and bombs were also dropped at Barnstone railway station, The Old Rectory at Plungar and Granby. A total of 18 high explosives and 120 incendiaries were dropped on Sherwood and Mapperley. Judges bakery is now a public house called 'The Bread and Bitter'. The first of a stick of bombs caused slight damage to Hucknall aerodrome.

MONDAY 2nd SEPTEMBER 1940

Two bombs were dropped on Carlton, Nottingham.

TUESDAY 3rd SEPTEMBER 1940

2345 hrs — Training

Hampden I L4182 of 106 Sqn from Finningley overshot the flarepath, swung out of the wind at speed to avoid a hedge and the undercarriage collapsed. The pilot was P/O T Dawson.

WEDNESDAY 4th SEPTEMBER 1940

1930 hrs — Training

Battle I P5230 of 18 OTU from Hucknall was on practice glide landings from 1,200 feet when the aircraft landed on rough ground at Hucknall and the undercarriage collapsed. The ground was rough and hard due to lack of rain. The pilot LAC P/780497 Nikodem Plotek PAF was not injured but was killed on 3rd July 1941age 24 and is buried in Manchester Southern Cemetery.

He was the pilot of Blenheim IV Z5870 of 12 Gp AAC Flight from RAF Digby which flew into a hill at 2,800 feet, in mist, at Lee Farm, Edale, Derbyshire, killing him and the other three crew members. Although engine failure was considered to have been unlikely, the cause of the accident was not known.

THURSDAY 5th SEPTEMBER 1940

504 Sqn, operating from RAF Hendon enters the Battle of Britain.

Battle I L5273 of 18 OTU from Hucknall undercarriage collapsed when the aircraft ran through a pile of stones and a hedge at Hucknall. The pilot was LAC P/780410 E Najoukiewicz PAF.

A Polish servicing crew prepare a Battle for a practice bomber sortie at Hucknall. Courtesy of Jerzy B Cynk

FRIDAY 6th SEPTEMBER 1940

0915 hrs — Training

Lysander II P1692 of 613 Sqn from Netherthorpe returning from a photo reconnaissance flight, made a long low approach to land in calm conditions, hit a moving truck which was screened by trees owing to the size and shape of the landing area, and crashed at Netherthorpe. The aircraft immediately caught fire and Sgt Letham, the air gunner, escaped, but the truck driver died. The pilot, P/O 51565 Grosvenor Louis Edmonds age 23, had to be rescued around exploding ammunition but suffered from 3rd degree burns to his legs and was admitted to hospital.

He died on Sept 13th from septicaemia and was buried in Worksop (Retford Road) Cemetery.

In September 1993 1325 Sqn ATC unveiled a plaque mounted on a wall of Netherthorpe Airfield clubhouse to the memory of P/O Edmonds.

P/O Edmonds death was the second in the family within three months. On 7th June 1940 P/O Edmond's brother, F/O 39971 John Dudley Edmonds, serving with 43 Sqn was killed over France age 21. He was flying Hurricane I L1931 on patrol over Amiens when he was shot down by a Me 109. He is buried in St Valery-en-Caux Franco-British Cemetery.

Grave of P/O G L Edmonds and his brother F/O J D Edmonds

A Lysander Mk II

Operations

Battle I L5593 of 150 Sqn from Newton on return from operations the starboard leg would not lower by mechanical and manual methods and the aircraft belly landed. The pilot P/O C H Elliot and his crew were not injured.

2015 hrs — Training

Hampden I P1311 ZN- of 106 Sqn from Finningley swung violently during take-off for a cross country training run probably due to the pilot, Sgt 566066 John Edwin Hills RAF, opening up the engines too quickly. The undercarriage collapsed possibly due to undue strain placed on the undercarriage on the application of the brakes. There were no injuries.

Sgt Hills was killed 18 days later on 24th September and is buried in Oxford (Rose Hill) Cemetery. He was piloting Hampden X2911 when he took off for a raid on Calais and collided with Hampden P4397. His three crew members were injured.

WEDNESDAY 11th SEPTEMBER 1940

Night — Op; Bologne

Battle I L5237 of 150 Sqn from Newton landed too far down the flarepath and at a slightly too fast a speed and overshot into a wire fence because the brakes had failed to arrest the aircraft in time. The aircraft had been returning from operations, probably to attack the shipping at Boulogne. Neither the pilot P/O Rafter nor his crew were injured. Six aircraft were dispatched from 150 Sqn on this raid and all returned safely.

MONDAY 16th SEPTEMBER 1940

1555 hrs — Operations

Battle I R7402 of 300 Sqn from Swinderby landed on one wheel, with port undercarriage leg retracted, and the aircraft belly landed. The pilots were F/O Konarzewski PAF and P/O P/7650 Kurowski PAF. There were no injuries.

WEDNESDAY 18th SEPTEMBER 1940

While a large parachute flare was being secured on a Battle of 301 Sqn at Swinderby its detonator was activated and its striker ejected, wounding LAC Stefan Nowak, an armourer fitter, in the arm. Realising the danger to the aircraft and maintenance crew working on it, he pulled the flare off its hooks and ran away from the aircraft before it exploded in his hands. He sustained injuries and severe burns. LAC Nowak's bravery earned him the first Polish decoration to an airman in Great Britain.

1834 hrs — Training

Hampden I X2960 of 106 Sqn from Swinderby was unable to maintain height on one engine and landed with the undercarriage retracted in a small field and ran into a hedge near Cantley. The pilot was P/O I H Grant. There were no injuries.

SATURDAY 21st SEPTEMBER 1940

Night — Taxiing

Battle I L5339 of 18 OTU from Hucknall taxied into a pile of stones at night. The night was extremely dark and the pilot, LAC 780152 D J Bakanacz, had difficulty in estimating his speed and was considered not to blame. LAC Bakanacz, by now a F/S, was also involved in an incident on 8th February 1943 when he was the pilot of Wellington DV671 which belly landed after both engines cut.

MONDAY 23rd SEPTEMBER 1940

2050 hrs — Training

Battle I K9480 of 18 OTU from Hucknall took off for a circuits and landings exercise piloted by LAC P/780509 Edmund Rozmiarek PAF age 25. After successfully completing 3 solo landings the aircraft had reached a height of 500 feet, it went into a right hand turn against the circuit, lost height and crashed into two houses at the corner of Ruffs Drive and Laughton Crescent, Hucknall. LAC Rozmiarek was killed and was buried with full military honours in Hucknall Cemetery on 27th September.

All the family in the house were also killed. They were Albert Evans, age 28, his wife Alice, age 30, and their children Ronald age 8, Alice (junior) age 6 and John age 2, all are buried in Hucknall Urban District Cemetery. Next door, Mr Smith and his six children were slightly injured. A soldier who attempted rescue received injuries and was admitted to the City Hospital. One Auxiliary Fire Service member was injured fighting the fire.
Crash location grid ref: sheet 129 523480.

There is a plaque mounted in a wall in West Lane, Hucknall, dedicated to LAC P780509 Edmund Rozmiarek.

Damaged house at Ruffs Drive.
Courtesy Nottingham Evening Post

THURSDAY 26th SEPTEMBER 1940

Night — Op; Ostend

Battle I L5336 of 103 Sqn from Newton overshot the flarepath and hit a boundary hedge on its return from Ostend. The pilot was Sgt 581733 Ralston. There were no injuries.

FRIDAY 27th SEPTEMBER 1940

2115 hrs — Training

Hampden I P1256 of 106 Sqn from Finningley on local flying practice was approaching to land and turning in on final stage when it dived into the ground at Highwood Farm, Misson Springs, three miles south east of Finningley airfield.

Of the crew, Sgt 967910 Lloyd Haig Beatty McLeod was killed and is buried in Edinburgh (Mount Vernon) Roman Catholic Cemetery. The pilot P/O 42373 John Edgecombe Lowe, age 20 and on attachment from 44 Squadron was seriously injured but died later and is buried in Finningley (St Oswald) Churchyard Extension.

R H Juby who was a volunteer with the home guard of the 3rd Battalion Doncaster Group attempted to rescue the occupants of the crash and was awarded the BEM. His citation reads:

'On 27th September 1940 an aircraft from the Royal Air Force Station at Finningley struck the ground near Misson and immediately burst into flames. The pilot, after being thrown from his seat, was caught by his parachute harness and remained hanging from the aircraft. Volunteer Juby, who immediately ran to the aircraft when it crashed and burst into flames, cut away the parachute harness and freed the pilot. He then carried him to the windward side of the aircraft. The pilot was later taken by ambulance to hospital but he died from the injuries he had sustained in the accident. Volunteer Juby disregarded personal safety and danger when he approached the burning wreckage and entered the flames to cut away the pilot's harness. Had it not been for the injuries he had received in the accident, there is little doubt that Volunteer Juby's prompt action would have saved the pilot's life.'

THURSDAY 3rd OCTOBER 1940

1600 hrs — Training

Tiger Moth T5701 of 7 EFTS made a forced landing and damaged the undercarriage at Kingston-on-Soar when the pilot, LAC 961448 K A Edwards, became lost due to weather deterioration.

1620 hrs — Training

Battle I L5081 of 18 OTU from Hucknall was on low level bombing practice when it was damaged in a forced landing in bad weather at Clifton Pastures bombing range, south west of Clifton, Nottingham. The pilot was Sgt P/980414 W Kulczycki PAF.

SUNDAY 6TH OCTOBER 1940

1250 hrs — Training

Hampden L4100 of 106 Sqn from Finningley was on a cross country training flight with Sgt 745021 D A Howard RAFVR at the controls when it was attacked by Spitfires. The aircraft had fired recognition signals on sighting the Spitfires but they still attacked and one crewman was killed. There are conflicting reports on the fate of L4100. One report says that the aircraft returned safely to base, albeit damaged by gunfire, another suggests that it crashed 6 miles north west of Stradishall. Adding credence to the Stradishall report is the fact that the 2nd pilot (says navigator in the crash log) was killed and his buried in Stradishall (St Margaret) Churchyard.

The aircraft landed safely. The attack happened 6 miles north of Stradisall or that is where the aircraft landed.

FRIDAY 11th OCTOBER 1940

1315 hrs — Ferrying

Battle I L5593 of 3 FPP engine cut and the aircraft belly landed in a field near Newton. The pilot was P/O S Reyman. This aircraft was also involved in an incident on 6th September.

SUNDAY 13th OCTOBER 1940

Ten bombs were dropped on the western edge of Swinderby airfield by a German bomber. One airman was injured receiving slight head injuries, one Battle aircraft of 301 Sqn was destroyed and two aircraft of 300 Sqn were damaged.

The gallant conduct shown by the Fire Tender crew, AC1 Rayner, AC1 Powell, AC1 Dugdale, AC1 Widows and AC1 Ladd, prevented a serious explosion as one of the bombs fell and ignited a flare which was stowed near a 'standby load' of 250 lb bombs.

1925 hrs Training

Hampden I L4184 ZN-Q of 106 Sqn from Finningley swung on take-off for a cross-country flight and the undercarriage collapsed. The pilot Sgt 958212 R Grainger failed to check swing at the start. No-one was injured.

Night Op; Calais

Battle I L5428 WT- of 142 Sqn from Binbrook on return from operations the pilot, P/O T Stevenson was unable to land the aircraft at Waddington at night owing to bad weather. He decided to gain altitude and when the aircraft subsequently ran out of fuel the crew abandoned the aircraft which crashed two miles west of Torksey. The two other crew members were Sgts Green and Whitcher none injured.

2300 hrs Op; Boulogne

Battle I L5427 BH-E of 300 Sqn from Swinderby was returning from Operations when the pilot Sgt 780466 W Koczwarski PAF became lost in bad weather and made a short landing in a narrow field, near Hucknall. At the end of its run the aircraft rolled to the right and broke a wheel. The crew, which included Sgt Sztul PAF, escaped unhurt.

Battle L5427 BH-E of 300 Squadron being prepared for operations. Courtesy of Jerzy B Cynk

Battle L5427 BH-E of 300 Squadron. Courtesy of Jerzy B Cynk

2350 hrs **Op; Calais**

Battle I L5499 BH-Y of 300 Sqn from Swinderby was returning from Operations on the invasion port of Calais when it crashed at Watchwood Plantation, between Calverton and Blidworth, due to control being lost, after meeting extremely adverse weather conditions including fog. The aircraft had been airborne for nearly six hours.

Staff at Papplewick Waterworks Pumping Station at Sansom Wood heard the crash and saw a vivid flash ½ mile away. A Home Guard unit from Ramsdale Park was on the scene soon after the crash.

The three crew members, F/O P/76605 Jan Gebicki PAF (Pilot), Sgt P/780113 Edward Morawa PAF (Observer) and Sgt P/780231 Tadeusz Egierski PAF (Air Gunner), were killed in the crash and are buried in Southern Churchyard, West Bridgeford. A memorial to the crew was erected 50 yards north of the crash site. (see memorials section).

Crash location: OS sheet 120 603519; Memorial location: OS sheet 120 605517.

Graves of Sgt Morawa, F/O Gebicki, Sgt Egierski.

MONDAY 14th OCTOBER 1940

A parachute mine was dropped on Winthorpe aerodrome making a crater 38 feet across and 20 feet deep.

THURSDAY 17th OCTOBER 1940

0322 hrs **Op; Bremen**

Wellington IC N2773 KX-K of 311 Sqn from East Wretham was returning from Operations when the radio failed over the Dutch coast and the crew became lost in bad weather. Unable to locate their position, the aircraft ran out of fuel and the crew abandoned the aircraft which then crashed near Papplewick Water Works, near Blidworth.

There was a crew of six who all baled out before the crash but the Czech pilot, F/L Josef Snajdr, who was injured was taken by ambulance to RAF Station Hucknall. P/O 82533 Miloslav Vejrazka RAFVR, (W/Op) age 29 was killed because he pulled his parachute cord too soon after leaving the aircraft and he is buried in Honington (All Saints) Churchyard, Suffolk.

Some reports have suggested that P/O Vejrazka was shot and killed by over zealous members of the Home Guard. The rest of the crew were un-injured: P/O 787563 Leo Anderle, P/O Richter, P/O 82599 Jan Furbach and Sgt 82557 Bohumil Landa.

F/L Snajdr eventually became a Wing Commander and was awarded a DFC. He was Flight Commander of 311 Sqn 'A' flight from 27.5.41 to 20.4.42 and Squadron Commander from 20.4.42 to 1.2.43.

Wellingtons of 311 Squadron in formation with N2773 'K' acting as No.2

SATURDAY 19th OCTOBER 1940

Three incendiary bombs fell on West Bridgford.

MONDAY 21st OCTOBER 1940

DH.84 Dragon X9398 of 7 AACU was lost in bad visibility near Clipstone, north east of Mansfield, and during a forced landing overshot in a small field, landing down a slope and ran into a hedge when the undercarriage collapsed. The pilot Sgt 742700 C L Harris RAFVR was unhurt.

TUESDAY 29TH OCTOBER 1940

1105 hrs Training

Battle I L5356 BH-R of 300 Sqn from Swinderby took off on a co-operation flight with roof watchers of Leicester. This entailed flying to Leicester and over flying roof spotters to enable them to readily spot Battle aircraft in the future. However 5 minutes after take off en route to Leicester the aircraft was observed manoeuvring in the vicinity of Sutton-on-Trent at a height of 4,000 feet, go into a dive and during its recovery the port mainplane became detached. The remainder crashed at high speed and burst into flames in Darley's Orchard, Sutton-on-Trent, eleven miles south south east of Retford. The three crew members, who all died, are buried side by side in the Polish Cemetery at Newark-upon-Trent.

Sgt P/780040 Gerhard Goebel aged 26, F/O P/76828 Stanislaw Firlej-Bielanski aged 33 (Pilot), and Sgt P/780068 Tadeusz J Szmarjdowicz aged 21. Their funerals took place on 1st November.

The enquiry concluded that the accident was due to structural failure whilst the pilot was pulling out of a dive.

A Polish airman's funeral party at Newark Cemetery. (There are over 300 Polish airmen buried in this Cemetery.)

THURSDAY 31st OCTOBER 1940

The first daylight air raid in the Nottingham area took place. Five bombs were dropped in Chilwell Lane, Bramcote, possibly targeting the Royal Ordnance Factory at Chilwell.

SUNDAY 3rd NOVEMBER 1940

1235 hrs — Training

Wellington IC L7817 of 4 FPP was attacked by a Hurricane three times and the pilot was forced to land at Long Eaton, whereupon the tail wheel collapsed after being damaged by bullets. The pilot was P/O W E J Lunn.

1300 hrs — Flying Test

Hampden I X2978 OL-K of 83 Sqn from Scampton was carrying out a night flying test and low flying up the River Trent. At a bend in the river it turned over land and collided with an ash tree in a field near Laneham, and crashed with the loss of three of the four crew members. The accident card states that the cause was obscure and only two crew members were killed: the pilot, Sgt 740422 Basil Edward Redgrove RAFVR age 24, and Sgt 639031 John Henry Green RAF age 20, are both buried in Scampton Churchyard. P/O Harwood and Sgt Evans were injured.

Records in the Nottingham Public Records Office state that the crash occurred at Laneham road, Rampton. Three of the crew killed, bomber completely burnt out. One occupant identified by papers in a pocket as 1108295 AC2 Robert Rankin McHarry Rowlands, 18 years was also killed and is buried in St Helens Cemetery.

It is likely that AC2 Rowlands was aboard the aircraft for flying experience and this was not recorded in the aircraft crash log.

A Wellington on its way to RAF Swinderby for delivery to 300 Sqn was attacked by a Hurricane at Long Eaton. Approximately 12 bullet holes were found in the aircraft when it finally landed at Swinderby.

A 300 Sqn damaged Wellington.
Courtesy of M J Ingham

FRIDAY 8th NOVEMBER 1940

2145 hrs — Training

Hampden I P2129 of 61 Sqn from Finningley undercarriage collapsed on landing after a cross country flight because it was not fully locked down. There were no injuries to the crew. However the pilot, Sgt 531180 John Hopkins age 24, was killed eighteen days later, on 26th November, he is buried in Darvel Old Cemetery. He was the pilot of Hampden X3064 of 61 Squadron which took off from Hemswell for a raid on Kiel and crashed at 0140 hours, on the return journey, at Spital-in-the-Street about a mile to the east of the airfield. X3064 was the only loss on the raid.

WEDNESDAY 13th NOVEMBER 1940

1940 hrs Training

Wellington IC L7813 PM- of 103 Sqn undercarriage collapsed in a heavy landing on one wheel at Newton and subsequently burnt out when hit by Wellington N2998 at 2005 hrs. The pilot Sgt 742211 C H Muggeridge RAFVR, and his crew escaped injury.

2005 hrs Training

Wellington IA N2998 JN- of 150 Sqn landed on Newton airfield and ran into the wreckage of Wellington L7813.

THURSDAY 14th NOVEMBER 1940

2045 hrs

The Lutwaffe dropped a landmine by parachute onto the south side of Winthorpe Airfield, a satellite of Swinderby, and it exploded and blew up a guard hut leaving a crater 39 feet across and 20 feet deep. 2 dispersed aircraft were undamaged. The landmine had been preceded by a bomb which had burst prematurely in the air and gave the alarm to the airmen in the guard hut who ran for cover.

FRIDAY 15th NOVEMBER 1940 Two bombs were dropped on Wollaton, Nottingham.

SUNDAY 17th NOVEMBER 1940

0340 hrs Operations

Hampden I X2970 ZN- of 106 Sqn from Finningley overshot the runway in bad weather after returning from Operations, probably a raid on Hamburg, turned to avoid an obstruction and the undercarriage collapsed. The pilot was P/O R D Wilson. There were no injuries. This aircraft was involved in another incident on 12th August 1941.

WEDNESDAY 20th NOVEMBER 1940

1630 hrs Training

Master I T8324 of 5 FTS took off on a solo flight for map reading practice when the pilot, LAC 916776 E A G C Bruce became lost. The aircraft crashed due to fuel shortage, with undercarriage retracted, in a ploughed field at Edingley one mile west of Kirklington, on the north side of the Mansfield/Southwell LMS railway line. LAC Bruce was un-injured.

A Miles Master Mk I

THURSDAY 21st NOVEMBER 1940

1820 hrs — Operations

Hampden I P1337 of 83 Sqn from Finningley on loan from 106 Sqn took off and after the pilot, Sgt 142412 J K Shreeve, found himself airborne he attempted to turn the aircraft, overshot the flarepath on landing, struck a gun post and barbed wire on trying to avoid a hedge and came to a halt. This aircraft was also involved in an incident on 9th February 1941.

FRIDAY 22nd NOVEMBER 1940

1600 hrs — Training

Hampden I L4204 of 14 OTU from Cottesmore force landed with undercarriage retracted in bad visibility four miles north of Willoughby-on-the-Wolds, near Nottingham. The aircraft was on an instrument and cross country training flight from Cottesmore to East Rufford (Retford), Northampton then back to Cottesmore. The pilot P/O Neill and crew were not injured.

MONDAY 25th NOVEMBER 1940

2050 hrs — Training

Hampden I L4120 of 106 Sqn from Finningley undershot the runway on approach to land and struck a tree 400 yrds from the airfield boundary. The pilot was Sgt 742786 Boyall. There were no injuries. This aircraft was also involved in an incident on 16th December.

TUESDAY 26th NOVEMBER 1940

1530 hrs — Training

Wellington I P9228 of 300 Sqn from Swinderby had the undercarriage retracted while on the ground by the pilot under instruction, Sgt Halabuda PAF. He had operated the landing gear instead of flaps, and the port landing wheel retracted and the aircraft received wing, aileron and engine damage. F/O Kaluza PAF was the instructor.

THURSDAY 28th NOVEMBER 1940

Day — Training

Oxford II N4839 of 11 FTS from Shawbury took off with LAC 908066 Garrould at the controls for a cross country trip from Shawbury to Peterborough and back. Unfortunately LAC Garrould became lost due to bad visibility and he made a forced landing in a field at Hickling Lane Farm, Stapleford, ran through a hedge and the undercarriage collapsed.

FRIDAY 29th NOVEMBER 1940

1750 hrs — Training

Hampden I L4183 ZN-P of 106 Sqn from Finningley swung on take off for a night exercise and the pilot, F/O 72251 William Kelman Burr Thomas, overcorrected. The aircraft flew over the bomb dump and struck the bomb dump fence and the undercarriage collapsed. No injuries were reported to the crew who were F/O Thomas, Sgt J E Sowden, Sgt J C Wiggall and Sgt Flynn.

F/O Thomas was killed on 4th February 1941 whilst piloting Hampden AD750 ZN- in a mining operation off St Nazaire when the aircraft crashed. He is buried in Pont-du-Cens Communal Cemetery.

2150 hrs Training

Hampden I L4185 of 106 Sqn from Finningley was practicing circuits and landings when at the end of the exercise its landing was delayed for nearly five hours due to another aircraft crashing on the flare path, probably Hampden L4183 above. The accident necessitated alteration to the flare path but fog descended before it was laid properly and as flight control was unable to communicate with the wireless operator due to failure of the intercom the pilot, P/O R M Broadhead, who was attached from 44 Sqn, made a heavy landing and the undercarriage collapsed.

R M Broadhead was promoted to P/O on 9th February 1936 and on 18th May he resigned his commission on the conversion of the Special Reserve to the Auxiliary Air Force. He was immediately granted a commission in the same rank with 504 (County of Nottingham) Bomber Sqn.

WEDNESDAY 4th DECEMBER 1940

1300 hrs Taxiing

Tiger Moth II N9279 of 613 Sqn was taxiing after a successful forced landing during a circuits and landings flight when the pilot, Cpl 327251 Ernest Kirby of the Yorkshire Hussars, who had only had two hours flying time, ran the aircraft into a post.

Cpl Kirby died age 36 on 6th September 1945 when serving with the Royal Army Service Corps. He is buried in Milan War Cemetery.

SATURDAY 7th DECEMBER 1940

1200 hrs Taxiing

Wellington I P9214 of 301 Sqn from Swinderby piloted by P/O 76678 Boleslaw Roland Murawski PAF, had a tail wheel collapse after it had struck a hole in the aerodrome surface while taxiing to position.

P/O Murawski was killed on 2nd January 1941 piloting Wellington T2518. He took off from Swinderby for a raid on Bremen and on return was shot down by a fighter and crashed at Wellingore. One crew member was injured and the five who died are buried in Newark-upon-Trent Cemetery. T2518 was one of four aircraft lost over England after the raid.

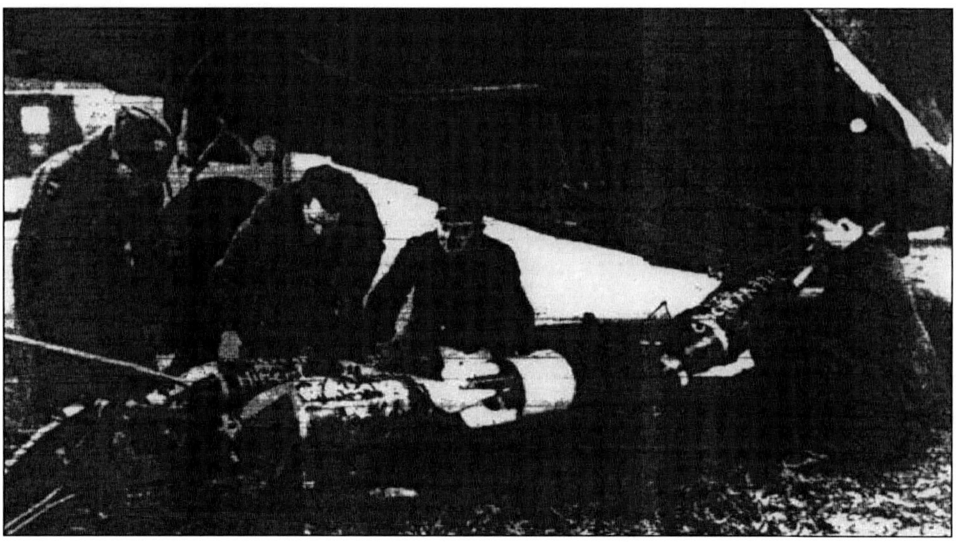

Bombs being loaded onto a Wellington bomber before a raid by Polish Airmen at Swinderby

1900 hrs — Training

Hampden I L4103 of 106 Sqn from Finningley was on circuits and landings practice when an engine cut in circuit and the aircraft struck the ground in a shallow dive, 1½ miles north west of Blaxton, near Finningley. Two crew members died: Sgt 741468 Joseph Donald Shilling RAFVR (Pilot) on loan from 50 Sqn buried in Farnborough (Victoria Road) Cemetery and Sgt 647064 John Thomson RAF (W.Op/Air Gnr) buried in Finningley (Holy Trinity and St Oswald) Churchyard Extension. The cause of the crash was obscure but thought to be an engine failure due to a lightning strike.

THURSDAY 12th DECEMBER 1940

2045 hrs

High explosive bombs were dropped on Kinoulton and also Grange Farm, Torworth, near Retford. 1 ewe, 1 beast and 2 sows were injured.

FRIDAY 13th DECEMBER 1940

2020 hrs

A bomb was dropped on Balderton, on an old colliery tip at Pyehill Colliery, Basford, and north of the Fosse Road, Kinoulton.

SATURDAY 14th DECEMBER 1940 — Engine Test

Wellington I R1227 of 301 Sqn from Swinderby was having engine tests when the pilot F/L J W Piotrowski PAF opened up both engines at the same time and the aircraft tipped onto its nose.

—

A bomb was dropped on Flatts Lane, Calverton.

SUNDAY 15th DECEMBER 1940

A parachute was found in a field near Moor Lane, Bramcote.

MONDAY 16th DECEMBER 1940

1450 hrs — Flying Test

Hampden I L4120 ZN- of 106 Sqn from Finningley had the port engine fail while on engine and air frame test, pulling the aircraft to the left. The port wing dropped, and unable to straighten out to fly on one engine the pilot, Sgt 741065 I P Mapp, recovered the situation near the ground and force landed with the undercarriage retracted ½ mile south east of Finningley. Sgt Mapp, on attachment from 61 Sqn, was not injured. This aircraft was also involved in an incident on 25th November.

—

2048 hrs

Bombs were dropped on Hucknall, Thurgaton, Gibsmere, Hazelford Ferry, Hoveringham, Newton, East Bridgford, Elston, Balderton, Annesley and the fields behind Bartons garage, Mansfield Lane, Calverton.

TUESDAY 17th DECEMBER 1940

1240 hrs

Lysander II P9068 of 7 AACU from Wittering crashed at Westfield Farm, Warsop, in bad weather. The undercarriage collapsed and the aircraft was completely wrecked. The only occupant, a Polish Sgt Pilot received slight injuries to a hand.

WEDNESDAY 18th DECEMBER 1940

1610 hrs Training

Tiger Moth II R4762 of 9 EFTS from Ansty near Coventry crashed in a field off the Great North road at Weston. The aircraft struck a small obstacle on landing and was damaged but no personnel were injured. The instructor pilot was F/L Keown and the pupil Sgt 954201 D E Bell RAFVR.

THURSDAY 19th DECEMBER 1940

2200 hrs

Bombs were dropped near Salterford Dam, Calverton, Giltbrook, Newthorpe, Kimberley and Kegworth.

SATURDAY 21st DECEMBER 1940

2040 hrs Training

Hampden I P1304 ZN-Y of 106 Sqn from Finningley undershot and struck a tree at Mount Pleasant, near Bawtry, five miles south of Doncaster, while practicing night take-off and landings. The aircraft was a write-off but no injuries were reported to the crew, Sgt 748775 P C Wells and Sgt Richardson. The accident report states that the crash may have been due to the pilot having difficulty in judging the approach due to landing lights having been turned off owing to an air raid warning.

Hampden P1304 of 106 Squadron undershot Finningley

Franz von Werra (1914-1941) was a German World War Two fighter pilot who was shot down over England and captured. He was the only German airman to succeed in escaping and return to Germany. In 1936 von Werra joined the Luftwaffe and at the beginning of the war he served in the French campaign. By September 1940 it was claimed that he had 9 victories in combat, 4 in the air and 5 on the ground. On 5th September 1940, during the Battle of Britain, von Werra's Bf 109 was shot down over Kent by P/O Basil Gerald 'Stapme' Stapleton of No.603 Sqn. Von Werra crash-landed in a field, was captured by the unarmed cook of a nearby army unit and eventually sent to the London District Prisoner of War Cage. He was interrogated and eventually sent to POW Camp No.1, at Grizedale Hall between Windermere and Coniston Water, Lancashire. On 7th October he tried to escape for the first time, during a daytime walk outside the camp. He was recaptured on 12th October and subsequently transferred to Camp No.13 in Swanwick, Derbyshire on 3rd November.

Franz Von Werra

In Swanwick he joined a group who were digging an escape tunnel and on 20th December Von Werra and 4 others escaped. The others were recaptured a few days later. Von Werra decided to go it alone. He had taken along his flying suit and decided to masquerade as Captain Van Lott, a Dutch RAF pilot. He claimed to a friendly locomotive driver that he was a downed bomber pilot trying to reach his unit, and asked to be taken to the nearest RAF base. In Codnor Park Station, a local clerk became suspicious, but eventually agreed to arrange his transportation to the RAF aerodrome at Hucknall. The police also questioned him, but von Werra convinced them he was harmless. At Hucknall, a Squadron Leader Boniface asked for his credentials and he claimed to be based at Dyce near Aberdeen. While Boniface went to check this, von Werra excused himself and ran to the nearest hangar, trying to tell a mechanic that he was cleared for a test flight. Boniface arrived in time to arrest him at gunpoint. He was sent back to Swanwick and put under armed guard.

In January 1941 von Werra was sent to Canada from where he escaped on 21st January to neutral U.S.A. From there he eventually made his way back to Germany. On 25th October 1941 von Werra disappeared while on a routine patrol in the Netherlands north of Vissingen, probably due to engine failure. Werra's story was the subject of a film called 'The One That Got Away' starring Hardy Kruger as von Werra.

Franz Von Werra's crashed aircraft in a Kent field

SUNDAY 22nd DECEMBER 1940

0145 hrs — Operations

Hampden I X3131 OL- of 83 Sqn from Scampton made a forced landing in a field with undercarriage retracted when returning from operations, probably minelaying in Kiel Bay. The aircraft ran through a hedge and across a road, adjoining Bacons Lane, South Leverton, five miles east of Retford. The aircraft had a fuel shortage after nine hours flying due to having to operate at an un-economical height in bad weather and the relatively high fuel consumption of the aircraft.

The crew of four, Sgt 748341 Arthur John Garwell, Sgt F S Kirke RNZAF, Sgt 646895 Robert James Flux RAF, and Sgt Dring survived.

The Lancaster made its first raid on the enemy on 3rd March 1942. However the public was still unaware that Bomber Command had a new heavy bomber and the Air Ministry took the occasion of a successful, and costly, daylight mission to unveil their new weapon to both the Third Reich and the British public. On 17th April six aircraft each from 44 and 97 Sqns were sent to carry out a daylight raid against one of the largest factories in Germany, the submarine diesel engine producing plant at Augsburg. In four formations of three each the bombers headed out toward Bavaria, 1500 miles of flying there and back. Just after crossing the channel 44 Sqn was attacked by fighters and one after one, four Lancasters were shot down. With little hope of reaching their target, the two remaining aircraft carried on, and having left the coastal area, had few problems until they reached Augsburg. Going in at chimney top level the two aircraft were unable to miss their target. However, meeting heavy defensive fire R5510 was set on fire and crash landed about two miles outside Augsburg.

Some of the crew of R5510 were Sgt Garwell, by now a F/O, the pilot, Sgt Kirke DFC, DFM now a W/O and Sgt Flux, now a F/S. F/O Garwell and Sgt Kirke survived and were made POWs but F/S Flux was killed and is buried in Durnbach War Cemetery.

F/O Garwell and F/S Flux had both been gazetted with the DFM in 1941.

Four Lancasters from No.97 Squadron and one from No.44 Squadron returned.

Squadron Leader John Dering Nettleton received the Victoria Cross for leading 44 Sqn on this raid.

—

Bombs were dropped on Weston, Laxton, Kneesall, Wiverton Hall, Gamston and Langford.

SATURDAY 28th DECEMBER 1940

2127 hrs **Op; Antwerp**

Wellington IC R1035 BH-A of 300 Sqn from Swinderby was one of six aircraft detailed to attack Antwerp from 300 Sqn. R1035 attacked the target and on the return flight, following the opening up of the engines to go round again after a shaky landing in a cross wind it side slipped to lose height and hit some trees. The pilot noticed that there was no airspeed registering on the indicator so put his nose down, struck the ground and crashed, the aircraft bursting into flames, one mile west south west of base. Flames and exploding ammunition made rescue work almost impossible and the Pilot, F/L P/76611 Stefan Krynski PAF, aged 35 was killed. The Front Air Gunner, Sgt P/781192 Henryk Wegryzn PAF age 25, was severely injured and was admitted to the Station Sick Headquarters where he died the next day. Both airmen are buried side by side in the Polish Cemetery at Newark.

The four other crew members, F/O Jerzy Golko (2nd Pilot) broken collarbone, P/O Zygmunt Karol Szymanski (Observer) broken ribs, Sgt Aleksander Szuczynski (Gunner) and Sgt Wladyslaw Graczyk (Gunner) were admitted and treated for their injuries in the Station Sick Headquarters. F/L Krynski was killed instantly in the crash but the rest of the crew were providentially thrown clear when the aircraft disintegrated.

1941

WEDNESDAY 1st JANUARY 1941

2230 hrs **Op; Bremen**

Wellington IC R1006 GR-H of 301 Sqn from Swinderby crash landed at Swinderby after bombing Bremen.

Wellington IC R1006 GR-H being bombed up before a previous operation. courtesy of Jerzy B Cynk

The beginning of 1941 was marked by tragic events for 301 Sqn following the raid on Bremen. Bremen was considered one of the most difficult targets to attack and it was to be the unit's first nearly seven-hours sortie. Since the Wellingtons of 301 Sqn were to be the first over the target they were each bombed up with 360 incendiaries. The crews reached the target and dropped their loads. On the way back to England they encountered a snow blizzard with nil visibility. Three of the squadron's aircraft crashed, killing 11 airmen, including S/L Floryanowicz the OC of Flight 'A'. Two Wellingtons crashed at RAF Waddington with only one tail gunner surviving and the other was R1006.

In view of the bad weather it was considered that the pilot of R1006, Sgt 780172 Stanislaw Klosowski PAF, took the best possible action by crash landing.

Wellington R1006 did not survive the war. When based at RAF Bramcote with 18 OTU it caught fire on the ground and was destroyed.

FRIDAY 3rd JANUARY 1941

2055 hrs **Training**

Hampden I P4314 ZN- of 106 Sqn from Finningley took off at 1730 hrs for navigational training on a North Sea sweep and after a flight of 2 hours 25 minutes force landed in a field one mile south of the airfield, on approach to land. The pilot Sgt 741065 P Mapp RAFVR was on attachment from 61 Sqn and also involved in an incident on 16th December 1940. The rest of the crew were Sgt Asson, Sgt Breen and Sgt Lund.

THURSDAY 9th JANUARY 1941

Six high explosive bombs were dropped in fields and woods around Walesby.

FRIDAY 10th JANUARY 1941

0005 hrs | Ops; Gardening

Hampden I X2968 of 106 Sqn from Finningley took off at 1705 hrs on a Gardening operation and on landing returning from the operation the undercarriage collapsed. The crew were Sgt 748585 R J West (Pilot) RAFVR, P/O Parramore, Sgt Harker and Sgt Hunt.

WEDNESDAY 15th JANUARY 1941

2215 hrs

Bombs were dropped in the area of Porchester and Colwick Road, Nottingham.
12 people were killed in Hutton Street and three killed in Trent Lane.

FRIDAY 17th JANUARY 1941

1930 hrs | Training

Oxford I P9034 of RAF College (I) from Cranwell took off on a solo flight with LAC 1158274 P Brown at the controls and passenger LAC 1057897 V D Croft. Some time later they became lost due to inexperience and bad visibility and force landed the aircraft at Daneshill Farm, near Torworth, and ran into a hedge. Neither of the airmen were injured.

The following is taken from a Notts Constabulary report, Retford Divsion 17.1.41.
'At about 16.45 hours an Airspeed Oxford Trainer plane No.9034 piloted by 1158274 LAC Peter Brown stationed at Cranwell aerodrome and accompanied by No.1057897 LAC Valentine Dixon Croft, also stationed at Cranwell, made a forced landing in a grass field 500 yards south west of Daneshill Farm between Lound and Torworth. It appears that they were out on a training flight and lost their way, and being short on petrol, decided to land. In doing so the brakes of the machine appear to have failed to function properly with the result that the landing wheels dropped into a dyke about three feet deep. This together with the adjoining hedge brought the machine to a standstill. Neither of the occupants were injured, but slight damage was done to the propellers by coming in contact with the hedge. The rear landing wheel was also damaged. PC836 Musson and myself remained on duty near the machine until 20.30 hours same date, when guard duties were handed over to Lieutenant Bastin, 9th Devons stationed at Wiseton Hall. The pilots and guard were given accommodation at Daneshill Farm, Lound which is tenanted by Mr Tuplin. The pilot of the machine stated that after minor repairs the machine can be flown away.'

Oxford Mk I aircraft

Sgt Peter Brown was subsequently killed on 21st June 1941 age 21 when he took off from Watton in Blenheim IV V6450 YH-L of 21 Sqn, one of twenty three, for a raid on Circus. His was the only aircraft lost on this operation when he was shot down by Me 109s before reaching the target, near St Omer airfield. He is buried in Longuenesse (St Omer) Souvenir Cemetery, France.

THURSDAY 30th JANUARY 1941

1600 hrs

In the afternoon an enemy bomber flew through low lying cloud and dropped fourteen High Explosive bombs in the area around the River Trent and Muskham Road, Newark.
Two young men were killed and several other people were injured.

TUESDAY 4th FEBRUARY 1941

1949 hrs

Bombs were dropped on Lucknow Drive Mapperley, Nottingham and also at 175 Wollaton Road and 28 Denison Street, Beeston but did not explode.
An enemy aircraft dropped a bomb on the edge of Swinderby airfield. No damage was done.

THURSDAY 6th FEBRUARY 1941

1445 hrs — Training

Wellington IC R1014 NZ- of 304 Sqn from Syerston took off and after a short run climbed very slowly and shortly afterwards began to lose height until it struck the ground and burst into flames in line with take-off, in a field ¼ mile south of Bleasby village. Evidence strongly suggested that the pilot took off with the elevator trimmer tabs in the 'up' position and was not aware of the fact until the aircraft became airborne. All the crew were killed in the partly burnt out bomber and are buried in the Polish plot at Newark-upon-Trent Cemetery.

The crew were Sgt P/782062 Stanislaw Tofin PAF age 35 (Pilot), Sgt P/781604 Wejciech Lichota PAF age 31, Cpl P/782182 Jan Adam Cymborski PAF age 35 and Cpl P/793311 Josef Jonczyk PAF age 24.

1640 hrs

Hampden I AD736 of 106 Sqn took off at 1430 hrs from St Eval on a flight to Finningley with plans to refuel at upper Heyford or Cottesmore if necessary. The 2nd engine faded out during circuit, and as there was insufficient height to reach the aerodrome the aircraft crash landed in a field ½ mile west of Finningley airfield. The pilot, Sgt 740380 W F Osborne RAFVR, had relied on the fuel gauge instead of landing en route for refuelling. The rest of the crew were Sgt Boyall, Sgt Wiseman and Sgt Davies.

SATURDAY 8th FEBRUARY 1941

1220 hrs — Training

Wellington II W5365 PH- of 12 Sqn from Binbrook was provisionally posted to Tollerton for bombing and gunnery practice. The aircraft took off for an air to ground firing practice training flight and when turning into the wind to land at Tollerton it stalled at 500 feet, over a small hill fringed with a row of high trees, which may have been a contributory factor, the engines were opened up and continued to run at high speed before crashing into a tree on what is now Cotgrave golf course. Of the 9 crew, 2 were injured and 7 members died. Crash location: OS sheet 129 631374.

Sgt Boyle

There is a plaque mounted adjacent to the Cotgrave Golf course commemorating the crew and also one mounted on a pillbox at Tollerton airfield (see memorials).

Those who died were: S/L 32228 Phillip Cutliffe Lawrence RAF age 27 (Pilot), cremated at Nottingham Crematorium, P/O 46325 Robert Atkinson age 29 (Pilot), also cremated at Nottingham Crematorium, Sgt 525889 James John Castleman Batty 26 buried Garston (St Michael) Churchyard Lancashire, Sgt 550950 Robert Tod Tomlinson DFM age 22 buried Mount Jerome Cemetery County Dublin, Sgt 636137 Arthur Crooks age 20 (W.Op/ Air Gnr) buried Barnstable Cemetery, Sgt 650974 Edward Frederick Ted Carter age 20 (W.Op/Air Gnr) RAF, buried Cotgrave (All Saints) Churchyard Extension.

Sgt 903054 Neil Colin Jim Boyle RNZAF age 25 (Air Gnr) buried Cotgrave (All Saints) Churchyard Extension.

The two surviving members of the crew were Sgt William Cecil Percy Watkins who was seriously injured and Sgt Henry William James Gill slightly injured.

A commemorative service was held at the crash site on 8th February 1994 attended by many people including F/S Gill who unfortunately collapsed and died during the service.

Postscript to this incident: George W M Purslow, a Wireless Operator/Air Gunner, was a regular member of this aircrew but, just prior to take off, he was approached by Sgt 'Tommy' Tomlinson DFM and asked if he would change crews for this particular exercise to which he reluctantly agreed. He flew off with another crew on an air firing exercise. On his return over the airfield he could see a crashed Wellington and the emergency services in action. On landing he discovered that all of his crew had been killed and two extra aircrew members were seriously injured. When he appeared in the crew room his friends were amazed to see him as they thought he was dead. George Purslow survived the war as a Flight Lieutenant and had been awarded the DFC on 14th June 1945.

Sgt Batty had already had a narrow escape on 14th June 1940. He was involved in the Battle of France at Souge when he was the observer in the crew of Battle L5396 of 12 Sqn which took off from Souge for a raid on Eureux and was shot down by Me109s at Coulonges, France. Crew member LAC D L Grant was killed but he and the pilot, P/O 77782 P H Blowfield, initially avoided capture. Sgt Batty succeeded in reaching England where he reported that P/O Blowfield had been shot and killed by machine gun fire from a Panzer.

Sgt Tomlinson received his DFM under the following circumstances.

He was a member of the crew of Battle L4949 PH-V which was hit by intense ground-fire and an engine was set alight during a low level attack on an enemy column near Luxembourg. The aircraft crash landed on fire near Virton on 10th May 1940. F/L William Simpson, the pilot, was seriously burned and LAC R T Tomlinson who received burnt hands and Sgt E N Odell who was unhurt both rescued F/L Simpson from the aircraft.

Sgt Simpson was later awarded the DFC and the other two crew members the DFM.

SUNDAY 9th FEBRUARY 1941

1100 hrs

Hampden I P1337 of 5gp TF from Finningley stalled from a low height and crashed 1½ miles south east of the airfield. The pilot was F/O A D Stewart.

MONDAY 10th FEBRUARY 1941

1935 hrs

17 bombs were dropped on Finningley airfield but only one aircraft was damaged.

WEDNESDAY 12th FEBRUARY 1941

0115 hrs Op; Bremen

Wellington IC R1238 KO-A of 115 Sqn from Marham took off at 1900 hrs for a raid on Bremen and on the return journey was diverted to Finningley where it stalled and crashed on landing hurriedly in bad visibility, due to fuel shortage, and hit an obstruction. The crew were Sgt 902513 J Whittaker (pilot), Sgt Thompson, P/O Searle, Sgt Kerr, Sgt Welch and Sgt Tough. Two other aircraft from 115 Sqn crashed in England on the return from the raid.

0122 hrs Op; Bremen

Hampden I AD722 OL-X of 83 Sqn from Scampton took off at 2010 hrs with ten other aircraft for a raid on Bremen and on return owing to increased fog at base was diverted to Lindhome. The pilot seeing a flarepath at Finningley, which was a strange aerodrome, attempted to land there but in very poor visibility, down to 200 feet, and struck the roof of the married quarters. 3 of the crew were killed and Hampden AD722 was one of two 83 Sqn Hampdens lost on this operation.

F/L 70043 Desmond Wallace Ferguson Barker DFC age 27 RAF (Pilot) buried Finningley Churchyard Extension, Sgt 754883 William Harry Lowson age 20 RAFVR (Pilot) buried Welton Church Cemetery, F/S 76021 Frank Selby Wilson age 34 RAFVR (Air Gnr) also buried Finningley Churchyard Extension. Sgt George Targett DFM was injured. His DFM was gazetted on 18th April 1941 and the citation read: 'Awarded for gallantry and devotion to duty displayed in the execution of air operations.' The funerals of F/L Barker and F/S Wilson were held on 15th February.

F/L Barker was awarded the DFC on 24th December 1940. The citation read, 'Flight Lieutenant Barker has consistently displayed gallantry and skill during his 19 operational missions against the enemy. On 15th October,1940, when returning from a raid on Magdeburg, his port engine was hit by anti-aircraft fire, and the airscrew flew off when he was flying over the Dutch coast. This officer regained control of his aircraft after it had lost some 3,000 feet, and flew across the North Sea on one engine until forced onto the water, by the failure of the second engine, 20 yards from the beach. roor gallantry and devotion to duty in the execution of air operations.'

His brother P/O R P W Barker died in a similar incident on 22nd December 1941 and is buried in Grantham Cemetery'.

WEDNESDAY 19th FEBRUARY 1941

Eight bombs were dropped on Finningley airfield but only one exploded destroying a crew training school hut.

SATURDAY 1st MARCH 1941

1630 hrs Training

Battle I K7683 of 1 (P)FTS from Hucknall took off for circuit and landings practice and crash landed at Watnall. The pilot Cpl 783658 A Damm was un-injured. This aircraft was also involved in an incident on 22nd July.

—

Two land mines were dropped on Finningley airfield.

SUNDAY 2nd MARCH 1941 Taxiing

Battle I K7676 of 12 FTS (I) from Tollerton was blown into barbed wire defences by a gust of wind whilst taxiing despite having an airman on a wing tip. The pilot was Cpl 518631 J E Butcher. This aircraft was also involved in incidents on 11th July and 31st October.

FRIDAY 7th MARCH 1941

1335 hrs

A raid was carried out on the Ransome and Marles factory at Newark. A single Heinkel He 111 bomber flying so low that those on the ground could see its markings, approached from the south following the railway line. As it neared its target it dropped 4 high explosive bombs. Two of these landed in the works, one on the road at the side of the factory and the other on an air raid shelter adjacent to Stanley Street. The plane also machine gunned the site before circling, passing over the factory again and dropping another bomb which did not explode.

1428 hrs
Another aircraft approached and dropped 5 more bombs but only 1 exploded. This was near the road and caused more damage and casualties. As a result of both raids 36 people were killed, 47 seriously injured and 20 slightly injured.

FRIDAY 14th MARCH 1941

A total of 12 bombs were dropped on Ribblesdale Road, Sherwood, Nottingham and a woman was killed.

Bombs were also dropped at Tuxford, Gedling Colliery, Bleasby Hall, Goverton, and Thurgaton.

A bomb damaged house on Ribblesdale Road.
Courtesy Nottingham Evening Post

2357 hrs

Nine short delay bombs were dropped on Syerston Aerodrome by unidentified enemy aircraft from a height of 500/1000 feet and exploded near the south perimeter track creating 2 craters 25 feet diameter by 15 deep and 7 craters 12 feet by 7 feet. There were no casualties. The aircraft were engaged by 2 machine gun posts and 2 Armadillos without visible results.

TUESDAY 18th MARCH 1941

1430 hrs Stationary

Wellington IC R1347 of 300 Sqn from Swinderby was struck by an army truck. The driver stated that when engaging gear the knob of the gear lever came off in his hand and whilst paying attention to this he unknowingly put pressure on the accelerator and the truck hit the aircraft.

300 Squadron Wellington IC BH-T at Swinderby. Courtesy of Jerzy B Cynk

1920 hrs — Taxiing

Wellington IC R1042 of 150 Sqn from Newton was taxiing to dispersal over a runway of railway sleepers placed over soft ground when the tail wheel struck the end of a sleeper and collapsed. The pilot, F/O 40263 Frederick Henry Savage RAF, and crew were unhurt but he was killed 2 months later, on 8th May. F/O Savage took off from Newton piloting Wellington R1374 of 150 Sqn for a raid on St-Nazaire and crashed near Nantes. He and the crew are buried in Nantes (Pont-du-Cens) Communal Cemetery.

FRIDAY 21st MARCH 1941

0120 hrs — Training

Wellington IC L7874 GR-S of 301 Sqn from Swinderby was on a practice landings flight and on its landing approach, came in too high. The pilot opened up the engines to carry out an overshoot, and it is thought he probably retracted the flaps too quickly at too low an altitude. The aircraft stalled on the climb, crashing about 2 miles from its base at Swinderby airfield, killing three of the crew: Sgt P/780108 Kazimierz Lenczowski PAF age 28 (Pilot), P/O P/76670 Josef Korycinski PAF age 29 (Observer), and Sgt P/793330 Bernard Chrzanowski PAF age 24 (W.Op/Air Gnr). All three airmen are buried in Newark-upon-Trent Cemetery and their funerals took place on 23rd March.

2340 hrs — Op; Lorient

Wellington IC R1452 PM- of 103 Sqn from Newton overshot landing on return from an operation to Lorient and hit an obstruction on the perimeter of the aerodrome. The pilot, S/L K J Mellor was also involved in another incident 10 days later.

SATURDAY 22nd MARCH 1941

0015 hrs

Wellington IC R1380 BU- of 214 Sqn from Stradishall ran into soft ground at Swinderby airfield after running off the flare path, probably returning from operations. The captain, Sgt 741780 Russell Arthur Williams RAFVR age 20, was considered not to blame.

Sgt Williams was killed only 17 days later when piloting the same aircraft, Wellington R1380, on a raid on Kiel. He took off from Stradishall and he and his crew were lost without trace, all are are commemorated on the Runnymede Memorial.

SUNDAY 23rd MARCH 1941

1220 hrs — Training

Battle I P6572 of 1 (P)FTS from Hucknall undershot approach to land and crash landed through the boundary hedge. The pilot was P/O Gazech.

2210 hrs

Wellington IA P9214 of 301 Sqn from Swinderby made a heavy landing at high speed and the undercarriage collapsed. The pilot, Sgt P/782266 Marian Kleindeshmidt PAF, was later killed on 29th June 1943 when the pilot of Wellington HZ438 of 300 Sqn on a raid on Koln. He took off from Ingham and was shot down by a night fighter near Eindhoven where the crew are buried.

WEDNESDAY 26th MARCH 1941

1630 hrs — Training

Tiger Moth I L6925 of 1(P)FTS from Hucknall took off with dual pilots to give an experienced pilot a refresher course on landings. During the flight the pupil pilot allowed the airspeed and altitude to get too low before opening the throttle and was unable to clear rising ground ahead. The aircraft struck a hedge in a field adjoining the airfield. Neither pilot was injured.

The enquiry concluded that F/O W Shearman, the instructor pilot, had placed too much confidence in the pupil pilot who already had 1000 hours flying experience.

THURSDAY 27th MARCH 1941

A man was killed during a bomb raid in Warton Avenue, Nottingham.

SUNDAY 30th MARCH 1941

1434 hrs — Training

Wellington IC T2574 of 300 Sqn from Swinderby took off on a flying test and cross country exercise. When flying at 6000 feet in cloud, snow and icing conditions promoted the pilot, Sgt P/782067 Leszkiewicz PAF to lower the undercarriage to lose height quickly, but then the aircraft struck the top of a mountain with the undercarriage and tail wheel. On return to Swinderby the pilot landed on one wheel and ran into a soft patch of ground which swung the damaged undercarriage and locked it.

MONDAY 31st MARCH 1941

0025 hrs — Op; Brest

Wellington IC W5612 PM-G of 103 Sqn from Newton was on return from operations when the aircraft was attacked by a Ju88 Intruder aircraft as the crew prepared to land and force-landed in a field, one mile from the airfield. The pilot, S/L Mellor, was injured and the rest of the escaped unhurt: Sgt Elliott, F/O Roberts, F/S McCudden, Sgt Davies and Sgt S E Hamblin.

Crash of Wellington IC W5612 PM-G

TUESDAY 8th APRIL 1941

0215 hrs

Ten bombs plus incendiaries were dropped on Beeston, Nottingham,at Glebe Street, Mona Street, Windsor Street and Middle Street. One woman was killed.

FRIDAY 11th APRIL 1941

Nine Bombs were dropped on Western Boulevard, Nottingham. One woman was killed.

MONDAY 14th APRIL 1941 Taxiing

Oxford II V3654 of 1 (P)FTS from Hucknall was being taxied without authorisation by Sgt Mechanic P/782210 Ludziejewski when it collided with Oxford T1027.

TUESDAY 15th APRIL 1941

1723 hrs Training

Wellington IC R1212 NZ- of 304 Sqn from Syerston was on a cross country training flight when the pilot overshot on landing due to a cross wind blowing along the longest length of the aerodrome. He opened up the engines, climbed in a gentle turn and nose dived into a tree in Flintham Woods. Evidence pointed to a problem with the port engine. Those who died were the pilot F/O P/0006 Rudolf K Christmann PAF age 35, Sgt P/793339 Wieslaw Leszely Pietruszewski PAF age 21 and Sgt P/793337 Antoni Berger PAF age 26, who are all buried in Newark-upon-Trent Cemetery. 3 other members of the crew were injured, 2 seriously: P/O Z Galczynski PAF, Sgt T Aranowski PAF and Sgt J F Jarosz all PAF.

Wellington's of 304 Squadron

2345 hrs

Enemy aircraft dropped a number of incendiaries ½ mile from Swinderby airfield. There were no casualties.

WEDNESDAY 16th APRIL 1941

Eleven aircraft from Swinderby were detailed to attack Bremen and all the aircraft returned to base on time without incident. During the landing operations a Heinkel He 111 arrived and attacked one of the landing aircraft with machine gun fire without causing damage. The enemy aircraft also dropped six small bombs on the north east corner of Swinderby airfield. Two failed to explode.

SUNDAY 20th APRIL 1941

1230 hrs Training

Whitley V T4332 KN-Q of 77 Sqn from Topcliffe crashed near Edwinstowe due to engine failure and caught fire despite the use of fire extinguishers. No injuries were reported. The pilot was Sgt 1000337 P Singleton.

2330 hrs Taxiing

Wellington X R1349 of 301 Sqn from Swinderby was taxiing to take off from the flarepath and ran into a gun emplacement. The pilot was Sgt P/780096 Weiss PAF.

MONDAY 21st APRIL 1941

AC1 914129 Albert Victor Hawkins RAFVR from RAF Syerston was fatally injured and two more airmen seriously injured in a motor accident outside the aerodrome. AC1 Hawkins is buried in Fulford Cemetery, York.

WEDNESDAY 23rd APRIL 1941

1200 hrs Taxiing

Wellington I T2999 of 103 Sqn from Newton was taxiing to dispersal when the tail wheel caught in a rut.

The pilot, P/O 40979 Mervyn Sydney Lund RNZAF from Auckland, was killed 4 months later on 24th July age 23. He was the pilot of Wellington R1397 of 103 Sqn which took off from Elsham Wolds for a raid on Brest and was lost without trace. He and his crew are commemorated on the Runnymede Memorial. P/O Lund had only completed his training in New Zealand, at Woodbourne Flying School on 23rd October 1940.

P/O Lund

THURSDAY 24th APRIL 1941

1120 hrs Training

Tutor K4814 of 2 CFS from Cranwell hit a tree at Langford Moor, north of Coddington, when the pilot, P/O 64300 Henry Robert Lanchester RAF age 28, was flying the aircraft below the regulation minimum height of 250 feet. P/O Lanchester was killed and is buried in Cranwell Churchyard. One other crew man died. The enquiry suggested that the aircraft probably lost further height during a turn.

FRIDAY 25th APRIL 1941

Night | Operations

Wellington I R1216 of 150 Sqn from Newton was returning to base from operations when the aircraft struck two balloon cables in quick succession. The port engine controls were made unserviceable and the undercarriage hydraulic system was affected as the wheels were lowered and locked but would not retract. The aircraft landed without further incident by the pilot Sgt 565240 V G Coleman.

SATURDAY 26th APRIL 1941

2155 hrs | Training

Wellington IC R1619 GR- of 301 Sqn from Swinderby crashed and caught fire after landing slightly heavy, the starboard tyre burst causing the starboard undercarriage leg to be wrenched off. No blame was attached to the pilot as it was rare that a tyre should burst on such a slight impact. No injuries were reported. The crew were: F/L S M Krzystyniak PAF (Pilot), F/L P/0375 Pawel Whilem Tobolski PAF, F/L Prazniewski PAF, W/O Przybylski PAF, W/O Szymankiewicz PAF and W/O Kwiatkowski PAF.

Two of the crew members were later involved in serious incidents. F/L Tobolski took part in the famous escape from the Stalag Luft III POW Camp but was re-captured at Stettin and shot at Breslau on 2nd April 1944. He was cremated at Breslau and his ashes taken back to Stalag Luft III.

Stanislaw Krzystyniak, by now W/Cdr, of 301 Sqn was the pilot of Wellington Z1479 GR-A which took off from Hemswell for a raid on 25th June 1942. 14 aircraft from 301 Sqn were detailed to take part in the '1000 a night' bombing raid on Bremen when his aircraft was hit by flak and crashed in the target area. He was taken prisoner. His aircraft was the only one of the 14 not to return to base.

301 Squadron Wellington

Night | Training

Anson I N9848 -CE of 25 OTU from Finningley took off to practice night circuits and landings. On return to base the pilot approached with the aircraft too close to the floodlights and ran into part of the Chance Lighting System. There were no injuries. The crew were the pupil pilot F/L E Coton and Sgt 904836 H A Church.

MONDAY 28th APRIL 1941

0030 hrs — Training

Hampden I P1287 of 25 OTU from Finningley overshot landing when going too fast in a light wind and ran into a heap of stones and mound of earth at the aerodrome boundary. The pilot, P/O 62269 Peter Dixon-Spain RAFVR, and the crew were unhurt but he was killed only 20 days later on 17/18th May. He was the pilot of Hampden P1233 of 25 OTU which took off from Finningley on a training exercise and was lost without trace probably over the North Sea. The crew are commemorated on the Runnymede Memorial: Sgt A Halbert, Sgt E K Dawson, Sgt T Morgan and P/O Dixon-Spain.

TUESDAY 29th APRIL 1941

1620 hrs — Training

Tutor K3448 of 2 CFS from Cranwell was on a dual low flying exercise when it dived and turned slightly at 250 feet, at 50 feet the aircraft speed was 140mph and continued to increase until it crashed at Beckingham near Newark. The aircraft had flown by itself for 2 minutes because each pilot thought the other was in command. One of the pilots was P/O R L Davies. Both crewmen were slightly injured.

Night

Four aircraft from 304 Sqn Syerston were detailed for night operations captained by F/L Blazajewski, F/O Czetowicz, P/O Iszkowski and P/O Sym. Before the 4th aircraft had taken off the operation was cancelled and the other 3 were recalled. Of the 3, P/O Iszkowski had experienced some difficulty lowering the undercarriage on his aircraft and after landing his rear gunner was involved in an accident with a propeller and very seriously injured.

THURSDAY 1st MAY 1941

Twenty bombs were dropped on Newton aerodrome and one hangar was damaged.

2030 hrs — Training

Hampden I P4317 of 25 OTU from Finningley landed with undercarriage retracted. When operating the flaps and the undercarriage the airspeed of the aircraft became so reduced that approach to the airfield was made with throttles advanced. The pilot Sgt 1163584 Harold Lewis Davies RAFVR, who was on his first flight on this type of aircraft, did not throttle back to bring warning lights into operation. He was later lost on 2nd June 1942 now a F/L, age 25, when the pilot of Lancaster R5571 OF-A of 97 Sqn. He took off from Woodhall Spa for a raid on Essen and is buried in Reichswald Forest War Cemetry.

MONDAY 5th MAY 1941

1200 hrs — Training

Oxford I T1028 of 1 (P)FTS from Hucknall was taking off for solo circuit and landings training when, due to the throttles being opened too quickly, the aircraft swung, the tail wheel struck a pile of concrete and the aircraft struck the ground nose first. The pilot was P/O W Bohuszewicz PAF.

Taxiing

Oxford I T1077 of 1 (P)FTS from Hucknall had been taxied to a hangar for servicing of the port engine and braking system. The pilot Sgt 742462 S E Lucas left the aircraft on sloping tarmac pointing towards the hangar which then ran forward and hit it due to lack of sufficient pressure in the braking system.

WEDNESDAY 7th MAY 1941

0340 hrs

Five bombs were dropped on Finningley aerodrome and one Avro Anson was destroyed on the ground. A hangar and married quarters were also hit.

THURSDAY 8th MAY 1941

0050 hrs Training

Hampden I P1236 of 25 OTU from Finningley overshot the runway and hit the boundary fence. The flare path was not lit due to enemy aircraft in the vicinity. The aircraft landed too fast, the flaps failed to lower apparently due to excessive speed on approach.

The pilot, Sgt 951819 Lesley Alexander Robertson was un-injured but was later killed on 3rd September. He was the pilot of Hampden AE254 of 44 Sqn from Waddington when his aircraft crashed at Wittenberg, Germany, during a raid on Berlin. He is buried in the War Cemetery in Berlin.

0030 hrs

Heinkel He111 H3 3210 A1-BA Heinkel of 1 Staffel KG53 Legion Condor, crewed by Oberlieutenant Emil Komel (Beobacher), Feldwebel Gunter Merton (Flugzeugfuhrer), Gefreiter Erhardt Schonberger (Dordfunker), Feldwebel Hans Muller (Bordmachaniker) and Gefreiter Oskar Wilfingeseder (Bordachutze), took off from its base in Vitry, Northern France, to bomb Liverpool. When over the Everton/Scaftworth area it was attacked by Sgt Johnson and Sgt Aitchinson flying a Defiant from No.255 Squadron, Kirton-in-Lindsey, who proceeded to shoot it down. The Heinkel crashed in flames into Scrooby Sand Quarry, 4 miles north of Retford, at 0030 hours with the bomb load exploding on impact. Eye witnesses who saw and heard the attack say that the Heinkel returned fire but was soon a blazing mass with burning debris falling from the bomber which set fire to undergrowth in Scaftworth Woods.

All five crew members baled out but the parachute of Emil Kolmel was found unopened on his body near the River Idle Bridge. Whether the aircraft was too low for his parachute to deploy when he left the aircraft is not known. He was later buried at Gringley-on-the-Hill Cemetery with full Military Honours. In the 1960s his body was exhumed and buried in the German War Cemetery at Cannock Chase, Staffordshire.

Three of the German airmen were later found walking along the dual carriageway at Scaftworth by a Special Constable and Fire Watchers who were out searching for them. They gave themselves up without a struggle, one of them handing over a revolver. Later during the night the other airman was captured and all four were taken to Ranby Army Camp, near Retford. On the 22.12.41 they were shipped to No.23 Prisoner of War Camp in Canada.

Heinkel He 111

FRIDAY 9th MAY 1941

0037 hrs

The Blitz of Nottingham

This raid started at 0037 hours and was made during a moonlit night by approx 50 German aircraft flying at an average height of 10,000 feet and lasted for approximately 3 hours. A total of 201 people were killed, 134 seriously injured and detained in hospital, 160 injured but not detained in hospital. The high proportion of dead and wounded was due to 2 shelter incidents. The first was the underground shelter at the Co-Op Bakery, Meadow Lane and the second a public shelter in the basement in Dakeyne Street. Approximately 50 men died in the bakery and 21 men, women and children in the Dakeyne St shelter.

The destruction extended from the edge of Mapperley Park across Woodborough Road and St Anne's Well Road areas to the Lace Market, Sneinton, Sneinton Dale, Leenside, Station Street, Carlton Road, Carlton hill and the Meadows, Colwick Road and Meadow Lane Trentside.

0547 hrs Operations

Wellington IC R1026 GR-R of 301 Sqn from Swinderby returned from operations and on landing struck a bomb lying on the flare path and the aircraft was damaged. The bomb had dropped from another aircraft. The pilot S/L 76687 W J Piotrowski PAF and crew were uninjured. This aircraft was lost on 23rd June at Winkburn, Notts.

SATURDAY 10th MAY 1941

A lone Ju 88 aircraft operating from France attacked Nottingham Ordnance Factory, dropping high explosive and incendiary bombs as it flew low over Wilford and Queens Drive, Nottingham. One hit a house killing two women.

MONDAY 12th MAY 1941

The following were killed at Grange Farm, Cropwell Butler: May Parker age 41yrs, Barbara Stewart age 15yrs, and Mary Ward age 21yrs of Beeston.

The following is an extract from the Beeston Gazette and Echo published 12 months after the event: Miss Barbara Mary Ward was asleep at the Grange Farm, Cropwell Butler, when enemy planes visited the district and showered down incendiary bombs, setting fire to the farm buildings. Barbara was employed at the farm as a Land Girl. She was awakened along with a maid by Mr Parker, her employer, who is a farmer. He along with his wife and the two girls at once began extinguishing the incendiaries. While thus employed the swish of falling bombs was again heard by Mr Parker who called to the others to lay flat on the ground. A stick of high explosive bombs straddled the farm buildings and grounds. One fell among the gallant party and the two girls and Mr Parker's wife were killed outright, the farmer alone escaped. Though the farmhouse was damaged by blast and splinters the three children in bed escaped unhurt.

WEDNESDAY 14th MAY 1941

During a daylight raid on Nottingham 3 bombs were dropped on Canal Street, Nottingham.

SATURDAY 17th MAY 1941

0025 hrs Training

Hampden I P2139 of 25 OTU from Finningley undershot the flarepath slightly, bounced and then landed heavily and the tail wheel collapsed. This was only the 2nd flight on this type of aircraft for the pilot, Sgt 1160143 F A Read and he had been flying for two hours without landing because of enemy aircraft in the area.

0030 hrs Taxiing

Hampden I P2111 of 25 OTU from Finningley piloted by Sgt 1154131 Kenneth Harry Hart RAFVR, taxied left at the end of the flarepath after landing instead of right and ran into a bomb fusing hut. There were no injuries.

Later Sgt Hart, now a F/S, was a member of the crew of Lancaster L7543 of 207 Sqn which took off from Bottesford for a raid on Danzig and was lost on 12th July 1942. The crew are buried in Malbork Commonwealth War Cemetery, Poland.

0350 hrs Training

Hampden I L4124 of 25 OTU from Finningley took off for practice floodlight landings but crashed vertically from 200 feet soon after becoming airborne, ½ mile north of Rossington Hall, 4 miles south east of Doncaster. The accident report stated that as the pilot wore glasses and goggles over his glasses it was possible that his goggles and glasses blew off and he lost control. All 3 crew members were killed.

Sgt 1162408 Richard Samuel Keith Hickmott RAFVR age 29 (Pilot) buried Tunbridge Wells Cemetery, Sgt 997005 David George Crichton RAFVR age 19 (W.Op/Air Gnr) buried Dundee Western Cemetery, Sgt 999277 Ernest David Foster RAFVR age 24 (W.Op/Air Gnr) buried Whiston (St Mary Magdalene) Churchyard.

SUNDAY 18th MAY 1941

0020 hrs Training

Blenheim I L8675 of 68 Sqn from High Ercall stalled at low altitude and spun into the ground, whilst on night local flying, 1½ miles south of Ruddington village. The crash report is not conclusive but states that the Officer Commanding thought that the pilot, P/O 60825 Geoffrey Robert Butcher, RAFVR age 21, did not realise he was so low, probably through talking on the RT, and the sudden realisation made him pull the control column back too quickly. He is buried in Wombridge (SS. Mary and Leonard) Churchyard Shropshire. Another crew member was also killed.

MONDAY 19th MAY 1941

1600 hrs

Battle I N2031 of 1 (P)FTS from Hucknall overshot landing in bad visibility, low cloud and drizzle and hit the boundary hedge. The pilot was Sgt P/780653 B Peislak PAF.

MONDAY 26th MAY 1941

1700 hrs Training

Oxford II V3683 of 1 (P)FTS from Hucknall overshot landing in an atmospheric hailstorm, ran into a hedge and tipped onto its nose. The brakes were ineffective on the wet and slippery ground.

The pilot, P/O P/0111 Leon Ryszard Osmialowski PAF, was later killed on 31st August 1943. He was the pilot of Wellington JA116 BH-Q of 300 Sqn which was one of 15 crews briefed for a night bombing operation over Munchengladbach. He took off from Ingham for the raid and became one of three crews failing to return having been shot down by a night fighter. All the crew members rest in Crooswijk General Cemetery.

WEDNESDAY 28th MAY 1941

0255 hrs Training

Hampden I P1177 of 25 OTU from Finningley overshot on landing and went through a hedge. The pilot, Sgt 970361 Alfred William Wilson RAFVR age 28, was later lost with rest of his crew on 8th July on a raid on Hamm. He was the pilot of Hampden AD840 of 44 Sqn. All the crew are buried in Reichswald Forest War Cemetery.

Taxiing

Wellington X R1760 of 103 Sqn from Newton was taxiing and got bogged down. The pilot Sgt 904243 Denis Maxwell Greey RAFVR tried to free the aircraft by use of the engines but it tipped onto its nose.

Sgt Greey was killed just 10 weeks later age 28 on 6th August. He was the pilot of Wellington W5656 which took off from Elsham Wolds for a raid on Frankfurt and crashed near Calais where he and his crew are buried: Sgt Jonston Playfair Taylor RCAF, Sgt Jack Moules, Sgt Frederick William Alleway, Sgt Robert Grattan Griffin and Sgt Carl Deges.

The crew of W5656. Courtesy of the Aircrew Remembrance Society

FRIDAY 30th MAY 1941

1745 hrs Training

Hampden I P1220 of 25 OTU from Finningley took off for local flying practice and on return overshot the airfield in bad visibility and hit a gun post bursting a tyre on barbed wire. The port undercarriage broke off. The pilot was Sgt 933275 K Richardson.

SATURDAY 31st MAY 1941

Intimation had been received from higher authority that the Polish Government had expressed their intention of recommending AC2 1162702 W J Abley and LAC 747023 G N Biddle RAFVR both from Swinderby for the award of the Polish Cross of Merit (Krzyz Zaslugi) for their gallantry in rescuing Polish airmen from a crashed aircraft on 28th December 1940. The aircraft in question was Wellington R1035.

The Polish Cross of Merit is awarded to Civilians, Foreigners and Military personnel, for outstanding service to Poland, for acts of bravery, philanthropy and various other meritorious acts. Awarded in 3 classes.

SUNDAY 8th JUNE 1941

2130 hrs Training

Magister I P2426 of 16 EFTS took off from base with LAC 1072955 Allen at the controls who was on solo map reading practice with the intended destination of Nottingham. When the weather deteriorated he turned back to base. However he then changed his mind and tried to reach Nottingham but got into trouble and force landed near to Gotham, Nottingham. The undercarriage was badly damaged but he escaped injury.

MONDAY 9th JUNE 1941

1200 hrs Training

DH.82A Tiger Moth X9318 of 150 Sqn from Newton hit a tree after failing to recover from a dive whilst on local low flying practice at Colston Hall, Bingham, three miles north east of Newton. Two crew members were killed one of which was the pilot F/L 76448 Denis William Mahon RAFVR age 26, who was on secondment from 103 Sqn. He is buried in Harpenden Westfield Cemetery Hertfordshire. The Court of Enquiry stated that the pilot was contravening regulations on low flying around Car Colston Hall and diving down on personal friends standing on the lawn in the Hall grounds.

TUESDAY 10th JUNE 1941

1000 hrs Training

Battle I N2104 of 16 (P)FTS from Hucknall undershot approach and landed through the boundary hedge. The pilot was P/O P/1316 W H Rabowski PAF.

WEDNESDAY 11th JUNE 1941

1900 hrs Training

Oxford II P6819 of RAF College Cranwell took off for a cross country flight to Dishforth but landed at Tuxford with undercarriage retracted. The pilot, LAC P T E Pugson, was un-injured and survived the war. He died on 9th May 2007.

—

Twenty aircraft from 301 Sqn Swinderby were tasked to attack Dusseldorf but 2 failed to take off. One of the 18, Wellington of F/O Kurzenpa, was attacked by an enemy aircraft over the wash and his rear gunner was seriously injured in the head and received a number of hits from cannon shells but F/O Kurzenpa managed to land is aircraft without further incident.

One of the 2 aircraft that failed to take off was being examined by Cpl P/781252 Waclaw Andrzejczuk PAF when he was killed when he walked into the airscrew of a running engine. He is buried in Newark-upon-Trent Cemetery.

THURSDAY 12th JUNE 1941

1140 hrs Training

Wellington IC R1017 SM-K of 305 Sqn from Syerston crashed following a mid-air collision with Oxford T1334 from 2 SFTS over Elton, 12 miles east of Nottingham. The Oxford struck the Wellington near the astro-dome and carried away the tail unit. Both aircraft crashed from a height of 900 feet and fell about 700 yards apart. The crew of the Wellington were all killed and their the funerals took place at Newark-upon-Trent Cemetery on 14th June at 1530 hrs.

They were F/L P/0057 Tadeusz Jan Stefanicki (Pilot) age 36, Sgt P/782362 Kazimierz Mruk age 24, F/O P/0080 Stanislaw Kowalcze age 28, AC1 P/781563 Jerzy Krawczyk age 24, F/O P/0076 Marian Jan Wojtowicz age 27 and F/O P/0074 Aleksander A Zirkwitz age 42 all PAF.

305 Squadron Wellington IV SM-. Courtesy of M J Ingham

1140 hrs Training

Oxford II T1334 of 2 SFTS See above. The pilot under training was LAC 1018127 William Robson Newton, RAFVR, age 26 who is buried in Newark-upon-Trent Cemetery.

1415 hrs Training

Hampden I L4165 of 25 OTU from Finningley was on flare path approach training when the pilot Sgt 402177 William John Fulton RNZAF made a slightly heavy landing in a cross wind, the aircraft swung, he braked fiercely and the undercarriage collapsed. The enquiry stated that this aircraft does not normally have the tendency to swing but once it starts, either on take off or landing, it is impossible to regain control. Sgt Fulton had a similar accident four days later.

FRIDAY 13th JUNE 1941

0115 hrs Training

Hampden I X2916 of 25 OTU from Finningley was practicing floodlit landings when the pilot Sgt 402189 Jack Kendrick Ibbotson RNZAF overshot the flarepath on landing and ran through the boundary hedge.

Sgt Ibbotson, now a F/S, was lost on 4th February 1942 age 21and is buried in Catania War Cemetery, Sicily.

This aircraft crashed on 11th August at Missom with a different crew killing all four airmen aboard.

0150 hrs Training

Wellington IC R1708 of 25 OTU from Finningley had been on a cross country flight and when completing the 1st circuit for landing the aircraft was shot down by an intruder and crashed at Misson near Finningley. All 6 of the crew were killed.

F/S 748379 Walter Robert Laidlow Collyer age 22 RAFVR (Pilot) buried Aberdour Cemetery, Sgt 960989 James Francis Markham RAFVR age 20 (Obs.) buried Finningley Churchyard Extension, Sgt 1250304 John Ernest Jackson age 20 RAFVR buried Norwich Cemetery, Sgt 1100675 James Marron Taylor age 26 buried Forfar Cemetery, Sgt 915475 Gordon Eric Blake buried Slough Cemetery, F/S 653716 Terence Alfred Grosvenor age 21 (W.Op/Air Gnr) buried Carisbrooke Cemetery, IOW.

0127 hrs Ground

Wellington IC X3163 GR-K of 301 Sqn from Swinderby was one of 22 aircraft detailed to attack the marshalling yards at Osnabruck and because of serious icing problems over the North Sea had to abort the mission and jettison their bomb load. The aircraft returned to base and landed safely at 0127 hrs. During taxiing the aircraft got stuck in mud and was then hit and damaged by Wellington R1348 which had overshot the runway. The pilot of X3163 received cuts around an eye.

0201 hrs Op; Osnabruck

Wellington IC R1348 GR-O of 301 Sqn from Swinderby took off for an attack on Osnabruck and because of severe icing problems over the North Sea also had to abort the mission and returned to its home base. The aircraft overshot on landing and crashed colliding with Wellington X3163 GR-K that had landed 34 minutes earlier. The crew were F/O Teofil Pozyczka (Pilot), P/O Plawski, F/O Voelnagel, Sgt K Brzozowski, Sgt Pchalek and Sgt Zuk all of the PAF. There were no injuries.

Wellington R1348 GR-0 of 301 Squadron being bombed up at Swinderby 1941. Courtesy M J Ingham

1115 hrs — Training

Battle I P6721 of 16 (P)FTS from Hucknall prepared to land but the undercarriage failed to lower and the aircraft landed on its starboard wheel. The pilot P/O P/0376 L Slomski PAF was commended on his airmanship as he was inexperienced on this type of aircraft. This aircraft was involved in another incident on 16th December.

1620 hrs — Training

Wellington I R1077 of 25 OTU from Finningley made a heavy landing and the undercarriage collapsed. The pilot was P/O 62267 Ralf Athelsie Pole Allsebrook.

P/O Allsebrook was ultimately promoted to F/L and awarded the DSO and DFC but was killed on 16th September 1943. He was the pilot of Lancaster EE130 of the famous 617 Sqn which took off from Coningsby to bomb the Dortmund-Ems Kanal and was believed shot down by flak. He and his crew lie in Reichswald Forest War Cemetery. Four other aircraft from 617 Sqn were lost on this raid including some crew members who had taken part in the Dams raid with W/C Guy Gibson VC. P/O Allsebrook was also involved in an incident on 15th February 1942. He took off from Scampton in Hampden AE397 of 49 Sqn for a raid on Mannheim and on return ran short of fuel and with both engines cutting he ditched the aircraft off the Isle of Wight with no injuries to the crew.

F/L Allsebrook was awarded the DFC on 14th April 1942 and the DSO on 9th July 1943.

F/L Allsebrook

F/L Allsebrook is third from the left. Courtesy of Malcolm Brooke 49 Sqn

2300 hrs Taxiing

Wellington I X9609 of 103 Sqn from Newton was taxiing to its take off position for an operational flight when the tail wheel collapsed without injuries to the crew.

The pilot S/L Dermot Daly Aloysius Kelly MiD RAF was killed just 3 days later age 23.

On the 16th June between 2250 and 2305 hours seven Wellingtons of 103 Sqn took off from Newton to bomb the harbour installations at the river Rhine in Duisburg. Each aircraft was loaded with three 500 lb bombs with direct ignition, one 250 lb bomb with delayed ignition and 6 units with 4 lb incendiaries. After dropping their bomb load, the seven Wellingtons were tasked to scatter leaflets above the German cities of Gladbeck and Krefeld. They flew to their target at Duisburg where the visibility was good to moderate and dropped their bombs. Above Duisburg the Wellingtons were caught in searchlights, encountered heavy flak and attacked by several German night fighters. On their way home N2849 piloted by S/L Kelly was shot down by the German Messerschmidt Me 110 of Lt Reinhold Knacke of 2NGJ/1. The Wellington went out of control and crashed at 0225 hours at Hamont.

S/L Kelly and his crew are buried in Heverlee War Cemetery, Belgium, which contains over 900 allied dead. Three times he had been mentioned in despatches and was the son of Brigadier Denis Patrick Joseph Kelly, OBE, MC.

S/L Kelly

S/L Kelly and crew buried in Heverlee Cemetery

SUNDAY 15th JUNE 1941 Taxiing

Oxford I R5959 of 16 (P)FTS from Hucknall landed and ran into a wire fence. The pupil pilot failed to apply the brakes properly. The instructor was F/O P/76778 M Smogor.

MONDAY 16th JUNE 1941

1220 hrs Training

Hampden I AD743 of 25 OTU from Finningley touched down with brakes on, one more than the other, causing the aircraft to swing and the undercarriage to collapse. The pilot Sgt 402177 William John Fulton RNZAF had a similar incident four days previously.

He was lost on a raid on Mannheim on 20th May 1942 when as pilot of Wellington W5458 of 12 Sqn his aircraft probably crashed into the North Sea. He is commemorated on the Runnymede Memorial.

WEDNESDAY 18TH JUNE 1941

1850 hrs — Air Test

Hampden I P4389 VN- of 50 Sqn from Lindholme took off normally for a night flying test before operations, turned to port at about 1000 feet, wobbled, lost height rapidly and crashed near Finningley. The cause of the crash was obscure. The 5 crew were all killed: Sgt 926469 Lawrence Rex Hinde age 20 RAFVR (Pilot) and Sgt 974217 Alexander Campbell age 19 RAFVR W.Op/Air Gnr both buried in Hatfield (Woodhouse) Cemetery, Cpl 969301 Morris Ernest Balkin RAFVR buried Glasgow (Glenduffhill) Jewish Cemetery, LAC 1250704 Harry Barton age 26 RAFVR buried Bacup (Fairwell) Cemetery, AC2 1141845 Percy Charles Kemp age 26 RAFVR buried Worthing (Durrington) Cemetery.

THURSDAY 19th JUNE 1941

1845 hrs — Training

Hampden I P1210 of 16 OTU from Upper Heyford overshot the runway on attempted landing at Balderton after a cross country flight. The pilot opened the engines up again but the aircraft failed to maintain height, the engines cut altogether and the aircraft landed with wheels and flaps down in a nearby field at The Hall, Balderton. The pilot P/O R R Mitchell from Rhodesia survived the crash. Sgt J/18431 Edward Alexander McDougall Grange RCAF, who had only been in the country 2 months, also survived the crash but then spent 17 months in hospital. P/O 81417 Alexander Elder Sinclair age 34 (W.Op/Air Gnr) was killed and is buried in Bedlay Cemetery as also was Sgt 1105549 Robert Alexander Crawford Connell age 21 RAFVR who is buried in Lochwinnoch Cemetery.

Sgt Grange recovered from his injuries but was then shot down by a night fighter on 15th August 1943 when acting as navigator of Lancaster JA675 of 467 Sqn, after he took off from Bottesford for a raid on Milan. He had completed more than 20 raids and is buried in Dreux Communal Cemetery, France.

SATURDAY 21st JUNE 1941

Two 250lb and six 50lb bombs were dropped on Plum Tree Farm, Bawtry, a satellite to Finningley. One failed to explode.

SUNDAY 22nd JUNE 1941 — Ground

Wellington I R1593 from Finningley was being prepared for operations when an airmans right arm became trapped between the turret door window and the baulk head door.

MONDAY 23rd JUNE 1941

0220 hrs — Training

Hampden I P1299 of 25 OTU from Finningley overshot the runway when landing on a dark night and went through the boundary hedge. The pilot was Sgt 979538 N F Turner.

0415 hrs — Op; Bremen

Wellington IC R1026 GR-R of 301 Sqn from Swinderby was nearing base on the return from operations, flying low to identify the ground beacons due to ground mist when the port airscrew sheared off at 1000 feet. The rapid increase in engine revolutions caused the engine to overheat and burst into flames. The aircraft was too low for the crew to bale out so a quick forced landing had to be made but the aircraft struck some trees and crashed in a barley field at Roe Wood Farm, Winkburn. It immediately burst into flames killing two members of the crew, P/O P/1379 Stansilaw Pietruszka PAF age 24 (Pilot) and Sgt P/781654 Czeslaw Tegowski PAF age 21 (Front Air Gnr). Both are buried side by side in the Polish Cemetery at Newark-upon-Trent. Crash location: OS sheet 120 697584.

The rest of the crew, some seriously injured, and some trapped in the blazing aircraft, owe their lives to Mr Harry and Mrs Amelia Broadberry, who, ignoring the flames, exploding ammunition and tracer bullets which were flying about, ran from their house and rescued the trapped airmen. For this heroic rescue Mr and Mrs Broadberry were awarded the BEM. Sgt Zygmunt Poplawski, PAF (2nd Pilot), and Sgt Mieczyslaw Grzymski, PAF (Rear Gnr), were both seriously injured and F/O Henryk Sawlewicz, PAF (Air Bomber), and Sgt Feliks Florczak PAF suffered minor injuries.

The award of the BEM to Mrs and Mr Broadberry was announced in The London Gazette on 5th September 1941 which read:

'When an aircraft crashed and caught fire in Nottinghamshire, Mr and Mrs Broadberry heard the crash and hurried to the scene. They went first to the assistance of the two badly injured pilots who were lying close to the burning plane. With the aid of the two members of the crew who were in a very dazed condition, they managed to drag the injured airmen clear of the flames. The rear gunner was trapped in his turret. Mr Broadberry obtained an axe and worked in intense heat for one and a half hours before he finally extricated the gunner. Meanwhile, Mrs Broadberry rendered first aid to the injured airmen. She also managed to give some assistance to her husband in his efforts to free the gunner. During this time, the petrol tanks blew up and ammunition was continually exploding. Mr and Mrs Broadberry showed complete disregard of their own safety and, as a result of their courage and endurance, three lives were saved.'

TUESDAY 24th JUNE 1941 — Training

Battle I P6630 of 16 (P)FTS from Hucknall was practicing forced landings when the pupil pilot turned in too close and attempted a final low right hand turn, stalled and crashed at Grange Farm, Hockerton near Southwell. Both the pilot, F/O P/662 Z Roter PAF, and his pupil were un-injured.

WEDNESDAY 25th JUNE 1941

0040 hrs — Training

Hampden I P1222 of 25 OTU from Balderton during a flarepath practice landing the pilot, Sgt 776003 Neville Hamilton Page, thought that the aircraft was about to swing, opened up an engine to counteract and as a result of this burst overshot and ran through the boundary hedge. There were no injuries.

Sgt Page was the pilot of Hampden AE121 of 144 Sqn which took off from North Luffenham on 12th September for a raid on Rostock and on return the aircraft ran out of fuel and crashed landed at Empingham, Rutland. He and one other member of crew died. He is buried in Jevington (St Andrew) Churchyard.

THURSDAY 26th JUNE 1941

1210 hrs — Air Test

Wellington I R2475 of 150 Sqn from Newton reached the end of its landing run when the pilot F/O 40642 C L Roy selected undercarriage up in mistake for flaps.

FRIDAY 27th JUNE 1941

1215 hrs — Training

Wellington IC R1662 of 23 OTU from Pershore was on a cross country flight when the aircraft crashed in a field and hit a tree in a forced landing 3 miles north of Bawtry on the Great North Road when engines cut and the aircraft lost height rapidly. The aircraft caught fire. The crash report stated that the pilot made every endeavour to save the aircraft.

The crew of eight survived including the pilot F/L 70363 B R Ker but Sgt R/62251 Howard John Kellough RCAF age 22 (W.Op/Air Gnr) RCAF sustained a broken leg and very serious burns and died due to his injuries the next day. He is buried in Doncaster Cemetery.

MONDAY 30th JUNE 1941 — Training

Hampden I P4302 of 25 OTU from Finningley overshot landing and crashed through the boundary fence and the undercarriage collapsed. There were no injuries to the crew.

This aircraft was involved in a fatal accident on 16th September 1941.

The pilot Sgt 402184 Lester Louis Harrison RNZAF was lost on 21st October when a member of the crew of Manchester L7462 OF-Z of 97 Sqn which took off from Coningsby at 2030 hrs for a raid on Bremen and was lost somewhere over the sea. A message had been received at 0030 hrs stating that the receiver was u/s. He is commemorated on the Runnymede Memorial.

L7462 had completed only one previous operation.

Sgt Harrison

—

AC2 1162702 W J Abley and LAC 747023 G N Biddle RAFVR from Swinderby were both awarded the Polish Cross of Merit (Krzyz Zaslugi) for their gallantry in rescuing Polish airmen from a crashed aircraft on 28th December 1940. The aircraft in question was Wellington R1035.

WEDNESDAY 2nd JULY 1941

1650 hrs — Training

Battle I N2031 of 16 (P)FTS from Hucknall was on a solo practice flight when, during landing, the port wheel would not lock down and the pupil pilot, LAC P/782883 J Szymanski PAF, landed the aircraft on one wheel.

THURSDAY 3rd JULY 1941 — Operations

Wellington I W5664 PM-H of 103 Sqn from Newton returned from operations and made a heavy landing. The throttles were opened too late to check by the pilot Sgt 748538 John Cedric Addy DFM, RAFVR.

Sgt Addy, now a F/S, was killed on 17th January 1942 piloting Anson N5030 of 27 OTU. He was on a night navigation exercise from Litchfield with 6 other crew members/passengers when their aircraft flew into cloud on Snaefell mountain, Isle of Man. He is buried in Jurby (St Patrick) Churchyard.

F/S Addy was gazetted with his DFM on 21th October 1941. His citation read: 'Awarded for gallantry and devotion to duty in the execution of air operations.'

SATURDAY 5th JULY 1941

Blenheim I K7156 of 23 Sqn was abandoned after control was lost in a dive out of cloud over Bottesford and crashed at Granby, Notts.

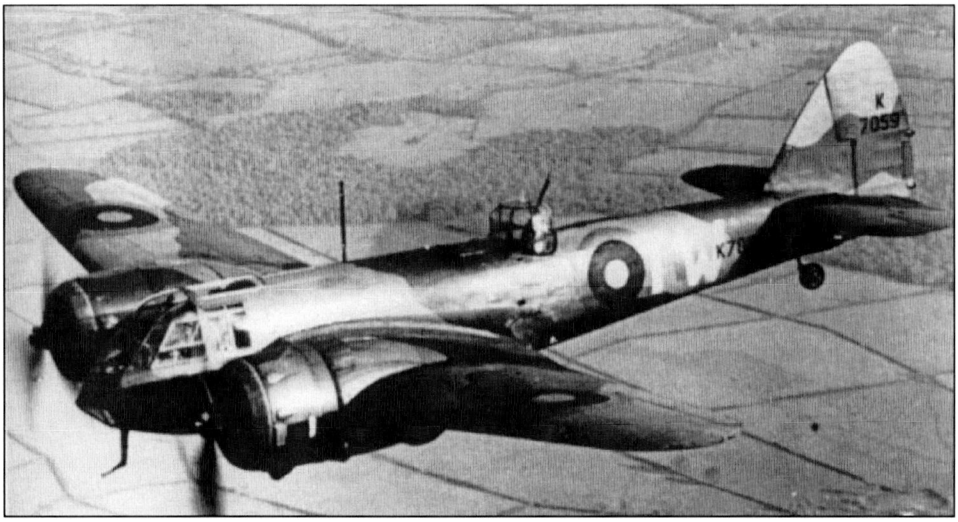

Blenheim I similar to K7156

THURSDAY 10th JULY 1941

0030 hrs Training

Hampden I P1287 of 25 OTU from Balderton was held off too high, made a heavy landing and damaged the tail wheel but with no injuries to the crew.

The pilot, P/O 88016 Gordon Geoffrey Watts RAFVR, was killed only 5 weeks later on 17th August during a raid on Dusseldorf. He was the pilot of Hampden AD756 of 106 Sqn which took off from Coningsby and was shot down by a night fighter and crashed in Belgium. He is buried in Gembloux Communal Cemetery.

1710 hrs

Wellington I X9622 of 25 OTU from Finningley with F/L Newton at the controls crash landed on the aerodrome with no injuries to the crew.

FRIDAY 11th JULY 1941

1130 hrs

Battle I P6627 of 16 (P)FTS from Hucknall landed from low altitude on difficult ground with obscured vision and the aircraft hit trees and a fence in Wood Lane near Hucknall. The pilot P/O P/0162 L Slazynski PAF was also involved in an incident on 5th July.

SATURDAY 12th JULY 1941 Training

Tiger Moth II N5481 of 17 EFTS piloted by LAC 655681 Rogan became lost on a training flight and on attempting to force land and when 15 feet from the ground he noticed an even surface. He opened up again but the engine failed to respond and the aircraft hit a ridge, turned and tipped on its nose, three miles south of Bingham.

TUESDAY 15th JULY 1941

The Polish Memorial in Newark Cemetery was unveiled by the President of the Polish Republic, Wladyslaw Raczkiewicz, and blessed by Bishop Gawlina.

WEDNESDAY 16th JULY 1941 **Polish Air Force Day**

301 Squadron at Swinderby The efforts of the squadron were not left unnoticed:
16.7.41. Command Routine Order, by Air Marshall Sir Richard E. C. Peirse, K.C.B., D.S.O., A.F.C., A. 54 Notable War Services. 'The Commander-in-Chief desires to bring to the notice of all ranks in the Command the coolness and courage shown by Flying Officer W. Butkiewicz of No.301 Polish Squadron. This officer was captain of a Wellington detailed for operations on the 16th June 1941. About 40 miles off the English coast he was attacked by a Messerschmitt 110. The rear gunner of the Wellington replied and the pilot took evasive action. He was again attacked, but fire was continued by the front and rear gunners until the enemy dived steeply out of sight. Fire broke out in the rear turret and was extinguished by the rear gunner. Despite this, the pilot determined to continue with his mission and flew on until again attacked. The rear gunner was now unable to return the enemy's fire as he was burned about the face and his turret was filled with smoke. Another fire broke out near the observer's seat and the aircraft was repeatedly hit. In these circumstances the pilot ordered the crew to stand by to abandon the aircraft and jettisoned his bombs. The fire, however, was successfully extinguished and a course set for the base.

The aircraft had suffered extensive damage and Fg. Off. Butkiewicz had the utmost difficulty in maintaining control. The undercarriage, flaps and emergency system were out of action, and the bomb doors would not close. He made a safe landing. This extremely difficult feat could not have been accomplished without the utmost co-operation and coolness on the part of the crew.'

General Sikorski addresses airmen of the Polish bomber squadrons at Swinderby during the Polish Air Force Day celebrations.
Courtesy of Jerzy B Cynk

FRIDAY 18th JULY 1941

0240 hrs Op; Rotterdam

Wellington IC N2840 GR- of 301 Sqn from Syerston took off at 2258 hrs for an attack on Rotterdam, having been borrowed by 305 Sqn who were based at Syerston. Four polish squadrons were involved in operations against Cologne and as the Wellington was manned by a 'fresher' crew it was customery to give them an easier task, the bombing of Rotterdam. On the return journey the aircraft was shot down by an intruder very close to base and crashed at Cowtham House Farm, Balderton, two miles south east of Newark. All the crew were killed and are buried in Newark-upon-Trent Cemetery.

F/O P/0401 Boleslaw Kuzian, PAF (Pilot) age 29, Sgt P/783678 Janusz Tomaszewski PAF age 25, F/O P/0486 Bronislaw Klatt PAF age 33, Sgt P/793771 Jan Sylwestrowicz PAF age 30, Sgt P/781767 Jan Podziemski PAF age 25, Sgt P/793025 Marian Czerniejewski PAF age 25.

A 301 Squadron Wellington IC ready to be bombed up. Courtesy Jerzy B Cynk

SATURDAY 19th JULY 1941

0045 hrs

High explosive bombs were dropped on Finningley aerodrome.

1100 hrs Training

Hampden I AD897 VN- of 50 Sqn from Finningley rolled over and flew on its back for a few seconds and then dived into the ground during formation practice just north of Finningley. The cause was unknown. All 4 crew members were killed.

Sgt 971237 Edward Ronald Bousfield RAFVR (Pilot) buried Liverpool (Toxteth Park) Cemetery, Sgt 995760 James Edward Stanley Burke RAFVR age 24 (W.Op/Air Gnr) buried Cupar New Cemetery, F/S 971149 James Hopkin Tittley RAFVR age 20 (W.Op/Air Gnr) buried Salford (Weaste) Cemetery, AC1 993639 Herbert Leslie Reed RAFVR age 27 buried Darlington West Cemetery.

SUNDAY 20th JULY 1941

0315 hrs Taxiing

Hampden I P4298 of 25 OTU from Finningley hit a taxiing post when taxiing off the flare path. The taxiing post was not illuminated due to the inability of the flare path party to locate it in the extreme darkness. All lights had been extinguished for two hours due to enemy activity. The pilot was P/O Alfrey. This aircraft was involved in a fatal accident on 30th August at Claypole, Notts.

0330 hrs Training

Hampden I AD987 of 25 OTU from Finningley approached Balderton too high and too fast and the pilot, Sgt 935332 C E Musgrave, was unable to stop the aircraft which then hit the boundary fence.

Sgt Musgrave had a lucky escape on 16th September 1941. He took off from Waddington in Hampden AD930 for a raid on Hamburg and on return the aircraft crashed at Harmston, near Lincoln, after flying into trees on approach to Waddington. He and and one other crew member was injured.

MONDAY 21st JULY 1941 — Training

Battle I R7407 of 16 (P)FTS from Newton during landing the undercarriage jammed and the aircraft was belly landed at Newton. The pilot, LAC 783168 Skadzien was on his first solo flight.

This aircraft collided with another aircraft on 25th November 1943 and crashed killing both crew members.

TUESDAY 22nd JULY 1941

0145 hrs — Training

Hampden I P1236 of 25 OTU from Finningley undercarriage collapsed after a good landing due to strains on previous landing occasions. The pilot Sgt 942610 Christopher George Furby RAFVR was unhurt but was killed on 26th March 1942 when piloting Manchester L7497 of 61 Sqn. He took off from Woolfox Lodge for a raid on Essen and was shot down by a night fighter. All the crew are buried in the Reichswald Forest War Cemetery.

0250 hrs — Training

Hampden I AE149 of 25 OTU from Finningley took off for night flying practice but while in the air Hampden P1236, piloted by Sgt C G Furby (see above) crash landed on the runway. While the runway was being cleared AE149 returned but was refused permission to land and instructed to circle. Whilst doing so the port engine cut and the aircraft crashed into a field next to the airfield and caught fire. One crewman was injured. The pilot was P/O W H Andrews.

1430 hrs — Training

Battle I K7683 of 16 (P)FTS from Newton took off on circuits and landings practice when the pilot became lost and overshot on a forced landing and hit trees at Bunny, 7 miles south of Nottingham.

Instructors had been told to impress noting landmarks and the relative position of the aerodrome on all pupils and to instruct them to look for pin-point of the aerodrome.

The pilot was LAC 780696 F Oprych PAF. This aircraft was also involved in an incident on 1st March.

1745 hrs — Training

Oxford I T1027 of 16 (P)FTS from Newton had engine failure due to fuel shortage and landed with undercarriage retracted near Newton. The pilot was LAC P/782705 Halkiew PAF. The aircraft had taken off with insufficient fuel.

FRIDAY 25th JULY 1941

2230 hrs — Op; Hanover

Hampden I AE234 VN- of 50 Sqn from Swinderby crashed 4 miles south of Swinderby after take-off en-route to a raid on Hanover. The crash report states that this was the 4th accident of this nature with cause not known. All the crew of 4 were killed and are buried in Thurlby (St Germain) Churchyard.

Sgt 902248 Charles George Montgomery RAFVR (Pilot), Sgt 749503 Robert Hooker Rampton RAFVR (Nav), Sgt 943709 Wilfred EllsleyRAFVR (W. Op/Air Gnr), Sgt 654720 Albert Edward Medden RAF (W Op/ Air Gnr).

Hampden P4318 of 25 OTU from Finningley piloted by Sgt Hiles crashed whilst taking off on the flare path causing the night flying programme to be abandoned.

SATURDAY 26th JULY 1941

Fairy Swordfish I L7699 of Station Flight Gosport crashed in a forced landing south of East Retford on the Great North road at Eaton Corner. The pilot was S/L 40673 J Clift who trained at 6 FTS.

TUESDAY 29th JULY 1941

0430 hrs **Op; Gardening**

Hampden I AD 902 VN- of 50 Sqn from Swinderby on return from operations undershot landing and hit a concrete post, 100 yards from the perimeter. The crew P/O 43025 W B Christophers, Sgt Glenn, Sgt Thompson and Sgt Bullin were not injured.

THURSDAY 31st JULY 1941

0200 hrs **Training**

Wellington I R1504 of 25 OTU from Finningley made a heavy landing and the undercarriage collapsed in difficult conditions but there were no injuries.

The pilot P/O 45522 Douglas Spencer Matthews DFM, RAF was killed on 9th January 1942 age 23.

He was the pilot of Manchester R5789 of 61 Sqn which took off from North Luffenham for a raid on Cherbourg and on the outward flight the starboard engine caught fire and the aircraft began to lose height. P/O Matthews ordered the crew to bale out, except for the 2nd pilot P/O T I R Wilson, as he was reluctant to jettison the bomb load for fear of injuring people on the ground. They both attempted to land the aircraft with a full bomb load but failed to see a line of trees and crashed at Wiltshire Cross. He is buried in Swindon (Christ Church) Burial Ground his home town. P/O Wilson survived.

SATURDAY 2nd AUGUST 1941

Tiger Moth N6602 of 25 (P)EFTS from Hucknall was completely burned out when an outbreak of fire occurred in No.1 hangar.

SUNDAY 3rd AUGUST 1941

0430 - 0530 hrs **Training**

Wellington IC X3177 of 25 OTU from Finningley flew into the ground 3 miles south west of Bawtry on a night navigation exercise at a very high speed and rolled over 2 or 3 times. It was a very dark night but there were no low clouds. The crew of 6 were all killed.

F/O 42833 Harry Trevor Gilbert, DFC RAF age 22 (Pilot), P/O 402567 William Henry Crane age 19 RAAF, P/O 402212 Geoffrey Landas Cohen RAAF age 27 all buried in Finningley Churchyard, F/S 748685 Harold Soar RAFVR buried Ticknall Churchyard, Sgt 1285469 Edgar James Matthews age 19 RAFVR buried Gellygaer Cemetery, F/S 755521 William Harrison age 29 RAFVR (W.Op/Air Gnr) buried Birtley New Cemetery.

Harry Gilbert had only been promoted to F/O on 20th April and his DFC announced on 18th April whilst with 61 Sqn.

P/O Geoff Cohen, who lived in Mosman, a suburb of Sydney, Australia, was a prominent member of the Manly Life Saving Club and was the first member of the club killed in WWII.

The black/white photograph on the opposite page depicts 6 members of the pre-war Manly Life Saving Club. P/O Cohen is the 2nd on the left with his surf board which became the MLSC club's War Honour roll. The member on the right is P/O 403778 Kenneth McDonald Simpson age 28 who was killed on 13th August 1943 serving with the RAF.

Above: **The Manly 'surf board' WWII roll of honour.**
Courtesy N A McMurtry

0512 hrs — Operations

Wellington IC W5688 of 304 Sqn from Swinderby crash landed with the undercarriage up when the pilot, F/O P/0403 Iszkowski PAF, misread his petrol gauge reading to believe that he had fuel shortage.

WEDNESDAY 6th AUGUST 1941

1310 hrs — Training

Magister I T9692 of 5 EFTS was on a training flight and became lost and force landed at Gedling. The pilot LAC 1382681 W A Eacote had reached for the brake but accidentally knocked the throttle open and the aircraft ran through a hedge damaging the undercarriage.

FRIDAY 8th AUGUST 1941

2210 hrs — Op; Mining

Hampden I AE124 VN- of 50 Sqn from Swinderby took off for a mining operation off the Friesian Islands, but the port engine cut shortly after being airborne and the Hampden swung and crashed near the airfield and caught fire. 3 injuries were reported. The crew were the pilot P/O N S Milnes, P/O 61983 Roy Frederick Benson Temperley, Sgt Graver and Sgt Bigby.

P/O Temperley was killed on 25th August when Hampden AE320 of 50 Sqn crashed during a raid on Mannheim. He is buried in Rheinberg War Cemetery.

SATURDAY 9TH AUGUST 1941 — Training

Magister I L8087 of 5 EFTS with pilot LAC 1330297 J Denton at the controls on a solo training flight became lost and he force landed 1½ miles south west of Worksop without injury.

SUNDAY 10th AUGUST 1941

1735 hrs — Training

Battle I R7383 of 16 (P)FTS from Newton was on dual circuits and landings training when the pilot belly landed in error, due to not lowering the undercarriage. The instructor pilot was W/O P/794087 Kania PAF.

MONDAY 11th AUGUST 1941

2230 hrs Training

Hampden I X2916 of 25 OTU from Finningley was on a photography and bombing exercise when it crashed 1½ miles south west of Misson. The accident report states that the pilot entered the circuit and was given permission to land and then there were two loud reports. After the first a Verey cartridge was seen showing the incorrect colour and after the second the aircraft was seen burning on the ground. It was thought that the crash may have been due to a structural defect. All four airmen were killed.
P/O 68769 Anthony William Genth age 26 RAFVR (Pilot) from London, P/O J/4765 Thomas Gerald Boucher age 25 RCAF (Obs), Sgt 1165625 Terence Vincent Gerard Clarke age 28 RAFVR (W.Op/Air Gnr.) all buried Finningley (Holy Trinity and St Oswald) Churchyard Extension, Sgt 1168622 Raymond John Moss age 24 RAFVR (W.Op/Air Gnr) buried Birmingham (Yardley) Cemetery.

TUESDAY 12th AUGUST 1941

1545 hrs Training

Hampden I X2970 of 25 OTU from Balderton took off on a training flight in gusty wind but climbed at too steep an angle, stalled and crashed within a minute. The pilot was Sgt 1253038 E F Groves. All 3 crew members were injured. This aircraft was also involved in an incident at Finningley on 17th November 1940.

SATURDAY 16th AUGUST 1941

0030 hrs Training

Hampden I X2959 ZP- of 25 OTU from Balderton took off on Friday the 15th for night circuits and landings training but undershot on landing and hit some high trees, then four houses in the London Road end of Grove Street, New Balderton and burnt out.

Three of the four houses were totally wrecked and at No.84, the home of Mr and Mrs William R Brumpton, six of their seven children were killed. Their ages ranged from five to eighteen years old. They were Geoffrey (18), Joyce (14), Mary Elizabeth (13), Alan (12), Lucy (9) and Sheila (6).

Mrs Brumpton was able to lower her youngest child, 3 year old Roy, to safety before making a safe exit through a bedroom window.

Mr W H F Judson, of Grove Street, tried to release the pilot from his cockpit but was unable to free him due to the intense heat.

Mr Brumpton, a railway worker, was on duty at the time and had seen the flames and though realising his home was in the vicinity of the fire he was not aware of the consequences to him and his family. Funeral services were held for the children on 20th August.

The pilot, Sgt 778405 Sydney Douglas Baldachin age 20 RAFVR, from S Rhodesia, was killed and is buried in Doncaster (Rose Hill) Jewish Cemetery. Sgt 1105933 Thomas Grahame Wood age 20 RAFVR (W.Op/Air Gnr) was also killed and is buried in Woodford Churchyard. Sgt D Macdonald was injured.

Sgt Baldachin was an experienced pilot with 190 hours 40 minutes to his name but this was his first trip in this particular aircraft.

At the inquest Sgt Macdonald stated 'towards the finish (of the flight) it was dark I had no means of knowing the exact height at which we were flying, and I could not tell whether we were over the town or open country. Just immediately before the aeroplane crashed I felt a bump and heard a crack, and this was followed at once by the crash. I did not know what we had struck. The plane burst into flames. The floor of the cockpit had been ripped open and I got through it and dropped to the ground'

SUNDAY 17th AUGUST 1941

0002 hrs — Op; Cologne

Wellington II W5532 EP- of 104 Sqn from Driffield took off at 2350 hrs for a raid on Cologne and was then attacked and shot down, crashing with full bomb load at 0002 hours and the loss of all 6 crew members between South Leverton and Cottam 6 miles south south west of Gainsborough.

Sgt R52876 William Thomas Ross Stephenson (Pilot) RCAF age 28 is buried in Scampton (St John the Baptist) Churchyard, Sgt 928472 John Walter Nowlan (2nd Pilot) age 21 RAFVR buried Eltham Churchyard, F/S 755954 Stanley Charles Steward (Observer) age 21 RAFVR buried Scampton (St John the Baptist) Churchyard, Sgt 961049 Kenneth Hutchinson (1st W/Op) age 24 from Long Eaton buried Long Eaton Cemetery, Sgt 918442 Ivor Howard Arthur Henderson age 23 (2nd W/Op) RAFVR buried Chickerell (St Mary) Churchyard, P/O 106682 Patrick Joseph Murphy (Air Gnr) buried Scampton (St, John the Baptist) Churchyard.

PC Hollingsworth of the Retford Police, who was on duty in the area at the time stated in his report that, at 00.01 hours on the night of the 16/17th of August 1941 he heard machine gun fire to the north east of South Leverton and observed tracer fire, and a minute later observed an aircraft falling in flames. At 00.02 hours he heard the aircraft hit the ground and explode and proceeded to the crash as quickly as possible and took charge. He was unable to approach the burning aircraft owing to the fierce heat of the fire but remained in close proximity.

At 0030 hours there was a terrific explosion caused by the bomb load exploding and PC Hollingsworth was hurled 70 yards by the blast, but luckily he suffered no serious injury.

At 1500 hours on 22nd August 1941 the funeral of P/O Murphy, Sgt Steward and Sgt Stephenson took place at Scampton Cemetery at which W/C Simonds, DFC, P/O MacCaughan, P/O Bradley and three Sgt Pilots from No.104 Squadron attended.

Lt Hans Hahn

The Wellington had been shot down by one of the all black Ju 88s from 3/NJG2 piloted by Lt Hans Hahn based at Gilze-Rijen airfield in Holland. Part of the Wellington had damaged the Ju 88 and it had to return to base on one engine.

Hans Hahn was considered an 'ace' in Germany. He trained as a bomber pilot and was assigned to a Kampfgeschwader in January 1940. In May he sank a 4,000 ton freighter off Dunkirk and shortly after transferred to the Nachtjagd and was posted to NJG 2 in September 1940 and assigned to 3./NJG 2. He gained his first victory on the night of 24th October on an intruder mission over England, Whitley P5073 of 102 Sqn as it took off from Linton-on-Ouse. He operated over England at night and was awarded with the Ritterkreuz (Knights Cross) on 9th July 1941 for 11 victories, the first night fighter pilot to receive this decoration. His 12th victory was to be his last.

On 11th October 1941 after attacking Oxford AB767 over Grantham, they were involved in a mid-air collision with the Oxford and both aircraft crashed with the loss of the crews. Lt. Hans Hahn (F) (Pilot), UFFZ Ernst-Wilhelm Meissier (BF)(Flight Engineer).

The crew of the Oxford AB767 were, Sgt 1101590 Thomas Daye Graham age 19 RAFVR buried New Kilpatrick (or Hillfoot) Cemetery Dumbartonshire and Cpl 655962 Samuel John Edwards untrained pilot RAF age 29 buried Downend (Christ Church) Churchyard.

TUESDAY 19th AUGUST 1941

2150 hrs — Training

Oxford II T1099 of 16 (P)FTS from Newton took off, swung and flew into barbed wire on the boundary due to the pupil pilot holding the aircraft on the ground too long. The aircraft landed without damage on the flarepath. The instructor pilot F/O P/0650 Jan Winiarek was later killed in an accident, see entry for 6th September 1945.

2200 hrs Training

Wellington IC R1073 of 25 OTU from Balderton took a long take-off run due to temporary loss of power from the port engine and the tail hit a hedge but the aircraft still had a successful take off. During landing, the tail wheel collapsed possibly due to some structural failure from hitting the hedge on take off without injuries to the crew.

The pilot, F/L 73022 Gilbert William Walenn RAFVR, had a tragic end to his life later on in the war. 22 days after the above incident, on 10th September, F/L Walenn was the pilot of Wellington N2805 of 25 OTU which took off from Finningley on night bombing practice and failed to return to base. It was thought that the crew may have become lost and found themselves over the sea, with the pilot deciding to force land the aircraft, having drifted over enemy territory. The crew were initially listed as 'missing' at 1955 hrs on 10th September. On the 8th October a telegram was received quoting information from Berlin which stated that F/L Walenn was a Prisoner of War. He later died on the 29th March 1944 having been one of the 50 RAF personnel shot by the German authorities in the Danzig area, whilst attempting to escape from Stalag Luft III, Sagan, Silesia, and was cremated in Danzig. His ashes are now buried in a collective grave in Poznan Old Garrison Cemetery.

F/L 'Tim' Walenn was the escapees' master forger and devised passes, permits and other 'official' documents. Both he and F/L Desmond Plunkett (who survived the escape) provided role models for Donald Pleasance's character in the film 'The Great Escape'.

F/L Walenn was twice Mentioned in Despatches.

WEDNESDAY 20TH AUGUST 1941

0015 hrs Training

Oxford I N4608 of 16 (P)FTS from Newton on dual training failed to turn into the wind early enough, undershot landing and hit trees. The instructor pilot was F/O P/76728 J P Pfeiffer PAF.

FRIDAY 22nd AUGUST 1941

2330 hrs Taxiing

Manchester I L7309 EM-O of 207 Sqn hit trestles taxiing to dispersal.
L7309 was lost on a raid on Hamburg on 15th January 1942. The aircraft was shot down by Oblt Schoenert II/NJG2. One crewman died and five became Prisoners of War.

SATURDAY 23rd AUGUST 1941

0030 hrs Training

Wellington IC X9626 PP-R of 25 OTU from Balderton took off for night training, became lost, and was directed by RT to Newton. The pilot, Sgt 1104095 Lyster Warren-Smith RAFVR, who thought he was landing at Syerston, an airfield he was familiar with, overshot the flarepath and ran into the bomb dump, surprisingly without injuries to any of the crew.

Sgt Warren-Smith was lost on 24th March 1942 when piloting Lancaster R5493 KM-M of 44 Sqn. He took off from Waddington to lay mines in French waters off Lorient and was believed shot down in the target area. The crew are buried near Brest.

SUNDAY 24TH AUGUST 1941

1215 hrs Training

Tutor I K6117 of RAF College Cranwell was on dual instruction in low flying when it hit high tension cables on approach to land at Cranwell and crashed near Coddington 4 miles east of Newark. The instructor pilot, F/O 44358 W D Beddow had failed to see the cables due to them being obscured by a wood. Both pilots were injured.

Wellington IC X9626 overshot Newton on 23rd August

0925 hrs — Training

Hampden I AE221 of 25 OTU from Balderton took off for local flying practice and developed a yaw when just airborne, lost flying speed, flew through a flock of birds and side slipped into the ground at Balderton. The pilot was Sgt 778473 D J Smith.

TUESDAY 26th AUGUST 1941

1650 hrs — Training

Hampden I P1322 of 25 OTU from Balderton swung on take off and the undercarriage collapsed. The pilot Sgt 778492 Evan Moffat Price RAFVR overcorrected the first swing but finally the aircraft took charge. He was un-injured but was killed on 26th March 1942 when piloting Manchester R5831 of 83 Sqn. He took off from Scampton with five other aircraft for a raid on Krupps, Essen and on his return flew into a barrage balloon cable near the Kent coast. 83 Sqn lost 2 aircraft. He is buried Leysdown (St Clement) Churchyard.

WEDNESDAY 27th AUGUST 1941

2250 hrs — Op; Mannheim

Hampden I X2991 VN- of 50 Sqn from Swinderby took off but failed to gain height and the aircraft appeared to slip back onto the ground and hit the aerodrome boundary. No injuries were reported. The crew were P/O 60570 William Pat Ferrie, Sgt Redwood, Sgt Holland and Sgt Hawkins. S/L Ferrie AFC, DFC was subsequently killed on 25th April 1946 age 33 and is buried Habbaniya War Cemetery near Bagdad in Iraq. S/L Ferrie was awarded the DFC on 22nd May 1942 flying with 50 Sqn.

FRIDAY 29th AUGUST 1941

1340 hrs — Training

Hampden I P4412 of 25 OTU from Balderton was on flare path approach landing training when the pilot lost control, the aircraft got into a stabilised yaw and crash landed. The pilot was Sgt 1253038 Groves and was not injured but Sgt 1257957 Sidney Victor Beaumont RAFVR age 20 (W.Op/Air Gnr) was critically injured and he died in Newark General Hospital on 6th September 1941. He is buried in Gravesend Cemetery. Sgt Groves had a previous incident on 12th August.

SATURDAY 30th AUGUST 1941

0115 hrs Training

Hampden I P4298 of 25 OTU from Balderton was on a circuits and landings exercise when the pilot, Sgt 1167740 Charles John Harvey Blunt age 20 RAFVR, lost control on turning in to land, stalled, undershot and crashed at Claypole.

Sgt Blunt was killed on 30th November 1941 age 20. He flew a 455 Sqn Hampden, AE430 UB-M, from Swinderby for a raid on Hamburg and did not return. He and his crew are buried in Kiel War Cemetery.

MONDAY 8th SEPTEMBER 1941

1500 hrs Training

Oxford II R6148 of 16 (P)FTS from Newton tipped up on landing when the brakes were applied too harshly. The instructor pilot P/0650 Jan Winiarek PAF was also involved in an incident on 19th August and was killed in 1945. See entry for 6th September 1945.

WEDNESDAY 10th SEPTEMBER 1941

1825 hrs Training

Oxford II P1087 of 16 (P)FTS from Newton was on circuits and landings training and during a landing a Battle aircraft overtook and came straight across 15-20 feet from the ground. The pilot F/O P/0424 J Kulakowski PAF, turned his aircraft too near the ground to avoid the Battle and a wing hit the ground. The pilot of the Battle never saw the Oxford. There were no injuries.

Training

Hampden I AE244 of 408 Sqn from Syerston returned from 'air firing' practice and on reaching dispersal point there was no brake pressure and the aircraft collided with a YMCA van. The air bottles for the brakes had been turned off before the flight. There were no injuries but the pilot P/O 84689 James Andrew Caldwell RAFVR age 22 was killed on 28th November when the pilot of Hampden AE437 of 408 Sqn. He took off from Syerston for a raid on Dusseldorf and was lost without trace. All the crew are commemorated on the Runnymede Memorial.

THURSDAY 11th SEPTEMBER 1941

1755 hrs Training

Battle I L5311 of 16 (P)FTS from Newton engine cut and aircraft landed on the edge of the aerodrome and hit a barbed wire fence and car, on approach to Newton. The pilot P/O P0377 J Salski PAF was on solo practice. There were no injuries.

2135 hrs Training

Wellington IC R1078 of 25 OTU from Finningley overshot landing when approaching too fast, overran the flarepath and hit the petrol dump on the boundary with no injuries to any of the crew. The pilot, Sgt 933510 Peter Hollowell Foster RAFVR, was killed 7 months later on 13th March 1942 age 21. He was a member of the crew of Manchester L7423 of 83 Sqn which took off from Scampton with five other aircraft and part of a mixed force of 135 aircraft for a raid on Koln and crashed near Nijmegen. He is buried in Jonkerbos War Cemetery.

TUESDAY 16th SEPTEMBER 1941

0022 hrs **Training**

Hampden I P4302 PP- of 25 OTU from Balderton overshot a landing and while attempting to go round again, climbed steeply and crashed to the ground. At 300 feet the aircraft turned to port and dived into the ground and caught fire. The crash report says that it is possible that dazzled by undercarriage warning lights, the pilot switched them off, automatically switching off the port engine.

The pilot P/O J5916 David Darling Christie RCAF from Lindsay, Ontario aged 21 years, was killed and is buried in Newark-upon-Trent Cemetery. His funeral was held on 20th September. Sgts R G Henderson was seriously injured and Sgt Hawkins escaped with minor injuries.

SUNDAY 21st SEPTEMBER 1941

0910 hrs **Training**

Oxford I V4036 of 1507 Flt from Finningley was on a blind take-off when it swung and hit a girder of No.4 hangar. The pilot P/O 86324 Richard Francis Keighley RAFVR age 23 was killed and is buried in Hornsea Cemetery. S/L 37036 Arthur John Frank Churchill age 27 was also killed and is buried in Finningley Cemetery. The other crew member F/S E Groves was very badly shocked but not seriously injured.

FRIDAY 26th SEPTEMBER 1941

1620 hrs **Training**

Wellington IC R1143 of 25 OTU from Balderton was on single engine flying practice when the port engine cut. The pilot Sgt 400475 Jack Marchant RAAF opened up the starboard engine and approached to land but then this engine cut. The aircraft then crash landed outside the aerodrome, ran through the boundary hedge into the aerodrome, hit a mound of earth and the undercarriage collapsed.

400475 Marchant, now a F/L, was killed on 20th December age 26. He took off from Wyton as pilot of Lancaster ED353 of 83 Sqn for a raid on Duisburg and crashed near the target. All the crew are now buried in Reichswald Forest War Cemetery. F/L Marchant was awarded the DFC on 23rd October 1942 whilst flying with 83 Sqn.

SUNDAY 28th SEPTEMBER 1941

0915 hrs **Training**

Hampden I P1194 ZP- of 25 OTU from Balderton took-off and control was lost due to engine failure, the aircraft made a steep rapid turn and crashed into a field next to the airfield, injuring two of the crew.

The pilot P/O J/5791 James Stewart Coulter RCAF was subsequently killed on 12th August, age 22 when flying with 408 Sqn. He had been promoted to F/L and was the pilot of Hampden AE150 which took off from Balderton for a raid on Mainz and his aircraft was lost without trace. All the crew are commemorated on the Runnymede Memorial.

THURSDAY 2nd OCTOBER 1941

1630 hrs **Training**

Oxford II AB 691of 12 SFTS was on a solo navigation exercise when the pilot, Lt 93859 J Readhead overshot a forced landing at Hucknall, while lost in bad weather, and hit trees at Weir Mill Farm, Linby, 3 miles north of Hucknall.

FRIDAY 10th OCTOBER 1941

1945 hrs Training

Wellington IC X9928 PP- of 25 OTU from Balderton took-off and on selecting 'undercarriage up', the nose was allowed to drop and the aircraft hit obstruction poles in a field on Staple Farm, Hawton, adjoining the aerodrome and crashed. The pilot, S/L 37648 John Carlton Betts, was killed and is buried in Elstree Churchyard. 2 other crew members, Sgt Morris and Sgt Byford, were seriously injured and treated in Newark Hospital.

MONDAY 13th OCTOBER 1941

0050 hrs Training

Wellington IC N2762 of 25 OTU from Finningley took off for a night exercise. On return the aircraft landed without flaps due to hydraulic failure, undershot and hit a hut on the aerodrome boundary. The crew were: the pilot P/O D L Atkinson, injured, P/O A G Burt, Sgt 929868 Dann also injured, Sgt 1057551 Titterington, Sgt 645045 R Jones and Sgt 913939 T A Evans.

WEDNESDAY 15th OCTOBER 1941

1230 hrs Training

Tiger Moth II T6266 of 25 (P)EFTS from Hucknall was being piloted by LAC P/?83102 L Dunajewski PAF on a solo flight when he became lost, landed cross wind and struck a hedge one mile west of Farnsfield.

THURSDAY 16th OCTOBER 1941

2130 hrs Training

Anson I W2626 ZP of 25 OTU from Balderton was on circuits and landings practice when it turned in to land and flew into the ground on an even keel, bounced, crashed and disintegrated at Claypole. Sgt 1062691 Eric Henry Charles Hardman RAFVR (W.Op/Air Gnr) was killed and buried in Tinsley Churchyard. The pilot Sgt R/68763 G S Douglas was seriously injured.

TUESDAY 28th OCTOBER 1941

1030 hrs Training

Tiger Moth II N9313 of 25 (P)EFTS from Hucknall took off, attempted to turn back, stalled and the aircraft crashed at Hucknall. The pilot was LAC P/793826 J Mazurkiewiez PAF.

FRIDAY 31st OCTOBER 1941

1130 hrs Training

Battle I K7676 of 16 (P)FTS from Newton was on circuits and landings practice when it crash landed in a field with undercarriage retracted near Long Clawson. There were no injuries. The pilot was A Czernecki PAF. This aircraft was also involved in incidents on 2nd March and 17th July.

Training

Battle I R7406 of 16 (P)FTS from Newton was on dual low flying exercise when the engine cut and the pilot belly landed the aircraft at Wiverton near Bingham. The pilot W/O P/780466 W Koczwarski PAF was also involved in an incident on 14th September.

SUNDAY 2nd NOVEMBER 1941

1715 hrs

Blenheim IV Z5947 of 17 OTU from Upwood took off from Upwood and while flying in cloud control was lost and the aircraft crashed at 1715 hrs at East Leake. The crew were killed. P/O J/5768 Charles William Bush age 23 RCAF (Pilot) buried Ramsey Cemetery, P/O104414 Arthur Thomas Sims age 25 RAFVR (Obs.) buried Bristol Cemetery, and Sgt 1375816 Edward John Bush age 28 RAFVR buried City of London Cemetery.

A Blenheim Mk IV being bombed up

FRIDAY 7th NOVEMBER 1941

1810 hrs Taxiing

Hampden I X3116 of 25 OTU from Finningley was taxiing to dispersal in very bad light when the aircraft hit a telegraph pole with no injuries to the crew.

The pilot Sgt 1281447 Bernard Edward Brown RAFVR was killed on 6th February 1942. He was the pilot of Hampden AE308 UB-L of 455 Sqn which took off from Swinderby on a Gardening operation and was shot down by a night fighter flown by Helmut Lent of Stab II./NJG2, his 30th victim. He and his crew are commemorated on the Runnymede Memorial.

Helmut Lent had been credited with 110 victories when he was killed age 26 when an engine failed on his Ju88 and it crashed.

SUNDAY 9th NOVEMBER 1941

1700 hrs Training

Oxford I P9044 of RAF College, Cranwell was on a solo flight when the aircraft climbed to 50 feet and stalled then hit an obstruction when force landing at Wigsley before darkness fell. The pilot, LAC 1382497 F G Brown was not injured.

2115 hrs Training

Wellington N2783-Q of 25 OTU B Flt from Finningley took off for a cross country and bombing exercise and flew into the ground at a shallow angle and crashed near Rossington village. The pilot probably did not realise he was flying at such a low altitude. 4 of the crew were killed and 2 injured.

Sgt 400471 Henry Clifford Howard RAAF, age 22 is buried Finningley Churchyard Extension, Sgt 1308648 Frank Morton Oddy RAFVR age 26 (W.Op/Air Gnr) buried Shipley Cemetery, Sgt 992165 Willie Holden RAFVR age 22 (W.Op/Air Gnr) buried Bradford Cemetery, Sgt 407201 Reginald Wilton Durdin RAAF age 27 buried Finningley Churchyard Extension.

The 2 injured crewmen were Sgt 404530 Arthur John Coe RNZAF and Sgt 406149 Clifford William Musto RAAF.

Sgt Coe was killed on 6th April 1945 whilst flying with 487 Sqn and is buried in Villers-Bretonneux Military Cemetery.

Sgt Musto was killed on 11th August 1942 age 28 when serving with 207 Sqn. He was a member of the crew of Lancaster R5499 which took off from Bottesford on a Gardening operation and was lost without trace. He is commemorated on the Runnymede Memorial. His brother-in-law F/S 406010 Ernest Louis Haffner was killed on active service just 7 weeks previously on 24th June.

SATURDAY 15th NOVEMBER 1941

0014 hrs Operations

Hampden AE436 of 408 Sqn from Syerston made too low an approach to land, probably affected by downdraught from the escarpment on which the aerodrome is situated. The starboard undercarriage struck an earth mound surrounding the bomb dump and was torn off. The pilot P/O J/ 5917 S Brackenbury landed the aircraft on one wheel.

SUNDAY 16th NOVEMBER 1941

1215 hrs Training

Oxford II R6129 of 16 (P)FTS from Newton was on a solo cross country flight when, due to rapidly deteriorating weather, the pilot unable to see the ground well enough to land, baled out. The aircraft crashed at Morton Grange near Retford. The pilot, LAC 783221 Uram PAF, was possibly trying to find and land at Gamston airfield which was only one mile away.

MONDAY 17th NOVEMBER 1941 Operations

Manchester I R5788 of 207 Sqn from Bottesford was held off too high during landing by the pilot F/S 564896 Colin Wathey, who was making his first landing on a runway, and the subsequent heavy landing damaged the tail wheel.

C Wathey, now W/O, was killed on 4th June 1942. He was the pilot of Lancaster R5847 EM-Y of 207 Sqn which took off from Bottesford for a raid on Bremen and was shot down by a night fighter and crashed at Zwiggelte near Assen, Holland. All the crew are buried in Westerbork General Cemetery.

TUESDAY 18th NOVEMBER 1941

0335 hrs Training

Hampden I P2113 of 25 OTU from Finningley undershot when landing on the flare path with a slight cross-wind and hit an inner marker beacon then landed when the pilot, Sgt 778494 R N B Sinclair, regainined control of the aircraft.

1632 hrs Training

Manchester I L7428 of 25 OTU 'D' Flight from Bircotes took off on a night training flight when 10 minutes into the flight the port engine started vibrating badly with smoke coming from the port air inlet. The pilot decided to force land and both engines were throttled back, the port wing dropped and the aircraft caught fire. The aircraft struck the ground, went through hedges at Scaftworth, near Bawtry and landed in a ditch. Three crew members were killed and two injured.

The pilot F/S 742983 Linford Herbert Adams DFM age 26 RAFVR is buried in Southend-on-Sea Cemetery, F/S 742962 Ronald William Hazard Baxter DFM RAFVR is buried in Letchworth Churchyard and F/O 404091 Desmond Barton Elleray age 22 RAAF is buried in Finningley Churchyard Extension. P/O C Danielson (Pilot) and Sgt 1061453R Rowell (W.Op/Air Gnr) were injured. F/S Adams's DFM was gazetted on 25th April 1941.

SATURDAY 22nd NOVEMBER 1941

Night Operations

Manchester I L7515 of 207 Sqn from Bottesford taxied off the flare path on the runway, became bogged down and was damaged when being towed out by a tractor. The pilot was F/L 33397 William Denys Butterworth Ruth.

F/L Ruth was awarded the DFC on 22nd November 1940 when serving with 50 Sqn and the Bar to the DFC on 6th November 1942 whilst serving with 207 Sqn. He was killed on 12th June 1944 with the rank of S/L when a member of 201 Sqn.

He was the Captain of Sunderland ML760, RAF Pembroke Dock, which was carrying out an anti-submarine patrol off the Bay of Biscay and was shot down by flak from a U-Boat in the North Atlantic and was reported missing, with the deaths of the 12 members of the crew presumed to have occurred on that day, 12th June 1944. On 11th April 1947, it was stated that as nothing had been heard of S/L Ruth since reported missing it was assumed that he had lost his life at sea, since when he has been commemorated on the Runnymede Memorial.

S/L Ruth. Courtesy of V Holyoak

MONDAY 24th NOVEMBER 1941

Training

Hampden I AE190 of 408 Sqn was on low level practice bombing at Clifton Pastures when a bomb hung up. The pilot P/O J/5917 Brackenburg dived to shake it off and the bomb dropped and struck the leading edge of the tail plane.

TUESDAY 25th NOVEMBER 1941

1400 hrs Training

Battle R7407 of 16 (P)SFTS from Newton was on a routine training flight when a Battle, possibly N2177, collided with it in mid-air. As one Battle sliced the wings off the other, F/O P/0379 Stefan M Dubas PAF, an instructor, and LAC Stanislaw Waskowiak PAF, a pupil, fell to their deaths together with the pupil in the other Battle, LAC P/782800 Emil Manka PAF age 20. They are all buried in Newark-upon-Trent Cemetery.

MONDAY 8th DECEMBER 1941

1800 hrs | Training

Wellington IC X9612 of 25 OTU from Finningley took off for the pilot, F/S 742468 P Sleight, to practice take off and landings. During the exercise the aircraft had engine and hydraulic failure which was then abandoned and it crashed on the Great North Road at Rossington. F/S Sleight and the other crew member, Sgt 619406 H Kitto, landed without injury.

WEDNESDAY 10th DECEMBER 1941

Night | Training

Oxford II T1077 of 16 (P)FTS from Newton landed with the undercarriage retracted. The OC suggested that the pilot Sgt P/784183 Knapik PAF had a moment of mental aberration.

THURSDAY 11th DECEMBER 1941

1010 hrs | Training

Manchester I L7524 of 25 OTU from Bircotes undershot the airfield when practicing flapless landings, closed throttles and dropped heavily on uneven ground on the edge of the perimeter track bounced and the undercarriage collapsed on the 2nd touch down. The pilot was P/O Metcalfe.

THURSDAY 18th DECEMBER 1941

0120 hrs | Training

Battle I P6640 of 16 (P)FTS from Newton was on solo circuits and landings when the aircraft overshot the flare path. The pilot, LAC P/792401 Wojsa PAF, opened up to go round again and struck a barbed wire fence damaging the undercarriage and landed ahead.

TUESDAY 23rd DECEMBER 1941

1600 hrs | Training

Manchester I R5782 of 207 Sqn from Bottesford was damaged by an engagement with a Spitfire during formation flying practice. The Spitfire had failed to identify the Manchester and opened fire. The pilot was A/F/S 741869 Dawkins.

1942

THURSDAY 1st JANUARY 1942

1310 hrs — Training

Manchester I L7526 of 25 OTU from Finningley was on circuits and landings training when the tail wheel fork failed and a tyre burst landing on rough ground at Bircotes. Because of this incident it was decided to practice future circuits and landings at Finningley. The pilot F/S 742920 F Ormonroyd was also involved in an incident on 15th March.

1710 hrs — Testing

Wellington I L4212 of RAE from Farnborough was on a test flight to climb to its ceiling height when the pilot F/L 40629 A S McCracken lost touch with base in deteriorating weather conditions. He broke through cloud and decided to force land in a field and ran into a depression in the ground and the undercarriage collapsed at Edwinstowe. There were no injuries.

FRIDAY 2nd JANUARY 1942

0010 hrs — Training

Manchester L7431 of 25 OTU from Finningley was on a sodium flarepath landings exercise for the pilot, P/O C G Hughes. During take off an engine emitted loud bangs and a panel behind an air intake blew off. Unable to maintain height on one engine the aircraft was landed undercarriage up at Cotterill Woods Farm, Woodsetts, Worksop, without injury to the crew. The enquiry concluded that the pilot was not to blame as he had a good 'one engine' performance but the initial loss of height after the engine failure and the low speed at the commencement of the failure gave the impression that turning was hazardous.

1045 hrs — Training

Manchester I L7421 of 25 OTU from Finningley was on dual instruction training when the tail wheel collapsed on landing at Bircotes due to a rough aerodrome surface. The pilot was Sgt 936266 D C Busby. Due to this incident it was decided that it was asking too much for a newly laid grass aerodrome to operate Manchester aircraft during the winter months and in future only light aircraft would operate from Bircotes during that time.

TUESDAY 6th JANUARY 1942

1745 hrs — Taxiing

Manchester I L7485 EM-G of 207 Sqn from Bottesford struck a bomb trolley on the edge of the runway whilst taxiing in bad visibility due to its ineffective brakes on the frosty surface. The pilot, Sgt 401470 John Justin Neville McCarthy RNZAF age 27, was also involved in an incident on 8th April and was killed on 24th July. He was the pilot of Lancaster R5867 also of 207 Sqn which took off from Bottesford for a raid on Duisburg and crashed near Krefeld where all the crew were laid to rest.

SATURDAY 10th JANUARY 1942

Spitfire I R6882 PR- of 609 Sqn from Digby in the course of a practice dog fight, Sgt B W Andrews was diving his aircraft almost vertically when structural failure occurred during recovery from the dive. He abandoned the aircraft 2½ miles south east of East Stoke.

2345 hrs

Three high explosive bombs were dropped at Hucknall at the junction of Beaufort Lane and Wynbush Road. Buildings at Beaufort farm were damaged.

Night | Training

Battle I P6751 of 16 (P)FTS from Newton was on a solo flight in moon light when the landing approach was made too low by the pilot LAC P/783109 Lewandowski PAF. The undercarriage struck the rifle range and was torn off and the aircraft landed without it.

THURSDAY 15th JANUARY 1942

1500 hrs | Ground

Tiger Moth II T7747 of 25 (P)EFTS from Hucknall was stationary on the aerodrome when it was struck by Spitfire R6889 of the Aeroplane & Armament Experimental Establishment, coming in to land from an engine consumption test flight, flown by S/L J H Heyworth, Assistant Chief Test Pilot for Rolls-Royce, Hucknall. Visibility was poor when approaching from air to ground whilst landing, and S/L Heyworth looking ahead did not see any aircraft in its landing path. Given the congested state of Hucknall aerodrome, the pilot failed to see T7747 immediately in front of the blind spot of his aircraft. F/O P/0921 Josef Gaudyn PAF, age 34, a pilot instructor, the pilot of T7747 was killed and is buried in Hucknall Cemetery. The investigators into the incident cleared S/L Heyworth from any blame for the accident and were surprised that there were not more accidents at Hucknall owing to the congestion of the airfield and notorious poor visibility.

S/L Heyworth was the pilot of a Rolls-Royce Lancaster which force landed on Hollingwell Golf Course on 22nd January 1954.

2230 hrs | Op; Hamburg

Wellington IV Z1265 BH-K of 300 Sqn from Hemswell was one of 8 aircraft and crews from 300 Sqn detailed to attack Hamburg. The aircraft took off at 1745 hours and completed the raid successfully and on its return encountered severe icing and bad visibility and the pilot could not see his base or lights when circling overhead and decided to find a landing ground. Apparently the aircraft stalled, crashed and caught fire at Clipstone, near Mansfield. Cause of the crash was unknown. All 6 crew were killed.

F/L P/78626 Jan Bak PAF (Pilot) age 40, LAC P/792071 Franciszek Chylewski PAF age 25, F/L P/1156 Waclaw Mosiewicz PAF age 44, P/O P/1541 Stefan Berdys PAF age 22, Cpl P/780831 Pawel Konaad Krenzel PAF and AC2 P/784658 Marian Wajeech Lagodzinki PAF age 28. All are buried in the Polish Plot at Newark-upon-Trent Cemetery.

Investigation in the PRO indicated that a Wellington crashed at 2230 hours at Brooms House Farm (probably Blooms Gorse Farm) in the Parish of Rufford. 300-400 leaflets printed in German was found at the scene. The leaflet was headed 'Terror' with a photograph of two bodies in a grave at the foot of a swastika suspended from gallows and the rising sun.

A Church parade and burial took place at Newark for the airmen on 20th January.

WEDNESDAY 21st JANUARY 1942

1130 hrs | Ground

Manchester I L7391 EM-Y of 207 Sqn from Bottesford was parked and struck by a lorry driven by AC2 Fawkner who was found to be guilty of negligence. He had failed to ensure that, when attempting to pass under a wing of an aircraft, the canopy of the lorry was sufficiently low to pass under safely. This aircraft was nicknamed the 'Glider' because of its high un-serviceability.

300 Squadron Wellington similar to Z1265 which crashed on 15th January

TUESDAY 10th FEBRUARY 1942

Ferrymead, New Zealand, Roll of Honour

0541 hrs — Op; Gardening

Hampden I AD783 UB-U of 455 Sqn from Wigsley took off at 2345 hrs to drop mines off Emden, Germany but returned early due to engine trouble. The aircraft stalled from 800 feet whilst circling the airfield and crashed at Eagle village, behind Sutton Farm, whilst preparing to land at Wigsley. All 4 crew were killed.

F/S 402874 John Bernard Kennedy RNZAF age 27 (Pilot) is buried in Newark-upon-Trent Cemetery, Sgt 778346 Verner James Hopwood age 26 RAFVR, is buried in Thurlby Churchyard, Sgt 1000480 William Leonard Kelly age 21 (W.Op/Air Gnr) RAFVR buried in Ashton-in-Makerfield Churchyard, Sgt 1375863 George Arthur Metcalfe RAFVR (W.Op/Air Gnr) buried in Edmonton Cemetery.

F/S Kennedy was on his 13th Operation and is listed on the Roll of Honour at Ferrymead, Christchurch, New Zealand. The inscription reads: 'Addington Workshops, Members of Staff, who made the supreme sacrifice, 1939-1945'.

1430 hrs — Training

Manchester I L7478 of 25 OTU from Finningley was coming in to land when an engine cut and the pilot, P/O J/5794 Elwood Raymond Seibold, was unable to counteract a swing, undershot the aerodrome and struck the ground heavily. The aircraft crashed 1½ miles north of Bawtry. The crash log suggested that the pilot failed to diagnose the fault as engine speed and approached with undercarriage and flaps down. The 2nd pilot inadvertently cut-off the fuel to the standby engine instead of closing radiator shutters. A civilian lorry was struck by the plane and damaged beyond repair and the driver received slight facial injuries.

Sgt 1127538 Frederick King age 26 RAFVR Air Gnr was the only fatality amongst the 7 man crew and was cremated at Newcastle-upon-Tyne Crematorium. There were no other injuries. P/O Seibold was involved in another incident on 5th May at Syerston.

FRIDAY 13th FEBRUARY 1942

1215 hrs | Training

Tiger Moth II R4919 of 25 (P)EFTS from Hucknall with P/784052 J Karobuk PAF in the cockpit was practicing turns and side slipping when he descended to 2000 feet and, because the engine was not warm enough on a very cold day, he opened the throttle too quickly resulting in the engine becoming choked and then seizing. The aircraft glided ahead without regard to wind direction and whilst trying to avoid some trees, stalled and crashed at Annesley Park. He was injured.

THURSDAY 19th FEBRUARY 1942

1030 hrs | Taxiing

Oxford II R6113 of 14 (P)AFU from Ossington was taxiing along the runway down wind on a slope when the brakes failed and the aircraft ran across the perimeter track into the runway exit and hit a contractors saloon car. The brake failure was due to negligence of the rigger. The pilot was P/O J C Perriatt.

THURSDAY 26th FEBRUARY 1942

0057 hrs | Operations

Hampden I AT150 of 455 Sqn from Wigsley returned from operations with a full bomb load, overshot landing and ran off the end of the runway onto broken ground and the tail wheel collapsed. The pilot was Sgt 778452 E H Busfield.

0530 hrs | Stationary

Oxford II X7065 of 14 (P)AFU from Ossington had crash landed and while stationary was hit by Wellington Z1255 whilst it was landing (see below).

0530 hrs | Op; Kiel

Wellington IV Z1255 of 301 Sqn from Hemswell was detailed with 8 other aircraft from 301 Sqn to attack Kiel. The mission was successful but on returning they had to make a precautionary landing at Ossington, having been given permission to land there because of fuel shortage due to icing. Both pilots had to operate the aircraft due to difficulty with the controls. Unfortunately the runway allocated for landing was already obstructed by Oxford X7065 which had previously crash landed also due to difficulty with the controls because of icing, and a collision occurred. The Oxford should have been marked by lights.

The pilot of the Wellington F/L Kurzempa PAF, 2nd pilot Sgt Niegrecki PAF and 5 other crew members were not injured. One aircraft did not return from the operation. This aircraft was lost on operations on 9th October.

MONDAY 2nd MARCH 1942

1530 hrs | Taxiing

Hampden I P2056 of 455 Sqn from Wigsley was taxiing along the runway when the tail wheel collapsed with no injuries to the crew.

The pilot P/O 3200 Robert Charles Roberts RAAF was killed a month later on 11th April age 29. He was the pilot of Hampden AT221 of 455 Sqn which took off from Wigsley for a raid on Essen and crashed at Sturzelberg. He and the crew are buried in Rheinberg War Cemetery.

WEDNESDAY 4th MARCH 1942

1125 hrs — Air Test

Blenheim I L6804 of 17 OTU from Upwood took off and an engine then failed at 1000 feet due to a fault in the oil system. As it was in bad visibility it was impossible to land so the pilot climbed to 3200 feet on one engine and the crew abandoned the aircraft which crashed near Colston Bassett. The enquiry discovered that the flight was not properly authorised because the weather was unsuitable for an air test. The Pilot of this aircraft was Sgt 613198 G D Jessup.

SUNDAY 8th MARCH 1942

1100 hrs — Ground

Oxford X AP480 of 14 (P)AFU from Ossington engine had switched off and the propeller had come to rest. AC1 1117507 J C Money approached the front of the engine to feel the cylinders and the propeller struck him a heavy blow on the head causing injuries.

1130 hrs — Training

Oxford II P8971 of 14 (P)AFU from Ossington port engine failed on landing approach to the airfield due to fuel shortage. The pilot, Sgt 1377128 W J L Leg, retracted the undercarriage and belly landed the aircraft in a field ½ mile east of Ossington. The crash enquiry stated that the pilot should have switched onto auxiliary tanks when he knew the aircraft had already done 2 hours 40 minutes flying time. No injuries were reported.

TUESDAY 10th MARCH 1942

1230 hrs — Ferrying

Hampden AT113 I UB-P of 455 Sqn from Wigsley swung to port on the runway and the starboard undercarriage collapsed during take off to ferry the aircraft to Swinderby. This was due to the port engine being throttled back quickly causing it to cut. This point had been stressed to all pilots but the pilot, P/O Gandy, had not been informed. This aircraft crashed near Balderton on 29th July.

WEDNESDAY 11th MARCH 1942

0050 hrs — Op; Essen

Hampden I P2085 UB-U of 455 Sqn from Wigsley landed on the starboard wheel only on returning from Operations which caused the Hampden to swerve violently onto nearby rough ground and hit obstructions. The crew were: Sgt 778452 E H Busfield (Pilot), Sgt Waites, Sgt Gower and Sgt Biggin.

1030 hrs — Training

Manchester I R5829 of 25 OTU from Bircotes swung to starboard on take off and hit a chance light. The pilot, P/O 103051 Alfred Henry Paget RAFVR, was considered at fault although he had a good record. There were no injuries.

P/O Paget was killed on 27th August when he took off from Grimsby in Wellington Z1338 of 142 Sqn for a raid on Kassel and the aircraft was lost. 4 aircrew lie in Rheinberg War Cemetery and one was taken prisoner.

THURSDAY 12th MARCH 1942

1300 hrs Air Test

Hampden I P5326 UB-V of 455 Sqn from Wigsley dived into the ground whilst banking steeply to port after suffering engine failure on take-off during an air test. The pilot Sgt 404823 Keith Alexander Andrew RAAF age 24 was killed and is buried in Thurlby Churchyard. His navigator Sgt Miflin was injured.

FRIDAY 13th MARCH 1942

1200 hrs Training

Hampden I AE264 of 455 Sqn from Wigsley was taxiing along the runway when a lorry travelling in front of the aircraft stopped. The pilot, P/O Bunbury, tried to pass without running off the track into boggy ground but the aircraft struck it with the port wing which was damaged.

1425 hrs Training

Tiger Moth II T7220 of 25 (P)EFTS from Hucknall stalled on gliding approach to a practice forced landing. Bumpy air conditions caused a wing to drop and the aircraft spun into the ground at Blidworth. The pilot, LAC P/793442 M Bronisz PAF, applied the engine in an endeavour to correct but this made the crash much worse. LAC Bronisz was injured.

SUNDAY 15th MARCH 1942

2315 hrs Taxiing

Wellington IC DV440 of 25 OTU from Finningley was taxiing to dispersal along the runway when the pilot, Sgt 655001 E H Burgess, saw a tractor coming towards the aircraft. He applied the brakes and swung the aircraft and the propeller and the underside of the port engine struck the bowser. No-one was injured.

TUESDAY 17th MARCH 1942

2210 hrs Training

Hampden I AD749 of 14 OTU was recalled from a training flight due to appalling bad weather. Unable to receive permission to land, the pilot, Sgt R/81403 Hershel Homer Davis RCAF, flew away from his home aerodrome and attempted a landing at Newton. He overshot the short flare path but there were no injuries.

Sgt Davis was subsequently killed just 5 weeks later, on 20th April 1942. He was piloting a 420 Sqn Hampden AD869 from Waddington when it crashed on a night cross country exercise near Horncastle. All the crew are buried in Waddington (St Michael) Churchyard.

MONDAY 23rd MARCH 1942

0930 hrs Training

Oxford II P6805 of 14 (P)AFU from Ossington was on dual instructional low flying training when it hit a tree with the starboard wing tip, hit the ground about 250 yrds away, then hit another tree and completely disintegrated. It eventually came to rest ½ mile north of Laneham. The pilot did not keep to the height laid down by his flight plan. Both crew members were killed. Sgt 1381487 George Walter Dawson RAFVR age 27 (Pilot) buried in Harrow Cemetery, Sgt 1292391 Stephen Youngs RAFVR age 20 (Pilot) buried Chislehurst and Sidcup Cemetery.

2307 hrs Training

Lancaster I R5486 OF-P of 97 Sqn from Woodhall Spa was on a non-operational bomb load flight due to operations being cancelled because bad weather was coming in from the east. The aircraft was diverted to Finningley on completion of its flight and on landing the undercarriage collapsed as a result of the aircraft swinging, caught fire and burnt out. The pilot, F/S 754106 G H Hartley, landed the aircraft at excessive speed due to his inexperience of landing on this type of aircraft at night. The crew were not injured.

F/S Hartley

TUESDAY 24th MARCH 1942

1530 hrs Training

Oxford I P1891 of 15 (P)AFU from Kirmington had engine failure in flight, failed to maintain height and struck a tree on a forced landing. The aircraft caught fire and burnt out ½ mile south of Collingham.

The pilot F/O 405315 Leon George Lyons RAAF age 26 was uninjured but was killed 5 months later on 29th August. He was flying with 408 Sqn piloting Hampden AT228 from Balderton on a raid to Saarbrucken and crashed near Liesse where he was laid to rest.

WEDNESDAY 25th MARCH 1942

2212 hrs Ferrying

Hampden I AE135 UB-C of 455 Sqn on arrival at Wigsley aerodrome the flare path had not been completely changed and the pilot was informed by control to land at Waddington. When the flare path had been changed, prmission was given to land at Wigsley but the pilot P/O 403403 Jack Napier Davenport RAAF failed to notice the correct direction for landing, landed downwind and overshot. There were no injuries.

P/O Davenport went on to have a distinguished and meritorious career in the RAAF with 455 Sqn and survived the war. He achieved the rank of Wing Commander and received the following decorations: DFC 25.5.43, DSO 9.6.44, Bar to the DFC 19.9.44, GM 5.1.45 and Mentioned in Despatches 1.1.46.

The citation for the DSO read: 'This officer has taken part in a large number of sorties, including many attacks on shipping, during which must loss has been inflicted on the enemy. Recently he led a formation of aircraft in an attack on an enemy convoy which was escorted by 16 armed ships. In spite of fierce opposing fire a most determined and successful attack was made. Two medium sized merchant vessels and one of the escorting vessels were very severely damaged. In this well executed operation, Wing Commander Davenport displayed high powers of leadership, great skill and determination which contributed materially to the results obtained. This officer has rendered great service and his sterling qualities have impressed all.'

P/O Davenport

The citation for the GM read: 'One night in September 1944, a Beaufighter attached to a RAAF squadron in the

United Kingdom, crashed on a runway and burst into flames. The hatch was seen to open partially and fall shut again. Davenport immediately dashed forward, opened the top hatch, and struggled to free the pilot. The pilot was severely burned, and his feet were jammed. Davenport pulled him out of his flying boots and lafted him bodily through the blaze to safety. Davenport sustained shock, with burns to his face, hair, and hands.'

The Beaufighter in question was NT892 which had just returned to its base at Langham from a reconnaissance flight when during landing the undercarriage collapsed and the aircraft caught.

The biography of W/C Davenport can be read in 'Jack Davenport – Beaufighter Leader' by Kristen Alexander.

SUNDAY 29th MARCH 1942

1400 hrs Ground

Oxford II V3684 of 16 (P)SFTS from Newton was undergoing undercarriage repair when LAC P/792071 Z Piszczeck PAF selected undercarriage lever 'up' instead of 'neutral' and he was trapped under the mainframe suffering injuries.

THURSDAY 2nd APRIL 1942

2100 hrs Training

Master III W8775 of 16 (P)SFTS from Newton made a heavy landing and crashed. The pilot LAC P/782846 Ilnicki PAF, who was on a solo night training flight, mis-judged his third approach and did not hold off in time.

FRIDAY 3rd APRIL 1942

1832 hrs Ferrying

Hampden AE361 of 408 Sqn overshot Syerston on landing in a small area after ferrying. The pilot, A/S/L 402167 D S N Constance was unable to pull up soon enough owing to lack of wind, a rough surface and wet grass. This aircraft was involved in another incident on 23rd October 1941.

SATURDAY 4th APRIL 1942

1330 hrs Training

Master III W8503 of 16 (P)SFTS from Tollerton pilot LAC P/783261 S Nawarski PAF was practicing forced landings and struck a tree on approach. He was not injured

MONDAY 6th APRIL 1942

0115 hrs Training

Lancaster I R5498 EM-Z of 207 Sqn from Bottesford was practicing circuits and landings and landed out of the wind on a runway. The tail plane struck a marshalling van at the intersection of the runways when the pilot P/O 61471 Gerald Antony Ings RAFVR, was correcting a swing with no blame to himself. The 2nd pilot was Sgt 1076769 Raymond Bell-Berry RAFVR. Lancaster R5498 was also involved in an incident near the aerodrome 2 days later.

Both pilots were killed just 4 months later on 6th August. Both took off in Lancaster R5761 of 207 Sqn for a raid on Essen when it was shot down by a night-fighter and crashed at Altforst, near Nijmegen. They are buried in Uden War Cemetery.

WEDNESDAY 8th APRIL 1942

0114 hrs

Training

Lancaster I R5498 EM-Z of 207 Sqn from Bottesford was training in circuits and bumps when the booster pump failed on approach. This caused both starboard engines to cut out, starved of fuel. The airspeed dropped, the aircraft turned to starboard and crashed onto the road running along the north south boundary of the aerodrome (adjacent to Willow Farm) and was completely destroyed by fire. Two of the crew were injured. It was considered that the pilot had committed an error of airmanship in taking off the last time when it was obvious that there was a defect in the fuel system which caused the petrol to be drawn in from one tank only. The pilot had made a statement that the port inboard tank showed its contents gauge that it contained 500 gallons and starboard in-board tanks 60 gallons indicating that all engines had been running on the starboard in-board tank only. The above statement is the official account of the incident.

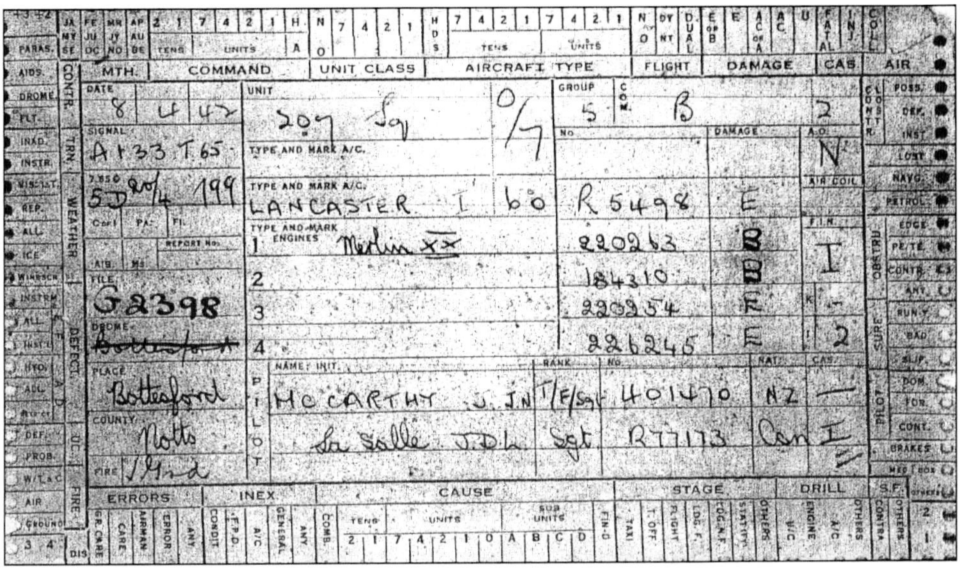

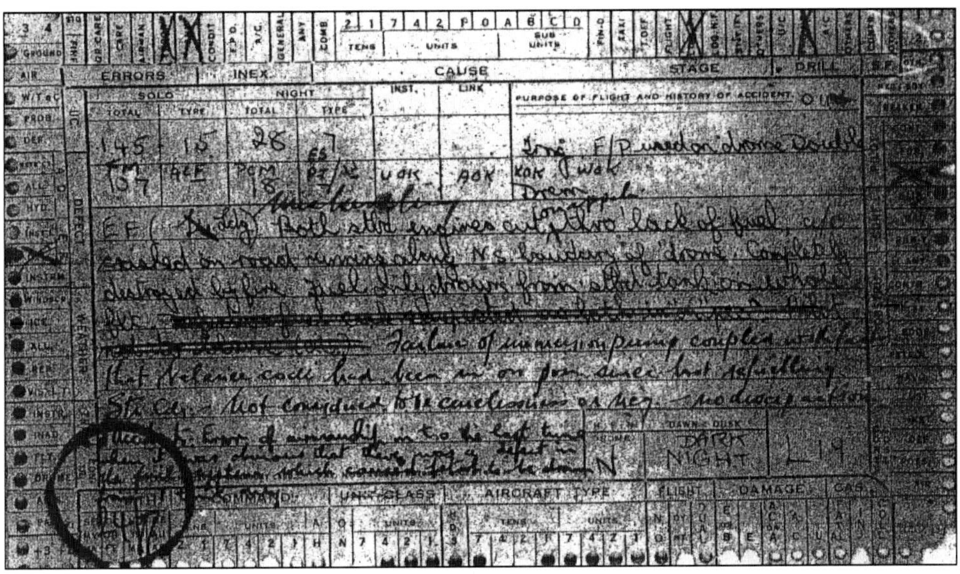

Official crash log sheets 1 and 2. Courtesy of DORIS Hendon

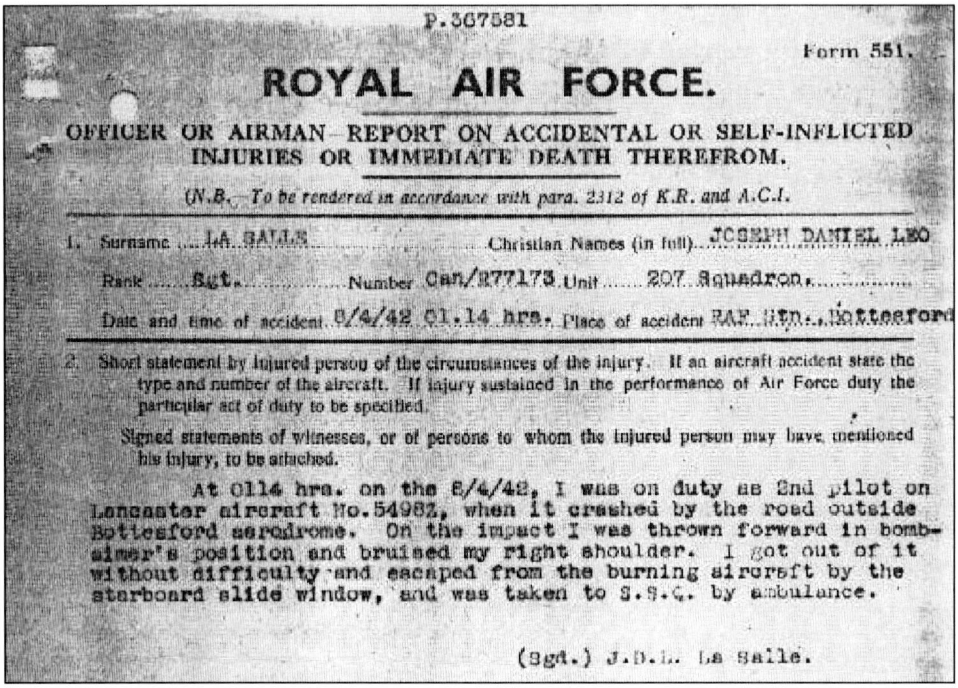

P.367581

Form 551.

ROYAL AIR FORCE.

OFFICER OR AIRMAN REPORT ON ACCIDENTAL OR SELF-INFLICTED INJURIES OR IMMEDIATE DEATH THEREFROM.

(N.B.—To be rendered in accordance with para. 2312 of K.R. and A.C.I.

1. Surname LA SALLE Christian Names (in full) JOSEPH DANIEL LEO

Rank Sgt. Number Can/R77173 Unit 207 Squadron.

Date and time of accident 8/4/42 01.14 hrs. Place of accident RAF. Stn. Bottesford

2. Short statement by injured person of the circumstances of the injury. If an aircraft accident state the type and number of the aircraft. If injury sustained in the performance of Air Force duty the particular act of duty to be specified.

Signed statements of witnesses, or of persons to whom the injured person may have mentioned his injury, to be attached.

At 0114 hrs. on the 8/4/42, I was on duty as 2nd pilot on Lancaster aircraft No.5498Z, when it crashed by the road outside Bottesford aerodrome. On the impact I was thrown forward in bomb-aimer's position and bruised my right shoulder. I got out of it without difficulty and escaped from the burning aircraft by the starboard slide window, and was taken to S.S.Q. by ambulance.

(Sgd.) J.D.L. La Salle.

Form 551 (part), the official injury report for F/S La Salle

The crew were: the skipper F/S 401470 (Mac) John Justin Neville McCarthy RNZAF, 2nd pilot F/S R/77173 Joseph Daniel Leo La Salle RCAF (W/Op) injured, Sgt 929931 J K (John) Banfield RAFVR, Sgt 982476 John Michael (Mike) Leahy RAFVR.

Some publications list Sgt 759163 Denis Leonard Worthington RAFVR (W.Op/ Air Gnr) as a member of the crew but the transcript of the incident written by F/S McCarthy indicates otherwise. F/S McCarthy was also involved in an incident on 6th January 1942.

The authors are indebted to Dwight Blok of London, Ontarion, Canada, nephew of F/S La Salle, for providing the following hitherto unpublished information on the incident, and the photographs of his uncle and of the incident.

The following is an extract from the transcription, with annotations, of a journal kept by the late A/410470 Flying Officer John Justin Neville McCarthy, Royal New Zealand Air Force, between August 1941 and July 1942 showing a unique snapshot in the life of a pilot during WWII.

'Monday, 13th April,1942.

Just a week since I've recorded anything herein. Last Tuesday I was too lazy and had nothing worth bothering about except that the weather was "looking up". However, since then my lapse has been more or less enforced being as follows.

On Wednesday I was down for an hour's local flying commencing at about 5/30 p.m. Assembled the boys in the crew room and reported to the Control Office at about 5 p.m.only to find that F/O. Ings who was to use the "kite" before me hadn't yet become airborne. Seems that the cause of the hold-up was my old friend "Do-Do". This is the second time he has definitely been behind time off the ground. In the finish when Ings went out to take over the a/c, he discovered that the jettison outlet on the s'board side had become U/S. That put a stop to our local flying as the Flight had to get the "kites" ready for our second lot of local night flying.

I was second off in my "kite" – Z for Zebra *(R5498)*. Didn't have the opportunity of doing an N.F.T. but Colin Wathey was doing a couple of hours in it ahead of me. Was a swell night for night flying – dark as pitch but a clear sky and a strong wind without much drift. Had with me Mike Leahy, Leo La Salle and John Banfield. We took over on the end of the runway without stopping the motors. The port fule guage *(sic)* appeared to be either "duff" – as Larry Lea informed us when he left the machine, or else all four motors were using the gas from one tank. However, having faith in a petrol system designed for the "finest and best" a/c in the world I didn't think that I had any cause to worry.

We filled in just over an hour doing only a couple of landings, which were quite passable, and also carrying out the overshoot procedure a couple of times. With just about 70 minutes flying done we landed and after checking the guages *(sic)* and finding that our port guage *(sic)* was reading in the vicinity of 50 gallons in the S'board inboard tank I decided that we'd have sufficient to take us round another time after which we'd pack in – and "pack in" we did certainly did.

Did a smart take-off and leveled out at 1500 feet. Did a circuit of the 'drome at that height and coming round down wind the second time I asked Leo to check the guages *(sic)* and instruments on his panel. After take-off the S'board guage *(sic)* had risen to just over 60 gallons but on this check it was showing between zero and 5 gallons. Things didn't look so good so I called up John to turn on the "balance cock". Theoretically, having done this, I should have been quite safe. However, I wasn't taking any chances as I didn't want to be the first one on the Squadron to "write off" a Lancaster in view of the dire threats which had been made to us in a C.O.'s lecture a few days previously. Little could I forsee just what what *(sic)* coming up for us. Called up Control and asked for immediate permission to "pancake" which they gave us. Let down about 15 degrees of flap, lowered the undercart and stepped up the revs.

The above two photographs of the Lancaster crash were taken by the pilot F/O McCarthy. Note farmhouse minus a chimney. Above the originals is written 'What one 4-engine Lancaster a/craft, valued approximately 100,000 pounds, looks like when successfully (?) pranged by 'Chester Crash' McCarthy. Farmhouse thrown in for good measure'. Both courtesy of D Blok

The same farmhouse in 2010 with chimney intact.

Did a tight circuit and came in to make my approach in the top of the green of the glide path indicator. Shoved on full flap when coming in on the first stage of my approach and then changed my mind and took of *(?off)* 20 degrees as I hoped to hurry my approach by making it more shallow and faster – which would have meant that I had just a little more height, at that time, to come and go on.

At this stage Leo called me up and told me that the "fuel pressure" indicator lights for the S'board motors were on which boded no good for us. Continued the approach hoping for the best. Think now that I must have forgotten to cross my fingers for our luck didn't hold and with the flare-path right ahead and only a short distance to go the two s'board motors decided that they'd had "nuff" for the night and they "packed in". More or less, left to myself, the boys and the "kite" both literally and figuratively "in the air." Height was then under 200 feet, airspeed on the clock at about 105 m.p.h. – as any good pilot would have for a good approach, and wheels and 40 degrees of flap down. As the fellows on the Squadron term it I was caught "with my pants right down." Tried to power in but the "kite" swung so badly it was out of the question, couldn't glide in as we didn't have any excess height and couldn't do an "overshoot" on two motors on the same side because I couldn't use sufficient power without a tendency to throw the "kite" into a spin into the deck. Took the only course open to me and using as much power as I dared to keep me in the air and as straight as possible I tried to get over first the WAAF site and then the Sick Quarters both of which were right in our line of approach. No signs of panic among the boys who were really grand. From the time our motors cut until we "arrived" I have calculated that were not in the air more than 40 or 50 seconds. In that short, but seemingly interminable space of time I was pretty busy – as busy as the proverbial "one-armed paperhanger". Guess I wrestled a good fight with the old "kite". Finally had to put it down. If I'd tried to keep it in the air any longer I had no idea just where we might finish up. Saw below me what I took to be the perimeter track on the 'drome and decided that I'd try to pancake as near to on it as possible.

However, due to an unfortunate error – couldn't be called an error of judgment, but an error, it wasn't the perimeter track at all but the roadway running parallel to it. Guaged *(sic)* and throttled back to stall about 10 to 20 feet about *(above)* the ground at as low a forward speed as possible. Achieved this much better than I had hoped but unfortunately some "so-and-so" had put a tree and a house directly in our track. Didn't feel the plane touch anything until we actually "arrived."

From inspection of the wreckage – or what was left of it, I reconstructed the final part of our trip as being something like this. Our port undercart fouled the tree smashing both the tree and wheel and caused our s'board wing to dip and flick the corner of the roof off the two-storied house. From then on we did a good landing except that a couple more trees got in the way. Port motors and wing were ripped off and the fuselage swung almost at right-angles to our line of approach. Then came the actual crash as the nose of the kite and the belly hit the ground. It must have been some wallop because I still can't sit down comfortably yet. Had been too busy trying all I knew to avoid a crash to think just what might happen or what we might be in for. In fact, it didn't accur *(sic)* to me that there was a very distinct possibility that we mightn't get out of it.

Came the crash – just the same as it is so often represented in the movies. A terrific noise and with it a confusion of sound and movement. Seemed that a state of chaos existed and yet none of us had any part in it. Then came a momentary silence and of a sudden we came to life again. It was just a scramble to sort ourselves out and do the best to get out of the "kite" before it caught fire. However, we were too late for the hungry flames were already at work on the port side. This made it all the more imperative that we should get out as quickly as we could for petrol tanks seem to have an awkward habit of exploding after crashes.

John Banfield was already trying to get through the bulkhead doors while Mike Leahy was right behind him. Leo La Salle had been thrown down into the bomb-aimer's position when we crashed and I stood right on his back when I tried to get out of my seat as he was crawling back along the floor to the rear of the front compartment. Also as I swung out of my seat I nearly hanged myself with my inter-com which was still plugged in. There we were, the four of us, in an orderly line – John, Mike, Leo and myself with John doing his best to get through the door on the port side as the s'board side had jammed and wouldn't open. My advice was "For Christ's sake hurry and get out before this bloody tank blows up." John's only answer was "Don't push, I'm stuck." Only one thing left for us to do was to try and get out of the front of the "kite".

The pilot's escape hatch was above my seat and the flames were licking over it so that I didn't think it would be too nice even trying to get out that way. The front escape hatch was flush on the ground and our only chance of getting out at all seemed to be through the sliding window on the s'board of the cupola. In went McCarthy "boots and saddle" and the boys lost no time in following me the same way. To my dying day I will never be able to recall whether I went through that window feet or head first. Regardless I found myself on my feet outside the fuselage waiting on the other boys who came behind me without a lapse between us. Not even one of the boys can remember just how they came out of that damned window – feet or head first.

On reaching "terra firma" we found ourselves in a small pen made up one side the inboard s'board motor of the "kite", a second side by the wing, the third side by the fuselage and the fourth side by a high hedge which was further reinforced by barbed wire. It didn't take us long to size up just which way we had to go to get out and in true Commando style we were over that hedge without any of us touching it or the barbed wire. It was here that we discoved that we were on the roadway just outside the 'drome. We scuttled along the roadway and lay on the far slope waiting for the petrol tanks to explode, However, it didn't look as though *(they)* were going to for the fire continued to spread until within a few minutes the ammunition in the mid-upper turret was popping off in grand style.

It was just at this stage that I spotted the house behind the wreck. Me thought I had better go back to the house to see if the good folks were al Okel Dokel. However, I didn't get far along the road before Leo and Mike were up with me and made me go back in case some of the stray bullets should decide that I'd been lucky enough for one day. We then decide that if no-one was interested enough to come looking for us the only thing for us to do was the try to find some-one ourselves. In due course we nipped through a couple of further barbed wire entanglements until we found ourselves on the 'drome having been unchallenged. We eventually located one of the "drome defence fellows and finally the "blood waggon" in which we proceeded to the Watch Office. It was rather amusing to see us huddled in the back of the old ambulance trying to be amused but each of us wondering just how things were going to work out.

The "blood waggon" dropped me off at the Watch Office with John Banfield while the other two boys went down to the Sick Quarters. Explained just what "the score was" to the Control Officer and while waiting to hear news from the crash the F/Commander, S/Ldr. Beauchamp phoned up and of course I had to "render an account". From there to the hospital where I found Mike and Leo both pretty woozey having been given and *(sic)* injection of morphia. Leo was suffering from a badly wrenched shoulder and shock, the former having probably happened when he was thrown down in the bomb-aimer's position. Mike had bad body and arm bruises and a couple of bent fingers and shock. However, they didn't give any cause for worry so I talked the Doc out of keeping me in the Hospital and took my time and wandered back to the Mess for a late supper. Then down to the billet where I woke up Bill Blair, my "sting-in-the-tail", to whom I told the whole story.

Believe me, I was still pretty worried about just they might do to me for having written off nearly one hundred thousand pounds worth of aircraft. Lay on my bed fully dressed and got very little sleep. Had seen the Wing-Co. in Sick Quarters but he hadn't said much except to tell me not to worry. Learned at a later date that immediately he had learned of the crash he had rushed down and dashed into the burning wreckage to see if we were all out – and that's "pukka gen." I take a rather high view of him but find that very few others on the Squadron do.

The day following the crash I occupied myself by interviewing the people who occupied the house which we so narrowly missed. They weren't the least bit put out and seemed extremely pleased that we had all managed to get off so lightly.

Visited the scene of the wreck a couple of times and naturally enough got as many "illegal" snaps of the mess as I could. The result was certainly no tribute to the manner in which I had

F/S John McCarthy

landed the "kite" and the only definite good indication was that we had all "walked away from it".

Saw P/O. Oliver, A.G. whom I class as one of the finest officers on the Squadron and on the Station, while I was in one of my more worried moods. He assured me that I had no cause for worry and that I had "managed to get away with it" which he added was something he didn't think any other pilot on the Squadron would have done – and, he added, there are some pretty experienced pilots on the Squadron, too. Guess after that I'll have to go to stores for a new Cap, F.S.

Later interviewed S/Ldr. Warren, Inspector of Accidents who was investigating the accident for the Air Ministry or maybe it was just the Group. Made a full statement to him and certainly didn't leave anything to chance. They recovered the main petrol cocks and the balance cock from the wreckage and these were all in the positions which they should have been and in which I stated they would be, if found. Since then, it's been just a case of waiting to hear the verdict. Everyone seems to think that I'm definitely "in the clear" but I'm not so sure for they certainly do some very strange and funny things in the RAF. I'm hoping for the best for having come so far with my flying and having managed to do so well I would hate to have serious setback at this stage.

The bottom of my spine is still very tender and sore from the bounce I took when we landed. Can't sit down for any length of time and when I do I have to shuffle from one side to the other. It's funny to everyone but myself. Have just noticed Roddy, one of my gunners, sitting opposite, grinning from "ear to ear" as I type this. He's a good kid done up in "half-pint" measure. All my crew are the same.'

John McCarthy, by now a P/O on his 24th operation, F/S Leo La Salle, John Leahy, now F/S, and Sgt Denis Worthington along with other crew members F/S 2060393 Ronald Alfred Edmonds RAFVR (Obs), F/S 646781 Arthur Rowland RAF (W.Op/Air Gnr) and P/O 126810 Eric Lionel Hayward RAFVR (Air Gnr) were all killed on 24th July. They were the crew of Lancaster R5867EM-T which took off from Bottesford for a raid on Duisburg and crashed near Krefeld, 10km south east of the target. They were all buried in the principal cemeteries of Krefeld but later re-interred in Reichswald Forest War Cemetery.

F/S La Salle, graduation photograph takenJuly 1941, one year to the month before he was killed. Courtesy of D Blok

F/S La Salle on leave, Spring/ Summer 1942. Courtesy of D Blok

Grave of F/S La Salle. Courtesy of D Blok

WEDNESDAY 8th APRIL 1942 (continued)

Puss Moth DD821of 6 FPP from Tollerton tipped up after taxiing.

2000 hrs — Training

Master III W8762 of 16 (P)SFTS from Tollerton piloted by LAC P/784758 Dabrowski PAF landed in a cross wind, was blown off the runway by strong gusts and hit the wreckage of Puss Moth DD821 (see above) which had been dragged off the runway.
Both accidents were the result of difficult landing conditions and inexperienced pilots.

FRIDAY 10th APRIL 1942

1020 hrs — Ground

Hampden I AE186 of 408 Sqn from Balderton was being prepared for a flight when there was an accidental firing of a Verey pistol which created a fire in the aircraft. The Verey pistol should not have been loaded but the primary cause was insufficient care being taken on the part of the Wireless Operator. There were no injuries.

The pilot, P/O J/7076 Kenneth Henry Taylor RCAF, was killed in action just 2 months later on 3rd June still flying with 408 Sqn. He was the pilot of Hampden AT154 which took off from Balderton for a raid on Essen and was shot down by a night fighter. He is buried in Medemblik General Cemetery.

SATURDAY 11th APRIL 1942

1440 hrs — Training

Hampden I AT186 EQ- of 408 Sqn from Balderton swung to port during flight indicating an engine failure on low level bombing practice at Clifton Pastures bombing range and crashed at Clifton Pastures, Nottingham and burnt out. No injuries were reported.

The pilot, Sgt 41922 M Marment RNZAF, had been on a bombing mission to Le Havre the previous night and returned without incident. He was also involved in incidents on 26th April and 21st June.

WEDNESDAY 15th APRIL 1942

0500 hrs — Op; Dortmund

Wellington II Z8586 of 305 Sqn from Lindholme took off at 2221 hrs for a raid on Dortmund and on returning ran out of fuel and force landed hitting the ground at Wroot. The aircraft swung round and broke its back. Two of the Polish crew of six were killed and one injured: F/O P/0612 Stefan Sznidel PAF (Pilot) and Sgt P/784835 Kazimierz Pasich PAF (W/Op.) both buried in Newark-upon-Trent Cemetery, F/O P/1208 K Konopasek PAF, F/O K Joszt PAF injured, Sgt B Sedzimir PAF and Sgt Szmidt PAF.

1620 hrs — Ferrying

Master III W8725 of 16 (P)FTS from Newton took off on a ferry flight from Newton to Tollerton but did not turn up and was later reported as crashed and burnt out at Burrows Farm, Clifton. Both crew members were killed.

The Commission of Enquiry stated that the aircraft stalled and developed a spin and although partially recovered from the spin there was insufficient height to prevent the aircraft from hitting the ground from the subsequent dive.

The pilot was S/L 70036 Herbert Baker age 32 (the husband of Edith Mary Baker of West Bridgford) is buried in Ruddington (St Peter) Churchyard. He was a Chartered Accountant by Profession.

A Miles Master

THURSDAY 16th APRIL 1942

0420 hrs — Op; Mining

Hampden I P2073 of 408 Sqn from Balderton returned from operations and on landing overshot the runway and crashed into the boundary hedge because the starboard engine cut due to shortage of fuel. The pilot was F/S R70723 J R Dillon of the USA. One of the crew was injured.

1245 hrs — Training

Tiger Moth II T7185 of 25 (P)EFTS from Hucknall collided with Tiger Moth T7972 and both crashed at Blidworth. See below.

1245 hrs — Training

Tiger Moth II T7972 of 25 (P)EFTS from Hucknall and Tiger Moth T7185 were both practicing steep turns, final landing approaches and landings when they collided at 800 feet and crashed. It was presumed that both pilots, who were killed, F/O /P3334 Stanislaw Walczak PAF and LAC P/784235 Stefan Pliszke PAF failed to keep a good lookout. LAC Pliszke PAF attempted to use his parachute. He was aged 25 and is buried in Hucknall Cemetery. F/O Walczak is buried in Weston-Super-Mare Cemetery.

SUNDAY 19th APRIL 1942

1745 hrs

Tutor K6120 of H.M. Kings Flight, Benson force landed four miles north east of Worksop. One injury was reported.

MONDAY 20th APRIL 1942

0154 hrs — Operations

Hampden I P1145 UB- of 455 Sqn from Wigsley made a heavy landing in poor visibility when returning from Operations, a tyre burst causing the aircraft to swing to port and then skid sideways and the undercarriage collapsed. The pilot was F/S 402185 Holding RNZAF. There were no injuries.

TUESDAY 21st APRIL 1942

1346 hrs | Ferrying

Manchester R5791 EM-Y of 207 Sqn made a very heavy landing at Bottesford when being ferried from Coningsby. The pilot, Sgt 748087 Laurence John Lea RAFVR failed to keep the aircraft straight on the runway and the port wheel ran along a ditch that had been dug along side of the runway and the undercarriage collapsed.

Laurence Lea, now a F/S, was killed with all the crew 5 weeks later. He was the 2nd pilot of the crew of Lancaster R5847 of 207 Sqn which took off at 2337 hrs from Bottesford for a raid on Bremen and was shot down by a night fighter flown by Major Gunter Radusch, II./NJG2. He is buried in Westerbork General Cemetery

2245 hrs | Training

Hampden I AD829 of 455 Sqn from Wigsley overshot the runway because the aircraft came in too fast too far up the runway and ran into a ditch. This was the third time that the pilot F/S 402185 E N Holding had damaged an aircraft.

FRIDAY 24th APRIL 1942

Manchester I L7386 of 25 OTU from Bircotes overshot on landing and went through a hedge into a field adjoining Bircotes airfield. This aircraft also was involved in an incident on 5th October when it crash landed at Scampton airfield.

SATURDAY 25th APRIL 1942

0250 hrs | Training

Manchester I L7289 of 50 Sqn from Swinderby was involved in a heavy landing when the pilot, F/O 62338 Sproule, held off too late, the aircraft bounced and a wing touched the ground. This aircraft was lost on a raid on Bremen on 26th June. It took off from Swinderby and was hit by flak and crashed at Grembke.

Manchester I L7289. Courtesy of E. Mike Penick

0945 hrs Training

Master II DK880 of 17 PAFU from Watton was on a cross country training flight when it landed at Newton with the undercarriage retracted. The pilot was Sgt 1271847 J A Round.

A Miles Master Mk II

SUNDAY 26th APRIL 1942

1045 hrs Training

Oxford I BG181 of 14 (P)AFU from Ossington was on a training flight practicing single engine landings with pilot Sgt P/106599 G G Sawatzky PAF when the aircraft swung on landing and hit a paint barrel which had been left about 15 yards from the runway. This aircraft was abandoned in the air and crashed on 18th December 1942 (see report for 18th December).

WEDNESDAY 29th APRIL 1942

1750 hrs Training

Oxford X7251 of 16 (P)SFTS took off from Newton at 1700 hrs on a map reading exercise and to land a passenger at Cranwell. After 15 minutes take off from Cranwell on the return journey the pupil who was at the controls of the aircraft encountered a violent bump and shortly after this occurred the aircraft started to vibrate. The instructor took over and landed the aircraft in a field one mile west of Radcliffe on Trent station. The crew were Sgt 780712 Slagowski and ? Piasecki.

MONDAY 4th MAY 1942

1730 hrs Training

Tiger Moth II T7742 of 25 (P)EFTS from Hucknall crashed at Wood Close Farm, near Kneesall and burnt out after hitting some high tension cables whilst carrying out unauthorised low flying. The safety pilot, Cpl P/793936 Jozef Kutcha PAF age 31 died from multiple injuries and incineration and was buried in Hucknall Cemetery.

The pupil LAC P/781696 M Zawadski PAF received a compound fracture of the right femur and after being treated by a local doctor for his injuries he was taken to Newark hospital and the following morning transferred to the RAF Hospital at Rauceby, Lincolnshire.

Burnt out Tiger Moth T7742. Courtesy of W Taylor

TUESDAY 5th MAY 1942

1145 hrs Ferrying

Lancaster I R5540 of 61 Sqn was being ferried from Woolfox Lodge to Syerston. The aircraft was to be flown on the centre tanks only as the immersion fuel pump in the port inboard tank was unserviceable. The pilot was incorrectly told to fly on the inboard tanks only. When nearing Syerston the starboard inner engine failed followed a few minutes later by the starboard outer engine then both port engines. The aircraft landed at Balderton with undercarriage retracted. No fault was attached to the pilots P/O J/5794 Elwood Raymond Seibold RCAF age 21 and Sgt R/62668 Albert Winston Armstrong RCAF age 23.

However both pilots were lost one month later on 3rd June when flying with 61 Sqn. P/O Seibold was the pilot of Lancaster R5562 with F/S Armstrong as 2nd pilot, which took off from Syerston for a raid on Essen and crashed at Rees. One of the crew was taken prisoner and the rest lie in Reichswald Forest War Cemetery.

P/O Seibold's brother F/O Herbert Stanley Seibold was killed on 6th September 1944 flying with 423 Sqn. He is commemorated on the Runnymede Memorial.

FRIDAY 8th MAY 1942

0240 hrs Training

Hampden I AE366 of 408 Sqn from Balderton undershot on landing and hit Hampden AT227 but went round again and landed safely. 5 weeks previously this aircraft had been used by 35 Sqn to attack the German Battleship *Tirpitz*.

The pilot, Sgt R/70722 Robert Lorne Locker RCAF, after being promoted to W/O 1st Class was killed on 18th April 1943 flying with 1659 HCU. He was a member of the crew of Halifax R9448 which took off from Topcliffe on a training flight and crashed at Crockney Hill near Dishforth where he is buried. He was 23 years of age.

1500 hrs Training

Oxford I BG211 of 14 (P)AFU from Ossington took off at 1400 hrs for the pilot to give dual instruction in circuits and landings at Ingham RLG to the pupil. The aircraft dived vertically into the ground from 2,000 feet at Darlton, near Ossington, and caught fire with the loss of both crew members. The cause was obscure as no defect was found with the aircraft.

The pilot, Sgt R/82860 Emory Andrew Mason RCAF (Instructor) is buried in Ollerton Cemetery and Sgt 1138267 Wilfred Benson, the pilot under training, RAFVR age 26 buried in Farnworth Cemetery, Lancashire.

WEDNESDAY 13th MAY 1942

1645 hrs Training

Manchester I L7519 of 50 Sqn from Swinderby was on local flying practice when it was seen to nose dive into the ground from around 800 feet and caught fire on impact at North Farm near Thurlby. The crew of five were killed:

F/S 1165296 Peter James Widdell Blake RAFVR (Pilot) buried in Thurlby Churchyard, P/O 120996 Alan Bartlett RAFVR age 32 (Obs.) cremated at West Norwood Crematorium, F/S 755113 Raymond Leslie Cunningham RAFVR age 22 (W.Op/Air Gnr) buried Coventry Cemetery, LAC 931022 William Stanley Stevens RAFVR buried Thurlby Churchyard, AC1 1142647 Leslie Harrison RAFVR age 21 buried in Sherburn Churchyard.

FRIDAY 15th MAY 1942

1630 hrs Training

Tiger Moth II T6261 of 25 (P)EFTS from Hucknall was on dual pilot training when the aircraft ran out of fuel and the engine cut on approach to land and crashed one mile north of Hucknall, near Ruffs Drive. The fitter was to blame for not filling up the fuel tanks and the pilot for not checking the gauges. P/O P/1696 T Wierzbowski PAF (Pilot) received a fractured right ankle and LAC P/793165 B Graft PAF suffered concussion and they were both admitted to the City Hospital. The aircraft was named 'City of Windsor'.

SATURDAY 16th MAY 1942

0255 hrs Training

Oxford I BG183 of 14 (P)AFU from Langar took off with flaps down and crashed on a night take-off in a field adjoining the airfield perimeter track. The crew P/O J/9355 George Milne (Pilot) RCAF and Sgt R/102287 R L Clearwater RCAF were injured.

P/O Milne, from Calgary, was killed age 21 on 14th January 1943 whilst serving with 426 Thunderbird Sqn. He took off from Dishforth piloting Wellington BK165 OW-F for a raid on Lorient when the aircraft was lost without trace. He is commemorated on the Runnymede Memorial. P/O Milne's elder brother F/O J/5968 Harry David Milne was killed age 22, 5 months later. He was a resident of the Palace Hotel, Torquay, which was being used as an RAF Officers hospital, when it received a direct hit from an enemy bomb. He is commemorated on the Runnymede Memorial.

1415 hrs Air Test

Manchester I L7286 of 61 CF from Syerston hydraulics failed on landing and then the emergency system failed and only the starboard wheel could be lowered. The pilot was A/S/L 74702 Rupert Arthur Victor Gascoyne-Cecil and 2nd pilot Sgt 928863 R S Fenner. A/S/L Gascoyne-Cecil was awarded the DFC 10 days later (see entry for 4.6.42).

THURSDAY 21st MAY 1942

0400 hrs — Training

Oxford I BG207 of 14 (P)AFU from Ossington took-off to carry out night instructional circuits and landings. The Oxford carried out a very low circuit over the airfield due to sudden deterioration of the weather and low cloud, disappearing into the mist and struck the ground, crashing into a field at Hall Farm, near the village of Egmanton, with the loss of both crew members. The Meteorological section had neglected to warn the unit that the weather was likely to deteriorate and ground mist would develop over an area north and east of Ossington after midnight. The crew pilot Sgt 934645 Norman Clements Keenan age 22 (pilot Instructor) and Sgt R/103921 Thomas Henderson Campbell RCAF (pilot under training) aged 23 years were killed. Sgt Keenan is buried in Belfast City Cemetery and Sgt Campbell in Tuxford Cemetery.

Sgt Campbell had gained his pilots wings on 12th March 1942 at 10 SFTS, Dauphin, Manitoba. His grave stands alone at the top of Tuxford Cemetery but was never forgotten by members of the Tuxford Methodist Chapel who regularly place flowers on it and each Remembrance Sunday the Tuxford Scouts and Girl Guides place Poppy Crosses.

Sgt Campbell. Courtesy of W Taylor

Grave of Sgt Campbell

1035 hrs — Training

Master III W8449 of 16 (P)SFTS from Tollerton landed with the undercarriage retracted when the attention of the pilot, LAC P/793993 H Rawicz PAF, was distracted.

1515 hrs — Training

Manchester I L7385 OL-C of 207 Sqn CF from Bottesford swung off the runway during take off for solo circuits and landings apparently damaging the tail wheel. The tail wheel then collapsed on landing after a further swing. The pilots were F/S 1160143 F A Read and Sgt 1378917 Lawrence Ritelli Wright. This aircraft was involved in another incident on 6th August.

Lawrence Wright, now a F/S, was killed on 24th October. He was the pilot of Lancaster W4121 of 207 Sqn which took off from Langar for a raid on Milano and crashed in the sea 30km south east of Jersey. He is commemorated on the Runnymead Memorial.

SATURDAY 23rd MAY 1942

0542 hrs — Operations

Lancaster I R5563 of 61 Sqn from Syerston undercarriage collapsed on landing on return from an 8 hour flight on operations. The pilots were F/O 60571 L D Gunter and Sgt 924352 A J C Timmins.

MONDAY 25th MAY 1942

1451 hrs Air Test

Wellington IC R1151 -L of 25 OTU from Bircotes took off for an air test and after 10 minutes attempted to land. The aircraft bounced on touching down on the downwind half of the aerodrome so the pilot opened up to go round again. The wing dropped twice due to a gusty wind but the aircraft was then approaching a thick wood and although he could have cleared it he turned to the left stalled, crashed and caught fire. 3 of the crew were killed and one injured. F/O 89608 Stanley Le Vesconte Wood DFC age 20 RAFVR (Pilot) is buried in Woodchurch Churchyard, Cheshire, F/S 751410 Ronald Alfred Coles age 23 (W.Op) RAFVR buried in Stivichall Churchyard, LAC 930367 Graham Langley Emms age 21 RAFVR is buried in King's Lynn Cemetery.

Sgt 946003 Livingstone was injured. F/O Wood was awarded his DFC on 13th March whilst a member of 49 Sqn.

THURSDAY 4th JUNE 1942

0500 hrs Ground

Hampden I AT220 EQ-G of 408 Sqn from Balderton caught fire while being re-fuelled. It appeared that some quantity of fuel lay on the ground due to a bad leaking hose and was ignited by a spark from the steel binding of the hose against a small flint on the ground.

1445 hrs Training

Master III W8443 of 16 (P)SFTS from Newton collided with Master W8476 during formation practice and crashed near Newton. The pilot LAC P/783357 Waclaw Kocon PAF age 24 was killed and is buried in Newark-upon-Trent Cemetery.

The pilot of W8476 gave a signal to change leadership. W8443 climbed, turned left and lost sight of W8476 and struck him on top of the engine. W8476 landed on the aerodrome and W8443 burnt out.

A Master of 16(P)SFTS at Newton (note the Polish chessboard on the nose)

1445 hrs Training

Master III W8476 of 16 (P)SFTS from Newton collided with Magister W8443 (see above). The pilot LAC P/793627 W Kempka PAF survived.

1720 hrs Air Test

Hampden I AT180 of 408 Sqn from Balderton was on an air frame and engine test when it went into a flat spin and the bomb doors were torn off when control was lost by the pilot, P/O 119813 Harry John Randall RAFVR, due to over use of the rudder. He decided to crash land straight ahead at Claypole and ran through a hedge.

On 17/18th August 1943 Bomber Command was tasked to attempt a 'special' night time precision raid on the German research establishment at Peenemunde. It was here that the V-2 rockets were built and tested. Such was the importance of the raid that most of the squadrons taking part were led by their Wing Commanders. 596 bombers took off for the raid including P/O Randall in Lancaster JA691 and 11 other Lancasters of 49 Squadron. For the first time the German fighters were using a new weapon, codenamed 'Schrage-Music'. This consisted of two 30mm cannon mounted to point upwards from the fuselage and the fighter pilot flew beneath a bomber and aimed shells up into the wing fuel tanks.

Forty aircraft were shot down by strong flak defences and fighters. JA691 was hit by flak as it flew over the junction of the Dortmund Ems and the Mittelland Canals. The Lancaster tried to make an emergency landing but collided with the roof of a house and then a crane on the canal bank before crashing into the water. The next day the Germans found that the crew had all been decapitated by the impact with the crane. P/O Randall and his crew are all buried in Aabenraa Cemetery, Denmark.

A unique aspect of the crew was that P/O Randall had previously been a member of the Grenadier Guards and re-trained as a pilot and one of the crew, Sgt Les Henley, the Flight Engineer had also been in the army, joined the RAF in 1940 and managed to get on operations at the age of 43.

The remains of Lancaster JA691

F/O Randall and crew. Courtesy Malcolm Brooke 49 Sqn

SATURDAY 6th JUNE 1942

0046 hrs — Training

Lancaster I R5491 of 61 Sqn from Syerston made a heavy landing by the 1st pilot Sgt 928863 R E Fenner who held off too high and the undercarriage collapsed. The Captain of the aircraft was A/S/L 74702 Rupert Arthur Victor Gascoyne-Cecil DFC and the 2nd pilot Sgt 1260392 S Noosden.

A/S/L Gascoyne-Cecil was awarded his DFC on 26th May 1942. He was also awarded a Bar to his DFC on 11th June1943 still flying with 61 Squadron. The citation read: 'This officer has taken part in numerous operational sorties since the award of the DFC. Many of these sorties have been against such strongly defended targets as Berlin, Lubeck, Essen and Spezia'.

1230 hrs — Flying Test

Hampden 1 AD980 EQ-Y of 408 Sqn from Balderton took off for a night flying test with pilot, P/O 149857 Harry John Randall, at the controls in readiness for operations to Emden. He lost control in the air as he was about to commence a cross country flight. In the circuit preparatory to setting course and on making a flat port turn he was unable to recover and crash landed in a field north east of the airfield. The aircraft had got into a 'stabilised yaw'.

The three crew: P/O Randall, P/O 400907 Rodger Perryman Wishart RAAF (Rear Gnr) and Sgt H E Elliott were all injured and admitted to Newark Hospital. Sgt Elliott had completed his tour of operations and was awaiting posting. Two days previous P/O Randall had been involved in a minor accident and was killed on 17/18th August (see entry for 4.6.42).

F/L Wishart was killed in action on 30th January 1944 age 33. He took off from Bourn in Lancaster JB535 OF-Q of 97 Sqn with F/L E S Clarke at the controls, on his 2nd raid on Berlin in two days. It was believed a wing and an engine were shot on fire by a fighter which caused the wing to break off, the aircraft then exploded in the air and crashed at 2210 hrs local time at Kolhorn, northern Holland. He was assigned as rear gunner and was found dead, sitting behind his guns in the tail section of the aircraft and he is buried in Barsingerhorn General Cemetery, Netherlands. The following is the translation of a Dutchman's story of the crash:

'Kolhorn 30th/31st January 1944
Kolhorn escaped a disaster on 30 Jan 1944 when a British bomber exploded above the village. All seven crew members died. Round about midnight all hell let loose above Kolhorn. A huge four-engine Lancaster appeared for the second time. The locals thought their last moments had come. The Lancaster flew lower and lower. It was directed at the village. All of a sudden a ball of fire appeared. The bomber seemed to disintegrate. It blew up above the village. The crew had no chance to escape. They met an horrifying death.

According to witnesses, Flip Timmerman and Simon Groot, everything was like a huge nightmare. Thinking back, Timmerman can recall all that happened as though it was only yesterday. He explained it all took place on a Saturday night. "We thought we were going to have a pleasant evening. We had been to the Theatre that evening. The church clock sounded midnight. My wife and I were on our way home, early for us, the usual dance had been forbidden by the Germans. We heard the aircraft and saw it come over on the way back from a raid on Germany. It flew in the direction of Schagen and the coast. It had probably dropped its bombs on Germany. It was being followed by a German night fighter which was firing tracer all the time. It was from the 'Flieqhorst Leeuwarden' whose fighters were always present above this area. The gunners of the Lancaster were firing back with everything they had. Unfortunately, the German managed to hit one wing and an engine. When the bomber was over Schagen it turned and came back, burning, in the direction of Kolhorn. It was a frightening sight."

The crew of the Lancaster was a mixed Australian and British one under the pilot 22 year old Ernest S Clarke. He probably realised he would never make it all the way home and was looking for a suitable place to crash-land. This explanation is offered because the Lancaster turned to starboard just before the village. It was then flying toward the Waarder Polder and the Wierirgmeer lake.

Those watching from the Dijk saw the pieces falling everywhere. The crew never had a chance to escape. Between Oude Streek and the Church one of the crew was found on a roof; one of his legs was missing and he was badly burned. He had tried to jump at the last minute; his chute was half open. He was dead.

A little nearer the bakery, an Australian with red hair was found. Kleas Keuns managed to take his watch and some personal papers from him. These belongings were later returned to the next of kin. Keuns's contact with the family later resulted in him emigrating to Australia.

The tail went through the roof of Piet Pool's house. The tail turret landed in the garden of Lsjf.

The gunner was still strapped in behind his guns. His body appeared to be unmarked; he probably broke his kneck. Along the area in front of the carpenter's shop the main fuselage hit the ground. Two crew members were in it. It was here that something shameful happened and who was responsible was never found. The two crew members were robbed of their flying boots during the night's panic.

On the other side of the Kolhorner Diep, an engine landed in the middle of the road. The sound of bullets could be heard going off everywhere. The nose lay at the farm of Blaauboer. It is probable that bodies were in it. Unfortunately the area was sealed off by the Germans so we will never know.'

For the village of Kolhorn the 30th January was a night that will never be forgotten. Under the trees, close to the spot where the crew lost their lives, in their last resting place, a simple monument was erected by the population for these brave young men. It reads: 'They died for us. The citizens of Barsingehorn, 31st August 1945'.

SUNDAY 7th JUNE 1942

1100 hrs — Engine Test

Oxford I V4173 of 1524 BAT Flt from Newton swung on take off but the pilot, Sgt 405352 Forsyth, was unable to correct owing to the passengers foot jamming the rudder bar, and the undercarriage collapsed. There were no injuries.

1800 hrs — Training

Master III W8780 of 16 (P)SFTS from Newton with pupil pilot Cpl P/780132 Szewc PAF at the controls was practicing glide approach training, approached over a hangar, stalled and crashed on the airfield. There were no injuries.

MONDAY 8th JUNE 1942

2345 hrs — Flying Test

Lancaster I R5503 of 207 Sqn from Bottesford was on landing approach and stalled from 5-10 feet and the starboard outboard engine fell out. The sub-frame of the engine had been badly welded which was considered negligence on the part of the rigger who carried out the daily inspection. The pilots were F/O 42850 F H LeLand and A/S/L 40256 K H P Beauchamp.

A/S/L Beauchamp was the pilot of Lancaster R5499 on a gardening operation on 22/23th May when one engine failed over the Baltic, and soon after turning for home a second engine failed. The Lancaster struck the sea as it crossed out over the Danish coast, damaging the propellers of the remaining two engines but A/S/L Beauchamp brought R5499 back to base and a safe landing, for which he was awarded an immediate DSO.

THURSDAY 11th JUNE 1942

1340 hrs — Training

Wellington IC R1454 of 25 OTU from Finningley took off on circuits and landings training and on returning to land the airspeed was too low, a wing dropped, the aircraft swung on touch down and skidded into trees and the port engine caught fire. There were no injuries.

The pilot Sgt 1058969 Frank Hutchinson subsequently was killed, age 22, on 25th June 1943 whilst with 289 (Anti-aircraft Co-operation) Sqn, Turnhouse, Scotland. He took off in Oxford HN173 at 1400 hrs, lost control in cloud, partially recovered, pulled up into a steep climb, entered a high-speed stall and crashed at Innellan. He is buried in Salford (Weaste) Cemetery.

FRIDAY 12th JUNE 1942

0235 hrs — Training

Wellington IC R1375 of 25 OTU from Bircotes was on a cross country training flight when the pilot undershot on landing and the wheels passed through a hedge and ripped its undercarriage off on a pile of stones and cinders. The pilot was Sgt 90251 W B Barrett RCAF.

TUESDAY 16th JUNE 1942

1608 hrs — Training

Stirling I N6088 LS-X of 1651CU C Flt from Waterbeach was tasked to take off at 1525 hrs on a cross country training flight with instructions to fly to 18,000 feet and practice bombing from 10,000 feet carrying a full crew and enough practice bombs to make up a typical operational load. On take off the aircraft swung and bounced onto the front wheels from about 5 feet and subsequently left the ground climbing normally. At 1600 hrs the aircraft was seen to be flying above clouds approaching Retford from Gamston direction when an explosion was heard. The aircraft emerged at 3,000 feet in a spiral right hand dive with the port wing on fire. At 2,000 feet the port outer wing and the outer portion of the portside mainplane fell away and the aircraft dived vertically into the ground near the main London to Edingburgh railway line and the Great North Road 2½ miles north of East Retford, near Barnby Moor. On inspection of the wreckage it was noticed that the pilots' and the gunners' hatches had been thrown clear indicating that bailing out may have been attempted. All eight crew died.

P/O 411491 Milan Roy Scansie RNZAF age 24 (Pilot), had 306 hours flying time, F/S 1001269 James Brian Tomlinson, RAFVR, Sgt 575984 Ernest William Morris RAF age 19 (F/Eng), who is listed on the 39th entry RAF Halton Aircraft Apprentices Roll of Honour, Sgt 1021190 Jack Titterton Smith RAFVR (W.Op/Air Gnr), Sgt 1184497 Roland Percival Broadbridge RAFVR age 20 (W.Op/Air Gnr), F/S R/70600 Harry Laverne Johnson RCAF age 26 (Air Gnr), Sgt 9119616 Raymond George Le-Blanc RAFVR aged 27 (Air Gnr), Sgt 1117295 David Barr Robinson RAFVR age 21 buried in Bedlay Cemetery Lanarkshire. All other crew members are buried Finningley, St Oswald Churchyard Extension.

SATURDAY 20th JUNE 1942

1630 hrs | Training

Oxford II W6564 of 16 (P)SFTS from Newton on return from a cross country training run landed but then tipped on its nose near the end of the landing run. The pupil pilot LAC P/781513 Jeziorowski PAF had apparently landed with the brakes applied. The instructor pilot was LAC P/780859 Daroszewski PAF.

1710 hrs

Lancaster I R5507 of 207 Sqn from Bottesford swung off the runway on take off when the tail struck obstructions on the runway. The enquiry stated that no damage would have been caused had the sides of the runway been clean. The aerodrome was in an extremely bad state. The pilots were F/S 1160143 F A Read and Sgt 1378917 Lawrence Ritelli Wright RAFVR.

Sgt Wright now a F/S was lost on 24th October when he was the pilot of Lancaster W4121 of 207 Sqn which was taking part in its first operation after only eight hours flying service. He took off from Langar for a raid on Milano and crashed in the sea off France. He is commemorated on the Runnymede Memorial.

MONDAY 22nd JUNE 1942

0032 hrs

Hampden I AE439 of 408 Sqn from Balderton overshot landing and crashed through two hedges and two ditches. The tail plane, centre section and undercarriage were damaged. The pilot was Sgt R/86808 E A Fitzsimmons RCAF.

TUESDAY 23rd JUNE 1942

1135 hrs | Stationary

Oxford II AP481 of 16 (P)FTS from Newton pilot F/O P/0977 J Kwapniewski PAF had started his cockpit drill prior to take off when the undercarriage slowly collapsed.

1840 hrs | Training

Lancaster I L7544 of 207 Con Ft from Bottesford on landing, a tyre burst and the aircraft swung towards a workmens' tent, the swing was increased to miss the tent because the pilot

S/L 33392 Thomas Charles Murray DFC believed it was occupied, and the undercarriage collapsed. There were no injuries. S/L Murray was awarded the DFC on 30th July 1940 and a Bar to the DFC on 11th August 1942.

WEDNESDAY 24th JUNE 1942

1430 hrs — Training

Oxford II V3191 of 1654 CU from Wigsley swung on take off on the runway, the pilot corrected with the throttle and, on opening up again the aircraft swung violently to the right and the starboard wing hit an air raid shelter, resulting in the undercarriage collapsing. The pilot, Sgt 1169304 L Haynes, had not received authorisation for the bombing practice flight.

1745 hrs — Training

Master III L8713 of 16 (P)SFTS from Tollerton with LAC P/784190 Budkiewicz PAF at the controls on take off hit a sodium flare and damaged the undercarriage. The aircraft was then flown to Newton to land but unable to lock the undercarriage down,the aircraft landed with it retracted with no injuries to the crew.

THURSDAY 25th JUNE 1942

0130 hrs

Twenty incendiary bombs were dropped ½ mile east of Gunthorpe village, and 700 incendiary bombs contained in a 10 foot long container were dropped near Bulcote Corporation Farm.

SATURDAY 27th JUNE 1942

0050 hrs — Training

Master III DL605 of 16 (P)SFTS from Newton overturned on landing at Newton due to excessive use of the brakes. The pilot was Cpl P/781374 W Strzala PAF.

2345 hrs — Operations

Lancaster I R5686 of 207 Sqn from Bottesford was taking off on an operational sortie when the aircraft swung, the undercarriage collapsed and an engine fell out and caught fire. There were no injuries. The enquiry stated that 'this pilot (Sgt 1205929 C B C Miller) is exceptionally keen and intelligent and was only recently converted to captain and it was considered that his accident was primarily due to use of brake for correcting swing which is contrary to instructions but not amounting to culpable ignorance. I do not recommend log book endorsement.' Sgt Miller was involved in another incident on 17th July'.

MONDAY 29th JUNE 1942

1430 hrs — Training

Blenheim IV R3848 of 13 OTU from Bircotes took off on a training flight when it was unable to maintain height due to engine failure and the weather. The pilot descended to 1000 feet and on opening the throttles the starboard engine spluttered, began to vibrate and an explosion took place. One cylinder became adrift and cowling was forced into the slipstream. The aircraft lost speed, was unable to maintain height, crash landed and caught fire with no blame to the pilot, at Brecks Farm, Moorhouse, two miles north of Ossington. The three crew P/O 4799 R D Robinson (Pilot), Sgt 1376642 Woodgate and Sgt 121378 Parsons were slightly injured.

1615 hrs Training

Master III DL604 of 16 (P)SFTS from Newton landed and ran into a tractor working in the middle of the aerodrome. There was damage to the starboard mainplane and undercarriage. The pilot was F/S P/780247 A Palul PAF.

2350 hrs Taxiing

Wellington I DV720 of 25 OTU from Finningley struck a member of the ground crew when parking. The pilot F/S 404847 F V Weckins RNZAF was taxiing to dispersal after landing and being guided by a member of the ground crew. On turning into dispersal he felt a slight bump but continued and parked the aircraft. The guiding airman lost his cap bent down to pick it up and the tail plane, which was swinging round, caught him on his arm. The pilot was not to blame.

TUESDAY 30th JUNE 1942

0230 hrs Training

Hampden I AD802 GL-V1 of 14 OTU from Saltby was on a training flight on a very dark night when the pilot attempted to land at his base at Saltby. He went around again and must have lost sight of the aerodrome and whilst looking for a pinpoint lost control and spun into the ground near Gunthorpe Bridge. All 4 of the crew were killed.

Sgt 1213919 Robert Thomas Pierson RAFVR age 21 (Pilot) is buried in Carlton Roman Catholic Churchyard, Yorkshire.

Sgt 404370 John Leonard Allison age 29, RAAF, Sgt 403743 Edmund Freeman Hunt age 20 RAAF and Sgt 403098 Arthur Hugh Stephens age 31 RAAF all buried in Shelford Churchyard Extension.

The brother of Sgt Stephens, Cpl Eustace Charles Stephens RAAF died on 20th October 1944 age 32 as a result of being a POW.

Left to right, Graves of Sgt Pierson, Sgt Allison, Sgt Hunt, Sgt Stephens

THURSDAY 2nd JULY 1942

1000 hrs Training

Oxford II ED154 of 14 (P)AFU from Ossington was on an instructional windspeed and direction finding flight when it flew into the ground after going into a spin at low altitude. The aircraft crashed onto the railway lines near the Northern Hotel, ½ mile south of Carlton-on-Trent, bursting into flames with the loss of all three crew members.

P/O J/9531 (R106529) Richard Sydney Horswill RCAF age 24 (Pilot) is buried in Ollerton Cemetery, AC2 1234171 Alwin Arthur Liddington RAFVR age 20 (W/Op) buried Wellingborough (Finedon) Cemetery, Sgt 413489 Frederick George Shears RNZAF age 21 (Pilot) buried in the Cemetery of St Mary Cray, Kent, the village from which his mother had emigrated to New Zealand as a war bride in 1919.

Sgt Shears, age 20 and his brother Douglas Leslie age 18 had left the family home together in June 1941 to begin their air force career. They both gained their wings and sergeant's stripes at Wigram, Christchurch in December 1941 then left New Zealand for the UK. After settling into the RAF both brothers were posted to Ossington in May 1942. A month later Doug was posted to Harrogate and subsequently joined 428 RCAF Sqn piloting Wellingtons. He survived the war.

Sgt George Shears

FRIDAY 3rd JULY 1942

0330 hrs — Training

Wellington HF911 of 11 OTU from Bassingbourne was on a cross country training flight when the port engine cut and the aircraft landed at Langar, the nearest aerodrome. On first approach at 800 feet the pilot received a red light but needed a green and with no time to lower the undercarriage, landed with wheels up. The pilot was Sgt 411922 D J Melbourne RNZAF.

1800 hrs

Manchester I R5835 of 1654 HCU at Wigsley was parked at dispersal and was damaged in a raid by 2 Ju 88s on a low level attack.

—

c.2020 hrs

A high explosive bomb was dropped on Holme Lane, Normanton-on-Trent and a enemy aircraft machine gunned Wigsley aerodrome.

SUNDAY 6th JULY 1942

1635 hrs — Training

Manchester I L7496 of 1654 HCU from Wigsley was on a non-operational flight when the starboard engine failed after the throttles were opened to carry out overshoot procedure. The pilot landed the aircraft straight ahead which subsequently caught fire. There were no injuries.

Two of the crew were F/S 78196 E W Lancey RCAF and F/S 71516 C W Brown RCAF. F/S Lancey was also involved in an incident on 16th July.

FRIDAY 10th JULY 1942

1950 hrs — Training

Tiger Moth II N6733 of 25 (P)EFTS from Newton hit a tree stump in a forced landing while lost, at Smalley, near Ilkeston. The pilot was F/S P/780753 Laskowski PAF.

SUNDAY 12th JULY 1942

0025 hrs — Stationary

Wellington I DV936 of 25 OTU from Finningley was stationary before a training flight on a very dark night when the pilot P/O G W Ross instructed his bombardier to inspect the tail wheel for damage. On returning to the front of the aircraft he walked into a propeller and was injured.

2337 hrs — Training

Hampden I X2974 of 14 OTU from Saltby took off for a night exercise and was hit in mid-air by Wellington Z8837 and crashed at East Stoke. Of the crew P/O 31160 Malcolm George Lees age 27 (Obs.) died and is buried in Bracebridge Churchyard. F/S R/87334 Gordon Edgar Pickel RCAF age 27 (W.Op/Air Gnr) also died and is buried in Newark-upon-Trent Cemetery. P/O 405315 Leon George Lyons RCAF, the pilot, survived un-injured.

The Wellington landed safely at Balderton.

P/O Lyons was born in Maidstone, Canada, joined the Air Force in February 1941 and came to England as an air gunner in December the same year. He continued training in England and had only been on active service a short time.

Leon Lyons, now F/O, was lost in action on 29th August 1942 when piloting Hampden AT228 of 408 Sqn on a raid on Saarbrucken. His aircraft crashed near Liesse, near Laon, France. All the crew rest in Liesse Communal Cemetery.

2337 hrs — Training

Wellington I Z8837 of 25 OTU collided with Hampden X2974 in the air causing damage to the aircraft and the pilot F/L 43090 E I J Bell force landed his aircraft at Balderton.

MONDAY 13th JULY 1942

0300 hrs — Ground

Manchester I L7476 of 50 Sqn from Swinderby caught fire on the ground when being re-fuelled by AC Voiels. The cause was obscure.

1320 hrs — Training

Oxford I V3874 of 1654 CU from Wigsley was training on high level bombing when the aircraft hit a tree and crashed at Gunthorpe while carrying out unauthorised low flying killing the 3 crew members.

Sgt 1000600 Leslie Arnold Dobie age 21 RAFVR (Pilot) is buried in Bebington Cemetery,

Sgt 404793 Richard Arthur Von Der Groeben RAAF age 25 (W.Op/Air Gnr u/t) buried Shelford Churchyard, Sgt 1184333 John Robert Warren age 22 RAFVR (W.Op/Air Gnr u/t) buried Idridgehay (St James) Churchyard.

Sgt Von Der Groeben

Night flying was stopped at Langar due to an enemy air raid but all bombs were dropped on the Q site.

SATURDAY 18th JULY 1942

On another raid on Langar a bomb was dropped demolishing the night flying hut.

SUNDAY 19th JULY 1942

1015 hrs Training

Oxford II N4739 of 14 (P)AFU from Ossington was taking off for an instructional flight when a swing developed. The pilot Sgt 1331522 H C G Creighton-Kelly was unable to correct it and the aircraft collided with a pile of logs.

TUESDAY 21st JULY 1942

0200 hrs Training

Oxford I N6339 of 14 (P)AFU from Ossington was taking off from Langar for a night flying exercise when the starboard wheel dropped off which was found in the morning in a field. Sgt J Corbishley (Pilot Instructor) with pupil pilot Sgt Freeman made a good landing on one wheel with no damage to the aircraft.

THURSDAY 23rd JULY 1942

Another air raid was made on Langar airfield.

FRIDAY 24th JULY 1942

0355 hrs Training

Wellington IC DV476 PP- of 25 OTU from Finningley collided in mid-air with Wellington T2701 and both crashed to the ground one mile north west of Finningley aerodrome. There seemed no reason why this aircraft was flying so low after only 30 minutes flight when it was scheduled for a 2 hour flight on high level bombing practice. As no bombs were released it was assumed that it had aborted bombing practice and was returning due to a fault. As a footnote to the accident one aircraft was under control from the ground and the other had not called control. The crew of 4 were killed: W/O 519241 John Lawrence Smith RAF (Pilot, W/O 561197 Charles Eade Lutwyche age 31 (Obs.), Sgt 54774 William McDonald age 24 all buried in Finningley Churchyard Extension, Sgt 1287636 Albert Edwin Barrows age 22 (W.Op/Air Gnr) buried Kensington (Gunnersbury) Cemetery.

0355 hrs Training

Wellington IC T2701 -L of 25 OTU from Finningley collided in mid-air with Wellington DV476 (see above).

All the crew of 7 died: P/O 402158 Richard Colvin Seddon Beck DFM RNZAF age 30 (Pilot) bried in Finningley Churchyard Extension, P/O 119240 John Vernon Robinson RAFVR age 20 buried in Sefton (St Helen) Churchyard, Sgt 1381351 Harry Champion Jellyman RAFVR (Obs.) buried in Llantrisant (Trane) Cemetery, P/O 116706 William Caufield Waterson age 22 (Air Bomber) buried in Uphall Cemetery, Sgt 1088309 Norbron Basil Hyde RAFVR age 21 (Obs.) buried in Wombwell Cemetery, Sgt 1376309 Stanley James Plume RAFVR age 28 (W.Op/Air Gnr) buried in Chingford Mount Cemetery, F/S 950909 Frederick Colin Ethell RAFVR age 21 (Air Gnr) cremated at Manchester Crematorium.

P/O Beck was awarded the DFM on 13th March while flying with 408 Sqn.

—

An enemy aircraft dropped 4 bombs on the Sneinton Dale district of Nottingham and on the sewage works at Stoke Bardolph. A firewatcher was killed and two women died later of their injuries.

SATURDAY 25th JULY 1942

0830 hrs — Training

Oxford I V3866 of 16 (P)FTS from Newton was on flying training when the aircraft went into a left hand spin during or after a steep turn. At a reducing height from 3,000 feet to 1,500 feet the spin became flat but the pilot failed to stop it. He was prepared for a crash landing and probably to abandon the aircraft by shutting main petrol corks, opening throttles, lowering flaps and trimming the aircraft to normal flying position. The pilot, Cpl P/780056 Marian Malczynski PAF age 26 left the cockpit and took up a position at the rear of the fuselage probably in an attempt to bale out. The aircraft crashed at Cropwell Bishop and Cpl Malczynski was killed. He is buried in Newark-upon-Trent Cemetery.

TUESDAY 28th JULY 1942

1800 hrs — Training

Oxford II N4647 of 14 (P)AFU from Ossington was on an instructional training flight when engine failure occurred and the pilot attempted to make a full circuit of the aerodrome at 300 feet carrying passengers and sodium equipment but crashed into the water tower killing the two crew and two passengers.

P/O J/9127 James Alexandra Brown RCAF age 20 (Pilot Flying Instructor) is buried in Ollerton Cemetery, Sgt 1385724 Ronald Charles Wootton RAFVR age 20 (Pilot) is buried in Paignton Cemetery.

Passengers AC2 1444915 Edward Claude Alton RAFVR age 20 (Flight Mechanic) is buried in Ollerton Cemetery, LAC 1124692 A E Fricker RAF age 33 an electrician is buried in Penarth (St Augustine of Hippo) Churchyard.

The following is an extract from 'The History of RAF Stations Ossington and Gamston' courtesy of Mr W Taylor.

'The evening of the 28th July 1942 was sunny and calm over Ossington. Children played on the green painted iron gates on the Hall drive, outside the airmens quarters. RAF personnel sat patiently in buses waiting the mile long journey to the airfield on the other side of the hamlet to continue their training courses, and inside the hastily erected airmans quarters other flyers were finishing their teas. Nobody noticed the twin-engined Airspeed Oxford flying over from the direction of the airfield. It was, after all, the most common sight in the hamlet. Just another trainer taking off with two more airmen to face the might of the Luftwaffe. What those on the ground did not know was that the Oxford was not taking off but trying to land and carrying the crew of two who had taken off earlier with two airmen who had hitched a lift from RAF Langar to Ossington.

The Oxford had been in the final stages of its approach to Ossington when it was ordered to overshoot. With its undercarriage down, it flew in a shallow arc just north of a few houses that comprised the Hamlet. As it neared the slightly higher ground on which the RAF camp was sited one of its engines cut out.

A gardener, Arthur Weaver who was working in the Hall gardens looked up, and horrified, watched the yellow painted plane continue ites gentle arc on a collision course with a 70 foot water tower on the edge of the RAF camp. Even though the aircraft was gradually losing the little height it had it would have cleared the oil rig shaped tower had its undercarriage been up, but one wheel hit the tower.

Gardener Weaver died in 1974 but ironically his son Arthur junior is able to take up the story. "I was seven at the time and playing on the green gates, it was a really warm evening. The first thing I remember was a tremendous crash. One of the wheels and part of the wing crashed down onto the drive not 10 yards from my friends and I. After a minute or so the plane just exploded. We ran to the airmen in their buses and passed the alarm, but there was nothing anyone could do. Ironically the aircraft was on top of 11,000 gallons of water, but the Fire Fighters were unable to reach the blazing aircraft with their equipment. Two airmen were burned to death in the remains of the plane on top of the black tar covered tower. The other two along with a section of the cockpit were catapulted across the drive into an orchard and were dead when the rescuers found them."

Gardener Weaver was the only civilian witness at the inquest that followed. He told how the engines spluttered, and how the aircraft lost just sufficient height to collide with the only object on the skyline that was high enough. The verdict was that the accident had happened because the aircraft was out of fuel, but Ossington residents hampered by secrecy that surrounded such events never found the answers.

If the aircraft was short of fuel why was it ordered to overshoot the airfield and make a second approach. One family did not wait to ask questions. Shortly after the catastrophe the occupiers of a farmhouse left for a village that did not have an airfield for company. Their home had been the next landmark on the flight path of the aircraft.'

WEDNESDAY 29th JULY 1942

1516 hrs — Air Test

Hampden I AT113 EQ-A of 408 Sqn from Balderton was taken for an air test during preparations for a raid on Saarbrucken by S/L Price, with two ATC cadets on board. The cadets were from 24 ATC and were on a visit to the station to spend a day with the squadron and to be given flight experience if a flight became available. The aircraft stalled 1½ miles south east of the airfield, crashed and burnt out with the cause unknown. Two airmen and the two cadets were killed.

S/L C/920 Lyall Basil Burman Price DFC RCAF age 22 (Pilot) is buried in Brookwood Military Cemetery Surrey, Sgt 984291 Idris Hughes RAFVR age 20 (W/Op/Air Gnr) buried in Moel-y-Tryfan (Hermon) Congregational Chapelyard, ATC cadet Keith Rollason Couzin Wood, 930 Westcliffe High School Sqn ATC age 16 buried in Newark-upon-Trent Cemetery, ATC cadet Geoffrey Hughes also age 16 is buried in Whittington (St Bartholomew) Churchyard.

S/L Price was awarded the DFC on 11th August 1942 and a citation read: 'Squadron Leader Price has completed 25 operational flights as Captain of a bomber aircraft. Throughout, his courage, cheerfulness and devotion to duty have been outstanding. He has been a fine example to all aircrew in his squadron, and the results he has achieved have gone far to inspiring his fellow crews to greater efforts. Squadron Leader Price has never failed to attack the most highly defended targets with the greatest determination and skill. He has brought back excellent photographs of the primary target taken whilst bombing, an outstanding example being that showing the actual sheds of the Heinkel Aircraft Works at Rostock which he was detailed to attack on the night of 26/27th April 1942.'

The funeral of S/L Price took place on 1st August and the chief mourner was his father Major General Charles Basil Price DSO, DCM.

1540 hrs — Training

Wellington I X9622 of 25 OTU from Finningley was carrying out overshoot action when the pilot, Sgt 655001 E H Bingers, retracted the undercarriage and reduced flaps from 70 degrees to 40 degrees and the aircraft sank to the ground. Sgt Bingers throttled back and allowed the aircraft to come to rest. The reason for the action is not known.

The second pilot, Sgt 778629 Dennis Arthur Green RAFVR, was killed 5 weeks later on 4th September age 22 having already been promoted to F/S. He was the pilot of Wellington X3940 of 25 OTU which took off from Finningley on a training flight and when an engine caught fire the aircraft was partially abandoned but 2 members of the aircrew died. He is buried in Kirkby Wharfe (St John the Baptist) Churchyard Extension.

SATURDAY 1st AUGUST 1942

1625 hrs Training

Spitfire Vb AB151 RF- of 303 (P) Sqn from Kirton-in-Lindsey was on a navigational exercise when it suffered engine failure due to an internal glycol leak and force landed in a field at Eakring, near Ossington. The pilot was Sgt P/793862 Karasinski PAF.

MONDAY 3rd AUGUST 1942

1305 hrs

An enemy aircraft machine gunned Harworth Road over the Coke Oven plant, Harworth Colliery.

THURSDAY 6th AUGUST 1942

0050 hrs Training

Manchester I L7385 EM-U of 207 Conv Flight from Bottesford collided with Lancaster R5550 whilst landing and burnt out. Of the crew 3 were injured: Sgt 1177661 Arthur S Pearson RAFVR age 20 (Pilot), Sgt 1536441 J Slater (Air Gnr) and Sgt A J C Whitehead RAFVR and 2 were killed Sgt 967145 John Forbes RAFVR age 22 (F/Eng) and Sgt 1112237 Caleb Stanley Kenneth Shepherd RAFVR age 20 (W.Op/Air Gnr). Sgt Forbes is buried in Aberdeen Cemetery and Sgt Shepherd in Chester General Cemetery. Sgt Pearson was admitted to the Burns Unit at the RAF hospital at Rauceby but he later returned to non-operational flying.

Manchester I L7385 EM-U of 207 Squadron

0050 hrs Taxiing

Lancaster R5550 EM-B of 207 Sqn from Bottesford had landed from a practice flight but because of repairs being undertaken on the perimeter track taxied back down the runway. Meanwhile, thinking that R5550 was clear, permission was given for Lancaster L7385 to land on the same runway, the two aircraft met head-on, there was an explosion and both aircraft caught fire. Two members of the crew were injured: Sgt 1255319 A F G Smart RAFVR (W.Op/ Air Gnr) and F/S 925453 F R Ikin RAFVR (Air Gnr). 3 of the crew were killed: Sgt 655412 Frederick Samuel Akerman RAF age 23 (Pilot) buried Uxbridge Cemetery, Sgt 537658 Harold Curson age 23 RAF (F/Eng) buried Bottesford (St Mary) Churchyard, F/S 924977 John Brooks RAFVR age 29 (Nav) buried in Arnold Cemetery. Sgt Ikin suffered shock and concussion.

SATURDAY 8th AUGUST 1942

0053 hrs

Three bombs were dropped on the perimeter track of Ossington airfield by an unidentified enemy aircraft damaging nissen huts and an Oxford aircraft. Flares were dropped on Cropwell Bishop, Tythby, Wyverton, Radcliffe-on-Trent, Cotgrave and Clifton.

0110 hrs Four more bombs were dropped on Ossington airfield runway.

MONDAY 10th AUGUST 1942

0300 hrs Taxiing

Manchester I R5776 of 1654 CU from Wigsley having landed at Swinderby collided with a armourers lorry parked on the edge of the perimeter track. Disciplinary action was taken against the lorry driver. The pilot was P/O A E Foster.

WEDNESDAY 12th AUGUST 1942

0255 hrs Training

Wellington I DV477 of 25 OTU from Bircotes overshot the aerodrome boundary after loss of engine power due to icing of the carburettor. The pilots were Sgt 1381720 R S Raymond and Sgt 1179388 P Siddons. There were no injuries.

Anson R9605 of 25 OTU from Bircotes force landed at Bircotes due to port engine failure.

—

Incendiaries and high explosive bombs were dropped on Epperstone and Woodborough.

SATURDAY 15th AUGUST 1942

0215 hrs Training

Oxford I BG206 of 14 (P)AFU from Ossington touched down, bounced, and took off again and then crashed into the ground from 50 feet. The pilot P/O L J Wood was taken to the Station Sick Quarters suffering from shock and injuries and was later transferred to RAF Hospital Rauceby.

WEDNESDAY 19th AUGUST 1942

0115 hrs Training

Lancaster I R5863 EM-K of 207 Sqn from Bottesford took off at night for the pilot, F/S Fordwyche, to practice landings and 3 engine overshoots. After one landing and two overshoots had been carried out the aircraft was then seen to make a normal approach for another overshoot but it failed to climb away and turned to the right, lost height and crashed to the ground at Normanton village, near Bottesford, just beyond the main runway. An outbreak of fire occurred on impact and the aircraft was totally destroyed. After examination of the aircraft it was considered that the accident was due to incorrect manipulation of the feathering switches. All 6 crew were killed outright.

F/S 591286 William Dundas Fordwych RAF age 21 (Pilot) buried Bottesford Cemetery; Sgt 401182 John Charles Murphy RAAF age 27 (2nd Pilot) also buried Bottesford Cemetery, P/O 117479 Denis Victor Morris-Edwards age 20 RAFVR (Obs) buried Stoke-on-Trent, Sgt 1181149 Stanley Oswald Spicer age 31 RAFVR (W/Op /Air Gnr) buried Hitchin Cemetery, Sgt 969690 Alexander John Boyne age 21 RAFVR, buried Logie Cemetery Stirlingshire. Sgt 1216295 Bernard Murray Smith, age 21 RAFVR (Air Gnr) son of William Bernard and Winifred Alice Smith of Lambley who is buried in Carlton (Gedling) Cemetery.

FRIDAY 21st AUGUST 1942

0125 hrs Training

Lancaster I L7580 of 207 Sqn from Bottesford made a very heavy landing with a bomb load and a strut buckled. The pilot, Sgt 656879 G Langdon, denied landing heavily and the enquiry concluded that many landings of the same aircraft had contributed to the failure. Sgt Langdon was involved in another incident on 31st August.

This Lancaster was displayed in Trafalgar Square during a 'Wings for Victory' fund-raising event in March 1943. The aircraft returned to 207 Sqn as EM-C and from late 1943 served with a succession of training units.

TUESDAY 25th AUGUST 1942

The Hon. C V Michael Strutt, age 28 was a pilot officer, service number J/15062 serving with 228 Squadron RCAF as an air gunner.

P/O Strutt was the Duke of Kent`s Equerry when a passenger in Sunderland W4026 -M, captained by F/L F Goyen (Australia) which took off from Cromerty Firth, Invergordon at 1310 hours. There were 15 men aboard, including Air Commodore HRH The Duke of Kent and W/C T L Mosely, Commander of 228 Sqn, who was acting as 2nd Pilot. Thirty two minutes later the aircraft crashed at Eagles Rock 3 miles inland from Dunbeath in Caithness. Eagles Rock is 928 feet above sea level and the aircraft hit at 700 feet. There was one survivor, F/S Andy Jack, the 21 year old rear gunner, who was flung clear on impact, bruised and badly burned. The court of enquiry into the crash partly blamed the pilot, but the cause has never been fully established. P/O Strutt was taking the place of S/L D J Ferguson, who was unwell.

The aircraft was officially heading to Iceland where the Duke of Kent was to meet senior members of the US military. The Duke's death led to various conspiracy theories some stating that he was actually heading to Sweden for secret peace talks with the Germans another that he was at the controls of the aircraft and his inexperience may have caused it to crash.

P/O Strutt is buried in Kingston-on-Soar (St Wilfrid) Churchyard and was the son of Algernon Henry Strutt, 3rd Baron Belper and of Lady Belper (nee Bruce), of Kingston-on-Soar; husband of the Hon. Mrs C V Michael Strutt.

WEDNESDAY 26th AUGUST 1942

LAC 1112945 Andrew Forrester RAFVR age 22 was killed when he was struck on the back by the propeller of a taxiing aircraft whilst driving a tractor at Tollerton aerodrome. He died later that day from a fractured spine and is buried in Glasgow (Sandymount) Cemetery.

FRIDAY 28th AUGUST 1942

2315 hrs Training

Wellington I T2468 of 25 OTU from Bircotes overshot on landing and the pilot Sgt R/88827 Paul Franklin Brawley RCAF applied the brakes, the aircraft swung and the undercarriage collapsed. There were no injuries however Sgt Brawley died just 23 days later when as a member of the crew of Wellington BJ689 of 101 Sqn he took off from Stradishall for a raid on Saarbrucken and the aircraft crashed in the Ardennes. He is commemorated on the Runnymede Memorial. Sgt Brawley came from Newcomertown, Ohio and was one of many Americans serving in the RCAF.

Another renowned American flying with the RCAF was P/O John Gillespie Magee, author of the classic aviation poem 'High Flight'.

SUNDAY 30th AUGUST 1942

1630 hrs Training

Manchester I L7416 of 1654 CU from Wigsley swung on landing in a cross wind and ran into trees due to brake failure which was due to lack of air pressure. All the crew including the pilot P/O 80222 William James Picken DFC RAFVR escaped injury.

P/O Picken was later awarded the DFC on 11th August when flying with 106 Sqn. His citation read: 'This officer has acted as captain on Hampden, Manchester and Lancaster aircraft. He is a pilot of great skill and resource who has achieved much success. He has many times attacked targets in the Rhur and on several occasions bombed the naval yards of Hamburg, Kiel, Bremen and Brest. He took part in the attack on the Renault armament factory scoring hits from 3,000 feet. He invariably presses home his attacks whatever the opposition. His courage and determination have been of a high standard.'

William Picken DFC, by now a F/L, was subsequently killed on 5-6th March 1943 when piloting Lancaster W4918 ZN-D of 106 Sqn on a raid on Essen. He is buried in the Reichswald Forest War Cemetery.

TUESDAY 1st SEPTEMBER 1942

1320 hrs Air test

Tiger Moth II T6267 of 25 (P)EFTS from Hucknall bounced on landing and tipped up. Aircraft mechanic LAC 781830 M Kaniewski PAF had taken off in the aircraft, made 6 circuits of the aerodrome and on landing struck the ground causing the aircraft to bounce up on its nose. The official accident card stated that this was 'a case of wilful damage to one of His Majesty's aircraft. No further action to be taken'.

2230 hrs Training

Oxford I T1002 of 14 (P)AFU from Ossington was on flying training when it made a heavy landing, bounced and the pilot, Sgt 1385475 T H E Harvey, endeavoured to carry out an overshoot. Unfortunately the aircraft hit a hedge and eventually landed in a field west of the aerodrome. Sgt Harvey was injured.

2315 hrs Training

Manchester I L7298 of 1654 HCU from Wigsley took off for night flying practice during which the fuel master cock was inadvertently partly closed causing fuel starvation and the engines failed. A wheels up landing was made a mile to the east of the airfield with no injuries to the pilot, Sgt 401449 Leslie Gordon Knight RAAF, or the crew.

F/L Knight

Leslie Knight DSO, now F/L and age 22 was killed whilst piloting Lancaster JB144 of 617 Sqn on 15-16th September 1943 on a raid on the Dortmund-Ema Kanal near Ladbergen. He died whilst attempting a forced landing but the rest of his crew survived. He flew on 26 operations and is buried in Denham General Cemetery. F/L Knight received his DSO when flying with 617 Sqn on the famous 'Dambusters raid' in May 1943.

The award was gazetted on 28th May 1943 and the citation for all those members of the squadron who received the DSO read: 'The KING has been graciously pleased to approve the following award in recognition of gallantry displayed in flying operations against the enemy:

On the night of 16th May 1943, a force of Lancaster bombers were detailed to attack the Moehne, Eder and Sorpe dams in Germany. The operation was one of great difficulty and hazard, demanding a high degree of skill and courage and close co-operation between the crews of the aircraft engaged. Nevertheless, a telling blow was struck at the enemy by the successful breaching of the Mohne and Eder dams. This outstanding success reflects the greatest credit on the efforts of the following personnel who participated in the operation in varios capacities as members of aircraft crew.'

FRIDAY 4th SEPTEMBER 1942

2330 hrs — Training

Anson I R9699 of 25 OTU from Finningley took off for a training flight but swung out of control and ran into Wellington DV494, also of 25 OTU, which was stationary. The Anson was wrecked. The pilot, who was very experienced, was W/C 44932 Ernest Edward Collins DFM, DSO.

Due to this incident instructions were given that the Drem flarepath should be augmented with goose neck flares as the contours of the grass interfere with the flarepath continuity when viewed from a low height. W/C Collins received his DSO while flying with 50 Sqn on 21st November 1941.

TUESDAY 8th SEPTEMBER 1942

1005 hrs — Training

Oxford II N4772 of 14 (P)AFU from Ossington swung on take off and collided with another aircraft because the pilot, Sgt R/104187 Frederick Eugene Gullison, RCAF, had failed to correct a swing. He was promoted to F/S but was killed on 8th February 1943 age 23 when piloting Whitley LA784 of 10 OTU from Abingdon on a training flight and on attempting to land at Harwell, the aircraft bounced and while going round again crashed near the airfield. All 4 crew men were killed and he rests in Brookwood Military Cemetery.

WEDNESDAY 9th SEPTEMBER 1942

2330 hrs — Training

Wellington IC DV433 -M1 of 25 OTU from Finningley returned from a training flight of five hours duration and landed heavily. The aircraft bounced 30-40 feet, overshot but then crashed into trees after failing to gain altitude ½ mile north of Finningley and caught fire. All the crew of four were killed: Sgt 657241 Reginald Victor Turpitt age 23 (Pilot) is buried in Tawstock Churchyard, Devon, P/O 118547 Peter Wren Dormon age 26 RAFVR buried Frinton-on-Sea Churchyard, Sgt 1289382 Leslie Hugh Davies age 22 RAFVR (W.Op/Air Gnr) buried Burry Port Cemetery, Carmarthenshire, Sgt 1289382 Dennis Charles Alfred Peter Denville RAFVR buried Halifax (Stoney Royd) Cemetery.

THURSDAY 10th SEPTEMBER 1942

1030 hrs — Training

Oxford I X6656 of 14 (P)AFU from Balderton was on an instructional training flight and landed with the undercarriage retracted. The Instructor had failed to notice that the pupil had not carried out vital actions and it can only be categorised as 'gross carelessness'. The pilots were Sgt 1147200 Whipp and Sgt 1525019 John Staniforth RAFVR.

Sgt Staniforth was killed on 5th May 1943 when as the pilot of Wellington HE162 of 196 Sqn on a raid on Dortmund when he crashed near Gelsenkirchen. He is now buried in Reichswald Forest War Cemetery.

SATURDAY 12th SEPTEMBER 1942

2123 hrs — Training

Hampden I AE385 of 408 Sqn from Balderton took off for circuit and landings practice. At 2123 hrs the aircraft stalled at 200 feet and crashed, bursting into flames, just over 2 miles north east of the airfield killing both crew members.

Sgt R/10151 George Murray Frame RCAF (Pilot) and F/S R/93149 William George Keogh RCAF (W.Op./Air Gnr) of Ontario, Canada are buried in Newark-upon-Cemetery.

MONDAY 14th SEPTEMBER 1942

0030 hrs — Taxiing

Manchester I L7457 of 83 Sqn CF from Wigsley collided with an air raid shelter. The pilot, F/S 404904 V S Moore, mistook one of the perimeter track lights for one of the runway lights, turned off, and braked when he realised he was on grass but the aircraft ran into the obstruction before the braking became effective.

This aircraft was involved in another incident on 24th January 1943 when it caught fire in the air and force landed at Saxilby.

0745 hrs — Inspection

Oxford I X6658 of 16 (P)FTS from Newton was being inspected by an airman when he accidentally moved the undercarriage selector lever causing the undercarriage to collapse. Disciplinary action was to be taken against the airman responsible.

TUESDAY 15th SEPTEMBER 1942

0955 hrs — Training

Master III DL603 of 16 (P)FTS from Tollerton undershot in an attempt to reach the aerodrome after engine failure and crash landed just outside the boundary. The pilot, LAC P/794623 L A Dowler PAF, was doing aerobatics and flew longer than he should and without a fuel gauge did not realise that he was out of fuel. He was not injured.

0130 hrs — Operations

Hampden I P2064 of 408 Sqn from Bottesford landed on Bottesford's No.2 Q site near Foston by mistake coming home from Operations and hit a tree, with no injuries to the crew. The pilot was P/O 110552 R H G Bossey.

FRIDAY 18th SEPTEMBER 1942

0130 hrs — Training

Wellington III BJ976 –G of 25 OTU from Bircotes took off for solo night bombing practice and on return after a 1 hour 50 minutes flight, overshot the runway and crashed into the ground from 2-300 feet, about a mile to the west of the airfield, and caught fire. All the crew of 4 were killed: Sgt 1165282 George Nicol RAFVR age 22 (Pilot) is buried in Wareham Cemetery, Sgt 1381154 Wilfred Bakes age 31 RAFVR buried Shipley Cemetery, Sgt 1383216 John Charles Dalton age 23 RAFVR buried Lambeth Cemetery, Sgt 1377795 Percy Benjamin Elliott Woodham RAFVR age 32 (W.Op/Air Gnr) buried Finningley Churchyard Extension.

SATURDAY 19th SEPTEMBER 1942

1015 hrs — Training

Master III W8530 of 16 (P)FTS from Newton whilst on a low level navigation exercise hit two trees some distance apart, despite the engine working satisfactory, and crashed at White House Farm, between Colston Bassett and Hose, and caught fire.

The first pilot, Sgt P/792276 Podbereski PAF was injured and the 2nd pilot, LAC 794679 E J Rewers (Pupil Pilot), an American, was killed and was buried in Newark-upon-Trent Cemetery. LAC Rewers was exhumed on 16th November 1949.

MONDAY 21st SEPTEMBER 1942

0950 hrs — Training

Master III W8794 of 16 (P)FTS from Newton had its engine cut whilst performing aerobatics and the aircraft undershot a forced landing and hit a hedge at Hockerton, near Southwell. The Instructor pilot LAC P/794402 Chrapkiewiez PAF was un-injured.

TUESDAY 22nd SEPTEMBER 1942

1720 hrs — Training

Master III W8998 of 16 (P)FTS from Newton was on flying training when the engine cut during flight and the aircraft struck a hedge and hit a bank in a forced landing on the Fosse Way, Nottinghamshire. Both the crew, F/O P/0644 Stefan Kleczkowski PAF and LAC P/794385 B Dobrzynski PAF, were injured.

MONDAY 28th SEPTEMBER 1942

0935 hrs — Training

Oxford I V4035 of 1507 BAT Flt from Finningley was approaching to land in fog on beam approach training and while following track 250 yards left of beam hit a tree or stalled in trying to avoid the tree. The aircraft crashed causing the death of two crewmen and injuring one.

P/O 117991 Basil Gordon Tree, DFM Pilot Instructor RAFVR age 25 is buried in Cottingham Cemetery, Sgt 413023 Hector Gordon Roch McCosker RAAF age 23 buried Finningley Churchyard.

F/S E Chamberlain was injured. P/O Tree gained his DFM on 29th November 1941 whilst serving with 49 Sqn.

THURSDAY 1st OCTOBER 1942

1749 hrs — Op; Wismar

Lancaster I R5703 QR-D of 61 Sqn from Syerston took off at 1745 hours with 10 other Lancasters detailed for an attack on Wismar but as the Lancaster cleared the end of the runway, the Immersion Switch on the dinghy pack activated and it became inflated causing the equipment to break from its stowage and become entangled with the tail unit causing loss of control of the aircraft. The bomber, which was carrying a 4000 lb bomb and incendiaries, turned to port and went into a shallow dive from 750 feet and hit the ground one mile north east of Gunthorpe. The 7 crew were all killed:

S/L 41885 George Ernest Weston DFC, RAF age 23 (Pilot) is buried in Hemblington Churchyard Norfolk, Sgt 1221132 Frederick George Bellchambers RAFVR (F/Eng) buried Newark-upon-Trent Cemetery, P/O 127491 George Alan Hawes age 22 RAFVR (Nav) buried Eastbourne Cemetery, Sgt 1365084 John McFadyen Ramsey age 22 RAFVR buried Lasswade

Cemetery, Midlothian, F/O 46968 Joseph Edward Hanson DFM age 24 (W.Op/Air Gnr) buried Shipley Cemetery Yorkshire, Sgt 1057338 Jack Machin Robinson, age 26 (W.Op/Air Gnr) buried Sheffield Cemetery, P/O J/16499 Lloyd George Gallaway RCAF age 26 (Air Gnr) buried Newark-upon-Trent Cemetery.

F/L Weston was awarded the DFC on 14th March 1941 whilst serving with 50 Sqn. The citation read: 'One night in February, 1941, Flying Officer Weston was detailed to attack an enemy vessel lying in the dock at Brest. Owing to extreme darkness and exceptional searchlight and anti-aircraft opposition, great difficulty was encountered in locating the target. Although his starboard engine failed, Flying Officer Weston persisted in his search and, in the face of an increasingly heavy and accurate barrage, eventually located his target and pressed home his attack with a full load of bombs. On the return journey, while over the English Channel his engine picked up but again failed. By skilful handling of his aircraft, however, he succeeded in reaching his base where he landed safely. He displayed outstanding gallantry, skill and determination throughout.'

F/L Weston's brother, F/S Godfrey Randal Weston RNZAF, was killed 18 months later age 22. He was Air Bomber aboard Stirling I R9353 of 1657 HCU which crashed at Stradishall whilst training. Both brothers hailed from Nelson City, New Zealand.

P/O Hanson gained his DFM while flying Hampdens with 50 Sqd, details being gazetted on 18th July 1941.

FRIDAY 2nd OCTOBER 1942

2125 hrs **Op; Krefeld**

Lancaster I W4238 ZN-C of 106 Sqn from Syerston took off at 1850 hrs for a raid on Krefield but on receipt of a recall message returned early. Unable to locate his own base he then inadvertently joined the circuit of RAF Newton aerodrome. The aircraft then landed on the shorter Newton runway, overshot and collided with a defence post. F/L 101532 W N Whamond (Pilot) had been told that that there was plenty of room for overshoot at his own base but this was not the case with Newton. The aircraft caught fire but only one injury was reported.

The rest of the crew were Sgt J P Humphreys, F/S E G McClelland, Sgt J L Cunningham, Sgt J R Hanson, Sgt B E Sutton, and Sgt E R Clarke.

SUNDAY 4th OCTOBER 1942

1428 hrs **Training**

Tiger Moth II T7781 of 654 Sqn force landed heavily on the port wheel, bounced and swung to port and tipped on its nose in a large field at Ollerton. The pilot Capt 95103 R M Carr was on a map reading exercise and had to land to check his position as industrial haze had limited the visibility to 500 yards.

MONDAY 5th OCTOBER 1942

2010 hrs **Op; Aachen**

Lancaster I W4102 ZN- of 106 Sqn from Syerston took off at 1915 hrs with nine other 106 Sqn Lancasters and eight 61 Sqn Lancasters for a raid on Aachen. Soon after both starboard engines of W4102 failed and the aircraft crash landed with undercarriage retracted while trying to land at Langar airfield. The captain, Sgt Lace, was unable to jettison his bombs owing to his aircraft being over land but the crew managed to leave the aircraft before a fire broke out and later there was an explosion of the bomb load, including a 4,000 pounder, which completely destroyed the aircraft. Failure of the starboard inner engine was caused by an internal coolant leak but failure of the starboard outer cannot be satisfactorily explained. The pilot, Sgt 1385008 G P

Lace, was unable to maintain height and did not have time to lower the undercarriage. The rest of the crew Sgt F E B Burgess, P/O W M Burnside, Sgt J R Bradshaw, Sgt L H Chester, Sgt H T Adams and Sgt J T Hunt were un-injured but a member of the crash tender was slightly burned. The crash crew arrived but scattered before the bomb exploded. There was slight damage to two Lancasters in a nearby dispersal, tiles were blown off nearby farm buildings and a crater 40 feet diameter by 25 feet deep was blown in the runway. The crash tender was sprayed with flying burning petrol and was a total loss. 50 civilian labourers and 50 personnel of the works squadron repaired the damaged runway.

WEDNESDAY 7th OCTOBER 1942

0052 hrs Op; Osnabruck

Lancaster I W4767 of 61 Sqn from Syerston took off with 7 other 61 Sqn Lancasters for a raid on Osnabruck and returned after a 5 hour 40 minute flight and landed near the end of the landing run and its wing tip struck the top of the rudder fin of an aircraft that had landed just previously. The enquiry stated that in future the landing procedure needed speeding up. The pilot, F/S 924352 A J B Timmins, and his crew escaped injury.

THURSDAY 8th OCTOBER 1942

1815 hrs Training

Oxford I R5945 of 14 (P)AFU from Ossington attempted a forced landing due to fuel shortage in the main starboard tank, hit high tension cables and crashed at Bates Farm, Kneesall. It was considered that either the pilot had failed to open the fuel cock or some undiscovered blockage occurred to check the fuel flow. The pilot, Sgt R104389 John Elliott Coombs RCAF age 23, missed the airfield which was enveloped in heavy rain. It was considered that there was a lack of judgement in taking off from a relief landing ground in the face of the approaching storm. The pilot was killed and is buried in Ollerton Cemetery.

The following is an extract from the Ossington ORB: At 18.17 hours all electric power on Ossington station failed suddenly. Enquiries to the Control tower were made and no news of any crash was available. Emergency lighting was tested and found to be working. At 18.35 hours a call was received from the duty pilot that a crash in the direction of Kneesall had been reported. The Medical officer proceeded in the large ambulance with the driver and one orderly. At Kneesall village they were directed to the scene of the crash, arriving at 18.55 hours and found Oxford R5945 which had crashed in a field belonging to Mr Bates, a farmer, about one and a half miles across the fields from the main road, and reached with great difficulty. The fire engine had already arrived, but no fire had occurred. The aircraft was lying near a hedge and brought down the main electric power cables for some distance on either side of the crash. The presence of the cables lying on the ground made access difficult. The aircraft was badly broken up and the pilot was found dead still strapped in his seat, face downwards on the front part of the weckage. With difficulty the wreckage was cleared and the body removed to Station Sick Quarters. Before leaving the scene a careful search was carried of the wreckage and surrounding area by torches and Ambulance Spot Light for any other bodies, but none were found.

On returning to the main road a message was received from the Duty Pilot stating that only one man should be in the aircraft who was on a solo training flight, that of Pilot R/104389 Sgt John Elliott Coombs RCAF Aged 23. The ID disc on the body confirmed that it was Sgt Coombs who had died from multiple injuries. No evidence of electrocution was evident. Sgt Coombs is buried in Ollerton Cemetery.

MONDAY 12th OCTOBER 1942

0515 hrs Training

Oxford I BG210 of 14 (P)AFU from Ossington called ground control and was given a green light to land and made a normal night landing on the flare path. At the end of the run the aircraft collided with Oxford T1140 which was stationary on the flare path with one engine stopped. Neither pilot, Sgt 1047258 William Henry Barrow RAFVR or Sgt 1483472 H S Gifford, were to blame.

Sgt Barrow was killed less than five months later on 2nd March 1943. He was the pilot of Wellington HE376 of 466 Sqn from Leconfield on a Gardening operation which was lost without trace. All the crew are commemorated on the Runnymede Memorial.

TUESDAY 13th OCTOBER 1942

1500 hrs

Spitfire IX BR371 of 6 FPP from Ratcliff (Leicester) took off from Hucknall, the engine misfired, cut and the pilot, 2nd Officer N Iredale, had to make a wheels-up forced landing at Greasley two miles west of Hucknall.

THURSDAY 15th OCTOBER 1942

2055 hrs Training

Wellington IC DV717 of 11 OTU from Westcott was on a solo night cross country exercise when it dived through the clouds straight into the ground at Breck's Farm, Maplebeck and caught fire. Cause was probably aircraft malfunction.

All 5 of the crew were killed and from New Zealand. The captain Sgt 414640 Vincent Xavier Kirby RNZAF (Pilot) age 23 had 336 flying hours experience, Sgt 411969 Richard John Fuller age 21 (Nav), Sgt 413282 Ivan Raymond Styles age 27 (Air Gnr), Sgt 413438 John Llewellyn Lloyd age 22 (Obs/Air Bomber), All the above are buried in Ollerton Cemetery.

Sgt 413264 Edward Alexander McCord age 26 (W.Op/Air Gnr) age 26 is buried in Ardagh Cemetery, Ireland.

In the preceding 5 weeks Sgt Styles had already experienced a crash landing and a take-off crash. As a poignant footnote to the tragedy, the body of Sgt McCord was repatriated to the land of his birth and buried in Ardagh Cemetery, County Longford, Eire. He had emigrated to New Zealand only 4 years earlier.

Sgt Kirby

Sgt Fuller

Sgt Lloyd

Ollerton Cemetery

0200 hrs Ground

Tiger Moth II T5976 of 25 (P)EFTS from Hucknall was wrecked in a gale. A gale warning had been received and handed to the Station Duty Officer whose duty it was to warn the duty crew but he had failed to do this.

SATURDAY 17th OCTOBER 1942

1510 hrs Training

Tiger Moth II T7293 of 25 (P)EFTS from Hucknall returned from a training flight and approached to land between a chequered flag and stationary Tiger Moth T6370 which the pilot LAC P/794178 K Jankowski PAF did not see. The aircraft undershot, bounced slightly, the pilot opened the throttle to correct and collided with T6370. The Officer Commanding stated that the reason for the incident could be that the airfield controller was an inexperienced pupil.

Day Op; Le Creusot

Lancaster I L7583 EM-A of 207 Sqn from Langar took off on a daylight raid on the Schneider Factory at Le Creusot piloted by Sgt R S Wilson. The aircraft turned back to base due to an engine failure and was attacked by 3 Arado Ar 196 sea planes, 20 miles west of Brest, of which two were shot down. Unfortunately the Flight Engineer, Sgt 576578 Kenneth Stuart Chalmers age 19, was hit by the only shot to hit the Lancaster and became the first airman of 207 Sqn to be killed flying from Langar. He is buried in Hanworth (St Bartholomew) Churchyard and is commemorated by a short write up in the church.

SUNDAY 18th OCTOBER 1942

1520 hrs Taxiing

Tiger Moth II DE147 of RAF Bottesford was taxiing behind a Lancaster when it was blown onto its back by the slipstream when the Lancaster opened up its engines. The pilot was F/O 43035 R Hannah.

MONDAY 19th OCTOBER 1942

1650 hrs — Training

Hurricane I V6606 RP- of 288 Sqn from Digby took-off for AA Co-operation flight. The engine caught fire at 6,000 feet and black fumes and then flames came into the cockpit and the aircraft was abandoned near Bottesford. 288 Sqn provided anti-aircraft co-operation and practice for anti-aircraft units in Lincolnshire and Yorkshire. The pilot, F/O P/847 W Wyganowski PAF, was injured. The enquiry concluded that F/O Wyganowski was probably burnt by flames from the exhaust whilst baling out.

TUESDAY 20th OCTOBER 1942

1300 hrs

AC2 704155 Kazimierz Wojciechowski based at RAF Hucknall died of gunshot wounds in Nottingham City Hospital. He was 21 years of age.

THURSDAY 22nd OCTOBER 1942

0930 hrs — Ground

Lancaster I L7579 of 1654 CU from Wigsley was on the ground being maintained when oxygen was used instead of air to top up the pressure in the tail oleo and an explosion took place damaging the oleo strut, tail plane and adjacent fuselage. An airman, LAC 1103933 L Hill, was injured. He had mistaken an oxygen bottle for air and the explosion occurred when the oxygen came into contact with grease.

TUESDAY 27th OCTOBER 1942

1140 hrs — Taxiing

Oxford II W6564 of 16 (P)SFTS from Newton was taxiing when the tail wheel was torn away as the aircraft crossed the concrete runway which was 5 inches higher than the surrounding ground. The pilot was F/O P/0813 J Filipowicz PAF.

THURSDAY 29th OCTOBER 1942

2240 hrs — Training

Lancaster I R5600 of 1654 HCU from Wigsley crashed on overshoot and hit a gun post whilst making a 3 engine landing. One engine had been feathered because the pilot, Sgt 1311858 Smith, thought it was on fire. There were no casualties.

SATURDAY 31st OCTOBER 1942

1915 hrs — Taxiing

Lancaster I W4765 of 61 Sqn from Syerston was taxiing with P/O 117679 D S Gillett at the controls and struck stationary aircraft Lancaster L7582. The aircraft were being marshalled prior to take off on a runway not in use as a part of the perimeter track was un-serviceable. Whilst marshalling was in progress the blue perimeter lights failed and a line of blue lamps were laid to assist marshalling. P/O Gillett mistook this lane for the aerodrome taxiing track and the wing of the aircraft hit the other aircraft which was unmarked.

1923 hrs — Training

Lancaster I L7545 of 1654 CU was taking off from its satellite at Wigsley, a swing developed and the flight engineer retracted the undercarriage. The pilot, F/L 43706 McKenzie, stated that when the aircraft swung he knocked the Flight Engineer's hand off the throttles and closed them. The enquiry stated that the accident was caused by slackness on the part of the pilot and flight engineer in not making themselves cockpit drill perfect. It was a failure of 'B' Flight in not ensuring this and panicking by the flight engineer.

MONDAY 2nd NOVEMBER 1942

2245 hrs

F/S 508012 Robert William Fayers age 34 RAF was brought into the SSQ at Ossington at 2230 hrs unconscious in a lorry, having had a cycling accident on the camp. He died at 2245 hrs and is buried in Stamford Cemetery.

FRIDAY 6th NOVEMBER 1942

1145 hrs — Training

Spitfire Vb EN825 DB-C of 288 Sqn from Digby was on a low flying training flight when it made a forced landing in a field one mile south of Norwell near Bathley, Newark. The pilot, Sgt R/87714 P Wallace RCAF, was injured. The accident log states that the crash may have been due to an internal coolant leak and subsequent engine failure.

TUESDAY 10th NOVEMBER 1942

2250 hrs — Training

Oxford II P6808 of 16 (P)SFTS from Newton was taking off for dual circuit and landing training, the pilot experienced engine trouble and attempted to land at the end of his run, the aircraft overshot the runway and crashed into a ditch.

The crew F/S P/782360 Jan Trembaczowski PAF (Pilot) and Cpl P/794480 K Palul PAF were injured. F/S Trembaczowski subsequently joined 305 Sqn.

FRIDAY 13th NOVEMBER 1942 — Ground

Lancaster I W4762 of 61 Sqn from Syerston had the undercarriage retracted by a member of the ground crew whilst on the ground. The enquiry stated that there was a lack of supervision by an NCO when operation of bleeding the hydraulic system took place and the pilot, W/O 969699 Rennie Lever, was partly responsible as he neglected to see that the undercarriage selector was in the down position.

W/O Lever was awarded the DFC 7 days later. His citation read: 'Warrant Officer Lever has participated in many operational sorties over some of the most heavily defended areas in Germany. In October 1942, he was captain of an aircraft forming part of the force which successfully attacked Le Creusot. He also captained aircraft which recently attacked Genoa and Milan. At all times this officer has displayed continuous courage and devotion to duty'.

SATURDAY 14th NOVEMBER 1942

0900 hrs — Training

Oxford N6334 of 14 (P)AFU became lost in poor visibity and overturned when making a precautionary landing in a field, at Skegby Farm, Normanton-on-Trent. The pupil pilot P/O R A Eadie had disobeyed rules by leaving formation and not looking carefully for an aerodrome.

WEDNESDAY 18th NOVEMBER 1942

1845 hrs — Training

Master III W8995 of 16 (P)SFTS from Tollerton was being flown by pupil pilot LAC 794488 Jan Wilhelm Opuchlik PAF. He took off at 1810 hrs on a solo night flying exercise and crashed on his 3rd solo landing, 1½ miles from the aerodrome, due to failing to maintain correct control of the aircraft. The aircraft was seen to enter a 45 degree dive whilst on down wind leg of circuit and failed to pull out. It is possible that LAC Opuchlik may have been seized by severe abdominal pains but post mortem failed to reveal the cause. The body was taken to the Newton Mortuary and is buried in Newark-upon-Trent Cemetery.

FRIDAY 20th NOVEMBER 1942

1605 hrs — Ferrying

Lancaster I R5745 of 207 Sqn from Langar attempted to land in conditions of very poor visibility and overshot the runway. The aircraft had been flown to Bottesford by F/S R/92063 James Barry Chester RCAF but due to failure of the RT he did not receive instructions to divert to another aerodrome and Control did not warn the pilot by red visual signal not to land at Bottesford.

F/S Chaster crashed over enemy territory on 3rd January 1943 when piloting Lancaster W4134 of 207 Sqn from Langar. They took off for a raid on Essen and on the homeward journey were shot down by a night fighter flown by Hptm Manfred Meurer, and crashed in Holland. 4 of the crew died, 2 were taken prisoner and he evaded capture.

THURSDAY 26th NOVEMBER 1942

1925 hrs — Training

Oxford I V3867 of 16 (P)SFTS from Newton landed wheels up on the aerodrome after the undercarriage system failed to function. The pilot was Sgt P/780992 Jan Danieluk

On the 3rd/4th March 1943 Sgt Danieluk's crew were one of three crews who laid mines off Lorient, Bomber Commands last operation to be made on Wellingtons.

He was killed on 26th July 1944 when the pilot of Lancaster PB252 BH-M of 300 Sqn which collided with a Lancaster aircraft near Orleans, France, where all the crew are buried.

SATURDAY 28th NOVEMBER 1942

1540 hrs — Training

Wellington IC R1786 of 28 OTU B Flt from Wymeswold took off for circuit practice, landed but as the aircraft gathered speed to go round again the engines cut. The pilot, W/O 754360 Ronald Joseph Fryer RAFVR immediately closed the throttles and raised the undercarriage and a few seconds later came to a stop just beyond the runway. The aircraft burnt out but the crew were unhurt.

W/O Fryer was later killed on 25th November 1943 in a crash at Wymeswold and was cremated at Nottingham Crematorium.

Nottingham Crematorium Memorial

1930 hrs **Training**

Wellington 1C X9941 of 28 OTU from Wymeswold was taking off at1932 hrs on a night training bombing exercise when it crashed at Hoton after hitting trees and shrubs and was burnt out.

F/S R/125364 John Bourne Jamieson RCAF Air Gnr age 25 was killed and is buried in Burton-on-the-Wolds Cemetery and Sgt 1148933 Duncan Potter RAFVR died 2 days later and is buried in Middlesborough Cemetery. The pilot, Sgt A98316 Leslie Arthur Peers, RCAF, was injured.

MONDAY 30th NOVEMBER 1942

1045 hrs **Ferrying**

Tiger Moth II DE159 of GPEU was making a powered approach over trees when its engine cut, the aircraft turned left to avoid the trees and landed on a hillside at Hardwick Hall. The pilot Sgt R/92749 G Petley RCAF was too low to select a suitable force landing area. Water was found in the petrol filter during investigations.

SATURDAY 5th DECEMBER 1942

2234 hrs **Training**

Beaufighter VIF X8140 KP- of 409 Sqn from Coleby Grange took off for a practice interception exercise. At 2217 hrs the pilot reported that he thought his engine was on fire and 10 minutes later he was at 800 feet with the starboard engine out but not on fire. At 2228 hrs he was instructed to climb if he could but he tried with out much luck and was then instructed to turn the petrol off and open the throttle. At 2232 hrs the pilot reported that the engine was still on fire, that he had opened the throttle and should he switch off. At 2233 hrs he was instructed to switch off and use the extinguisher and was asked 'is everything ok'. The reply was 'no I can't get the fire out and it is blinding me'. At 2234 hrs the aircraft flew into the ground six miles north of Mansfield near Langwith Colliery killing both crew members.

The pilot F/O J/10238 Kenneth Earle Warner RCAF age 26 from Lexington, Oregan, USA and Sgt 1398882 Herbert Pendleton RAFVR age 41 (W.Op/Obs) are both buried in Scopwick Church Burial Ground.

SUNDAY 6th DECEMBER 1942

1940 hrs **Training**

Wellington IC R1223 of 28 OTU from Wymeswold was on dual flying training when the pilot attempted an overshoot of the airfield approaching to land. The aircraft was off line of the flight path so the instructor decided to go round again and crashed into trees well upwind of the airfield after flap had been eased off too much and it caught fire. The crash occurred ½ mile south west of Hoton. Two of the crew, F/S 930239 R M Williams and Sgt 1332712 Frank Ronald Page RAFVR were injured. Sgt 138077 Norman Kenneth Millard (W.Op/Air Gnr) of 3 Sqn RAFVR age 22 was killed and the pilot Sgt 1435153 Donald Robert Loyd age 22 died the next day from burns. Both are buried in Burton-on-the-Wolds Cemetery.

Frank Page, now a F/S, was killed on 24th November 1943 age 21 whilst flying with 7 Sqn on a raid on Berlin in Lancaster JB 480 MG-N. He was lost without trace and is commemorated on the Runnymede Memorial.

TUESDAY 8th DECEMBER 1942

1747 hrs Ground

Lancaster I R5864 QR-K of 61 Sqn from Syerston caught fire prior to an operation on Turin when it is thought that several incendiaries exploded subsequently resulting in the explosion of the 4000 lb bomb it was carrying. G/C Walker saw something fall from the bomb bay and raced across the airfield to warn the crew but before he reached the aircraft the 4000 lb bomb exploded.

The crash party from the aerodrome also received injuries. LAC 1068871 Hughes received shrapnel wounds to his legs, LAC 1257587 Dowman received multiple leg injuries, LAC 1030510 A Davies received a fractured leg, Sgt 622461 Cox received injuries necessitating the amputation of his right foot above the ankle and AC1 1692614 John Thwaites age 39 RAFVR received severe head injuries from which he died in Sheffield hospital on 10th December 1942. He is buried in Walshaw (Christ Church) Churchyard. The pilot of the aircraft was Sgt 622461 J Cocker. The following report is taken from the Yorkshire Evening Post 21st September 2006.

'On December 8 1942 Lancaster bombers under the command of Group Captain Augustus Walker were preparing to take off on a night raid over Turin. All were fully armed, many with 1,000 lb bombs, and fuelled for the punishing raid over Italy. While taxiing to take off, Group Captain Walker saw something fall from the bomb bay of one of the heavy bombers and, thinking it might have been a bomb, instinctively rushed across the airfield to warn the crew to abandon the sortie. Suddenly there was an explosion. He was withing a few metres of the aircraft and was thrown nearly 80 metres by the blast, severing his right arm above the elbow joint. Incredibly, as he was being taken to hospital he asked one of his staff to telephone the RAF top brass to ask if they would take back a one-armed station commander in two month's time. Two months later he was back on duty. Only a month after that he became an Air Commodore at the age of 30 and continued to fly, having an artificial arm with leather loops which wrapped around the control column. During his 36 year RAF career he rose to be Air Chief Marshall Sir Augustus Walker, DSO, DFC, and died on December 1986 aged 74.'

A blue plaque was placed on his childhood home in the village of Garforth, near Leeds, on 11th October 2006. The plaque reads: 'Air Chief Marshall Sir Augustus Walker was born in Garforth and brought up in this house. Serving in the RAF he rose to its highest ranks. An inspirational figure, he led during raids with 50 Sqn on industrial targets in Germany and commanded a series of bomber stations during World War Two.'

G/C Walker

THURSDAY 10th DECEMBER 1942

0235 hrs Op; Turino

Lancaster I W4168 QR- of 61 Sqn from Syerston took off at 1745 hrs for a raid on Torino. On the return the aircraft was diverted to Swinderby, an engine cut and the pilot overshot a downwind landing and crash landed at Eagle, near North Scarle. This aircraft had completed 21 operations. The crew, who suffered only superficial injuries, were Sgt 66493 H Goodwin, the American pilot, Sgt H D Lewis, F/S J W Patterson, Sgt L S Hampnett, Sgt G Walker, Sgt S Smith and Sgt T R Jones.

FRIDAY 11th DECEMBER 1942

0120 hrs Training

Wellington III BJ620 -T of 25 OTU from Finningley was diverted to Wymeswold after a six hour training flight due to bad weather conditions, heavy rain, low cloud and severe icing. The aircraft struck trees on the boundary and crashed killing a crew member. The crew were: the pilot S/L 87066 C Anextein injured, P/O A Booth, Sgt 656044 Arnold Tanswell RAFVR age 23 buried in Manchester Southern Cemetery, Sgt J B Reay, Sgt H Ellis, Sgt W Hardaker and Sgt A L Payne.

Three members of the crew were later killed on Operations. Sgt 1025301 John Bowman Reay age 23 RAFVR of 12 Sqn died returning from a raid on Lorient on 13/14 th February 1943 when Lancaster W4836 crashed 3 miles from their home base, Wickenby. He is buried in Bentley-with-Arksey New Cemetery. Sgt 1577810 Albert Lewis Payne RAFVR (Air Gnr) of 100 Sqn died on a raid on Bochum on 13th June 1943 as a crew member of Lancaster W4989 which crashed at Essen-Frintrop. He is buried in Reichswald Forest War Cemetery. F/S 1125265 William Hardaker RAFVR of 115 Sqn died on 24th December 1943 when Lancaster DS773 crashed on a raid on Berlin. He is commemorated on the Runnymede Memorial.

2310 hrs — Training

Oxford I BG196 of 14 (P)AFU from Ossington was approaching the flare path too high and carried out overshoot action from about 100 feet and crashed on the edge of the airfield in line with the flight path. The occupants of the Oxford were taken from the crash scene by ambulance and conveyed to the SSQ. The pilot, Sgt 1237472 Horace Ralphs RAFVR, was injured and died at 0205 hrs the next day, 12th December, without gaining consciousness and is buried in Bagnall (St Chad) Churchyard, Staffordshire. A/C 1716915 B W Jacob had serious injuries and was eventually moved to RAF Rauceby, but survived.

2320 hrs — Training

Master III W850 of 16 (P)FTS from Newton was on circuits and landings training when the pilot lost direction in bad visibility, flew too low, and crashed approximately 3 miles south of Tollerton. The pilot P/792129 Jozef Benedyk PAF age 27 and his passenger LAC P/793822 Jan Kraus PAF were both killed and are buried in Newark-upon-Trent Cemetery.

2359 hrs — Training

Lancaster I W4255 of 1654 HCU from Wigsley took off for night training but due to a sudden deterioration in the weather, bad visibility and heavy rain, the pilot Sgt 1331831 Bernard Daniel Charles Cox RAFVR decided to land as soon as possible, hit the runway hard causing the undercarriage to collapse. Sgt Cox was killed on 7th July 1943 age 22 flying with 142 Sqn. He is buried in Malta Memorial Cemetery.

SUNDAY 13th DECEMBER 1942 — Taxiing

Lancaster I L7540 of 1654 HCU from Wigsley was being taxied by the pilot, Sgt 413373 Norman Clive Beer RNZAF, when it collided with a wrecked aircraft obstructing the perimeter track. The wrecked aircraft (possibly Lancaster W4255 – see above) had been improperly left obstructing the perimeter by personnel of 58 MU. Sgt Beer was killed on 18th February 1943 piloting Lancaster ED330 of 207 Sqn which took off from Langar for a raid on Wilhelmshaven and presumed crashed in the target area. He is buried in Sage War Cemetery.

MONDAY 14th DECEMBER 1942

1215 hrs — Training

Master III DK984 from RAF Cranwell made a precautionary landing in a field near Bilsthorpe Colliery and the undercarriage collapsed. This was due to poor navigation and airmanship by the inexperienced pilot LAC 1396936 S A C Peires from Ceylon.

FRIDAY 18th DECEMBER 1942

0900 hrs — Training

Oxford II BG181 of 14 (P)AFU from Ossington was abandoned mid-air due to the base and all nearby airfields being fog bound after running out of fuel. The pilot Sgt 1550900 I M Thompson, a pupil, made a safe parachute landing at Norton Disney. He had been airborne for 4 hrs 40 mins.

0900 hrs Dispersal

Stirling I BK628 WP-Q of 90 Sqn from Bottesford was being repaired by F/S 561820 Ian Malcolm James McGavin age 31, employed as a fitter first class, when he was fatally injured by the collapse of the port undercarriage. He died of his injuries at Bottesford Station Sick Headquarters and is buried at Hamble.

The official enquiry stated that 'due to the pilot taking off on his last flight with the "ground flight" switch in the "ground" position, thus throwing the whole electrical load on the engine driven generators. The resultant fall in voltage when undercarriage retracting was attempted prevented the port side chassis-in solenoid from making firm contact, causing arcing and subsequent welding of the main solenoid contacts thus leaving the port ac motor "live" on the "up" terminals immediately an electrical supply was corrected'. The pilot was held responsible for incorrect use of the switch resulting in the accident. F/S McGavin was Mentioned in Despatches.

MONDAY 21st DECEMBER 1942

1030 hrs Training

Wellington IC T2887 of 14 OTU from Cottesmore took off on a navigation exercise which was the first flight for the crew as a team. The aircraft had been in the air for 2 hours 15 minutes when 3 loud bangs were heard coming from the starboard engine. Flames were then seen to be coming from the engine, the pilot throttled back and he and the navigator then struggled to keep the aircraft on course. The aircraft descended from 1200 feet to 400 feet and then the starboard engine fell out of the airframe. The pilot was able to pull out of the dive and crash landed at Millhill Farm near Bingham. The cause of the crash was failure of No.6 cylinder due to fatigue.

There were 5 injuries, the pilot Sgt 1333582 G S Boyle and Sgts Tomlinson, Brown, Gay and Woods. Ground witnesses first saw the aircraft beyond the old windmill and then over the east side of Newton aerodrome. The aircraft crossed the Newark to Bingham road moved to the left and crash landed.

2028 hrs Op; Munich

Lancaster I R5699 QR-H of 61 Sqn from Syerston took off at at 1716 hours for a raid on Munich and returned to base early due to failure of the intercom system. Whilst approaching the airfield the Lancaster was caught in a severe down draft over trees and crashed short of the runway. One injury was reported. This aircraft had completed 34 operations.

The crew were P/O J/15123 W J Dierkes RCAF an American, Sgt L Pettigrew, P/O W Apps, Sgt R Inglis, Sgt R Andrews, Sgt J A Fairley and F/O J/10212 Harvey Sterling Glinz RCAF.

F/O Glinz was subsequently killed age 22 years flying with the famous Dambusters of 617 Sqn. He flew on a raid on the Sorpe Dam on 16th May 1943 and crashed after his aircraft collided with high tension cables. He was buried in the North Military Cemetery and then re-interned in the Reichswald Forest War Cemetery.

F/O Glinz

WEDNESDAY 30th DECEMBER 1942

1715 hrs Training

Lancaster I R5356 of 207 Sqn from Langar landed and overshot the runway, ran through a hedge and came to rest in a ditch. Visibilty at the time was worsening rapidly and caused misjudgement by the pilot F/S 1076962 N J Wilkinson.

1943

SATURDAY 2nd JANUARY 1943

1245 hrs Training

Wellington I L4379 of 18 OTU from Bramcote crashed after a 2½ hour flight when making a forced landing on navigational exercise between Holme and Langford near Newark, probably due to icing of the carburettor, and caught fire.

One of the crew AC1P/782472 Eugeniusz Antoni Korzeniowski PAF, age 27, was killed and is buried in Newark-upon-Trent Cemetery.

The following 5 crew members were injured: the pilot P/O P/1655 A Ratatczak, P/O C Czekalski, Sgt J Drapala, Sgt R Baszowski and Sgt M Nogacki all personnel of PAF. The crash location was OS sheet 121; 812 594.

On 27th July 1945, P/O Ratajczak was killed when his 301 Sqn Warwick III HG226 encountered bad weather over France and spun into the ground 32km South of Lyon. Along with 3 fellow countrymen, he is buried in the extension to Mazargues Cemetery, Marseille.

SUNDAY 3rd JANUARY 1943

1100 hrs Training

Lancaster I R5547 of 1661 CU from Winthorpe swung off the runway on take off due to a temporary failure of the port engines causing the swing. The pilot Sgt 408806 John Good RAAF tried to correct with brakes but the engines resumed full power at the same time causing a swing to starboard. Sgt Good ultimately rose to the rank of Squadron Leader and received the DFC with 467 Sqn and the Bar to the DFC with 466 Sqn.

SATURDAY 9th JANUARY 1943

1700 hrs

Lancaster I R5731 of 106 Sqn from Syerston was returning to unit after a diversion when the starboard undercarriage collapsed on landing due to the failure of the top bracket on the oleo leg. There were no injuries.

The pilot Sgt 1098655 Philip Noel Reed RAFVR age 23 was killed a few weeks later on 3rd February. He was the pilot of Lancaster W4770 of 106 Sqn which took off from Syerston for a raid on Hamburg and never returned. All the crew, which had an average age of 22, are buried in Hannover War Cemetery.

MONDAY 11th JANUARY 1943

2008 hrs Training

Lancaster I R5739 of 1654 CU from Wigsley on take off the pilot P/O J/8219 Lou Warren Somers RCAF overcorrected a swing and the aircraft struck an oak tree sustaining some damage.

P/O Somers, age 24, did not return from a raid on Wuppertal on 25th June. He was the pilot of Halifax DK135 of 427 Sqn which crashed near Rotterdam and is buried in Groesbeek Canadian War Cemetery.

2030 hrs Training

Wellington III BK189 of 16 OTU from Swinderby starboard tyre burst on touch down and the aircraft swung off the runway and the undercarriage collapsed after the pilot Sgt 1344401

David Douglas Laidlaw RAFVR made a forced landing due to W/T failure. It was a very dark night and there was a slight cross wind.

Sgt Laidlaw was killed 7 weeks later on 3rd March age 21. He was the pilot of Wellington Z1620 of 115 Sqn which took off for a raid on Hamburg and was lost. He and his crew lie in Becklingen War Cemetery.

2320 hrs — Training

Oxford I BG180 of 14 (P)AFU from Ossington had engine failure after a 2 hour flight and the pilot aircraft force landed in a field at Hall Farm near Laxton. The pilot Sgt 548363 R Dickenson stated that he checked fuel gauges and found 10 gallons in each tank and attempted to turn on a subsidiary tank but both engines cut.

Night — Training

Lancaster I W4183 of 1661 HCU from Winthorpe took off to practice night circuits and landings but yawed to starboard and the tip of the starboard wing dug into the ground.

No-one was injured but the pilot, Sgt 406634 Andrew Basil Reginald Airy RAAF, was subsequently killed on 26-27th June 1943 age 26 in Wellington HF544 of 466 Sqn when he was shot down on a raid on Gelsenkirchen. His rank was W/O and he is commemorated on the Runnymede Memorial.

Sgt Airy

WEDNESDAY 13th JANUARY 1943

1200 hrs — Training

Anson I DG830 of 14 (P)AFU from Ossington had been in the air for 2 hours when an engine failed and the aircraft force landed having stalled in clearing telegraph wires, the port wing struck the ground and the aircraft crashed at Thorpe-on-the-Hill near Swinderby. The pilot F/L 106370 J H Alldis said the port engine caught fire during circuit so he switched it off, lost the airfield in bad visibility and force landed as the aircraft would not maintain height. F/L Alldis sustained a compound fracture of the right tibia and the 2nd pilot, P/O Doubleday, sustained multiple abrasions. Sgt Doubleday's injuries were the result of him being pinned by one of the air screw blades which had to have the tip sawn off to release him.

SATURDAY 16th JANUARY 1943

2200 hrs — Ops; Berlin

Lancaster I W4357 QR-A of 61 Sqn from Swinderby was damaged by a flare whilst in flight, presumably by a friendly aircraft, and returned to base. The pilot was F/S A/403803 P L Elliott RAAF.

SUNDAY 17th JANUARY 1943

1555 hrs — Ferrying

Mustang I AG603 of 1 FPP was being ferried by 2nd Officer Diana Ramsey when the aircraft landed wheels up on Wigsley airfield. The pilot had failed to put the undercarriage selector lever into the lock position. There were no injuries.

MONDAY 18th JANUARY 1943

0120 hrs **Op; Berlin**

Lancaster I R5900 ZN-X of 106 Sqn from Syerston took off at 1635 hrs for a raid on Berlin joining 10 other 106 Sqn Lancasters and 11 61 Sqn Lancasters. During the raid R5900 was damaged by flak and on returning safely to base the undercarriage collapsed on landing but no injuries were reported. The nickname for this Lancaster was 'Admiral Airgoosk'.

The crew were: Sgt 1098655 Philip Noel Reed RAFVR age 23 (Pilot), Sgt 614340 Francis McNeil RAF age 23 (F/Eng), P/O 146345 Peter Edward Bevis RAFVR age 21 (Nav), Sgt 1382059 Roy Edward Cooke RAFVR age 20 (Air Bomber), F/S R/96684 Joseph Rosario Arthur Coulombe RCAF age 23 (W.Op), Sgt 983952 Kenneth Loach RAFVR age 23 (Air Gnr), Sgt 1437035 Arthur William Thomas RAFVR age 19 (Air Gnr).

All the crew but P/O Bevis was killed 15 days later on 3rd February when they took off from Syerston in Lancaster W4770 also of 106 Sqn for a raid on Hamburg and were lost over Germany. They are all buried in Hannover Cemetery.

The same fate befell P/O Bevis who was a member of the crew of Lancaster EE125 also of 106 Sqn from Syerston, which took off 25/26th June for a raid on Gelsenkirchen and was lost without trace. He is commemorated on the Runnymede Memorial.

SATURDAY 23rd JANUARY 1943

2330 hrs **Op; Lorient**

Halifax II DT678 EQ-C of 408 Sqn from Leeming took off at 1716 hours for an attack on Lorient. After 5½ hours flight and on the return leg the pilot changed the outer engines to No.4 tanks each containing 130 gallons of fuel. After 10 minutes the fuel pressure warning light came on for the starboard outer engine which then cut so the pilot changed over to No.3 tanks holding only 20 gallons of fuel and the engine picked up immediately. Shortly after the starboard inner engine warning light came on, the engine cut then picked up again then cut again. At this time it had been running for about 20 minutes on No.1 tank which contained about 90 gallons of fuel so the pilot decided that he had to make a forced landing at the nearest airfield. He received permission to land at Ossington but during approach the starboard engines cut and he crash landed with undercarriage retracted. The probable cause of the fuel starvation was the water found in the tanks probably freezing in the feed pipes. The flight had lasted 6 hours 14 minutes. No injuries were reported. The crew were Sgt 401309 K O Greig (Pilot), RAAF, Sgt J D Blewett RCAF, F/S W V Neumann RCAF, P/O C A Vogel RCAF, P/O N D Downie RCAF, Sgt W A Ivor RCAF, Sgt R/104910 Joseph Vincent John Raymond Veys RCAF (Air Gnr).

Joseph Veys, by now a F/S, was subsequently killed on 28th May 1943 age 21 years flying with 408 Sqn on a raid on Essen in Halifax DT674 EQ-A. His aircraft was shot down by a night fighter in the target area and he is buried Reichswald Forest War Cemetery.

SUNDAY 24th JANUARY 1943

1510 hrs **Training**

Manchester I L7457 of 1654 HCU from Wigsley took off for a combination of familiarisation, dual and circuit practice. Soon after becoming airborne the port engine burst into flames and the aircraft force landed at West Bank, Saxilby. The pilot was F/S 1182674 Taylor.

MONDAY 25th JANUARY 1943

1016 hrs **Training**

Lancaster I R5846 of 1661 CU from Winthorpe taxied off the perimeter track, struck a ditch and the undercarriage collapsed. The pilot Sgt 744872 G N Stephenson was unable to stop due to lack of brake pressure and swung the aircraft off the hard standing to avoid workmen.

TUESDAY 26th JANUARY 1943

1115 hrs — Training

Manchester I R5772 of 1654 CU from Wigsley took off with the pilot on his first solo on this type of aircraft for a 30 minutes dual instruction flight. After 20 minutes a white cloud and vapour was seen to be coming from the port engine which then caught fire. The graviner extinguishing system was operated with no effect so the aircraft force landed in a field and burnt out one mile north east of Wigsley. The incident report stated that the primary cause was the failure of No.3 exhaust valve. There were no injuries. The pilot, F/S R/80163 Schnier RCAF, was also involved in another incident on 10th February 1943.

1825 hrs — Ops; Lorient

Wellington IV Z1318 GR-L of 301 Sqn from Ingham was one of 7 aircraft detailed to attack Lorient Harbour. The aircraft took off at 1714 hours and during the flight the port engine gave trouble and finally stopped. The pilot, Sgt P/793854 M Krol, aborted the mission and returned on one engine. He decided to land undercarriage up but as he approached to land at Langar the starboard engine failed and the aircraft landed on rough ground at the side of the airfield. This was the last Wellington written off by 301 Sqn.

All the crew were injured: Sgt M Krol (Pilot), F/O W Pietrasik, Sgt C Harmuszkiewicz, Sgt S Ratlinski and P/O N Cywinski.

2300 hrs — Op; Lorient

Wellington X HE368 HD-L of 466 Sqn from Leconfield took off at 1704 hrs to bomb the submarine pens at Lorient in the north west of France and sustained flak damage. After being airborne for 6 hours 10 minutes with one engine feathered, loss of fuel and continuous loss of height it hit the top of small trees before crashing and bursting into flames in a field at Sutton-cum-Lound Railway Crossing, 2 miles north west of Retford. Three of the crew were killed, the Rear Gunner and Navigator, who later died from injuries, managed to escape from the wreckage and raise the alarm.

Sgt 414726 Donald Maxwell Lang McKenzie RNZAF age 22 (Pilot), P/O 126961 Harry Edwin Bonest RAFVR age 30 (Air Bomber/Nav), Sgt 411059 Colin Crawford Brownlee RNZAF age 23 (W.Op/Air Gnr) all buried in Finningley (St Oswald) Churchyard Ext.

Sgt 1385767 William Charles Bush age 21 RAFVR (Nav), died on 27th January from his injuries and is buried in Southgate Cemetery. F/S A R Ferris (Rear Gnr) was injured. Crash location: Cassini grid OS 1940 sheet 46 138042; OS 1992 sheet 120 672 843.

THURSDAY 28th JANUARY 1943

2140 hrs — Training

Lancaster I R5540 of 1661 HCU from Winthorpe was on circuit and landing training when overcorrection of a wing drop during approach to land caused the aircraft to land heavily on one wheel, stall and crash at Winthorpe and catch fire.

The pilot, Sgt 944872 George Noel Stephenson RAFVR, was not injured, however he was later killed piloting Lancaster ED665 of 44 Sqn on a raid on Berlin on 1st September 1943 when his aircraft crashed at Schonebeck. His rank was Pilot Officer and he is now buried in Berlin 1939-1945 War Cemetery.

FRIDAY 29th JANUARY 1943

1700 hrs — Training

Lancaster I R5658 of 1654 CU from Wigsley port tyre burst on take off and when landing the aircraft swung off the runway and came to rest on its belly.

The pilot, Sgt 1335643 Sydney Abel RAFVR age 21, did not return from a raid on Essen on 1st May. He was the pilot of Lancaster ED451 of 106 Sqn from Syerston which crashed at Wulfen and all the crew are buried in Reichswald Forest War Cemetery.

2115 hrs **Training**

Wellington IC N2764 of 28 OTU from Castle Donington made a heavy landing when the pilot, Sgt 1333399 Ronald Gordon Winchester RAFVR, held off too high, a tyre burst and the undercarriage collapsed.

Sgt Winchester took off in Lancaster W4901 of 103 Sqn on 16th June for a raid on Koln and his aircraft was shot down a few hours later by flak. He and his crew are buried in Uden War Cemetery.

MONDAY 1st FEBRUARY 1943

2225 hrs **Training**

Lancaster I L7530 of 1661 HCU from Winthorpe had been in the air for 20 minutes on a training flight when it crashed straight ahead immediately after attempting an overshoot coming to rest just off the Newark to Sleaford road.

It was thought that the pilot, Sgt 401083 Basil Frederick Wilmot RAAF was dazzled by headlights and flew into rising ground. The aircraft stopped off the Newark to Sleaford road with one fatality. The crew were Sgt 980916 Arthur Macdonald (F/Eng), Sgt 1388792 Thomas William Hill, P/O Pietsch, and Sgt 1345138 William John Fraser RAFVR (MUAG).

Sgt 401508 Hugh Herbert Lloyd RAAF (Rear Gnr), was killed age 29 and is buried in Newark-upon-Trent Cemetery. Sgt Fraser was taken to RAF Hospital Rauceby for specialist treatment. Sgt Wilmot was also involved in an accident with 1661 HCU on 19th Feb at Winthorpe but killed on 11th June with some members of this crew.

He took off from Bottesford at 2316 hours in Lancaster ED304 PO-C of 467 Sqn for a raid on Dusseldorf and was lost without trace with Sgts Macdonald, Hill, Fraser and other crew members. They had been posted to 467 Sqn in April and were on their 8th Operation when they were lost. They are commemorated on the Runnymede memorial.

TUESDAY 2nd FEBRUARY 1943

1325 hrs **Transit**

Halifax II DT682 EQ-F of 408 Sqn from Leeming was in transit from Syerston to base after repairs to the hydraulic system, a few minutes after take off and at 1300 feet when smoke and flames were seen coming from the port outer engine. The pilot pressed the fire extinguisher and the flight engineer feathered the propeller and the petrol was turned off. The flames died down but within a minute appeared again in the mainframe and the pilot crash landed the aircraft ½ mile to the south of Long Bennington and ran into an embankment adjacent to the Great North Road and collided with a passing truck. Following a technical inspection, the airframe was struck off charge on 20th February. All crew members were injured except for the pilot and one other. The crew were F/S A/76545 F W Wood RCAF (Pilot), Sgt D A Allen, F/S L J Palmer, F/O T B Moore RCAF, Sgt J B Cameron RCAF, Sgt W R Shellington and Sgt B L Lehew.

FRIDAY 5th FEBRUARY 1943

0440 hrs **Training**

Oxford I BG174 of 16 (P)FTS from Tollerton was on circuits and landing training when it had a slight overshoot on landing and stalled and crashed from approximately 200-300 feet about 200 yards north west of Tollerton aerodrome.

The pilot, LAC P/794400 Wladyslaw Baj PAF age 29, was killed and is buried in Newark-upon-Trent Cemetery.

The enquiry stated that the aircraft stalled during an inadvertent turn to the right with insufficient height to recover.

THURSDAY 10th FEBRUARY 1943

0212 hrs — Training

Lancaster I L7540 of 1654 CU from Wigsley had been in flight for 20 minutes when the starboard outer engine throttle jammed open and the pilot made a 4 engine landing, bounced and the starboard undercarriage collapsed. The enquiry stated that the pilot, F/S R/80163 Schnier RCAF, would have been better making a 3 engine landing.

FRIDAY 11th FEBRUARY 1943

2345 hrs — Training

Oxford II AP481 of 16 (P)SFTS from Tollerton was taking off on a night training exercise when the aircraft hit AC1 P/703000 Henryk Fisch, employed as an Electrician 2 at RAF Newton, who was cycling across the flare path. He was killed and is buried in Newark-upon-Trent Cemetery. The pilots F/O P/1555 M Goszcynski PAF and F/O P/1729 J Ochedzen PAF were exonerated from any blame.

F/O Jan Ochedzan was killed on 19th December. He was the pilot of Wellington X HF598 BH-E of 300 Sqn which took off from Ingham at 1100 hrs on an air test and crashed 11 minutes later one mile south west of Hackthorn, 7 miles north north east of Lincoln. The other crew member, Sgt Feliks Bluj PAF (Bomb Aimer), was also killed and both are buried in Newark-upon-Trent Cemetery.

Wellington X HF598 BH-E at Ingham, being loaded up before a mission, Summer 1943

SATURDAY 13th FEBRUARY 1943

1440 hrs — Ground

Tiger Moth II R5057 of 25 (P)EFTS from Hucknall had returned from solo practice with pilot LAC P/703824 W Jarnicki PAF as pilot when the aircraft was overturned by a strong gust of wind.

SUNDAY 14th FEBRUARY 1943

0135 hrs — **Op; Lorient**

Lancaster I W4167 EM-Q of 207 Sqn from Langar took off at 1914 hours for a raid on Lorient and on return over 6 hours later bounced on landing, aggravated by a strong gusty wind, stalled and the undercarriage collapsed at the aerodrome. Initially it was thought that the damage could be repaired but following a mechanical inspection the aircraft was struck off charge. The crew were: pilot Sgt 657231 Peter Evison RAFVR, Sgt 626498 Raymond Walter Ernest Holley RAF (F/Eng), Sgt C E Wittner, Sgt R/92287 William Victor Wallace RCAF (W.Op/Air Gnr), Sgt 402590 Melville George Delatorre (De La Torre) RAAF, Sgt 1253760 Lewis Reginald Thompson RAFVR and F/S R/85910 William Edward Cain RCAF (Air Gnr). 3 of the crew were injured entailing Sgt Evison being taken to the SSQ.

Sgt Evison was subsequently killed 17 days later, on 3rd March 1943 age 25, with 5 members of the above crew: Sgt Holley, Sgt Wallace, Sgt Delatorre, Sgt Thompson and F/S Cain.

They took off from Langar on a raid on Hamburg in Lancaster ED365 EM-U of 207 Sqn and crashed at Wedel, near Hamburg. They are all buried in Hamburg Cemetery.

THURSDAY 18th FEBRUARY 1943

2256 hrs — **Training**

Lancaster I W4270 QR- of 61 Sqn from Syerston crashed whilst on a training flight, after 6 hrs 45 minutes in the air, following a fire in the starboard inner engine during a circuit of Bottesford airfield. The fire seemed to spread towards the cabin. The crash occurred at Staunton, 2½ miles north west of Bottesford and all 7 of the crew were killed. The engine failure was caused by a fractured connecting rod and it was possible that a petrol tank exploded prior to impact.

W/O R/102085 Thomas Herbert Warne age 23 RCAF (Pilot) is buried in Newark-upon-Trent Cemetery, Sgt 576765 George Arthur Hitchon age 19 (F/Eng) buried in Padiham Churchyard, Sgt 1174086 Robert John Preece age 22 RAFVR buried Wembdon Churchyard, Sgt 1119116 Thomas Raine Newton age 21 (W.Op/Air Gnr) RAFVR buried Brandon and Byshottles Cemetery, Sgt 975551 James Milton Whitehead age 22 (W.Op./Air Gnr) RAFVR, age 22 buried Cambusnethan Cemetery, Sgt 950159 Edward John Loverock age 21 RAFVR buried Matlock Churchyard, Sgt 1276786 John Coaker age 22 RAFVR buried Leusdeon Churchyard Devon.

The Farndon Archaeological Research Institute researched the crash and crash site and many pieces of debris were found.

Sgt Hitchon is mentioned on the 41st Roll of Honour of Old Haltonians. The RAF Halton Apprentice Scheme was introduced in 1920 by Lord Trenchard, the father of the RAF. Over 40,000 young boys were trained at RAF Halton as skilled technicians and administrators. The school closed in 1993.

A memorial with a Lancaster propeller blade commemorating the crew stands near St Mary's church at Staunton (see memorials).

FRIDAY 19th FEBRUARY 1943

2122 hrs — **Training**

Lancaster I R5850 of 1661 HCU from Winthorpe took off on dual pilot practicing 3 and 4 engine overshoots. Coming in to land the aircraft failed to stop and overshot the runway, crashed through telephone wires and hedges after an engine lost power, hit a telegraph pole and then caught fire and burnt out. F/S R/133968 Melvin Samuel Kahn age 22 (Rear Gnr) from Toronto was the only casualty and he is buried in Wilford Hill (Jewish) Cemetery, Nottingham. He enlisted in August 1941 and received his wings at Fingal, Canada.

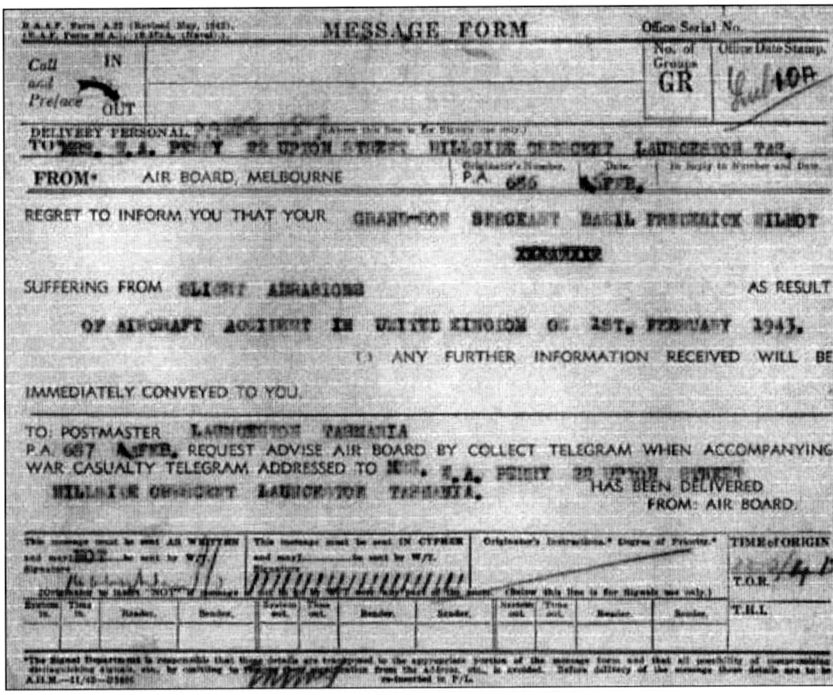
MESSAGE FORM

Office Serial No.

Call and Preface IN OUT

No. of Groups GR

Office Date Stamp

DELIVERY PERSONAL

TO MRS. E.A. PERRY 22 UPTON STREET HILLSIDE CRESCENT LAUNCESTON TAS.

FROM: AIR BOARD, MELBOURNE

Originator's Number P.A. 686 Date 4 FEB.

REGRET TO INFORM YOU THAT YOUR GRANDSON SERGEANT BASIL FREDERICK WILMOT XXXXXXX

SUFFERING FROM SLIGHT ABRASIONS AS RESULT OF AIRCRAFT ACCIDENT IN UNITED KINGDOM ON 1ST, FEBRUARY 1943.

ANY FURTHER INFORMATION RECEIVED WILL BE IMMEDIATELY CONVEYED TO YOU.

TO: POSTMASTER LAUNCESTON TASMANIA

P.A. 687 4 FEB. REQUEST ADVISE AIR BOARD BY COLLECT TELEGRAM WHEN ACCOMPANYING WAR CASUALTY TELEGRAM ADDRESSED TO MRS. E.A. PERRY 22 UPTON STREET HILLSIDE CRESCENT LAUNCESTON TASMANIA. HAS BEEN DELIVERED

FROM: AIR BOARD.

This message must be sent AS WRITTEN and may NOT be sent by W/T.

This message must be sent IN CYPHER

Originator's Instructions. Degree of Priority.

TIME of ORIGIN

T.O.R.

T.H.I.

Above: **Message sent to the grandmother of Sgt Wilmot**

Below: **Initial crash report**

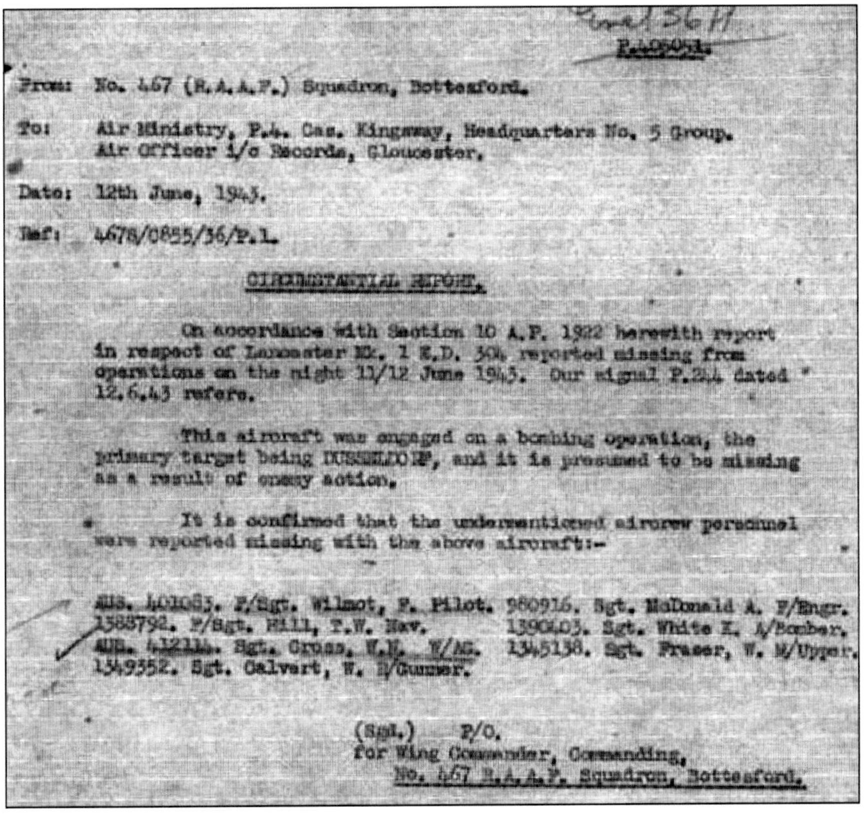
P.408081.

From: No. 467 (R.A.A.F.) Squadron, Bottesford.

To: Air Ministry, P.4. Cas. Kingsway, Headquarters No. 5 Group.
Air Officer i/c Records, Gloucester.

Date: 12th June, 1943.

Ref: 467S/C855/36/P.L.

CIRCUMSTANTIAL REPORT.

On accordance with Section 10 A.P. 1922 herewith report in respect of Lancaster Mk. 1 E.D. 304 reported missing from operations on the night 11/12 June 1943. Our signal P.244 dated 12.6.43 refers.

This aircraft was engaged on a bombing operation, the primary target being DUSSELDORF, and it is presumed to be missing as a result of enemy action.

It is confirmed that the undermentioned aircrew personnel were reported missing with the above aircraft:-

AUS. 401083. F/Sgt. Wilmot, F. Pilot. 980916. Sgt. McDonald A. F/Engr.
1388792. F/Sgt. Hill, T.W. Nav. 1390403. Sgt. White E. A/Bomber.
AUS. 412114. Sgt. Cross, W.N. W/AG. 1345138. Sgt. Fraser, W. M/Upper.
1349352. Sgt. Calvert, W. R/Gunner.

(Sgd.) P/O.
for Wing Commander, Commanding,
No. 467 R.A.A.F. Squadron, Bottesford.

F/O 122056 G N Hartley (Instructor Pilot) was injured. The rest of the crew were Sgt 401083 B F Wilmot (2nd Pilot) also injured SSQ at Swinderby, Sgt 980916 Arthur Macdonald RAFVR, Sgt 1388792 Thomas William Hill (Nav) RAAF and P/O 108779 Pietsch (W/Op).

Sgt Wilmot RAAF, and Sgt Macdonald (F/Eng), Sgt Hill, P/O Pietsch were also involved in an accident on 1st February. See previous crash ref.

F/S Wilmot, Sgt Macdonald and Sgt Hill subsequently lost their lives on 11th June 1943 when they took off in Lancaster ED304 of 467 Sqn from Bottesford for a raid on Dusseldorf and were lost without trace. They are commemorated on the Runnymede Memorial.

Sgt Wilmot

F/O J M Sullivan and Sgt Wilmot. Courtesy of V Holyoak

SUNDAY 21st FEBRUARY 1943

1610 hrs — Ferrying

Master III DL748 of 16 (P)SFTS was being ferried from Newton to Tollerton when the engine cut at 500 feet. The aircraft force landed with undercarriage retracted, hit a ditch and broke in two at Shelford. The pilot, F/S P780653 B Pieslak PAF, was not injured.

THURSDAY 25th FEBRUARY 1943

1500 hrs — Ground

Manchester I L7400 of 1654CU from Wigsley had a practice bomb explode in the bomb bay prior to take off. There were no injuries, however the pilot Sgt 416114 John Lawrence Hendry, RNZAF was killed on 31st August when he took off from Syerston as the pilot of Lancaster ED409 of 106 Sqn for a raid on Berlin. His aircraft was shot down by a night fighter and crashed near Lingen. 3 other crew members died and 3 were taken prisoner.

FRIDAY 26th FEBRUARY 1943

1020 hrs — Training

Oxford II T1048 of 14 (P)AFU from Ossington swung on take-off when on a solo instructional flight and crashed into a wood outside the windward boundary. The pilot was Sgt 413012 E A McGregor RAAF. There was one injury.

—

A Manchester aircraft of 207 Sqn from Bottesford was returning from operations, probably a raid on Nurnberg, when it was intercepted by a night fighter and the mid-upper turret was destroyed and the gunner killed by bullet wounds and the explosion of a shell in his lap. The gunner, Sgt 1053096 Thomas Bows age 31 RAFVR, is buried in Bramley (St Peter) Churchyard. The pilot was F/O Mappin.

MONDAY 1st MARCH 1943

1100 hrs Training

Master III W8533 of 16 (P)SFTS had an engine failure in flight and force landed with undercarriage retracted near Farnsfield. Metal deposits were found in the oil pressure filter. The pilots were P/O P/2080 Zakszewski PAF and F/O P/1758 J Kaminski PAF.

2345 hrs Training

Wellington IV Z1469 of 18 OTU from Finningley overshot landing and the pilot, P/O P/1916 S Tomicki PAF, swung the aircraft and struck a post.

TUESDAY 2nd MARCH 1943

0315 hrs Op; Berlin

Lancaster I W4242 of 106 Sqn from Wymeswold had just returned from Operations after being in the air for 8 hrs 45 minutes, and was taxiing round the perimeter track when it struck Lancaster R5677which had become bogged down just off the perimeter track. R5677 had not been marked with a red light and the R/T on W4242 had failed so no warning got through to the pilot Sgt 1334122 J Munro.

1500 hrs Training

Manchester I L7277 of 1654 HCU from Wigsley was on a dual training flight when on a feathering demonstration to the trainee pilot, the port propeller would not un-feather. The aircraft undershot the aerodrome at Wigsley, attempted a belly landing but struck a tree at North Scarle, and caught fire with one fatality.

F/L 66031 Philip John Stone DFC (Pilot), Sgt 1386402 R F Lee, Sgt 573620 Matthew William Hanley RAF, Sgt W C Brearley, Sgt M Y Smith and Sgt F A John were all injured. Sgt 924868 Patrick (Pat) Brook RAFVR age 27 was killed and is buried in Thornley (St Helen) Churchyard.

Following this incident feathering practice was discontinued on this type of aircraft. F/L Stone DFC was subsequently killed on 13th June at the age of 25 years flying with 50 Sqn whilst on a raid on Bochum. Piloting Lancaster ED828 VN-S, he took off from Skellingthorpe at 2312 hours and was shot down by a night fighter and crashed at Fleringen in Holland. He rests with 4 of his crew in Tubbergen Roman Catholic Cemetery. 2 crew members were taken prisoner.

F/S Hanley was killed in a flying accident on 22nd November 1944 and is buried in Epson Cemetery. He was the flight engineer aboard Stirling III EF201 of 1660 HCU from Swinderby which took off for a cross-country conversion training exercise, the port outer engine failed and the aircraft crashed out of control near Northleach airfield, Gloucestershire.

F/L Stone was awarded the DFC on 6th November 1942 when serving with 50 Sqn. The citation read: 'For gallantry and devotion to duty in the execution of air operation.'

1660 hrs

Halifax DG338 of 1660 HCU starboard wheel fully retracted on landing at Swinderby. There were no injuries to the crew. The pilot was Sgt Saxton.

WEDNESDAY 3rd MARCH 1943

1645 hrs — Training

Master III W8817 of 16 (P)SFTS from Tollerton had been in the air for 15 minutes on a solo training flight when the pilot, LAC P/794927 J Kuloszczykj PAF, while carrying out a gliding approach to land, did not open the throttle in time to prevent a crash on the aerodrome. He escaped unhurt.

THURSDAY 4th MARCH 1943

2351 hrs — Training

Lancaster I R5503 of 1660 HCU from Swinderby was on conversion training when it overshot the runway damaged the undercarriage and crashed at Swinderby. The long runway was not in use in conditions of no wind due to an overlap with the Winthorpe circuit. The pilot was P/O J/12811 Duncan McNaught Moodie DFC RCAF.

D M Moodie, by now a F/L, was killed on 18th October 1943, whilst piloting Lancaster JB220 OF-O from Bourn on a raid on Hannover. He took off at 1738 hrs carrying 4 x TI, 1 x 4000 lb and 6 x 1000 lb bombs and his aircraft crashed at Erichshagen near Neinburg. He is buried in Becklingen War Cemetery.

F/L Moodie's DFC was presented to his next of kin on 14th May 1946. The citation read: 'This pilot is captain of a most reliable and capable crew and has taken part in all the recent major operations against Germany including three on Berlin and four on Hamburg. In July 1943, when attacking Hamburg, his aircraft was illuminated by searchlights and sustained damage from heavy anti-aircraft fire which he succeeded in evading. Despite this he completed the attack and made a safe return to base.'

FRIDAY 5th MARCH 1943

0307 hrs — Op; Minelaying

Lancaster III ED549 HW-S of 100 Sqn from Waltham took off at 1832 hrs for a minelaying operation in the area of St Nazaire and crashed on return while trying to land at Langar airfield having been diverted twice from other airfields. The aircraft attempted to land on the 3rd circuit of the aerodrome in poor visibilty but the airspeed dropped and the aircraft sank into the ground in a semi-stalled condition at Plungar. The difficulties for the pilot were aggravated by failure of the port inner engine and failure in communication between the aircraft and the ground.

F/S 99993 Gerald Russell Avey RCAF (Pilot), buried Long Bennington (St Swithin) Churchyard, Sgt 1176108 Benjamin Thomas Hallett, age 23 RAFVR (F/Eng) buried Portsmouth Cemetery, Sgt 1535230 Alan Havelock Spence age 32 RAFVR (Nav) buried North Sunderland Cemetery, Sgt 1383404 Grey Doyle Cumberbatch age 21 RAFVR (Air Bomber) who came from Barbados is buried in Long Bennington (St Swithin) Churchyard, Sgt 1024294 John Robinson age 34 (W.Op/Rear Gnr) buried Thornton-le Fylde Churchyard, F/S R/100254 Rene Rodger Landry age 23 RCAF (Air Gnr) buried Long Bennington (St Swithin) Churchyard.

Sgt D S Davies (Rear Gnr) was injured. This was the first mission by 100 Sqn after they had received Lancasters

The photograph on the opposite page shows the Barbados Second Contingent of personnel who served during the war and were all recruited for the RAF and left Barbados in November 1940. The twelve men selected includes Errol W Barrow who became Barbados' first Prime Minister (1966-1976).

In 2008 the Barbados Postal Service issued a set of stamps commemorating their men who served in the Royal Air Force during World War Two, one of which was a copy of the above photograph.

(NB. It is interesting to note that in 1940 no so-called 'men of colour' could have joined the RAF, but by the end of the war in 1945 there were between 300 and 500 aircrew from the Caribbean out of a total of 6,000 volunteers who served during WWII. About 70 were commissioned and 103 received decorations.)

Sgt Cumberbatch is 1st on left

Grave of Sgt Cumberbatch

SATURDAY 6th MARCH 1943

1815 hrs — Training

Tiger Moth II T5690 of 25 (P)EFTS from Hucknall struck a tree and crashed 500 yards from the aerodrome during approach when practicing precautionary landings. The pilot, LAC P704065 A Chmielowiec PAF, was not injured but was killed on 13th July 1944 as a crew member of Wellington Z1696 of 18 OTU. The aircraft took off from Finningley for night training and crashed near the airfield with all crew buried in Newark-upon-Trent Cemetery.

THURSDAY 11th MARCH 1943

1235 hrs — Training

Master III W8446 of 16 (P)SFTS from Tollerton was landing off a glide, bounced, and the pilot, LAC P/794905 A Galwin PAF, opened the throttle stalled and crashed on the airfield without injury.

FRIDAY 12th MARCH 1943

1745 hrs — Training

Lancaster I R5556 of 1661 HCU from Winthorpe had a major overall at RAF Swinderby on 12th January where the port outer engine was changed. The aircraft took off from Swinderby for a test flight back to base and after 10 minutes flames were seen to be coming from the port outer engine which enveloped the wing which then broke away from the aircraft. The aircraft crashed at Cromwell, 3 miles north north west of Newark, near the river Trent killing all the crew of 9 which included two maintenance personnel. Their bodies were taken to the mortuary at RAF Swinderby.

F/L 411861 James Cowan (Pilot Instructor) age 30 DFC RNZAF, Sgt 1315656 Anthony Richard Burgess (Pilot), age 21 RAFVR, F/S R/115553 Albert Edward Hannay (Nav) age 24 RCAF all buried in Newark-upon-Trent Cemetery, Sgt 577026 Douglas William Lovelady (F/Eng) age 19 RAF buried Bootle Cemetery, who is listed on the 40th entry RAF Halton Aircraft Apprentices Roll of Honour, Sgt 1576096 Eric Hall age 22 RAFVR Bomb Aimer cremated at Birmingham Municipal Crematorium, F/S 1100855 Howard Victor Adams age 22 RAFVR (W.Op/ Air Gnr) buried Liverpool (Allerton) Cemetery, Sgt 900321 Stanley Charles Johnson

age 22 RAFVR (Air Gnr) buried Tottenham and Wood Green Cemetery, Sgt 1600432 Albert Edward Clark age 19 RAFVR buried Hammersmith New Cemetery, LAC 1160792 Kenneth Thomas Robson age 21 RAFVR buried Shepshed Cemetery, AC1 1462732 Leonard James Rogers age 21 RAFVR buried Pitsea Old (St Michael) Cemetery.
The cause of the crash was the siezure of No.6 big end assembly due to rag being found in the engine and oil pressure system.

F/L Cowan had logged a total of 727 flying hours and undertaken 26 operations while serving with 9 Sqn prior to his posting to the HCU as an instructor. He was also the pilot of Wellington Z1575 of 9 Sqn which took off from Honington 6th June 1942 for a raid on Emden and crashed almost immediately, caught fire and burnt out.

F/S Hannay came from McGee, Saskatchewan, and Hannay Bay, in the area, was named after him. Also Hannay Island was named after his brother Gunner Hugh Halbert Hannay who died in 1951 from wounds 7 years after receiving them at Caen.

F/L Cowan

Lancaster R5556. Courtesy of M Gladwin

SATURDAY 13th MARCH 1943

0330 hrs — Training

Oxford I V4154 of 14 (P) AFU from Ossington took off at 0315 hrs on a solo night flight when it dived vertically into the ground near Besthorpe, 5-6 miles from the airfield.
The cause was not known.

The Canadian pilot W/O R/90442 Stuart William Gunn RCAF age 27, was killed and is buried in Thurlby Churchyard. His body was taken to RAF Swinderby by ambulance. He enlisted on 15th March 1941, trained at No.3 EFTS, and won his Pilot's Wings at No.6 SFTS. He went overseas in January 1942 and flew in South Africa and Egypt before returning to England.

WEDNESDAY 17th MARCH 1943

1610 hrs — Training

Lancaster I ED409 ZN-B of 106 Sqn from Syerston landed normally and when running along the runway the tail oleo leg spun completely round then collapsed jamming all the controls. The pilot was Sgt 983743 N Glaholm.

Night — Training

Lancaster I R7576 of 1661 CU from Winthorpe was returning from dual pilot night landing training when the aircraft swung to port causing a tyre to burst and the undercarriage to collapse. The instructor pilot was P/O 125432 John Seymour Runnacles RAFVR and the pupil Sgt Sharples.

John Runnacles, now a F/L, returned to operations with 97 Sqn and was killed on 11th November 1944, age 31. He was the pilot of Lancaster PB450 OF-D which left Coningsby for a training run over France and was lost without trace. All the crew are commemorated on the Runnymede Memorial.

The 97 Sqn ORB stated: 'No news whatsoever has been heard of the missing crews (2) since they left base for the training which was carried out over the continent. F/L Runnacles was one of our most promising pilots together with his crew.'

THURSDAY 18th MARCH 1943

1645 hrs — Training

Tiger Moth II T7293 of 25 (P)EFTS from Hucknall had engine failure at 800 feet in the circuit immediately after take off. The pilot, LAC P/703220 J Osostoniez PAF, made a turn of 180 degrees and decided to land the aircraft cross wind. Due to over crowding on the airfield he was compelled to make the final turn at low altitude and when touching down a strut on the right of the aircraft bent. He was not injured. The con rod on No.3 cylinder had failed at the crank.

SUNDAY 21st MARCH 1943

2258 hrs — Training

Lancaster I R5895 of 1660 CU from Swinderby bounced slightly on landing and the instructor took over, eased the bounce with the engines but on closing the throttle the starboard outer engine did not respond and kept running causing a swing. The undercarriage collapsed when the aeroplane struck a bank. The instructor pilot was F/L 89597 S J Beard and the pupil Sgt 407853 J H Whiting RAAF who was also involved in an incident on 29th March.

MONDAY 22nd MARCH 1943

2158 hrs — Training

Lancaster I R5624 of 1661 HCU from Winthorpe port tyre burst on landing causing the aircraft to swing and the undercarriage to collapse. There were no injuries to the crew.

The pilot, P/O 1254721 Philip Gerard Herrin RAFVR, was killed 3 months later on 23rd June flying with 207 Sqn, age 32. He was the pilot of Lancaster ED692 which took off from Langar for a raid on Mulheim and crashed near Koln. He has no known grave and is commemorated on the Runnymede memorial.

Halifax DG315 of 1660 HCU landed at Swinderby when the Flight Engineer selected 'undercarriage' instead of 'flaps'. No injuries. Pilot P/O Mason.

Lancaster R5895 of 1660 HCU from Swinderby undercarriage collapsed on landing. Pilot F/L Reard, no injuries.

WEDNESDAY 24th MARCH 1943

1045 hrs — Training

Halifax V DG362 of 1660 HCU from Swinderby took off on conversion training in a cross wind. The pilot applied full right rudder to correct a swing and when he attempted to ease off, suddenly the controls became locked in the full right position and the aircraft came to a halt with both undercarriage legs ripped away. The crew were P/O 111552 James Leslie Cooper DFC and F/S 1076962 W J Wilkinson.

P/O Cooper was awarded the DFC on 12th January 1943 whilst a member of 106 Sqn.

1525 hrs — Training

Manchester I 7453 of 1661 HCU from Winthorpe landed with undercarriage retracted after the port engine caught fire shortly after take off necessitating an immediate landing. The 2nd pilot failed to lower the wheels in time and the aircraft belly landed at Swinderby. The fire was attributable to the burning of the exhaust manifold of 'A' block. The pilot was S/L 61011 R G W Oakley and 2nd pilot Sgt 1388306 George Stanley Cole, who was injured.

Sgt Cole was subsequently killed when piloting Lancaster ED432 of 49 Sqn from Fiskerton on a raid on Oberhausen on his crews' 8th operation. An all Lancaster force of 197 guided by 6 Mosquitoes made a successful attack and despite the target being covered by cloud, accurate sky-marking enabled the bombers to do considerable damage. Twelve Lancasters left Fiskerton, one returned early and the remaining 11 crews found themselves engaged in a savage battle from both flak and fighters which resulted in the loss of 17 aircraft. Sgt Cole and crew were caught by a night fighter and the aircraft crashed at Castle Doorweth, near Arnhem, Holland, on 15th June. Two of the crew survived and became POWs and Sgt Cole and the rest of the crew were buried in Renkum (Oosterbeek) General Cemetery.

Sgt Cole.
Courtesy Malcolm Brooke 49 Sqn

In the intervening years what was not known was that the graves of the crew members had been constantly tended by Geertruida Oosterhaar who was awarded the MBE in 1974. When a schoolgirl Geertruida remembers very well the night the aircraft crashed near her home. 49 Squadron held their annual reunion at Woodhall Spa in 1993 and Geertruida Oosterhaar was a very special 'guest of honour'. The squadron veterans took that opportunity to show Geertruida their deeply felt appreciation for the devotion she has shown over the years to some of their fallen comrades.

SATURDAY 27th MARCH 1943

2230 hrs — Training

Lancaster I W4132 of 1661 CU from Winthorpe had the undercarriage retracted during take off owing to violent vibrations the reasons for which were not definitely established but thought to be a faulty undercarriage. The pilots were S/L 116149 Mackenzie and Sgt 1287996 Sharples.

MONDAY 29th MARCH 1943

0121 hrs — Taxiing

Lancaster I W4887 of 1661 CU from Swinderby landed and the tail wheel juddered and then while taxiing the tail box beam collapsed. There were no injuries to the crew. The pilot F/S 407853 J H Whiting RAAF was also involved in an incident on 21st March.

2200 hrs — Training

Wellington IC DV804 of 18 OTU from Finningley took off at 2145 hrs piloted by Sgt P/784772 Michel Zarebowicz PAF, with Sgt P/794422 Stanislaw I Grabarczyk PAF as Wireless Operator, for the pilot to practice his first solo landings. Sgt Zarebowicz asked for, secured and acknowledged permission to land, but crashed on approach to Finningley 3½ miles from the aerodrome, at Upperthorpe Village with the loss of both personnel aboard. Although the aircraft may have stalled, the cause of the accident was unknown. Both crew members are buried in Newark-upon-Trent Cemetery with Sgt Grabarczyk's funeral taking place at 1530 hrs on 2nd April. Crash location: Cassini grid OS 1940 sht 38 22420?; OS 1992 sht 112 757003.

TUESDAY 30th MARCH 1943

Night | Training

Lancaster I R5504 of 1660 CU from Swinderby swung on landing and the undercarriage collapsed. There were no injuries.

The pilot Sgt 1347713 Adam Anderson RAFVR age 20 was killed only 22 days later on 21st April flying with 49 Sqn on only his 2nd operation. He was the pilot of Lancaster III ED620 from Fiskerton forming part of a mixed force of 339 Bombers on a raid on Stettin. 100 acres of the town were destroyed for the loss of 13 Lancasters, 7 Halifaxes and one Stirling but by 0615 hrs all of 49 Squadron Lancasters had returned with the exception of Sgt Anderson and his crew. Light flak had set fire to the incendiaries and his Lancaster began to burn furiously and he crash landed the aircraft, with the bombs still on board, near Ringkobing. Three crew members were killed, three taken prisoner and Sgt Anderson died later in hospital. He is buried in Lemvig Cemetery.

Remains of Lancaster III ED620. Courtesy of www.49squadron.co.uk

WEDNESDAY 31st MARCH 1943

1135 hrs | Training

SpitfireV AR431 of 317 Sqn from Kirton-in-Lindsey took part in one of 11 sorties programmed for the squadron this day due to limited flying. The sorties included formation flying, cine camera gun and low flying. During the exercises the pilot of AR431 P/O P/1951Kazimierz Maksymilian Kierski PAF was conducting a low flying and navigation exercise and when flying low over a field, after having missed the target, turned his aircraft to the left, hitting the ground with his port wing. The aircraft crashed and caught fire near Finningley on the Haxey to Gainsborough road, near the Misson range. He is buried in Northwood Cemetery.

THURSDAY 1st APRIL 1943

Cpl 1282543 Punter was involved in an accident at Hucknall aerodrome. A detonator exploded at a distance of only 2 yards and he received wounds to his abdomen and was transferred to the City hospital.

WEDNESDAY 7th APRIL 1943

1145 hrs | Stationary

Oxford II N6403 of 14 (P)AFU from Ossington was picketed on hard standing by means of concrete blocks. A gale had been blowing for approximately 48 hours when the wind increased suddenly with gusts of at least 70mph. The aircraft together with the blocks was lifted from the ground, blown backwards into an air raid shelter. The sudden increase in the wind velocity prevented sufficient extra men reaching the dispersal area in time to prevent the damage.

THURSDAY 8th APRIL 1943

1055 hrs Training

Master III DL747 of 16 (P)SFTS from Newton landed with undercarriage retracted due to forgetfulness by the pilot LAC P/794934 T Kuniewski PAF.

2100 hrs Op; Duisberg

Lancaster III ED623 EM-N of 207 Sqn from Langar swung on take off and over correction made the starboard undercarriage collapse after the pilot, W/C 26242 Thomas Alfred Boyd Parselle, Officer Commanding of 207 Sqn, decided to give up the attempt to take off. The aircraft slewed off the runway in a shower of sparks, the bomb doors were crushed and the 4000lb bomb dug a furrow in the grass but did not explode. There were no injuries.

Because of this incident both Lancaster I ED692 W-Willie and Lancaster III ED554 Q-Queenie were prevented from taking off for the raid on Duisberg.

W/C Parselle was taken Prisoner on 26th May. He was the pilot of Lancaster W5001 EM-J of 207 Sqn which took off from Langar for a raid on Dusseldorf and was shot down by a night-fighter and crashed near Nijmegen. After the war he had a distinguished career in the RAF rising to the rank of Air Vice Marshall.

Lancaster W5001 EM-J

Stationary

Manchester I L7297 of 1661 HCU from Winthorpe was parked when it was damaged by Manchester R5769 which was blown back in a gale. L7297 was also involved in an incident on 19th May.

SATURDAY 10th APRIL 1943

0125 hrs Training

Lancaster III ED823 of 1661 HCU from Winthorpe crashed off School Lane at Halam with the loss of all crew members. The aircraft crashed 8 miles from the airfield and in line of take-off. The Air Investigation Branch found it impossible to ascertain the reason for the crash owing to lack of evidence.

F/O 127064 Edward Lambert RAFVR age 34 (Nav) is buried in Fleetwood Borough Cemetery, F/S 411919 Leonard Wentworth Lean RAAF pilot age 22 buried Newark-upon-Trent Cemetery, Sgt 1087359 Henry Utley Oxspring RAFVR age 27 buried Hoyland Nether

Cemetery Yorkshire, F/S R/115799 Raymond David Lewis RCAF (Air Gnr) age 22 buried Newark-upon-Trent Cemetery, Sgt 1231524 William George Stephenson RAFVR age 21 buried Leicester (Gilroes) Cemetery, Sgt 14855 Frank Dunkin age 21 RAAF, buried Newark-upon-Trent Cemetery, Sgt 1345277 William Shearer Lindsay Graham age 20 RAFVR (W.Op/Air Gnr) interred Glasgow Western Necropolis.

The funeral of F/S Lean

2332 hrs — Training

Lancaster I R5848 of 1660 HCU from Swinderby took off for dual pilot conversion training, a swing developed and before it could be checked the aircraft swerved from the runway and lost its undercarriage. The pilot instructor and pilot were F/L 404890 Roy R O Calvert RNZAF and F/O 65071 W N Lewis. Sgt Corrie received a puncture wound to his right leg.

SUNDAY 11th APRIL 1943

1850 hrs — Training

Manchester I R5841 of 1660 HCU from Swinderby was on a training flight when the Swinderby Station Medical Officer saw the starboard engine of the aircraft catch fire in mid-air and followed it in his car until it crashed in flames at Bassingham Green. With the assistance of a civilian who had already arrived at the crash scene, the rear gunner Sgt 980759 Brookes was rescued. He was suffering from multiple injuries, burns and shock but was conscious. The captain F/L Whitwell and Sgt Davies were killed. 3 of the crew Sgt H M Scott, Sgt W J Robinson and Sgt B R Traves escaped with minor burns and bruises.

Unfortunately Sgt 908789 Arthur James Brooks age 30 RAFVR (Air Gnr) died of his injuries in Rauceby RAF Hospital at 2330 hrs and is buried City of London Cemetery.

It was considered that F/L 44540 John Martindale Whitwell RAF AFM age 36 (Pilot Flying Instructor) from Grantham and buried in Grantham Cemetery, by his expert airmanship had saved three lives. The fire was established as in the vicinity of the B block in the starboard engine, possibly due to hydraulic pipe failure. Sgt 1206039 Robert Davies age 28 RAFVR (F/Eng) is buried in Kinson (St Andrew) Churchyard.

MONDAY 12th APRIL 1943

1430 hrs — Ground

Oxford II N4755 of 14 (P)AFU from Ossington engine was being turned over when AC1 1396627 S J Torrison walked under the airscrew and was struck on the head and injured.

TUESDAY 13th APRIL 1943

1335 hrs — Training

Blenheim IV V6510 of 13 OTU landed on Hucknall airfield with undercarriage retracted after failure of the port engine. The pilot had insufficient time to lower the undercarriage fully with the hand pump. The engine had been serviced at Snaith for engine revs dropping and then continued its flight. The crew, Sgt 1320606 A E Fotherby, Sgt A Wallwork and Sgt E Price were unhurt.

THURSDAY 15th APRIL 1943

G/C A C Evans-Evans took command of Swinderby RAF Station. G/C Evans-Evans was the Station Commander of Coningsby when he was killed on 21st February 1945 age 43 on operations. He was the pilot of Lancaster NE165 OL-Y of 83 Sqn (a Pathfinder Force Squadron) which took off from Coningsby at 1707 hrs to mark the Mittelland Canal. The aircraft was shot down by a night fighter and crashed in Holland. He was also involved in another incident when with 115 Sqn returning from a raid on Bremen on 12th February 1941. He was the pilot of Wellington R3238 KO-H which was abandoned in Essex probably due to fuel shortage.

1345 hrs

Beaufighter JL120 of 232 Sqn from Lyneham piloted by Sgt Stokes crashed on landing at Bircotes.

1850 hrs — Training

Manchester I L7294 of 1654 HCU from Wigsley took off on a training flight and after 2 hours in the air, an engine misfired and caught fire and the pilot headed for base. As the aircraft reached the runway it stalled, crashed and burnt out. The crew of 7 were all injured: Sgt J/17626 William Hedley Eager RCAF, Sgt T D Viggers, Sgt 157326 Hubert Thomas Petts RAFVR, Sgt T H James, Sgt 160519 Frederick Richard Stone RAFVR, Sgt G E Hunnington and Sgt A Jones. Three of this crew were subsequently killed.

Sgt Eager with 1661 HCU on 16th December 1943 (see entry for 16th December 1943). H T Petts (Nav) now with the award of the DFC and promoted to F/L, was killed flying with 463 Sqn. He was a member of the crew of Lancaster LL892 on a raid on Braunschweig which crashed at Nieuwolda in the Dutch province of Delfzjjl on 23rd April 1944. He is buried Nieuwolda General Cemetery.

F R Stone, now a F/O, was killed on 22nd June 1944 flying in Lancaster ND531 of 630 Sqn on a raid on Wesmeling when his aircraft was lost without trace. He is commemorated on the Runnymede memorial.

Sgt Petts was awarded the DFC on 10th December 1943 when a member of 61 Sqn.

FRIDAY 16th APRIL 1943

0040 hrs — Ops; Gardening

Lancaster III ED649 ZN-X of 106 Sqn from Syerston when returning from operations overshot landing, ground looped and was unable to go around again due to the pilot having lowered the flaps. The pilot was P/O J/20017 E L Rosner RCAF. This aircraft went missing on a raid on Oberhausen on 15th June.

SUNDAY 18th APRIL 1943

0546 hrs — Ground

Oxford I MP407 of 14 (P)AFU from Ossington was hit by Oxford MP408 while awaiting take-off on the flare path. Neither pilot was to blame as the ground controller had signalled MP407 onto the flare path and gave MP408 permission to land. The crew were Sgt 1146872 A N Hadley and Sgt R89928 W L Miller RCAF who was slightly injured.

Oxford I MP408 of 14 (P)AFU from Ossington hit Oxford MP407 on the flare path when coming into land. The pilot P/O J20689 R G Rivers was injured.

MONDAY 19th APRIL 1943

0630 hrs — Ops; La Spezia

Lancaster I W4198 QR-H of 61 Sqn from Balderton was returning from operations after a 9 hour 45 minute flight when it made a heavy landing and the undercarriage collapsed. The weather conditions were bad and the flight had been long. The pilot was F/L 77777 Eric Arthur Benjamin. The undercarriage collapsed on this aircraft in a similar incident on 23rd August 1943 at Syerston.

F/L Benjamin DFC and Bar was promoted to W/C but was killed on 20th February 1945 flying with 627 Sqn. He was the pilot of Mosquito KB401-E and the Master Bomber assigned to a raid on Bohlen when his aircraft was hit by flak and crashed in the target area. He is buried in Berlin 1939-1945 War Cemetery. W/C Benjamin was awarded the DFC on 10th September 1943 and a Bar to the DFC on 18th January 1944.

TUESDAY 20th APRIL 1943

1650 hrs — Training

Tiger Moth II T8708 of 25 (P)EFTS from Hucknall struck the ground after a bad landing causing the aircraft to overturn. The pilot was Cpl P/703229 S Waydowicz PAF.

WEDNESDAY 21st APRIL 1943

0600 hrs — Ops

A Lancaster of 106 Sqn from Syerston was returning from operations when Sgt 1269176 R Kelly (MUG) was hit by shrapnel possibly from an attack by fighters or flak. On returning to base he received medical assistance on wounds to his right leg which was fractured and transferred to Rauceby hospital.

THURSDAY 22nd APRIL 1943

0232 hrs — Training

Oxford I BG208 of 14 (P)AFU from Ossington was on night flying dual training during heavy rain, low cloud and bad visibility. The pilot overshot the airfield believing he could follow the lights around the circuit but this proved impossible and the aircraft crashed and struck a telegraph pole whilst he was attempting to locate the outer aerodrome lights. The crash occurred two miles west of Ossington on the Kneesall to Newark road. Both occupants were killed.

F/O 120407 John Hamilton Barnes RAFVR (Flying Instructor) age 26 is buried in Armagh (St Mark) Church of Ireland Churchyard and Sgt R81378 Henry Fred Puder RCAF (Pilot) buried Ollerton Cemetery.

TUESDAY 27th APRIL 1943

0434 hrs — Ops; Duisburg

Lancaster II ED361 EM-R of 207 Sqn from Langar took off for a raid on Duisburg and attacked the target. W/O Rees's report was as follows: attacked at 0229 hrs from a height of 15000 feet, heading 200 degrees, air speed 200mph in moderate visibility. Target identified by markers. Concentration of green TIs in bomb site. Bombs seen to burst, rather scattered at the beginning, later the attack seemed to develop into a concentrated effort. Photo-fire tracks, ground detail, load – 1 x 4000 lb HC and 12 SBCs (8 x 30). SORTIE COMPLETED.

The aircraft then returned to base without incident and on landing the tail wheel tyre burst when it jammed in one position. The crew were: W/O 930246 Kenneth Royston Rees RAFVR

(Pilot), Sgt A/14063 George Tyler age 22 RCAF (F/Eng), Sgt 145353 Patrick Alfred Kingsley Mockford RAFVR (Nav), Sgt 1383884 Thomas Edward Ellingham age 29 RAFVR (Air Bomber), F/O 136345 Leonard Foulds age 23 RAFVR (W.Op/Air Gnr), Sgt 1578147 Stanley William Cowham age 20 RAFVR (Air Gnr) and Sgt 1370576 Alexander Wilson Cochrane age 20 RAFVR (Air Gnr). This same crew were all killed 2 days later. They were the crew of Lancaster W4945 EM-Z of 207 Sqn which took off from Langar at 2055 hrs for a Gardening operation off the coast of Denmark, in an area codenamed 'Daffodil'. On the return flight W4945 passed over the Oddesund bridge from where 3.Batterie Flak Abt.742 opened fire on the Lancaster. It was hit and W/O Rees tried to bellyland the aircraft which ended up in the water 100 metres off Remmerstrand at 0129 hrs. The aircraft broke into three parts and a fire erupted killing all the crew who are buried in Lemvig Cemetery.

The remains of Lancaster W4945. Courtesy of Soren C Flensted

WEDNESDAY 28th APRIL 1943

1058 hrs — Training

Master III DL778 of 16 (P)SFTS from Tollerton flew into the ground on take-off when the pilot, who was on solo circuits and landings, lost control and a wing hit the ground. The pilot, LAC P/703817 W Chorabik PAF, was injured.

THURSDAY 29th APRIL 1943

1240 hrs — Training

Oxford I N1190 of 14 (P)AFU from Ossington engine cut and height was lost on attempted overshoot and the aircraft crashed ¼ mile north west of Ossington, on the Kneesall road. The pilot, Sgt R/132079 O E Sauer RCAF, who was on solo training, was found lying on the ground outside the aircraft having got out himself. His condition was not serious with shock and lacerations of the left eye lid and scalp.

1730 hrs — Training

Manchester I L7468 of 1660 HCU from Swinderby took off for dual conversion to aircraft type training. An engine partly failed in circuit and then completely failed when the aircraft turned into the wind and an engine caught fire on landing. The crew were P/O 111552 James Leslie Cooper DFC RAFVR and Sgt 1246721 Terence Peter Murphy RAFVR.

T P Murphy, by now a F/S, was killed on 29th June 1943 when piloting Lancaster ED979 of 619 Sqn on a raid on Koln when he was shot down by a night fighter and crashed near Aalst 5km S of Eindhoven. He is buried in Eindhoven (Woensel) General Cemetery.

Sgt Cooper was also involved in an incident on 24th March 1943.

SATURDAY 1st MAY 1943 — Training

Wellington IC X9638 of 28 OTU from Wymeswold overshot on landing after a flight of 4 hours 45 minutes. The approach was good but rather too fast. The pilot, Sgt 1434323 Peter Francis Snape RAFVR, was suffering from tonsillitis and a high temperature and should not have flown.

Sgt Snape was killed on 30th July when as pilot of Halifax JD252 of 78 Sqn he took off from Breighton for a raid on Hamburg and was presumed lost over the sea. He and his crew are commemorated on the Runnymede Memorial. He was 22 years of age.

WEDNESDAY 5th MAY 1943

1630 hrs — Training

Master III W8730 of 16 (P)SFTS from Tollerton took off for landing practice for the pilot, LAC P/703844 Stanislaw Schmidt PAF, the engine lost power, the aircraft overshot a forced landing, and crashed at Tollerton causing the death of the pilot. The aircraft was damaged beyond repair due to the undercarriage not being lowered. LAC Schmidt's body was taken to Newton mortuary and he was buried in Newark-upon-Trent Cemetery. The cause of the accident was possibly due to engine failure.

1825 hrs — Training

Lancaster I W4775 of 1661 HCU from Winthorpe took off for solo circuits and landings and the undercarriage collapsed when the aircraft swung on landing due to a slight cross wind and caught fire. The pilot was Sgt 658045 R W (Bob) Petty.

Bob Petty, now W/O, was shot down near Berlin on 3rd December 1943 flying with 49 Sqn. He was the pilot of Lancaster JB371 EA-J which was one of 14 Lancasters from 49 Sqn and one of 450+ bombers which was detailed to attack Berlin. Near the target JB371 was attacked by a Me 110 but continued its bombing run and was then attacked by another Me 110. However during the run flak then hit the starboard inner engine which burst into flames and the crew baled out. He and 5 crew members who were on their 17th operation were made POWs in camp L3 Stalag Luft Sagan and Belaria. As a footnote to this incident the rear gunner, Ed Smith, had reported that his guns were un-serviceable but the crew still decided to press on with the mission. Unfortunately the bomb aimer Bill Walke was killed along with Ed Smith, who although seen to bale out has no known grave.

FRIDAY 7th MAY 1943

1100 hrs — Training

Tiger Moth II T6300 of 25 (P)EFTS from Hucknall stalled on approach to land in gusty weather while holding off high and hit a pillbox. The pupil pilot, LAC P/794885 Z Lawski PAF, was injured.

TUESDAY 11th MAY 1943

1325 hrs — Training

Tiger Moth II N6874 of 25 (P)EFTS from Hucknall was on a cross country flight when the engine failed and the pilot, LAC P/704255 M Foczpaniak PAF, crash landed the aircraft in a field at Owthorpe, near Tollerton.

THURSDAY 13th MAY 1943

1315 hrs — Training

Wellington IC DV714 of 28 OTU from Wymeswold took off on a circuits and landings training flight and on landing bounced into the air causing the locking bar on the control column to jam. The aircraft hit the ground again and caught fire.

P/O 145306 Dennis Ray Cooper RAFVR age 22 (W.Op/Air Gnr) died and is buried in Manchester Southern Cemetery. The rest of the crew, F/O 109370 W R Bean pilot, F/O 114994 J F Wright and Sgt W R Coleman were all injured.

FRIDAY 14th MAY 1943

0420 hrs — Training

Wellington IC DV572 of 28 OTU from Wymeswold was on night flying training and landing when the pilot, P/O 138150 Gerard Anthony Beaumont RAFVR, presumed that the flaps were not fully down, overshot and retracted the undercarriage to prevent the aircraft running over the boundary. There were no injuries to the crew.

P/O Beaumont was killed on 26th November flying with 7 Sqn. He was the pilot of Lancaster JB303 MG-F which took off from Oakington for a raid on Berlin and was shot down by a night fighter. He is buried in Hanover War Cemetery.

TUESDAY 18th MAY 1943

1235 hrs — Training

Tiger Moth II T7183 of 25 (P)EFTS from Hucknall side slipped into the ground and burnt out at Longdale Farm, Blidworth, whilst on a training flight. The pilot LAC 780696 F Oprych PAF was injured and unable to be questioned at the time of the accident report.

WEDNESDAY 19th MAY 1943 — Training

Wellington IC R1324 of 28 OTU from Wymeswold had a practice bomb explode in the aircraft during flight and injure Sgt 1344672 S W Gray.

0327 hrs — Ground

Wellington III X3541 of 18 OTU from Finningley had just been parked after a training flight and the pilot was preparing to switch off the engines. Sgt P/704360 Kwenewski PAF, a member of the crew, left the aircraft and walked into the starboard airscrew and was injured.

1430 hrs — Training

Oxford I V4022 of 14 (P)AFU from Ossington took off at 1415 hrs with Sgt R/6597 John Gregory O'Gorman RCAF at the controls, on a solo training flight. Immediately previous to this he had been given dual instruction in the same aircraft by a flight instructor. 15 minutes later his aircraft was seen to spin off a steep turn and crash between North and South Wheatley and burst into flames. Sgt O'Gorman was killed and is buried in Harpswell (St Chad) Churchyard, Lincolnshire.

1215 hrs — Training

Manchester I L7297 of 1661 HCU from Winthorpe was on conversion training when an engine caught fire in flight and an emergency landing was made at Winthorpe, and the undercarriage was retracted to stop overshoot of the aerodrome. The pilot was Sgt 1336560 J Clifford. There were no casualties.

A Manchester of 1661 of HCU at dispersal, Winthorpe. Courtesy of W Taylor

FRIDAY 21st MAY 1943

1500 hrs — Taxiing

Wellington III BK463 of 18 OTU from Finningley was being taxied when the port engine failed and caught fire. The crew were P/O 137443 J Lennox, P/O 133419 Robert Laval Proudfoot RAFVR and Sgt 1339320 D Baker.

P/O Proudfoot was killed on 16th December age 24. He was the pilot of Lancaster JB596 of 100 Sqn which took off from Grimsby for a raid on Berlin and crashed near base on return. He is buried in Orsett (St Giles and All Saints) Churchyard. The cause of the crash was partly due to low cloud, fog, and running short of petrol but a contributing factor was a faulty altimeter. Faulty altimeters on a particular batch of Lancasters was the subject of an investigation at the time. A memorial to this and three other Lancasters of 100 Sqn has been unveiled at Holton-le-Clay.

SATURDAY 22nd MAY 1943

1420 hrs — Training

Oxford II X7249 of 14 (P)AFU from Ossington overshot on landing in a heavy thunderstorm and hit the boundary fence. The pilot was Sgt 1388826 Patrick Keenan RAFVR.

F/S Keenan was subsequently lost on 28th April 1944 whilst piloting Halifax LV783 of 51 Sqn on a raid on Montzen railway yards. He is now buried in Heverlee War Cemetery, Leuvan, Belgium.

1620 hrs — Ground

Wellington IC R1216 of 28 OTU from Wymeswold was being repaired by Cpl 1088349 G L Bond with an engine running when flames from an exhaust caused the aircraft to be burnt out. No-one was considered to be blamed for the incident as defects were found in the carburettors and ignition system.

—

Albert Bell age 39 of Carlton-on-Trent was killed at RAF Station Ossington. Circumstances not known.

TUESDAY 25th MAY 1943

0020 hrs — Training

Master III W8450 of 16 (P)SFTS from Hucknall was on night circuits and landings practice when it is believed that the pilot lost sight of the flare path and hit a tree in a forced landing at Coppice Road, Arnold. The pilot AC1 P/794593 Evzebjusz Mroczek PAF age 24 was killed and is buried in Hucknall Cemetery.

1735 hrs Training

Master III W8769 of 16 (P)SFTS from Tollerton had engine failure during aerobatics and landing practice flight and undershot landing and crashed inside the airfield boundary. The pilot was F/O P/1955 W Czerwinski PAF.

THURSDAY 27th MAY 1943

0145 hrs Training

Master III DL607 of 16 (P)FTS flew into the ground at Landmere Lane, Wilford near Ack Ack battery 181AA2 after a night take-off. There was no evidence of technical failure. The pilot LAC P/794918 T Jasinski PAF was injured.

0840 hrs Training

Master III W8654 of 16 (P)SFTS from Newton landed and the undercarriage collapsed. The pilot was LAC P/794984 J Wiercmowicz (PAF).

FRIDAY 28th MAY 1943

0315 hrs Training

Wellington IC T2741 of 28 OTU from Wymeswold had port engine failure in flight and landed at base wheels up without injuries to the crew.

The pilot, P/O J/17065 James Warren O'Hara RCAF, was killed on 15th August. He was a member of the crew of Lancaster JA850 of 7 Sqn which took off from Oakington for a raid on Milano when it crashed at Sassenay where all the crew are buried in the churchyard. He was 21 years of age. There is a memorial in commemoration to the crew at Sassenay, France.

The memorial at Sassenay

SATURDAY 29th MAY 1943

1150 hrs Training

Master III DL608 of 16 (P)SFTS from Newton landed with undercarriage up due to error by the pilot LAC P/703326 W Wesolowski PAF.

SUNDAY 30th MAY 1943

0130 hrs Training

Master III W8723 of 16 (P)FTS crashed after a night take-off at Thurlbeck Dyke, one mile west of Tollerton. The cause was not known. The pilot Sgt P/703840 A Sroczvnski PAF was injured.

MONDAY 31st MAY 1943

1000 hrs Training

Master III DL568 of 16 (P)SFTS from Newton swung on take-off and the undercarriage was damaged when the aircraft crash landed. The pilots were F/L P/0815 F Skiba PAF and S/L P/0246 P Kaczmarczyk PAF.

MONDAY 7th JUNE 1943

1410 hrs Training

Master III W8793 of 16 (P)FTS during flight the pupil pilot LAC P/708865 S Zajchowski PAF was unable to operate the throttle, which had slipped out of its fixing, and force landed wheels up in a field two miles north of Bleasby. The instructor was F/O P/76787 P Sadowski PAF.

FRIDAY 11th JUNE 1943

1015 hrs

Lancaster I R5849 of RR & AAEE (Rolls-Royce & Aeroplane & Armament Experimental Establishment) from Hucknall took off at 0915 hrs for a one hour engine observation test for the merlin engines fitted to the aircraft. The flight was completed with all appearing to be satisfactory. During the approach to land and on crossing the airfield boundary a witness heard a backfire from the rear port inner engine ans saw flames emerging. The aircraft landed, fuel was turned off and the graviner extinguishers used but the aircraft burnt out after the crew had left the aircraft.

MONDAY 14th JUNE 1943

1715 hrs Training

Tiger Moth II N9348 of 25 (P)EFTS from Hucknall flew into a chimney of a farmhouse on overshoot at Hucknall and crashed. It was considered that the pilot did not open the throttles enough as there was no technical defect. The pilot, LAC P/704335 A Szymanski PAF, was slightly injured.

SUNDAY 20th JUNE 1943

1810 hrs Ferrying

Boston III W8266 of 6 FPP from Ratcliff (Leicester) overshot landing at Tollerton and the undercarriage collapsed after hydraulics failure. The pilot was F/O H S Mather. There was one injury.

TUESDAY 22nd JUNE 1943

1802 hrs Training

Wellington IC X9644 of 28 OTU from Wymeswold landed normally but at the end of the landing run the pupil pilot Sgt 1439610 William Ashurst RAFVR raised the undercarriage in mistake for the flaps.

Sgt Ashurst took off from Kelstern in Lancaster R5702 CF-Y of 625 Sqn on 15th February 1944 at 1725 hrs for a raid on Berlin and was shot down in flames by a night fighter and crashed at Fjelstrup, Denmark. On the outward bound journey, over the Jylland peninsula at 16,000 feet, R5702 was attacked by a German night fighter piloted by Oberleutnant Gerhardt Raht of 4./NJG3 and after having dropped its bomb load while trying to escape the fighter it exploded in the air at low altitude. F/O Harry Proskurniak RCAF survived and was taken prisoner. Sgt Ashurst, age 21, and the rest of the crew are buried in Aabenraa Cemetery.

A memorial dedicated to the crew was unveiled close to the crash site on 28.9.45: 'Here fell 6 English airmen on 15th February 1944. They sacrificed their lives. We won freedom'.

Above: **Memorial to the crew** Right: **Grave of Sgt Ashurst**

Above: **Lancaster R5702 had previously given service to 50 Sqn and this photo shows R5702 sometime before a raid on 9th November 1942 on its 31st operation.** Courtesy of the Roy Calvert Collection via Dave Homewood

Above: **R5702 after the raid, peppered with flak holes and minus its spinners and propellers, and sitting on its belly, the way it landed as its undercarriage was damaged. It was later rebuilt and saw service with 106, 460, and 100 Sqns before joining 625 Sqn and falling victim to a German night fighter on 15th February 1944.**

WEDNESDAY 23rd JUNE 1943

1355 hrs — Training

Oxford I N4566 of 16 (P)FTS engine cut in the air and the aircraft flew into a tree and crashed at Bircotes. The pilot F/S 780875 M Kita PAF was not injured.

FRIDAY 25th JUNE 1943

0135 hrs — Op; Wuppertal

Lancaster III LM326 EM-Z of 207 Sqn from Langar took off on an operation to Wuppertal and was involved in an incident that made the front page of the Daily Express. The aircraft was showered with incendiaries from another aircraft flying above them. Five came through the fuselage and one went into the port petrol tank. Two fell under the mid-upper turret and two fell near the rear turret, one exploding and blowing in the doors to the turret, but no one was injured. Sgt Mitchell and Sgt Toomey dealt with the fires. Sgt Toomey chopped holes into the bomb-bay with an axe allowing the incendiaries to drop through and out of the aircraft when the bomb doors were opened and the aircraft returned to base without any injuries to the crew.

The crew were: Sgt 1316799 Arthur Marcus Fitzgerald age 20 (Pilot), Sgt 1314020 Cyril Herbert Pratt RAFVR age 20 (Nav), Sgt 1503006 Sydney James Mitchell age 38 (F/Eng), Sgt 1313919 William Walter George Addison RAFVR age 21 (W.Op/Air Gnr), Sgt 1383991Henry Albert Toomey RAFVR age 22 (Bomb Aimer), Sgt 1541030 Stephen Preston RAFVR age 20 (MUAG), Sgt 1603332 John Goodwin RAFVR age 20 (Rear Air Gnr).

This crew came together in June 1943 and were posted to 207 Sqn at Langar. They took part in their first operation over Germany on 12th June 1943 to Bochum in Lancaster ED498. Over the next weeks in June they completed 3 further operations over Germany to Oberhausen, Mulheim and Wuppertal. On the operation to Wuppertal the above incident took place. During July they completed 3 further operations, twice to Cologne and once on a 9 hour operation to Turin in 2 different Lancasters.

During August the crew took part in further operations to Mannheim, Nurnberg, Milan, Peenemunde and Berlin all in Lancasters, and bizarrely were involved in a similar incident to the one above on one of these operations on 16th August. On the night of 23/24th August they took another Lancaster, ED627, on an operation to Berlin.

For their last and 13th operation together, again in Lancaster ED627 EM-N they took off from Langar at 2129 hrs on 27/28th August on a second visit to Nurnberg. They were shot down by a night fighter and crashed on Markung Hohenburg, 60 miles west of Nurnberg. The crew were buried in the St Nikolai Cemetery and re-interred in the Durnbach War Cemetery after the war.

A postscript to this sad incident was that Sgt Goodwin, the rear gunner, died on his 21st birthday and this was to be Sgt Pratt's last operation with this crew as he had been transferred to other duties.

Requiem for a Rear Gunner

My brief sweet life is over, my eyes no longer see,
No summer walks – no Christmas Trees –
no pretty girls for me,
I've got the chop, I've had it, my nightly ops are done
Yet in another hundred years, I'll still be twenty-one

(by R W Gilbert)

Top row: Sgt Addison, Sgt Toomey, Sgt Pratt;
Bottom row: Sgt Fitzgerald, Sgt Goodwin

Far left: **Sgt Preston**

Left: **Sgt Fitzgerald**

The photographs and report of the events of Friday 25th June 1943 are courtesy of Shaun McGuire the cousin of Sgt Fitzgerald.

MONDAY 28th JUNE 1943

1715 hrs — Training

Wellington III DF671 of 18 OTU from Finningley took off on a bombing and photography training flight and on return to base the flaps partially failed causing the starboard wing to drop and the nose of the aircraft to yaw away from the centre line. The pilot, Sgt 158583 Henry Wilson Heron RAFVR, raised the undercarriage and force-landed.

Sgt Heron was promoted to P/O and was killed on 31st August, when serving with 166 Sqn. He was piloting Wellington HE988 AS-U from Kirmington on a raid on Monchengladbach when his aircraft was shot down by Major Heinz-Wolfgang Schaufer, the highest scoring night fighter ace with 121 victories in 164 combat missions. The aircraft crashed in Belgium and he is buried in Heverlee War Cemetery.

Sgt Heron

FRIDAY 2nd JULY 1943

2330 hrs — Training

Wellington IC DV444 of 28 OTU from Castle Donington had port engine failure in flight and the aircraft landed wheels up back at base. The pilots were Sgt 1058736 J Price and Sgt 132247 D Langford. This aircraft also force landed at Castle Donington on 1st April 1944.

SATURDAY 3rd JULY 1943

1420 hrs — Training

Wellington IC R1157 of 28 OTU from Castle Donington had engine failure on take off and the pilot swung the aircraft to avoid a road and the undercarriage collapsed. There were no injuries to the crew.

The pilot, Sgt 1338065 William Richard Cooper RAFVR, was killed on 24th December 1943 age 21. He was the pilot of Lancaster ND327 of 100 Sqn taking off from Grimsby for a raid on Berlin when his aircraft collided in the air at 12,000 feet with a 550 Sqn Lancaster, resulting in a massive explosion, killing all 14 crew members, both crashing near Fulstow. He is buried in his home town churchyard of Harrow (St Mary).

SUNDAY 4th JULY 1943

1200 hrs Training

Manchester I R5770 ZN-G of 1660 HCU from Swinderby engine cut on take off for dual training, the aircraft swung and the undercarriage was raised to stop. Foreign matter was found in the carburettor. The pilot was P/O 111552 James Leslie Cooper DFC RAFVR. This aircraft was built by Metrovick at Trafford Park, Manchester and delivered to 25 OTU at RAF Finningley on 9th April 1941. It was then delivered to 106 Sqn at RAF Coningsby on 8th March 1942 with whom it completed several operational sorties. R5770 was then delivered to 1660 HCU at RAF Swinderby. This aircraft was also piloted by the famous W/C Guy Gibson VC, DSO and Bar, DFC and Bar, on 2 raids, Rostock on 25th April 1942 and the Heinkel works at Warnemunde on 8th May, when he was Commander of Avro Manchesters with 106 Sqn. Lancaster R5770 has also been painted and produced as an aviation print by M A Kinnear.

1543 hrs Training

Oxford I BG231 of 16 (P)SFTS from Bircotes after landing starboard undercarriage collapsed but there were no injuries.

The pilot, P/O P/1940 Mikolaj Kirkilewicz PAF, was killed on 2nd March 1945 flying with 300 Sqn. He was the pilot of Lancaster I PB854 which took off from Faldingworth for a daylight raid on Koln with 12 other bombers of the squadron. They joined an aircraft group of some 800 aircraft for a strike on German troop and armour concentrations in support of the 1st US Army making a bridgehead at Remagen. His aircraft was shot down by AA batteries.

Right: **A Lancaster of 300 Squadron being bombed up at Faldingworth.** Courtesy of Jerzy B Cynk

Below: **Faldingworth memorial**

WEDNESDAY 7th JULY 1943

0330 hrs — Training

Lancaster III ED546 PO- of 467 Sqn from Bottesford was returning from a training flight and when it made too fast an approach on the short runway and overshot into a field. There was one injury. The pilot was F/S 414407 B R Jones RAAF.

1220 hrs — Training

Master III W8706 of 16 (P)SFTS was on a training flight when the pilot made a left hand circuit and accidently went into a left hand spin, stalled and dived into the ground near the railway station at Radcliffe-on-Trent. The pilot, LAC P/703911 Jozef Gorski PAF age 21, was killed and is buried in Newark-upon-Trent Cemetery.

FRIDAY 9th JULY 1943

0445 hrs — Training

Lancaster I R5889 GP-M of 1661 HCU from Winthorpe had a starboard tyre burst during take off for night circuits and landings whilst travelling at high speed. The pilot Sgt 658571 A G A Barnet maintained control and became airborne. He circulated for the next 2 hours waiting for daylight. He then jettisoned part of his fuel load made a good landing and the aircraft then caught fire. There were 2 injuries including Sgt Barnet.

MONDAY 12th JULY 1943

1600 hrs — Ground

A fire broke out in No.3 room of the bomb store at Ossington among crates of 30 lb incendiaries but was extinguished before any explosions occurred.

TUESDAY 13th JULY 1943

0900 hrs — Op; Torino

Lancaster III LM311 PO-L of 467 Sqn from Bottesford took off at 2245 hrs on a raid to Torino and during the raid it was severely damaged forward of the tail section. At 0855 hrs the pilot was nearing base and requested that the crash tender stand by for a wheels up landing. Just before 0900 hrs between Plungar and Langar a witness saw light through the fuselage of the aircraft and when the flaps were lowered in readiness for landing, structural failure occurred and the Lancaster broke into two sections. The aircraft crashed about one mile from the aerodrome.

The pilot had had to do another circuit of the airfield due to another Lancaster being given an emergency landing. The Lancaster was called L for Liz'beth as this was the name of F/S Chapman's girl friend who was a WAAF transport driver at the aerodrome.

Apart from the pilot and Sgt Greenwood, all were Scottish. The crew were: P/O 415117 Cedric Arthur Chapman RAAF age 20 (Pilot), buried Oxford (Botley) Cemetery, Sgt 980381 Jack Greenwood age 25 RAFVR (F/Eng), buried Mankinholes Chapelyard Yorks, Sgt 1551320 Albert Edward Michaels age 22 RAFVR (Nav) buried Glasgow Roman Catholic Cemetery, Sgt 1349535 Norman Campbell Smith age 21RAFVR (Bomb Aimer) buried Edinburgh Cemetery, Sgt 1369188 Patrick Donlevy age 19 RAFVR (W.Op) buried Dalkeith New Cemetery, F/S 967187 William Bruce age 22 RAFVR (Air Gnr) buried Falkirk Cemetery, Sgt 1372826 William Stewart Buchanan age 20 RAFVR (Tail Gnr) buried in Glasgow Cemetery.

P/O Chapman and his crew were posted to 467 Sqn on 3rd April and had completed 16 Operations, 13 in Lancaster LM311. The Squadron ORB reads 'We're not superstitious but this was a dark and dismal 13th for the Squadron, for we lost 3 valuable crews, namely F/L Gibbs,

F/O Mitchell and F/S Chapman. F/S Chapman arrived back from the target OK, but turning to come in to land the tail appeared to break off and the aircraft crashed a short distance from the 'drome. All members of the crew were killed instantly and none of the Squadron personnel who were at the scene of the disaster could do anything'.

A memorial commemorating the crew of LM311 was erected by Jack Greenwood's family and the 467 RAAF Squadron Association in 1999.

Left to right: Sgt Donlevy, Sgt Smith, Sgt Michaels, Sgt Greenwood, Sgt Chapman, Sgt Buchanan, Sgt Bruce. Courtesy of Bottesford Council

Memorial erected near the site of the crash. OS sheet 130; 825 442

1620 hrs — Training

Mosquito II HJ 921 ZK- of 25 Sqn from Church Fenton stalled and spun off a steep turn at height of 500 feet over the pilot's fiancee's home at Road, Nottingham. The pilot P/O 144280 Jack Grundy age 20 RAFVR and his crewman were killed. Jack, the son of John Thomas and Annie Grundy of Sneinton, is buried in Nottingham Southern Cemetery.

THURSDAY 15th JULY 1943

0133 hrs — Training

Lancaster I R5862 of 1660 CU from Syerston took off with a slight swing to port. The pilot, F/S 412958 J E Hay RAAF, was hampered by his right hand being trapped between the elevator trimming wheel and the F/L's knee and was unable to close the throttle. The undercarriage seemed to strike something and collapsed.

TUESDAY 20th JULY 1943

1335 hrs — Training

Tomahawk I AH795 (No14) of 1685 BDT Flt from Ossington took off for a low level cross country training flight and after a one hour flight at 500-700 feet the engine seized and flames came into the cockpit and the engine caught fire. The aircraft had a connecting rod break in the Alison Engine smashing the crankcase. The pilot Sgt 413979 R L Gawn successfully belly landed the aircraft in a field 3 miles north east of Hucknall, near Papplewick, and was uninjured. He used the fire extinguisher but could not put out the fire and the aircraft was destroyed. Crash location: Cassini grid OS 1940 sheet 54 011703; OS 1992 sheet 120 549504.

Within 3 months Sgt Gawn was involved in a couple of controversial incidents. He took off from Ossington in another Tomahawk for a trip to Castle Donington but got lost and landed at Loughborough race course. 5 days later on the 9th he was tasked for another flight in a Tomahawk but refused to fly the aircraft. He was subsequently tried and court martialled on 22nd October and his rank was reduced.

SUNDAY 25th JULY 1943

1715 hrs Training

Wellington III BJ880 of 82 OTU from Ossington was on a dual instruction flight and when taking off the pilot thought that the aircraft was not developing sufficient power, throttled back and ran off the runway. The pilots were F/S 1375166 V H New and P/O J/23404 Thomas Leo Whigham Teasdale RCAF.

F/O Teasdale lost his life on 25th March 1944 age 21 flying with 166 Sqn. He took off from Kirmington in Lancaster ED731 (called Dantes Daughter) for his 12th mission to Berlin and while on the homeward flight crashed near Kempen. The crew were buried there and at the end of the war were transferred to the Reichswald Forest War Cemetery.

1900 hrs Taxiing

Lancaster I R5875 of 1660 CU from Swinderby was taxiing when it struck Lancaster ED808 which was unoccupied.

The instructor pilot was F/O 132129 N F Turner and the pupil P/O J/22780 Erle Keith Williams RCAF. P/O Williams died on 25th February 1944 while piloting Lancaster LM419 of 619 Sqn. He took off from Coningsby for a raid on Schweinfurt and was shot down by a night fighter. He and his crew are buried in Durbach War Cemetery.

TUESDAY 27th JULY 1943

0015 hrs Training

Lancaster I ED591 UG-L of 1654 HCU from Wigsley began take off but the starboard tyre blew out causing the aircraft to swing, leave the runway and crashed into some trees. The pilot P/O J/17323 N L Schofield RCAF and the pilot under training F/L 41660 Brain escaped injury.

THURSDAY 29th JULY 1943

0249 hrs Taxiing

Lancaster I W4232 of 1660 HCU from Langar taxied into Lancaster W4887 after the pilot failed to notice its tail light in time to stop. The rear gunner of W4887 did not display his inspection lamp or warn his pilot. P/O 146156 S S Warnock was the instructor pilot of W4232 and the pupil P/O J/22780 Erle Keith Williams who was also involved in another taxiing collision on 25th July. The pilots of W4887 were F/O 111547 G E Fawke (Instructor) and P/O J/20361 J A Hefferman, the pupil. Strangely enough F/O Fawke was also involved in a taxiing incident on 26th April. This aircraft crashed at Syerston on 17th April 1944 with the loss of the 7 crew members.

FRIDAY 30th JULY 1943

1315 hrs Training

Lancaster X R5845 of 1660 HCU from Langar took off at 1230 hrs for the crew to familiarise themselves with the Lancaster aircraft. 45 minutes into the flight the Lancaster force landed at Winthorpe, which was a strange airfield to the pilot, with wheels up due to engine failure. There were no injuries to the crew who were: P/O 143376 N Graham (Pilot), F/O A/403147 J H Nicholls RAAF (2nd Pilot), Sgt 1452977 J Gardner RAAF, F/S 416967 K Jolly RAAF, F/O 420166 R Easson and Sgt 995283 J Lambert.

SUNDAY 1st AUGUST 1943

LAC 1141603 T Whiteside was injured by an explosion of a flash bomb at Swinderby. He received burns to his face, scalp and right arm and was admitted to RAF Rauceby Hospital.

1531 hrs — Training

Lancaster I R5614 ZN- of 106 Sqn from Syerston returned from a training flight and landed heavily. The pilot had attempted an overshoot in a strong gusty cross-wind but crashed, caught fire and burnt out at Syerston. The pilot, Sgt 798628 Frederick Manuel Mifflin RAFVR, and his six crew members were all injured. This aircraft had flown a total of 440 hours.
F/O Mifflin DFC, and one other member of his crew, was killed on 27th April 1944 age 21 whilst piloting Lancaster ME669 ZN-O of 106 Sqn from Metheringham on a raid on Schweinfurt. They are buried in Durnbach War Cemetery.

The aircraft was intercepted by a night fighter whose fire set light to a fuel tank. With total disregard for his own safety, one of the crew, Sgt Norman C Jackson (F/Eng) slipped on his parachute and, with a fire extinguisher, climbed onto the fuselage of the aircraft which was travelling at 200mph at 20,000 feet. He tried to put out the fire, but his parachute partly opened and he slipped onto the wing. The fire spread and he was badly burned, then he was swept from the wing with his partly inflated, burning parachute trailing behind him. He landed heavily, breaking an ankle, was looked after by a woman and her daughter then taken prisoner. For his outstanding courage he was awarded the Victoria Cross. The citation read:

'The KING has been graciously pleased to confer the VICTORIA CROSS on the under-mentioned airman in recognition of most conspicuous bravery: 905192 Sergeant (now Warrant Officer) Norman Cyril Jackson, RAFVR, 106 Squadron.

This airman was the flight engineer in a Lancaster detailed to attack Schweinfurt on the night of 26th April 1944. Bombs were dropped successfully and the aircraft was climbing out of the target area. Suddenly it was attacked by a fighter at about 20,000 feet. The captain took evading action at once, but the enemy secured many hits. A fire started near a petrol tank on the upper surface of the starboard wing, between the fuselage and the inner engine.

Sergeant Jackson was thrown to the floor during the engagement. Wounds which he received from shell splinters in the right leg and shoulder were probably sustained at that time. Recovering himself, he remarked that he could deal with the fire on the wing and obtained his captain's permission to try to put out the flames. Pushing a hand fire-extinguisher into the top of his life-saving jacket and clipping on his parachute pack, Sergeant Jackson jettisoned the escape hatch above the pilot's head. He then started to climb out of the cockpit and back along the top of the fuselage to the starboard wing. Before he could leave the fuselage his parachute pack opened and the whole canopy and rigging lines spilled into the cockpit. Undeterred, Sergeant Jackson continued. The pilot, bomb aimer and navigator gathered the parachute together and held on to the rigging lines, paying them out as the airman crawled aft. Eventually he slipped and, falling from the fuselage to the starboard wing, grasped an air intake on the leading edge of the wing. He succeeded in clinging on but lost the extinguisher, which was blown away.

By this time, the fire had spread rapidly and Sergeant Jackson was involved. His face, hands and clothing were severely burnt. Unable to retain his hold, he was swept through the flames and over the trailing edge of the wing, dragging his parachute behind. When last seen it was only partly inflated and was burning in a number of places. Realising that the fire could not be controlled, the captain gave the order to abandon aircraft. Four of the remaining members of the crew landed safely. The captain and rear gunner have not been accounted for.

Sergeant Jackson was unable to control his descent and landed heavily. He sustained a broken ankle, his right eye was closed through burns and his hands were useless. These injuries, together with the wounds received earlier, reduced him to a pitiable state. At daybreak he crawled to the nearest village, where he was taken prisoner. He bore the intense pain and discomfort of the journey to Dulag Luft with magnificent fortitude. After 10 months in hospital he made a good recovery, though his hands require further treatment and are only of limited use.

This airmans attempt to extinguish the fire and save the aircraft and crew from falling into enemy hands was an act of outstanding gallantry. To venture outside, when travelling at 200 miles an hour, at a great height and in intense cold, was an almost incredible feat. Had he succeeded in subduing the flames, there was little or no prospect of his regaining the cockpit. The spilling of his parachute and the risk of grave damage to its canopy reduced his chances of survival to a minimum. By his ready willingness to face these dangers he set an example of self-sacrifice which will ever be remembered.'

MONDAY 2nd AUGUST 1943

1530 hrs — Training

Wellington III X3800 of 18 OTU C Flt from Finningley took off at 1510 hrs to practice single-engine flying, dived and crashed 20 minutes later at Wroot, near the airfield and caught fire killing all the crew. Cause of the crash was never established. The crew were:

Sgt 1333575 Leslie Albert Charlton RAFVR age 21(Pilot) cremated Golders Green Crematorium, Sgt Ronald Henry Smith RAFVR age 21 (Nav) buried Lewisham (Hither Green) Cemetery, F/S 410739 Eric Hempel Sherman RAAF age 19 (W.Op/Air Gnr) buried Finningley Churchyard Extension, Sgt 1439469 John William (Bill) Perry RAFVR age 28 also buried Finningley Churchyard Extension. The Worksop Fire Brigade attended the fire.

2350 hrs — Op; Nickel

Wellington X HE526 of 18 OTU from Finningley took off at 2350 hrs and crash landed almost immediately at Partridge Hill Farm, 1½ miles down wind of the flare path after an engine failed. All the crew of 6 were injured: Sgt 1180053 N Walker (Pilot), P/O L T Bowers, P/O H C Atkinson RCAF, Sgt J R Taylor, Sgt S Edwards and F/L Hill.

Night — Taxiing

Wellington IC R1645 of 28 OTU from Wymeswold was being taxied on a dark night prior to night flying training when a wing hit a tree. The pilots were Sgt Price and F/S 656076 H Thompson.

TUESDAY 3rd AUGUST 1943

0005 hrs — Op; Hamburg

Wellington X HE807 BH-O of 300 Sqn from Ingham and its crew were detailed along with 14 other crews of 300 Sqn to attack Hamburg. HE807 took off at 2342 hrs but developed starboard engine trouble which resulted in the good engine overheating and the captain aborted the mission. The bombs were jettisoned and the aircraft made a forced-landing in

Lancaster LM487 BH-J. Courtesy of Jerzy B Cynk

a corn field, near Truman's Lodge, Clumber Park. A fire broke out and the Wellington was destroyed. The crew were F/L P/1065 J Spychala PAF, P/O M J Bergner PAF, Sgt M Wiecek PAF, F/S C Pawlak PAF and Sgt J Stromski PAF. All but the pilot suffered some bruises and abrasions and the air bomber was slightly burnt on leaving the aircraft.

P/O Mieczyslaw Bergner (Nav) was killed on 22nd May 1944 flying with 300 Sqn. He took off from Faldingworth for a raid on Dortmund in Lancaster III LM487 BH-J when he crashed on the return journey near Krefeld. He rests in Reichswald Forest War Cemetery. He was on his 53rd Operational sortie. Lancaster LM487 BH-J was one of seven to take part in No.300 Squadron's first Lancaster raid on the night of 18/19th April 1944. The photograph on the opposite page was taken on 19th May, 3 days before its fateful mission.

0146 hrs — Training

Wellington IC DV823 of 14 OTU from Market Harborough was on a night training flight when the aircraft made a crash landing at Hose without injury to the crew. The exhaust stub on the starboard engine had burnt out and gave the pilot Sgt J/19632 Louis Curatolo RCAF age 20 the impression that the engine was on fire.

Louis Curatolo, now promoted to P/O, was lost on 14th January 1944. He was piloting Lancaster R5729 of 44 Sqn from Dunholme Lodge on a raid on Braunschweig when his aircraft was shot down by a night fighter. He is buried in Hannover War Cemetery. R5729 flew 70 operations with 44 Sqn.

1420 hrs — Training

Tomahawk I AH777 of 1685 Flt from Ossington took off for a fighter affiliation exercise. On return to base the pilot, Sgt 1322882 E J Golly, was unable to get the wheels to lock down and a wheels up landing was made with no injuries. An airman was charged due to the hydraulic reservoir cover being left loose after the daily inspection and the reservoir emptying during flight.

THURSDAY 5th AUGUST 1943

1525 hrs — Training

Master III W8464 of 16 (P)SFTS was on a training flight and had only been in the air for thirty minutes when the engine seized and the aircraft belly landed in a field at Owthorpe Lodge, near Cotgrave. The pilot, LAC 703719 W Grabowski PAF, was not injured.

FRIDAY 6th AUGUST 1943

1645 hrs — Training

Martinet I HP318 of 1485 Flt from Fulbeck took off for a fighter affiliation detail and after a 24 minute flight appeared to spin, crashed and caught fire at Eagle village. The pilot, W/O P/780559 K Felus PAF, received multiple injuries and burns and died. His remains were taken to RAF Swinderby mortuary. He is buried in Newark-upon-Trent Cemetery.

SATURDAY 7th AUGUST 1943

0203 hrs — Training

Wellington IC X9638 of 28 OTU was on a night bombing exercise when an engine caught fire and control of the aircraft was lost due to the burning away of fabric and it crashed in flames 2 miles from Wymeswold killing the five crew.

F/S 1237237 Ronald William Bagley RAFVR age 18 (Pilot) is buried in Wilnecote New Cemetery, Tamworth, Sgt 1410618 Richard Arthur Owens RAFVR age 21 (Nav) buried Llanfair Kilgeddin (St Mary) Churchyard, Sgt R/156117 George Albert Long RCAF age 26 (Air Bomber) buried Oxford (Botley) Cemetery, Sgt 656841 Ronald William Belmomt Pimm RAFVR age 23 (W.Op/Air Gnr) buried Streatham Park Cemetery, Sgt 1803836 John James Davidge RAFVR age 20 (Air Gnr) buried Burton-on-the-Wolds Church Cemetery.

MONDAY 9th AUGUST 1943

1500 hrs — Training

Wellington X MS471 -G of 82 OTU from Ossington crashed at Grimston Hill between Wellow and Ompton whilst in the circuit at Ossington. The aircraft was returning from a cross country flight with suspected starboard engine failure. The pilot attempted a crash landing, stalled at low altitude and the aircraft burst into flames with the loss of all five crew members.

P/O 150243 Walter Waldron Adams (Pilot) age 24 RAFVR cremated Bournemouth Crematorium, P/O 135747 Frank Graham Bell age 32 (Nav) cremated Golders Green Crematorium, P/O J/24024 Herbert Ibbott age 21 (Air Bomber) buried Bedford Cemetery, Sgt 1861770 Peter Baldwin RAFVR age 19 (Air Gnr) buried Ollerton Cemetery, Sgt 1390845 Roland Walter Ballauff RAFVR age 21 (W.Op/Air Gnr) also buried Ollerton Cemetery.

Police Sgt Ernest Flinders who was nearby attempted to rescue the crew. For this brave deed he was awarded the British Empire Medal (Civil Division) on 21st March 1944. The citation read: 'Ernest John Thomas Flinders, Police Sergeant, Nottinghamshire Constabulary. An aircraft crashed and immediately burst into flames. Sergeant Flinders, who was on leave, ran across two fields to the aircraft and, despite exploding ammunition, made a quick reconnaissance to locate the crew. He found three members who were seriously injured amongst the burning wreckage, dragged all three clear of the fire and cut away their smouldering clothing. With help he then extricated two more bodies from the wreckage. A portion of one wing of the aircraft was wrenched away and lodged upside down on a stook of corn nearby. Petrol was flowing from this wing and there was danger of it becoming ignited. After getting the bodies out Sergeant Flinders directed and assisted in extinguishing the burning sheaves of corn, a large area of which had become ignited. Sergeant Flinders showed outstanding courage without thought for his own safety'.

TUESDAY 10th AUGUST 1943

0135 hrs — Training

Blenheim I K7050 of 12 (P)AFU was on a night flying exercise flight when the pilot lost sight of the flare path for the aerodrome and the aircraft crashed attempting to land on a Q site at night and burnt out, on the Great North Road near Bottesford. The Danish pilot, P/O 151948 Sigfred Johannes Christopherson RAFVR, and the other two crew members were killed. He is buried in Grantham Cemetery.

P/O Christopherson had a very unconventional and eventful route to joining the RAF. He was born on 11th July 1914, the son of market gardener Johannes Christopherson and Ane Christopherson. He joined the Danish Royal Guards in November 1935 and was accepted for flying training at the Army Flying School from 1st April. He left the school on 10th September 1938 and was unemployed for the next six months. He then spent some time working in Germany as a gardener. In January 1940 he volunteered to become a pilot in the Finno-Russian Winter War but it is not certain if he was involved in hostilities. He returned to Denmark and worked for a while at the German occupied Vaerlose Air Station.

On 26th December 1940 he left Denmark and arrived in London on 23rd April 1941 via Istanbul, Cyprus, Suez and Cape Town. Having volunteered for the RAF at the British Air Attache in Istanbul, he apparently has second thoughts and accepts an offer by British Intelligence to be trained in radio-telegraphy. Without realising it he has enrolled in the Special

Intelligence Service. On 10th September 1941 at 1946 hrs a Whitley of 138 Sqn captained by F/S A W Reimer R/61467 takes off from Newmarket bound for Denmark, on board are Christopherson and Lt Thomas Christian Sneum. Flak is encountered during the flight but both agents are successfully dropped near Holbaek. Apparently they never succeeded together as agents since they never really trusted each other with Christopherson seemingly the one to blame. At the end of February 1942 Christopherson decides to leave Denmark and on 3rd/4th March he attempts to cross the ice covered waters between Stevns in Denmark and Falsterbo in Sweden with his brother and another resistance member. Due to the bad weather he is the only one to barely survive the crossing being picked up by Swedish fishermen. He is imprisoned in Malmo, and during interrogation compromises agent Sneum who then has to leave Denmark at the end of March. In mid-June Christopherson, Sneum and another agent are transferred to England in a Lockheed Hudson and imprisoned in Brixton Prison. Christopherson is offered a place in the RAF in recognition of his services. It is during his training that he loses his life.

1040 hrs Training

Wellington IC X9808 of 105 OTU from Bramcote had the port engine fail on take off from Tollerton and the aircraft overshot the end of the runway. The enquiry stated that the pilot had carried out the correct procedure promptly. The pilots were F/S 1365777 M McDonald and Sgt 1336369 S W Brant.

THURSDAY 12th AUGUST 1943

1752 hrs Training

Lancaster I W4952 EM-T of 207 Sqn from Langar was landing downwind after an air test and the pilot, F/S A414175 V H Trimble, overshot, swung the aircraft and the undercarriage collapsed. There were no injuries.

2350 hrs Operations

Lancaster I W4766 QR-J of 61 Sqn from Syerston took off at 2115 hrs for operations but the starboard outer engine caught fire in the air so the aircraft jettisoned its bombs at 5258N 0018E, returned and landed safely. The pilot, P/O 147998 Ronald Steer RAFVR age 21, was killed just 4 days later when as pilot of Lancaster DV186 the aircraft crashed near Lisieux during a raid on Milano. The crew are buried in St-Desir War Cemetery.

SATURDAY 14th AUGUST 1943

1545 hrs Training

Martinet I JN639 of 82 OTU from Ossington took off on a fighter affiliation exercise and the pilot made a force landing in a field and ran through a hedge between Carlton village and Ossington due to engine failure. The pilot F/S 1196381 W E Jenkins was un-injured.

Martinet I similar to JN639

SUNDAY 15th AUGUST 1943

No.1668 HCU was formed at RAF Balderton to convert crews on to the Lancaster and Halifax.

MONDAY 16th AUGUST 1943

0015 hrs | Op; Milan

Lancaster III EE141 EM-P of 207 Sqn from Langar was over the target area of Milan and struck by an incendiary bomb dropped from a friendly aircraft. The aircraft piloted by P/O 148125 Arthur Marcus Fitzgerald RAFVR returned safely.

12 days later P/O Fitzgerald did not return from operations. He was the pilot of Lancaster ED627 of 207 Sqn from Langar on a raid on Nurnberg and crashed at Schwabisch. He and his crew are buried in Durnbach War Cemetery. (see entry for 25th June)

0135 hrs | Training

Wellington III BJ671 of 18 OTU from Finningley caught fire when the engines were started up and the port engine burnt out. Two of the crew were F/O P/1999 L Rebinski PAF and F/S Bzmaxiarz PAF.

F/O Rebinski lost his life on 14th August 1944 during a raid on Falaise when his Lancaster DV278 of 300 Sqn was hit by flak and crashed at Pont d'Ouilly. He lies in the Polish Cemetery at Grainville Langannerie.

0540 hrs | Training

Lancaster I W4113 GP-J of 1661 CU from Winthorpe made a successful 3 engine landing after the airframe had been damaged by fire in the air.

The pilot F/O J/7891 Alexander Novick RCAF was killed on 22nd October flying with 57 Sqn. He took off from East Kirkby in Lancaster JB237 for a raid on Kassel and crashed at Polle. He and 2 other crew members were killed and buried in Hannover War Cemetery and 4 were made POWs.

Lancaster W4113. Courtesy W Taylor

1340 hrs | Training

Wellington X HE461 of 18 OTU from Finningley had a port engine failure in flight and made a belly landing on the aerodrome. The pilot was Sgt 1561190 W J Cleland.

TUESDAY 17th AUGUST 1943

1125 hrs — Taxiing

Wellington IC X9883 of 28 OTU from Castle Donington caught fire after a test flight and was totally destroyed. An engine caught fire and flames from the exhaust ignited the underside of the port mainplane. The pilot was F/S 114942 P Sleight.

1425 hrs — Operations

Halifax HR971 from Lissett landed at Ossington from operations, burst a tyre and obstructed the runway. Aircraft were diverted to other airfields while the runway was cleared.

2202 hrs — Training

Wellington III Z1694 of 23 OTU from Pershore was on a special exercise 22 miles off course when it crashed 2½ miles north west of Wymeswold. It seemed to dive into the ground at a high speed. Pieces of aircraft were found up to 1½ miles from the main impact point. All the crew were killed.

Sgt R103555 Frederick David Johnson RCAF (Pilot), F/O J/21361 Allan Thomas Duke age 23 RCAF (Nav), F/S R/140533 Gordon William Holditch age 20 RCAF (Nav), F/S R/159957 Joseph Taylor age 22 RCAF (Air Gnr), Sgt R/186823 Robert Hilliard Chisnell age 19 RCAF (Air Gnr) all buried in Oxford (Botley) Cemetery, Sgt 1443790 James Arthur Vanlint age 21 RAFVR (W.Op) buried Chingford Mount Cemetery.

F/O Duke was an American from East Orange, New Jersey and F/S Taylor was also American originating from Worcester, Massachusetts.

WEDNESDAY 18th AUGUST 1943

0305 hrs — Training

Wellington X HE279 of 18 OTU from Finningley took off to practice night circuits and landings and during take off had a tyre burst which caused the aircraft to swing, the undercarriage collapsed and the aircraft caught fire. The pilot was F/L 119009 W J Stevens and 2nd pilot P/O 144932 Kenyon Bowen-Bravery.

P/O Bowen-Bravery was the pilot of Lancaster LL811, named 'Bad Penny II', of 550 Sqn based at RAF North Killingholme which at 1134 hrs on the 5th June 1944 was the first aircraft to cross the French coast and drop its bombload on a German coastal gun battery in Normandy to begin Operation Overlord. In the late 1990s the French government awarded a collective Croix de Guerre to the crew and captain, Flying Officer (later Squadron Leader) Kenyon Bowen-Bravery, in recognition of this and a commemorative plaque was dedicated in the church of St Denys in North Killingholme.

Above: **Back row; Sgt Fysse, Sgt Thompson, F/S Keeley; front row; Sgt Bodill, F/S Thomas, F/O Bowen-Bravery, Sgt Davies**

Left: **Lancaster LL811 'Bad Penny II'**

0435 hrs Operations

Halifax DK269 MP-J of 76 Sqn from Holme-on-Spalding swung and struck an obstruction on landing at Wymeswold after a flight of 7 hrs and 40 mins, returning from Operations, probably a raid on Peenemunde. The pilot was F/S 1093921 C Kirkham.

THURSDAY 19th AUGUST 1943

2115 hrs Stationary

Wellington X HE420 of 18 OTU from Finningley was stationary with engines running when LAC 1542162 Ronald Cox, a wireless mechanic, walked into a propeller and was killed. The court of enquiry stated that there was no blame attached to anyone and the accident was probably caused 'due to misjudgement of aircraft distance by an airman possibly caused by sight not having adjusted to darkness again and airman having flashed a bright torch, coupled with slight fatigue due to having been on duty from 0800 hrs to time of accident 2115 hrs'.

FRIDAY 20th AUGUST 1943

Barracuda II BV759 of 5 FPP crashed near Rufford bombing range near Mansfield after engine failure. The pilot F/S 1316791 John Christopher Milliken RAFVR age 20 was killed and is buried in Butcombe (St Michael) Churchyard.

SATURDAY 21st AUGUST 1943

2327 hrs Training

Wellington X HE332 -J of 82 OTU from Ossington took off at 2115 hrs on night training and hit trees on a low landing approach to Ossington and crashed at the edge of the airfield. Two crew men were killed, P/O 133088 Frederick Gordon Ingham age 25 (Nav) who is buried in Brighouse Cemetery and Sgt 1333407 Ronald William Hughes age 22 RAFVR (Air Bomber) buried in Milton Cemetery, Portsmouth.

The pilot F/S 23748 H O Shaw RAAF and F/S 425408 Evered Austin McCasker RAAF were injured both suffering from fractured skulls and broken legs. 2 others Sgt Jennings and Sgt Bernard Dye were not injured. Sgt Dye completed his full tour of operations.

P/O McCasker aged 23, and 5 other crew members were killed on 5th November 1944 after taking off from Driffield in Halifax NR132 with 466 Sqn for a raid on Bochum. Their aircraft was shot down by Hptm Heinz Rokker near Julich on the outskirts of Cologne. He is buried in Rheinberg War Cemetery. The pilot P/O 428517 N C R Dodgson became a POW.

In 1945 N C R Dodgson, by then a F/O, produced a report stating: 'I did not bale out but was blown out by the explosion. The first fighter attack set fire to the fuselage and I told the Engineer to try to put out the fire and warned the crew to put on chutes. Another attack set fire to the starboard outer, I feathered the prop but fuel was leaking out and burning. The fire got worse and I told the crew to jump. A few minutes later the starboard wing broke off at the outer engine nacelle and the aircraft spun. I put on my chute and the aircraft exploded but did see the front crew position and it was empty with the front escape hatch open. Before the explosion I used the call light for the jump and continued to call jump on I/C later tossing off my helmet and yelling likewise. Received acknowledgement from the Mid Upper Gunner only. Had no indication that any of the crew were injured. The aircraft in about the centre of a triangle Koln, Duren, Dusseldorf. I fell near an Ack-ack battery and caught almost immediately. Landed besides the burning aircraft. A German interrogation officer said all the crew were dead found with their

Heinz Rokker

parachutes on but all failed to open. A Russian worker in the hospital said that some aircrew had been killed by civilians the night before (4/11) in the town about 4 miles from the crash'. Released 22.5.45.

Hauptmann Heinz Rokker was credited with 64 victories in 161 missions. He recorded 63 of his victories at night, including 55 four-engine bombers.

MONDAY 23rd AUGUST 1943

1645 hrs Training

Oxford II T1141 of 16 (P)FTS was abandoned after the pilot lost control of the aircraft in cloud in a dive and the aircraft began to break up, and crashed at Chestnut Farm, Sedgebrook. The pilot Sgt P/704075 Holubowicz PAF baled out and was injured. His crew member LAC P/704281 Jerzy Henryk Szylling PAF age 21 was killed and is buried in the Polish plot of Newark-upon-Trent Cemetery.

1812 hrs Training

Lancaster I W4190 GP-A of 1661 HCU from Winthorpe crashed on take-off. The port outer engine cut on take-off causing the aircraft to swing. There were no injuries. The pilot was F/O 126937 B S Turner.

TUESDAY 24th AUGUST 1943

1100 hrs Ground

Wellington III BK399 –W of 82 OTU from Ossington was preparing to taxi out for a flight when a Verey pistol, which was assumed to be unloaded, was accidently discharged inside the fuselage and it caught fire. F/O 41344 O L Macfarlane RNZAF and Sgt 1388461 Leslie William Charles Wheeler RAFVR were inside the aircraft but not injured.

F/S Wheeler then of 15 Sqn age 21 was piloting Lancaster LM490 on a raid on Berlin on 24th March 1944 when he was shot down when homeward bound. He is interred in Berlin War Cemetery.

THURSDAY 26th AUGUST 1943

1645 hrs Training

Wellington III BK145 of 82 OTU from Gamston had suspected engine failure on take off and the pilot, Sgt 1387400 R F Fleetwood, tried to stop the aircraft but crashed through the boundary hedge.

SATURDAY 28th AUGUST 1943

0200 hrs Taxiing

Wellington IC X9697 of 28 OTU from Wymeswold collided with dispersed aircraft Wellington R1700 when led into the dispersal pan by an airman. The NCO ground crew were to blame for not carrying out orders of the NCO. The pilot was P/O 150181 Sidebothom.

1301 hrs Training

Lancaster III ED946 DX-E of 57 Sqn from Swinderby took off at 1258 hrs on a training flight but due to lack of fuel to both inboard engines they cut and the Lancaster crash-landed in a field about one mile from the airfield. No injuries were reported. The pilot was Sgt 1318084 J B Josling. Crash location: Cassini grid OS 1940 sht 47 345795; OS 1989 sht 121 883600.

MONDAY 30th AUGUST 1943

0030 hrs — Training

Wellington X HE632 of 82 OTU took off from Bircotes but as the bomber gathered speed a swing developed and before this could be corrected came off the runway and crashed. The screened pilot Sgt 171757 Arthur Noel Stockdale DFM and pupil Sgt 1439768 Fisher were un-injured.

TUESDAY 31st AUGUST 1943

2128 hrs — Training

Wellington IC DV572 of 28 OTU from Wymeswold overshot landing due to inefficient brakes which were being tested. The pilots were W/O 754360 R J Fryer and Sgt R/150153 S Wilson RCAF. W/O Fryer was killed at Wymeswold see entry for 25th November.

2135 hrs — Training

Wellington IC R1697 of 28 OTU from Castle Donington had port engine failure on take off and the pilot made a good downwind belly landing with little damage to the aircraft. The cause was obscure. The instructor pilot was F/O R Kitson and the pupil Sgt 1556914 Caile.

WEDNESDAY 1st SEPTEMBER 1943

0330 hrs — Op; Berlin

Lancaster III JB 132 QR- of 61Sqn from Syerston took off from Syerston at 2008 hours for a raid on Berlin. On its return the aircraft collided head-on in the air with Lancaster R5698 of 1654 HCU. Both aircraft crashed between Bleasby and Morton near Southwell.

The crew of 8 were all killed: S/L 40965 Dennis Crosby Wellburn DFC age 27 RAFVR (Pilot) buried Newark-upon-Trent Cemetery, F/O 408968 Roy Leslie Clarke age 26 RAAF (2nd Pilot) from Victoria Australia, buried Newark- upon-Trent Cemetery, Sgt 1369957 John Knox Watson age 20 RAFVR buried East Calder Churchyard, Sgt 658923 John Reid Jack Forrest age 31 RAFVR (Nav) buried Newark-upon-Trent Cemetery, F/L 67648 Richard Edward Davies age 31 RAFVR (Bomb Aimer) buried Streatham Park Cemetery, Sgt 1092940 Jack Blackett age 20 RAFVR (W.Op./Air Gnr) buried Durham Churchyard, F/O 107718 Trevor Francis Joyce age 25 RAFVR (Air Gnr) buried Newark-upon-Trent Cemetery, Sgt 639330 Alan Paterson age 25 RAF buried Montrose Cemetery.

The enquiry surmised that it was a dark night and neither crew could have seen the navigation lights of the other aircraft. The total crew of eleven were all killed. Wreckage was found in 6 fields in the parishes of Bleasby and Fiskerton. S/L Wellburn was awarded the DFC posthumously on 15th October 1943 when serving with 61 Sqn. The citation read: 'For gallantry and devotion to duty in the execution of air operations'. August had been a black month for 61 Sqn as 13 crews had been reported missing.

Lancaster I R5698 UG-P of 1654 HCU from Wigsley took off for night training and at about 0330 hrs collided in the air with Lancaster JB132 and crashed near Southwell.

All the crew were killed and they were: P/O 156662 Joseph Widger Murphy Macdonald RAFVR age 30 (Pilot) buried Southport Roman Catholic Cemetery, Sgt 1238563 George Robert Joyce age 19 RAFVR (F/Eng) buried Gravesend Cemetery, F/O 120547 Walter Stephen Jobling DFC age 34 (Nav) buried Thorney Churchyard, Sgt 1087736 Edward Neilan Jones age 20 RAFVR (Air Bomber) buried Wallasey (Rake Lane) Cemetery, Sgt 1044676 George Herbert Tough age 23 RAFVR (W.Op/Air Gnr) buried Mount Jerome Cemetery, Sgt 853608 John Henry Hutchinson age 38 RAF Aux Air Force buried Liverpool (Anfield) Cemetery, F/S 415917 Robert William Rashbrook age 20 RAAF buried Thorney Churchyard. F/O Jobling had only just been awarded the DFC, on 17th August, when flying with 50 Sqn.

THURSDAY 2nd SEPTEMBER 1943

2315 hrs **Training**

Master III FL676 of 16 (P)SFTS from Newton took off with the pilot, Sgt P/703229 Stanislaw Waydowicz PAF, at the controls. The aircraft lost height on a turn after take off, hit trees and control was lost. The aircraft crashed at the junction of Edwalton Village Street and Melton Mowbray Road, Edwalton. Sgt Waydowicz was killed and is buried in Newark-upon-Trent Cemetery. A mystery remains as to the aircraft serial number as the official crash log gives the number as FL676 although that number was allocated to a Mitchell.

2230 hrs **Training**

Wellington IC Z8870 of 28 OTU from Wymeswold took off for practicing night circuits when the pilot, Sgt 1385735 J Rouse, discovered he could not lower the flaps fully and force-landed on the airfield with the undercarriage retracted.

MONDAY 6th SEPTEMBER 1943

The Station Commander of Syerston, Group Captain Francis 'Frank' Samuel Hodder, joined the crew of Lancaster DV182 ZN- of 106 Sqn for a raid on Mannheim. They took off from Syerston at 1950 hrs and during the outbound flight the aircraft was attacked by a night fighter whose opening burst of fire killed the pilot, P/O A A Robertson, and wounded the flight engineer. A fire broke out and the aircraft crashed with seven fatalities and one airman, F/O G Willatt, being made a POW. The crew are buried in Rheinberg Cemetery. GC Hodder had joined the RAF in 1925 and was stationed in France at the outbreak of World War Two where he was Mentioned in Despatches. In 1940 he became a Wing Commander and 2 years later a Group Captain.

0028 hrs **Op; Mannheim**

Lancaster III LM360 VN- of 61 Sqn from Syerston was returning from a raid on Mannheim and had been in flight for 4 hours 10 minutes when the port inner engine failed and caught fire. The pilot, F/O 117468 B C Fitch, ordered the crew to bale out and then landed the aircraft successfully at Winthorpe. The aircraft was successfully repaired and continued on operations.

Two months later, LM360 was badly damaged by an Fw 190 on the way to bomb Dusseldorf. The pilot, F/L William 'Bill' Reid of 61 Sqn, was wounded in the head, shoulders and hands when the windscreen was shattered. With his navigator dead and wireless operator fatally wounded he decided to continue rather than turn back, bombed the target and managed to get his aircraft home but the navigator, wireless operator and rear gunner died. For his tenacity, conspicuous bravery and devotion to duty he was awarded the Victoria Cross. F/L Reid died on 28th November 2001. F/L Reid's VC was sold at auction in 2009 for £348,000.

Lancaster LM360 after crash landing on 4th November 1943 in Norfolk.

F/L Reid

0332 hrs **Op; Mannheim**

Lancaster III DV232 QR-K of 61 Sqn from Syerston took off at 2015 hrs for a raid on Mannheim, only the crews' second operation, when the port outer engine caught fire on the outward flight. With the propeller feathered they carried out their operation, bombed and turned for home. On return the pilot P/O Todd came into land on 3 engines, the aircraft went into a turn to port, narrowly missing some station buildings, flew on at almost ground level and finally did a steep turn and 'belly flopped' into the river Trent, half a mile north of East Stoke. 2 of the crew were injured but not seriously.

The crew were P/O 149553 Peter H Todd (Pilot), Sgt 1624707 Sidney Robson RAFVR, F/O J Hodgkinson, Sgt V R Duvall, Sgt W Houseley, Sgt Pattrick and Sgt J Cartwright.

P/O Todd and most of this crews' luck ran out on 24/25th March 1944 on their 16th trip. They were shot down flying Lancaster III ND440 OF-H of 97 Sqn coming home from a raid on Berlin, before being picked up by a German launch and spending the remainder of the war as POWs. However Sgt Robson was killed and is commemorated on the Runnymede memorial.

The 97 Squadron Operation Record Book read: '24.3.44 Training was suspended for briefing.14 aircraft being detailed for operations.14 Lancasters set out to attack Berlin, weather over target was 4 to 9/10ths cloud, visibility good. Defences slight H/F. and moderate L/F. Searchlights ineffective, night fighters active. Bombing took place from approx 19,000 feet. The attack opened with Wanganui flares and were in fair concentration. Later red and green TIs were seen. This was kept up and marking was fairly well concentrated and constant. Fires were seen in the area of TIs. Built up area and lines of streets were clearly seen around the glow of incendiaries. Generally considered a good attack. 12 photos attempted. F/O Todd and crew and P/O Coates DFM and crew failed to return. A signal was received from F/O Todd and crew when near the Calais area on return, but nothing further heard. Well over 2500 tons were dropped on this attack and a total of 72 bombers reported missing.'

Lancaster DV232 in the river Trent at East Stoke. Courtesy of Newark Advertiser

Tomahawk AH802 of 1685 BDT Flight from Ossington swung off the runway on landing and damaged the port wing tip.

WEDNESDAY 8th SEPTEMBER 1943

1510 hrs — Training

Lancaster I R5547 GP-V of 1661 HCU from Winthorpe swung to starboard on landing as the brakes were ineffective and undercarriage leg collapsed at Balderton. Fire developed but this was quickly extinguished by competent fire fighting. There were no injuries.
The pilot was F/S A8315 Robert A Errey RAAF.

1320 hrs — Flight Test

Lancaster III JB153 PM-D of 103 Sqn Elsham Wolds took off at 1320 hours on a test flight from Wymeswold but dived into the ground about 2 miles south east of the airfield and exploded. Those who saw the incident say the Lancaster began a turn to port, the nose dropped and the bomber hit the ground. All those on board were killed. Three Air Training Corps cadets from 1180 Sqn ATC were also aboard the aircraft and are buried in Chapel-en-le-Frith (St Thomas-a-Becket) Churchyard, Derby. One, cadet P Bond, was age 14 and his two friends D J Fox and E L Hall were 17. The crew were:

F/S 406992 Alfred William Buxton age 23 RAAF (Pilot) is buried in Botley Cemetery and from Subiaco, Western Australia, Sgt 1684485 John Leeming age 21 RAFVR (F/Eng) buried Manchester Cemetery, Sgt 1554620 Normand Kidd age 21 RAFVR (Nav) buried Kirkcaldy Cemetery worked in the Art Department of Allen Litho in Kirkaldy, Sgt 1473130 William Stephen Whalley age 20 RAFVR (Air Bomber) buried Burton-on-the-Wolds Cemetery was a marine engineer prior to joining the RAF. Sgt 1367821 Gerald Sweeney RAFVR (W.Op/Air Gnr) buried Glasgow Roman Catholic Cemetery, F/S 409668 Gordon Alfred Joffre Daldy age 28 RAAF (Air Gnr) buried Oxford (Botley) Cemetery from West Coberg, Victoria, Australia.

Sgt Kidd

F/S Buxton

Sgt Whalley

The authors are indebted to David Fell and the RAF Elsham Wolds Association for the following extract from their website.

'F/S Buxton's crew commenced operations in August 1943 and was detailed to fly their first trip on the night of the 2nd/3rd August to Hamburg. Soon after take-off the port inner engine of their Lancaster became unserviceable and they had to jettison the bomb load in the sea and return to Elsham Wolds. The crew had more luck the following week and successfully completed operations to Mannheim, Nuremburg and Milan.

The German V weapons site at Peenemunde on the Baltic coast was attacked on the night of 17/18th August and F/S Buxton and his crew took part in this highly important and dangerous operation. The attack caused considerable disruption to the German flying bomb and rocket research programmes and delayed the introduction of these weapons into operational service for some months.

On the night of the 31st August/1st September the crew participated in an attack on Berlin and followed this up with another raid on the German capital on the 3rd/4th September. The target involved a long flight and was always heavily defended but F/S Buxton and his crew completed these sorties successfully and without any reported incident. The crew then participated successfully in two raids on successive nights, the 5/6th and 6/7th September, to Mannheim and Munich respectively.

Since the beginning of August F/S Buxton and crew had completed nine operations and must have been feeling more confident having negotiated the first part of their tour although it is worth mentioning that 103 Sqn had lost nine Lancasters and crews on operations during this period.

At the beginning of September the boys of 1180 Squadron Air Training Corps, based at Buxton in Derbyshire, were attending a one week camp at Elsham Wolds. The boys were all from the Chapel-en-le-Frith Flight of the Squadron under the command of Lt Commander E J Cook Royal Navy (Retired). His eldest son, Sgt Edward J Cook, had been an Air Gunner with 103 Sqn in the crew of F/S "Bunny" Austin. This excellent crew was killed on the penultimate operation of their tour with the Squadron on the 2nd/3rd March 1943.

Lt Commander Cook, who was also chairman of the Chapel-en-le-Frith Wings for Victory Committee, had subsequently helped to raise the money to purchase two Lancaster Bombers for 103 Squadron during the town's Wings for Victory Week. This was a truly splendid effort of fund raising for such a small town. One of the Lancasters was named E for Edward in memory of the late Sgt E J Cook.

Amongst the cadets at the camp were Desmond Fox aged 17, Leslie Hall aged 17 and Peter Bond aged 14. All three boys were amongst the keenest members of the Flight and had all recently flown in Derbyshire. All three worked together in the toolroom at Ferodo Ltd and were inseparable companions in work and leisure activities. They were all well known and very popular in their hometown.

On the 8th September 1943 F/S Buxton and crew undertook an air test in Lancaster JB153 PM-D. Cadets Hall, Fox and Bond accompanied the crew on this flight. The cadets had written permission from their parents to undertake air experience flights, which was normal practise for cadets to give them some flying time in a modern aircraft during any convenient and suitable routine flight. No doubt all three were thrilled at the opportunity to have a trip in an operational machine.

The Lancaster took off from Elsham Wolds at 1300 hrs and landed at Wymeswold in Leicestershire a short while afterwards and taxied up to the control tower. An airman left the Lancaster and reported to the watch office. Presumably this was Sgt Davidson, although it is not confirmed. The reason for this is not clear and whoever it was did not return to the aircraft. A member of the crash crew at Wymeswold noted with interest the Lancaster landing that day because this type of aircraft was rarely seen at their base.

The Lancaster immediately took off again with six crew members and the three air cadets. It was seen to be flying normally at between 300/500 feet in a circuit of the base when it turned to port and dived into the ground about two miles from the airfield killing all on board instantly.

The aircraft crashed next to the farmhouse of Arthur Knight and his son remembers to this day the sound of the Lancaster's engines running at full revs just above the house and the sound of the bomber hitting the ground nearby. There was no eye witness to the actual impact but it does seem, however, that the pilot made some attempt to pull out of the dive as, at the moment of impact, it was shallow and no part of the aircraft was buried in the ground. The Lancaster immediately collided with a large tree and simultaneously burst into flames about 250 yards from the first point of impact. The emergency services at the airfield were quickly on the scene but there was nothing that could be done for the crew or cadets.

An investigation was made of the wreckage and it was not possible to prove mechanical failure because the great extent of the damage and destruction to the aircraft. It was, however, established that all the engines were running at the time of the crash. The pilot did not make any distress call although the sudden nature of the dive will have meant there was no time in which to do so.

F/S Buxton and crew.
Courtesy of David Fell and the Elsham Wolds Association

The subsequent court of enquiry was unable to definitely establish a cause to the crash and it was attributed to an accident. It is, however, now considered that it is most likely that there was some form of mechanical failure, which could not be established due to the complete destruction of the aircraft.

The funeral of the cadets was held with full military honours at the Chapel-en-le-Frith Parish Church on the following Saturday 11th September. The service was attended by over 800 family, friends and representatives from the services and the local community which was united in grief at the loss of three popular and respected local boys.

Sgt Whalley was buried locally with full military honours at Burton on the Wolds Church Cemetery, Leicestershire and F/S Buxton and F/S Daldy were laid to rest together at Oxford (Botley) Cemetery, North Hinksey, Oxford. The other three were laid to rest in their home towns, Sgt Kidd at Kirkaldy (Dysart) Cemetery, Fifeshire, Sgt Leeming at Manchester (Philips Park) Cemetery, Lancashire and Sgt Sweeney at Glasgow (St Kentigems) Roman Catholic Cemetery.

Sgt Davidson resumed operations with 103 Sqn but sadly he too was to lose his life before the month was out. He flew as rear gunner in the crews of F/O H D Churchill to Hannover on 22/23rd September 1943 and S/L "Jake" Kennard to Mannheim on the 23rd/24th September 1943. On his second operation with S/L Kennard this highly experienced and decorated crew were shot down on the night of the 27/28th September 1943 whilst taking part in an operation to Hannover. Sgt Davidson is buried with the rest of the crew at the Hannover War Cemetery in Germany.'

SATURDAY 11th SEPTEMBER 1943

7 British sand filled bombs with live explosive system was found in a grass field at Fiskerton. Location Cassini grid sheet 54 172711,OS sheet 120 711513.

TUESDAY 14th SEPTEMBER 1943

1210 hrs — Training

Wellington III X3401 of 18 OTU from Finningley shortly after take off on a solo circuits and landing exercise the port engine caught fire and a creditable wheels up landing was made on the airfield by the pupil pilot Sgt 1537412 D H Woolrich.

1515 hrs — Training

Wellington III BK447 of 18 OTU from Finningley made a belly landing there after a 12 minute training flight due to pilot error. The pilot was F/S P780998 Poludniak. There were no injuries.

WEDNESDAY 15th SEPTEMBER 1943

2245 hrs — Taxiing

Master III DL688 of 16(P)SFTS from Tollerton was stationary on the wrong runway when it was struck by Master W8693. LAC P/703060 R Zacharewicz PAF, the pilot of DL688 disobeyed instructions and taxied on the wrong runway.

2245 hrs Training

Master III W8693 of 16(P)SFTS from Tollerton hit Master DL688 on the runway when landing (see above). The pilot was F/O P/1632 Antoni Widawski PAF and his pupil LAC P/704261 G Krok PAF.

F/O Widawski was killed in a tragic accident when he was the pilot of either Mosquito VI PZ302 or Mosquito VI LR262 of 305 Sqn, both of which collided and crashed to the ground near Lasham, Hampshire, on 24th September 1944. He is buried in Newark-upon-Trent Cemetery. A memorial at the entrance to Lasham airfield was dedicated on 14th September 2006 to those who served there between 1942 and 1948.

Memorial at Lasham

Mosquito VI at Lasham 1944

FRIDAY 17th SEPTEMBER 1943

1955 hrs Training

Lancaster I W4921UG-O of 1654 HCU from Wigsley took off on exercise and swung almost immediately which the pilot failed to correct and the aircraft hit the battle headquarters building with the port eleo and outer engine before finishing on fire near the camps 25 yard rifle range. The pilot was Sgt 1394128 D Matthews. There was one injury, the rear gunner receiving a broken leg.

TUESDAY 21st SEPTEMBER 1943

2230 hrs

Lancaster III JA902 JO-D of 467 Sqn from Bottesford bounced on landing and overshot the aerodrome without injuries to the crew.

The pilot, P/O 416418 Douglas Chapman Dunn age 22 RAAF, was posted from 467 Sqn to 463 Sqn on 25th November and after completing 7 operations was killed on 30th January 1944. He was the pilot of Lancaster ED949 from Waddington on a raid on Berlin when he was shot down by a night fighter. He is buried in the 1939-1945 War Cemetery at Berlin. P/O Dunn was a very experienced pilot and had also completed 16 operations with 467 Sqn.

WEDNESDAY 22nd SEPTEMBER 1943

1547 hrs Training

Wellington III BK493 of 18 OTU 'C' Flight from Finningley had port engine failure after an engine feathering demonstration to pupil pilot Sgt 1575059 A Botham. The pilot instructor P/O 149215 H C Jenner made a wheels up landing on the airfield but overshot into a field.

2210 hrs

A Spitfire piloted by a Polish pilot, Goea, crash landed at Wigsley and obstructed the runway.

THURSDAY 23rd SEPTEMBER 1943

0830 hrs Ground

Wellington IC DV511 of 28 OTU from Wymeswold caught fire in a hangar and was destroyed due to a pedestal lamp being accidentally knocked into a drip tray, the filament bursting and setting fire to oil in the tray.

0845 hrs Ground

Tiger Moth II T7126 of 12 Grp Com Flt from Hucknall engine started up prematurely and injured a member of the ground crew, AC2 1381519 E Harden. Disciplinary action was taken against the fitter responsible.

THURSDAY 24th SEPTEMBER 1943

1135 hrs Training

Wellington X HE992 of 82 OTU was on dual pilot training when the undercarriage collapsed on landing due to structural failure and the aircraft crashed at Bircotes with no casualties. The pilots were P/O 145193 A J Mott and Sgt 1790032 T M J Shervington.

SUNDAY 26th SEPTEMBER 1943

2209 hrs Training

Lancaster I W4937 of 1660 HCU from Swinderby was on night conversion training when the aircraft swung on landing. The pilot under training corrected but when centralising the rudder the staff pilot's foot became jammed between the rudder pedals, the aircraft swung again, the undercarriage collapsed and the aircraft caught fire. The crew were: P/O J/16384 M P C Cuelenaere RCAF (Pilot Instructor), Sgt R/1125832 Lancy (Pilot), Sgt 1531755 Banks, Sgt 1590663 Deardin, Sgt 1591475 Sgt Corbett, P/O 134208 Davis and P/O J/228054 Gennis.

MONDAY 27th SEPTEMBER 1943

1445 hrs Training

Master III DL612 of 16 (P)SFTS from Newton took off at 1345 hrs for formation flight training when it was involved in a mid-air collision with Master W8710 and crashed approximately 1,000 yards south west of Radcliffe-on- Trent. The pilot F/S P/782696 S Czachla PAF survived.

1445 hrs Training

Master III W8710 of 16 (P)SFTS from Newton made a faulty break away from formation flying and struck leader DL612 (see above) from below and crashed approximately 1,000 yards south west of Radcliffe-on-Trent. The pilot LAC P/703657 Tadeusz Eret PAF was killed and is buried in Newark-upon-Trent Cemetery.

1605 hrs Training

Wellington III BJ645 of 18 OTU 'A' Flight from Finningley took off for an exercise on feathering procedures. The pupil feathered the port airscrew and almost immediately the starboard engine cut. The aircraft lost height and at about 200 feet stalled and dived into the ground at Everton north of Retford. Four of the crew were killed.

F/O P/1599 Czeslaw Gozdz (Pilot), Sgt P/783846 Stefan J Majewski, F/S P/783556 Edmund Formaniewicz, Sgt P/703858 Stanislaw L Piorek. They are all buried in the Polish plot of Newark-upon-Trent Cemetery. Sgt J Duchaczek (Rear Gnr) PAF was injured.

TUESDAY 28th SEPTEMBER 1943

2006 hrs — Training

Wellington IC T2920 of 28 OTU from Wymeswold overshot landing. The aircraft unaccountably assumed nose down attitude on approach, speed increased and it went through a hedge and the instructor, W/O 1164430 G H Phillips selected undercarriage up.

The enquiry concluded that the cause was probably downdraught and that the pilot appeared to have done all he could.

SATURDAY 2nd OCTOBER 1943

1827 hrs — Op; Munich

Lancaster III DV184 EM-O of 207 Sqn from Langar took off on a mission to Munich and stalled almost immediately and crashed 400 yards north of Barnstone Lodge farm and caught fire.

The canvas cover had been left on the pitot head, a hollow tube located on the port side of the forward fuselage which enabled the airspeed of the aircraft to be measured. So devastating was the impact that all 7 crew were killed and only three bodies were identified: F/O Bremner, Sgt Smith and F/S Dyde. Their four companions are commemorated on the Runnymede Memorial. The crew had completed 17 operations together in 3 months and these were the last 207 Sqn casualties at Langar. The crew were:

P/O 52753 Archibald (Jock) Ferguson Bremner age 24 RAF (Pilot) buried Glasgow Cemetery, Sgt 1005599 Robert Mitchell Appleton age 23 RAFVR, F/S 1452094 Roland Reuben Woodhouse age 20 RAFVR, F/S 1287148 Arthur Dorrien Archer age 23 RAFVR, Sgt 951152 John Herbert Victor Horsley age 24 RAFVR, all 4 crewmen commemorated on the Runnymede Memorial.

Sgt 1589096 Arthur Edward Smith age 19 RAFVR is buried in Liverpool Cemetery and F/S 518808 Frederick William Dyde age 28 RAF buried Long Bennington Churchyard. Crash location: OS sheet 129 743345.

SUNDAY 3rd OCTOBER 1943

0100 hrs — Training

Wellington X LN545 of 18 OTU from Finningley was on a Bullseye training sortie when an engine cut and the aircraft crash landed in a field 3 miles east of Finningley near Wroot. The pilot F/S P781204 J Nalepa was injured along with 4 other crew members. The accident was caused by incorrect manipulation of the petrol cocks as the bomb aimer mis-understood the instructions.

F/S Nalepa was also involved in an incident on 22nd May 1944 with 300 Sqn from Faldingworth when 8 crews were allotted the target of Dortmund. The briefing was held at 1915 hrs and all the aircraft tasked for the operation took off with F/S Nalepa in Lancaster I LL857 BH-B taking off at 2240 hrs, but only 5 reached the target. Prior to crossing the enemy coast Sgt Nalepa had trouble with the oil pressure in the port engine and was compelled to feather the propeller and stop the engine. Part of the bomb load was jettisoned in the sea and the operation was aborted. While approaching to land at base with flaps fully lowered the port inner engine failed causing the aircraft to bank to the left at an angle of approximately 90 degrees. On losing height rapidly the aircraft hit the building of the shooting range and crashed in flames resulting in total wreckage. 3 crew members were killed and are buried in Newark-upon-Trent Cemetery and 5 injured, including Sgt Nalepa. The crew were: F/S Nalepa, F/S K Nieruchalski, F/S W Mroczkowski, F/S M Golec, F/S Nowak, Sgt P/780062 Czeslaw Rybinski (F/Eng) and Sgt P/704444 Antoni Leszkowicz (W.Op/Air Gnr). Sgt Rybinski and Sgt Leszkowicz are both buried in Newark-upon-Trent Cemetery.

A Wellington of 300 Squadron, Faldingworth, May 1944. Courtesy of Jerzy B Cynk

Subsequently F/S Napela PAF was killed on 2nd September 1944 whilst serving with No.1586 Special Duties Flight based at Brindisi in Italy.

On the night of 1st/2nd September 1944 two Polish Liberators were sent the Campinos Forest, Poland, and five Halifaxes to the Radom-Kielce area. In accordance with the newly introduced practice, all Halifaxes flew without 2nd pilots. The two Liberators accomplished their tasks successfully but for the Halifaxes the operation ended in disaster, only one returning to base. Halifax BB389 –M piloted by F/S Jozef Nalepa was destroyed by AA fire. Of its crew Sgt Nalepa, Sgt Jozef Pialucha, Sgt Konrad Staniewicz, F/S Jozef Jas, Sgt Adam Bialoszewski and F/S Jozef Derewieko were killed. F/S Tadeusz Jawor managed to jump to safety and was made a POW.

A Halifax II of No.1586 (Polish) Special Duties Flight, Brindisi (Italy) March 1944, with a Liberator in the background. (Note the Polish chessboard beneath the cockpit.).

2035 hrs Training

Wellington III BK242 of 18 OTU from Finningley took off at 1840 hrs for a training flight and after 1 hour 55 minutes an engine failed and the aircraft approached the runway on one engine. For some indeterminate reason the pilot decided to overshoot and go round again, the nose pitched up and the aircraft hit the ground and caught fire killing all the crew.

Sgt 1432841 Thomas William Hodgson Dalziel age 20 RAFVR (Pilot) is buried in Finningley (Holy Trinity and St Oswald) Churchyard Extension, Sgt 1344192 William Baird Jarvie age 21 RAFVR (Nav) buried Old Monkland Cemetery, Sgt 1562923 Edgar Farrer age 29 RAFVR (Air Bomber) buried Uphall Cemetery, Sgt 1235344 Murray Cohen age 21 RAFVR (W.Op/Air Gnr) buried Leeds Jewish Cemetery, Sgt 1611281 Louis Lazarus age 22 RAFVR (Air Gnr) buried East Ham Jewish Cemetery.

TUESDAY 5th OCTOBER 1943

1630 hrs Ground

Master III DL618 of 16 (P)SFTS from Newton caught fire in a hangar due to a portable lamp being dropped and broken. An enquiry came to the conclusion that it was an accident.

THURSDAY 7th OCTOBER 1943

0445 hrs Training

Wellington X LN291 of 82 OTU from Ossington took off for a cross country exercise and after 6 hours 30 minutes crashed at Clipstone Forest, near Rufford. An engine had failed due to the pilot's mishandling as he allowed the engine to become cold while gliding down and did not select warm air to the engine intake. The aircraft crash landed on top of small fir trees using landing lights and miraculously there were no injuries to the crew.

The pilot, Sgt 947234 Denzil Yorke Bishop age 24 RAFVR, by now a F/S, was subsequently killed on 21st April 1944 whilst flying with 625 Sqn. He was piloting Lancaster ME731 CF-S when he took of from Kelstern for a raid on Koln and crashed into the sea off the coast of Holland. He is commemorated on the Runnymede memorial.

SATURDAY 9th OCTOBER 1943

0347 hrs Training

Wellington X HE919 of 82 OTU from Ossington took off for night training and crashed in a forced landing when an engine cut at Blyth, with no casualties. W/O J D Rees and Sgt J/85822 Douglas Earl Aiken RCAF were both aboard the aircraft.

P/O Aiken was lost age 23 on 25th June 1944 when piloting Lancaster ND751of 44 Sqn for a raid on Pommerval. He is buried in the churchyard at Criquetot-sur-Longueville.

1045 hrs Training

Halifax V DK133 of 1660 HCU from Swinderby swung on take-off and the port aileron was torn off. The pilot Sgt 1221026 M R Lawler had handed control to the flight engineer before the aircraft had gained proper speed for rudder control.

2358 hrs Training

Lancaster III ED413 of 57 Sqn landed at Syerston and ran off the end of the runway in bad visibility. The pilot was P/O A/413909 J A Smith.

TUESDAY 12th OCTOBER 1943

1450 hrs Training

Wellington X HE201 of 82 OTU from Gamston crashed at Creswell Plantation, between Haughton Chapel and Bevercotes. The aircraft was on dual instruction pilot training and shortly after take-off trouble was experienced with the port engine, which caught fire. It was later discovered that the cause was a roller race failure in the main bearing. It also appeared that the pilot had tried to make a forced landing in difficult terrain ahead but had crashed into trees and the aircraft caught fire. Of the crew of seven, four were injured and three killed.

F/O 144293 John Coughlan DFM RAFVR (Screened Pilot Instructor) age 30 is buried in Kanturk Catholic Cemetery, County Cork, F/O J/24498 Harold Gordon Dayman RCAF age 24 (Pilot) buried Ollerton Cemetery, P/O J/28782 John Christie RCAF age 20 (Air Gunner) also buried Ollerton Cemetery. The funeral of F/O Dayman and P/O Christie was held at 1100 hrs on 16th October.

The rest of the crew F/O H C McGavin RCAF (WO1), R Tarling RCAF, Sgt J/92532 John Alfred Stuart MacGregor RCAF, and Sgt H D La Pointe RCAF were injured.

Sgt MacGregor was killed on 28th December 1944 age 26 when Lancaster KB738 of 419 Sqn came down at Leverkusen-Wiesdorf on a raid on Opladen. He is buried in Rheinberg War Cemetery.

SATURDAY 16th OCTOBER 1943

1230 hrs Training

Oxford I BG156 of 16 (P)SFTS from Newton had an engine fail due to the pupil pilot LAC P/794836 T Gesicki closing the throttles and then opening them too quickly. The instructor pilot belly landed the aircraft in field. LAC Gesicki was involved in another incident on 14th January 1944.

2203 hrs Training

Wellington IC R1727 of 28 OTU from Wymeswold made a heavy landing and the tail wheel collapsed. The instructor pilot was F/O 413108 P Muggeridge.

The pupil F/O 139595 William Andrew Lawrence Colhoun RAFVR was killed on 31st March 1944 age 25 flying with 49 Sqn on his 6th operation. He took off from Fiskerton as pilot of Lancaster JB466 for a raid on Nurnburg and was shot down by a night fighter. 2 of the crew were made POWs and the rest are commemorated on the Runnymede Memorial. Bomber Command suffered its biggest loss of the war on this raid: 31 Halifaxes and 64 Lancasters which was 11.9% of the total force sent on the raid. JB466 was the 64th Lancaster to go down.

2230 hrs Training

Lancaster III FD532 of 467 Sqn from Bottesford overshot landing due to too high and too fast an approach. Winthorpe Conversion Unit had borrowed 2 aircraft for training purposes and this was one of them. The 467 Sqn ORB stated: 'Winthorpe Conversion Unit borrowed two aircraft for training purposes and one had some fun landing, the plane overshooting into a paddock next to the drome and finished up amongst tree stumps but it was not damaged in any way. Can't afford to lose any more'.

The pilot, F/O 134533 John William Eunson Duncan McGilvray RAFVR, died on 11th April 1944 age 32. He was the pilot of Lancaster LL784 of 619 Sqn which took off from Coningsby and was lost on a raid on Aachen and is buried Eindhoven (Woensel) General Cemetery. LL784 was probably shot down by Lorenz Gerstmayr of 4./NJG3, his 15th victory.

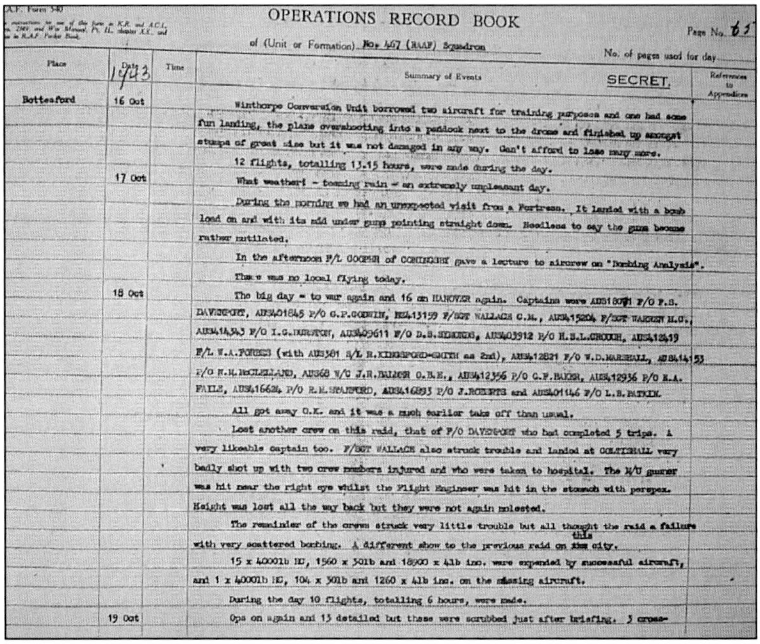

OPERATIONS RECORD BOOK

of (Unit or Formation) No. 467 (RAAF) Squadron — Page No. 65 — No. of pages used for day

SECRET.

Place	Date 1943	Time	Summary of Events	References to Appendices
Bottesford	16 Oct		Winthorpe Conversion Unit borrowed two aircraft for training purposes and one had some fun landing, the plane overshooting into a paddock next to the drome and finished up amongst stumps of great size but it was not damaged in any way. Can't afford to lose many more.	
			12 flights, totalling 13.15 hours, were made during the day.	
	17 Oct		What weather! - teeming rain - an extremely unpleasant day.	
			During the morning we had an unexpected visit from a Fortress. It landed with a bomb load on and with its mid under guns pointing straight down. Needless to say the guns became rather mutilated.	
			In the afternoon F/L COOPER of CONINGSBY gave a lecture to aircrew on "Bombing Analysis".	
			There was no local flying today.	
	18 Oct		The big day - to war again and 16 on HANOVER again. Captains were AUS180?1 F/O F.S. DAVENPORT, AUS401845 P/O G.P.GODWIN, NZ413159 F/SGT WALLACE C.M., AUS415204 F/SGT WARREN H.G., AUS414343 F/O I.G.DURSTON, AUS409611 F/O D.S.SIMONDS, AUS403912 P/O H.B.L.CROUCH, AUS412419 F/L W.A.FORBES (with AUS381 S/L R.KINGSFORD-SMITH as 2nd), AUS412821 F/O W.D.MARSHALL, AUS414153 P/O N.H.McCLELLAND, AUS68 W/C J.R.BALMER O.B.E., AUS412356 P/O G.F.BAKER, AUS412936 P/O K.A. FAILE, AUS416624 P/O R.M.STANFORD, AUS416893 P/O J.ROBERTS and AUS401146 P/O L.B.PATKIN.	
			All got away O.K. and it was a much earlier take off than usual.	
			Lost another crew on this raid, that of F/O DAVENPORT who had completed 5 trips. A very likeable captain too. F/SGT WALLACE also struck trouble and landed at COLTISHALL very badly shot up with two crew members injured and who were taken to hospital. The M/U gunner was hit near the right eye whilst the Flight Engineer was hit in the stomach with perspex. Height was lost all the way back but they were not again molested.	
			The remainder of the crews struck very little trouble but all thought the raid a failure with very scattered bombing. A different show to the previous raid on this city.	
			15 x 4000lb HC, 1560 x 30lb and 18900 x 4lb inc. were expended by successful aircraft, and 1 x 4000lb HC, 104 x 30lb and 1260 x 4lb inc. on the missing aircraft.	
			During the day 10 flights, totalling 6 hours, were made.	
	19 Oct		Ops on again and 13 detailed but these were scrubbed just after briefing. 3 cross-	

467 Sqn Operations Record Book for 16th October 1943

TUESDAY 19th OCTOBER 1943

1103 hrs — Training

Wellington HE750 of 82 OTU from Ossington suffered engine failure during take-off and the pilot retracted the undercarriage to stop the aircraft. No injuries were reported. The pilots were F/O 143940 M L Dewing and Sgt R/155145 M W Barr. This aircraft caught fire and burnt out at Gamston on 13th November 1944.

THURSDAY 21st OCTOBER 1943

1957 hrs — Training

Wellington III BK471 of 18 OTU of 'A' Flight Finningley took off and crashed at Rossington Hall 2 miles north of Bircotes whilst on a training cross country flight. The pilot requested permission to land saying that he had an engine failure but the aircraft undershot landing and crashed through trees into a field and burnt out. Sgt Z Maryknowski PAF was injured. 4 of the crew were killed and are buried in Newark-on-Trent Cemetery: Sgt P/793230 Mieczyslaw Solecki age 33 PAF (Pilot), F/L P/0031 Stefan Karol Alberti age 35 PAF, F/S P/780470 Roman Kot age 24 PAF, Cpl P/793799 Jerzy Sawicki age 29 PAF.

1105 hrs — Test Flight

Oxford I MP448 of 16 (P)FTS was on a test flight when an engine fell out without warning and the aircraft was abandoned near Langar. The crew who used their parachutes were W/C P/76623 S Grodzicki PAF and F/O P/?1633 W M Wlodarcymk PAF.

FRIDAY 22nd OCTOBER 1943

Fortress B-17G 42-37803 of 571 BS 390BG Group from Framlingham overshot landing at Hucknall. The pilot was Albert C Rood.

SATURDAY 23rd OCTOBER 1943

0026 hrs Operations

Lancaster I W4957 of 61 Sqn from Wigsley was returning from operations and at 300 feet in cloud and rain coming in to land the pilot P/O 156085 F J Nixon was blinded by a 'green' flare causing him to crash land along the sodium flares. The aircraft caught fire but there were no injuries.

SUNDAY 24th OCTOBER 1943

2140 hrs Training

Wellington X HE921 of 18 OTU from Finningley attempted landing in a ground haze and landed on the wrong side of the flare path, hit a mound with the tail wheel and damaged the nose. 2 members of the crew were slightly injured.

The pilot F/O 150244 Edwin Laurence Eames RAFVR was killed on 22nd May 1944 age 27 flying with 100 Sqn. He was the pilot of Lancaster LL960 which took off from Grimsby for a raid on Duisburg and was hit by flak and crashed. He is buried in Reichswald Forest War Cemetery.

WEDNESDAY 27th OCTOBER 1943

2300 hrs Training

Master III W8888 of 16 (P)FTS from Tollerton undershot landing at night at Tollerton due to the pupil pilot, LAC P/704016 T Pyzik PAF, mishandling the engine and flaps.

SATURDAY 30th OCTOBER 1943

Lightning P-38H 42-67072 of 343FS, 55FG Group was involved in an incident at Tollerton. The pilot was Clair A Penners.

TUESDAY 2nd NOVEMBER 1943

1935 hrs Training

Lancaster I W4249 of 1661 CU from Winthorpe was taking off when the instructor pilot F/O 160021 E K E Knight, for reasons unknown, throttled back and as the aircraft overshot the runway selected undercarriage up. There were no injuries. After the incident F/O Knight was taken to hospital with an unknown illness. The pupil pilot was P/O 156957 K D Smith.

SATURDAY 6th NOVEMBER 1943

1230 hrs Training

Wellington IC R1405 of 28 OTU from Castle Donington landed heavily in a slight cross wind and the undercarriage collapsed. The enquiry concluded that the undercarriage chassis may have been fatigued after 1032 hrs flying. The pilots were F/O 120892 M Smith and F/S 422999 G Paget.

1546 hrs Training

Lancaster I W4258 of 1661 CU from Winthorpe on landing bounced and the port wing dropped. The port undercarriage was torn off and the aircraft slewed round. The instructor pilot was F/O 145678 M P Crampton and the pupil Sgt 1099486 G R Phipps who was involved in another incident 7 days later.

WEDNESDAY 10th NOVEMBER 1943

0945 hrs | Training

Tomahawk IIA AH986 of 1685 BDT Flight from Ossington took off for fighter affiliation practice. At the completion of the detail, Sgt 1320149 R B T Adams (Pilot), found himself flying in poor visibility and lost contact with the Wellington which was leading him towards base. He decreased height to locate his position and flew into some high-tension wires and force-landed near the airfield. There were no injuries.

Thunderbolt P-47D 42-22508 of 495 Group was involved in an incident at Hucknall. The pilot was Robert L Baker.

SATURDAY 13th NOVEMBER 1943

1239 hrs | Training

Lancaster III LM308 of 1661 CU from Winthorpe made a fast approach, not in line with the runway and ran across the grass of the airfield and struck a ditch causing the undercarriage to collapse. The pilot Sgt 1099486 G R Phipps was also involved in an incident 7 days previously. This aircraft crashed near the Elm Tree Hotel, Hoveringham on 29th January 1945 with the loss of all 7 crew members.

2200 hrs

Sgt P/703431 Jan Gawlik PAF a Wireless Operator/Air Gunner of 18 OTU, Finningley, accidently walked into a propeller of Wellington BK448 on the Dispersal Point at Bircotes Aerodrome and was killed. His body was taken to Station Sick Quarters, Finningley, and he is buried in Newark-upon-Trent Cemetery.

MONDAY 15th NOVEMBER 1943

1805 hrs | Training

Master III DL751 of 16 (P)SFTS from Tollerton was on a duel training flight when the engine cut and the aircraft hit a tree in a forced landing at Tollerton with undercarriage retracted. The pilots were W/O P/780527 J Warchall PAF and LAC P/704441 Knikcik PAF.

MONDAY 22nd NOVEMBER 1943

2200 hrs | Op; St Marlow

Wellington X LN601 -B of 82 OTU from Ossington took off to drop leaflets on St Marlow. After reaching the height of 800 feet one of the locking rings in a bearing on one of the propeller shafts separated causing the loss of the engine. The aircraft dived into the ground and burst into flames killing all six crew at Norwell Woodhouse near Kneesall Lodge. F/L Brassington, the Units Gunnery Leader decided to fly with the crew as the Mid-upper Air Gunner.

The following 4 members of the crew are buried in Ollerton Cemetery: W/O II R/126451 Harold Winthrop Johnson RCAF age 30 (Pilot), P/O J/27696 Alexander Grant, RCAF age 33 (Air Bomber), F/O 139692 Oscar Geoffrey de Jongh age 26 RAFVR (Nav), F/S R/144200 Kenneth Ross Fallowdown RCAF age 21 (W.Op/Air Gnr), Sgt 1321739 Robert James Wannell RAFVR age 19 (Air Gnr) 19 is buried in Fulham Old Cemetery.

F/L 127175 John Gordon Brassington RAFVR age 28, an Air Gunner leader flying as a MUG, also died and is buried in Trentham Cemetery.

WEDNESDAY 24th NOVEMBER 1943

1855 hrs Training

Wellington IC DV950 of 28 OTU from Wymeswold took off but the pilot F/S 415800 Patrick William Laidler RAAF mishandled the engine controls and decided not to attempt to become airborne, retracted the undercarriage and overshot the runway. F/S Laidler was killed on 14th April 1944. See entry for that date.

THURSDAY 25th NOVEMBER 1943

2255 hrs Training

Wellington IC DV771 of 28 OTU from Wymeswold was on a cross country exercise when the pilot attempted a crash landing on approach after the aircraft caught fire and crashed in a field south of Wymeswold village. Six of the crew were killed and two injured, one of whom died 3 days later in Loughborough hospital.

W/O 754360 Ronald Joseph Fryer age 26 RAFVR (Pilot) cremated Nottingham Crematorium, F/S 415732 Francis William Greenwell age 29 RAAF buried Oxford (Botley) Cemetery, Sgt 1456213 Raymond Tasker McLean age 19 RAFVR (Nav) buried Wallasey (Rake Lane) Cemetery, Sgt 1567974 John Veitch Curry age 19 RAFVR (Air Bomber) buried Newburn (Lemington) Cemetery, Sgt 1558318 Andrew MacIntyre age 22 RAFVR (W.Op/Air Gnr) buried Oban (Pennyfuir) Cemetery, Sgt 2204598 Norman Ainscough Kenyon age 19 RAFVR (Air Gnr) buried Southport (St Cuthbert) Churchyard.

P/O 157736 Peter Emmerson age 25 RAFVR died on 28th November and was cremated at Glasgow Crematorium. Sgt S S Hewitt was injured. W/O Fryer had also been involved in another crash landing incident at Wymeswold on 28th November 1942.

THURSDAY 2nd DECEMBER 1943

1030 hrs Training

Wellington X LN186 of 18 OTU from Bircotes took off for circuit practice and after completion of the detail the undercarriage collapsed after a heavy landing. The pilot, F/O 127340 James Girvan McCall RAFVR, was injured but was lost flying Halifax JP162 of 148 Sqn during a Special Operations Executive sortie from Brindisi, Italy, to Poland on 5th August 1944. He was age 23 and buried in Krakow Rakowicki Cemetery, Poland.

2005 hrs Training

Wellington X HE242 of 17 OTU from Silverstone overshot landing at Gamston with engine trouble, the port engine scavenger oil pump partially seized and the undercarriage collapsed as the aircraft ran through a hedge. Injuries were reported. The pilot was Sgt 1107700 F Mountain.

FRIDAY 3rd DECEMBER 1943

0029 hrs Op; Berlin

Lancaster I DV334 WS-C of 9 Sqn from Bardney took off at 1645 hrs as one of 12 aircraft detailed for an attack on Berlin and reached the target successfully. On the return leg many aircraft were forced to divert to other airfields due to thick fog, including DV334, which was diverted to Ossington. After 7 hours 40 minutes flying time DV334 overshot the Ossington runway due to the fog and because of fuel shortage, possibly only 10 minutes air time left, attempted to land at Gamston. Again the the aircraft overshot the runway and on going round again for another attempt all four engines failed and the aircraft crashed in a field after hitting trees at Milton. There were 6 fatalities and 2 injuries.

P/O 155215 Kenneth Edgar Warwick age 20 RAFVR (Pilot) buried Winkfield Churchyard, F/S 1233713 Thomas Butterfield age 27 RAFVR (Bomb Aimer) buried Middleton Churchyard, Sgt 1540496 John Graham (Nav) age 23 RAFVR buried Carlisle Cemetery, Sgt 626828 Richard Emrys Jones age 22 (MUAG) buried Wallasey Cemetery, Sgt 991400 Robert William Davison age 29 RAFVR (F/Eng) buried Longbenton Cemetery, Sgt 1575881 Derrick Ivor Thomas Munn age 22 RAFVR (W.Op/Air Gnr) died en route to hospital and is buried in Much Cowarne Churchyard. Sgt C Rickard sustained a fractured arm and leg and F/S L B Owen received multiple injuries.

0250 hrs — Training

Master II AZ700 from RAF Cranwell on landing at Syerston struck wing tips on the overhead feeders to the sodium funnel on the Drem airfield lighting and crashed. The pilot LAC 1625450 Frank Bedford RAFVR age 20 was killed and is buried in Monk Fryston Cemetery.

SATURDAY 4th DECEMBER 1943

2048 hrs — Taxiing

Lancaster I W4824 of 1660 CU from Swinderby was taxiing down the perimeter track and Lancaster LM309 was turning onto the track after having crossed the runway and they collided. The pilot of W4824, Sgt 1334855 P E G Harford, and F/O 141683 P N Boyle of LM309 were found guilty of gross carelessness by the Court of Enquiry, by failing to keep a proper look out.

MONDAY 6th DECEMBER 1943

1145 hrs — Training

Oxford I MP304 of 16 (P)SFTS from Newton was taking off when the pilot believed that the aircraft would not become airborne, throttled back and selected undercarriage up. The occupants of the aircraft F/O P/1721 Z Kleniewski PAF, F/L P/76786 A Meginski PAF and F/L P/0091 T Martusewicz PAF were not injured.

SUNDAY 12th DECEMBER 1943

1140 hrs — Training

Wellington X HE818 of 18 OTU from Bircotes on taking off the port engine cut and the pilot, Sgt R/152283 J Downing RCAF, throttled back and checked a swing but due to very wet conditions the aircraft skidded off the edge of the runway into soft ground and the nose tipped.

MONDAY 13th DECEMBER 1943

1100 hrs — Training

Tomahawk AH825 from 1685 BDT Flight from Ossington took off with the pilot W/O 629622 Bidewell on his first solo flight in a Tomahawk, engine failed and immediately caught fire in the air and almost immediately the aircraft crash landed on the airfield.

THURSDAY 16th DECEMBER 1943

2016 hrs — Training

Lancaster I LM 307 GP-T of 1661 HCU from Winthorpe crashed 1 mile east of South Muskham, near Bathley. The aircraft flew into the ground in a turn and caught fire, cause obscure. An investigation gathered that there were several contributory factors; the chief cause was flying low and allowing attention to be distracted from instruments to look for aerodrome lights which were unserviceable. The runway flare path had been laid and the pilot found the airfield then lost it again and had lowered flaps and the undercarriage intending to land immediately. However he was told to stand by. Six of the eight crew were killed outright, one died later and one was injured.

F/O J/17626 William Hedley Eager DFC RCAF age 23 (Pilot Instructor) Canada buried Oxford (Botley) Cemetery, P/O 170426 Kenneth Clifford Hampson age 20 RAFVR (Pilot) buried Oxford (Botley) Cemetery, Sgt 1582751 Laurence Bert Lawrance age 19 RAFVR (F/Eng) buried Leicester (Saffron Hill) Cemetery, Sgt 1457372 William Stanley Austin age 29 RAFVR (Nav) buried Leeds Cemetery, Sgt 1316601 Roy Henry Woolcock RAFVR age 21 (W. Op/Air Gnr) buried Plymouth, F/S R/163624 Robert William Baldwin RCAF (Air bomber) age 28 buried Oxford (Botley) Cemetery, Sgt 2209717 Philip Dillon age 19 (MUAG) and Sgt 1304901 East (Rear Gnr) were transferred to Newark Hospital both suffering from severe injuries and shock. Sgt Dillon died at 6am on the 17.12.43 and is buried in Oxford (Botley) Cemetery.

F/O Eager was slightly injured on 15th April 1943 when making an emergency landing in a Manchester with its port engine on fire at Wigsley. He was awarded the Distinguished Flying Cross effective from 6th November 1943 whilst flying with 61 Sqn having graduated from initial training on 13th February 1942, No.19 EFTS on 24th April 1942 and No.10 SFTS on 29th August 1942. He was commissioned in 1943. His citation reads: 'completed many successful operations against the enemy in which he displayed high skill, fortitude and devotion to duty.'

F/S Baldwin was a former Saskatchewan and Western Canadian tennis champion and also well known in Rugby and Ice Hockey circles.

SUNDAY 19th DECEMBER 1943

0830 hrs — De-bombing

Lancaster III ED801 of 1661 CU from Winthorpe was being de-bombed of its practice bombs by an armourer when one exploded severely injuring AC2 Wheeler. AC1 Thompson had failed to replace safety pins.

1243 hrs — Training

Wellington X LM240 of 18 OTU from Worksop after a 2 hour flight the port engine failed so the pilot, Sgt 1546644 W Kuyser, decided to crash land on the airfield wheels up which he did and made a good landing.

MONDAY 20th DECEMBER 1943

1450 hrs — Training

Wellington III BK403 of 18 OTU from Worksop was approaching to land when the pilot, F/S 9763 F G Durrant RCAF, overchecked the aircraft at about 20 feet, stalled and on landing the undercarriage collapsed.

TUESDAY 21st DECEMBER 1943

At 1450 hrs it was reported that a Whitley machine gunned Broughton Pumping Station.

WEDNESDAY 22nd DECEMBER 1943

0640 hrs — Training

Wellington X LN160 of 29 OTU took off from Bruntingthorpe on a training flight when the aircraft crashed into a tree at Harby whilst attempting a south east landing at Wigsley. The port engine had cut out as a result of a fracture of the driving dogs of the pressure oil pump. When the ambulance arrived at the scene four of the five man crew were already free of the aircraft but the fifth was trapped in the wreckage in the Wireless Operator's compartment. A channel had to be dug in the ground below the aircraft to enable him to be freed. Burst petrol tanks and a short circuit in the wiring added the necessary stimulus for acting as quickly as possible. The four crew who escaped were Sgt H A S Russell (Pilot), Sgt 1082080 C Wilkins (Nav), Sgt 1217288 R Thomson and Sgt 1891865 F Fraser (MUG).

Sgt 1504087 Newby (Air Bomber) received fractured ankles to both feet during the crash.

Sgt 778936 Henry Alfred Scott Russell RAFVR (Pilot) was killed on 23rd October 1944 age 33 flying with 44 Sqn. He took off from Spilsby piloting Lancaster LM645 KM-P for a raid on Walcherenand and was presumed to have crashed in the target area. He lies in Bergen-op-Zoom War Cemetery, Netherlands with the rest of the crew.

1500 hrs — Taxiing

Lancaster I ED368 of 5 LFS from Syerston taxied into a lorry on the perimeter track. The pilot was P/O 156328 D H Matthews.

FRIDAY 24th DECEMBER 1943

1640 hrs — Training

Wellington X HE740 of 18 OTU from Bircotes had engine failure and belly landed on the airfield. The Flight Engineer had been unable to turn on the nacelle cocks and the engine cut, due to fuel shortage. The pilot was Sgt 152283 J Downing.

SUNDAY 26th DECEMBER 1943

1200 hrs — Training

Master III W8831 of 16 (P)FTS engine cut and the aircraft belly landed at Orston relief landing ground. The pilot was LAC P/782927 A Wieniorowski PAF.

1535 hrs — Training

Blenheim V AZ922 of 12 (P)AFU took off at 1440 hrs on a training flight with Sgt 1435357 Gavin Harvie RAFVR as the sole occupant. At 1535 hrs an engine cut, followed by loss of control and the aircraft crash landed at Bottesford Aerodrome. Sgt Harvie survived and was admitted to Rauceby Hospital. He died on 14th January 1945 with the rank of W/O, cause unknown, and is buried in Lesmahagow (or Abbey Green) Cemetery.

WEDNESDAY 29th DECEMBER 1943

1223 hrs

Tiger Moth II T7345 of 25 (P)EFTS from Hucknall collided with Tiger Moth T5980 on approach to land at Hucknall, despite the pilot taking violent avoiding action. The aircraft stalled and dived into the ground and caught fire. The pilot 2nd Lt Michal Bobitko of the Polish Army was injured. The pilot of T5980 was not aware of the collision until later.

Michal Bobitko was killed on 28th July 1944 and is buried in Newark-upon-Trent Cemetery.

1745 hrs — Training

Tiger Moth II T7176 of 29 EFTS piloted by 2nd Lt A Pilny became lost in bad weather and limited visibility and landed in a cornfield 1½ miles west of Edwinstowe. The aircraft skidded and swung in soft ground, the wheels dug in, and the aircraft overturned.

THURSDAY 30th DECEMBER 1943

1610 hrs — Training

Martinet I JN429 of 18 OTU took off from Bircotes and 10 minutes later spun into the ground during mock attacks on another aircraft at Scofton Village near Worksop, during a training flight. Both crew members were killed. F/O 141090 Peter Robert Street DFM, RAFVR age 24 buried Great Berkhampstead Church Cemetery, Sgt 1559295 James Maxwell Holmes RAFVR age 21 buried Cathcart Cemetery, Renfrewshire.

1944

MONDAY 3rd JANUARY 1944

Aircraft 'V' of 'B' flight from RAF Ossington was carrying out night practice bombing when it dropped one bomb through the roof of a house some 800 yards away from the target at Rufford bombing range.

WEDNESDAY 5th JANUARY 1944

1215 hrs — Training

Halifax II W7772 of 1656 HCU from Lindholme was on a training flight when it crash landed at Oatland Farm, Grimley-on-the-Hill. The starboard engines were feathered but were unable to be re-started, the aircraft lost height and crash landed in a field. The aircraft turned on its nose when the pupil applied the brakes fiercely because the undercarriage had not been lowered. There were 9 personnel in the aircraft all un-injured.

The pilot was P/O 155263 William Murray Addison DFC RAFVR and the pilot under training P/O 161735 Alfryn James Jenkings age 31 RAFVR.

P/O Jenkins, serving with 100 Sqn, was killed on 24th March piloting Lancaster ND642 on a raid on Berlin. He took off at 1857 hrs from Grimsby and was shot down by a night fighter and crashed 8km north of Eilenburg. All the crew rest in the Berlin 1939-45 War Cemetery.

P/O Addison was awarded the DFC on 10th December 1943 when serving with 51 Sqn.

THURSDAY 6th JANUARY 1944

1330 hrs — Training

Wellington X LN448 of 18 OTU from Worksop took off for dual circuits and landings, bounced badly on completion of the first circuit, flew around again but had damaged the undercarriage and on landing again it collapsed and the aircraft caught fire. The pilots were instructor P/O J/18861 R Dubois and pupil Sgt 1338028 Richard Howell Jenkins RAFVR.

Richard Howell, now a F/S, was killed on 13th August. He was piloting Lancaster ME617 of 101 Sqn from Ludford Magna when it was lost on an operation on Russelsheim. He is buried in Durnbach War Cemetery.

FRIDAY 7th JANUARY 1944

1115 hrs — Training

Tiger Moth II T5613 of 25 (P)EFTS from Hucknall inadvertently took off while taxiing in a strong cross wind, stalled and spun into the ground at Hucknall. The aircraft burst into flames on hitting the ground. The pilot, AC2 P/705414 M Wawrzaszek PAF, who was training was injured.

SATURDAY 8th JANUARY 1944

1230 hrs — Training

Wellington III BK300 of 18 OTU from Worksop had been in the air for 30 minutes when an engine failed and the aircraft crashed on the runway as the undercarriage could not be pumped down in time. The pilots were A/F/L 142852 John Edward Sanderson DFC RAFVR and P/O 150330 A C Hicks. F/L Sanderson, age 23, was a very experienced pilot having flown on many operations before being transferred to a training unit and was awarded the DFC on 13th August 1943 while serving with 76 Sqn.

He was the pilot of Halifax DT482 of 1656 HCU from Lindholme on a training exercise which crashed near Doncaster on 24th March killing all the crew. He is buried in Salendine Nook Baptist Chapelyard, his home town.

TUESDAY 11th JANUARY 1944

1225 hrs | Training

Wellington X LN570 of 82 OTU from Ossington overshot Gamston on demonstrating a flapless landing and crashed through a hedge. The pilot F/O J 15488 A A Sherlock was injured and the pilot under training P/O J/26755 Brown and four other crew members were un-injured.

1720 hrs | Ferrying

Oxford I HN529 of 16 (P)SFTS from Newton belly landed at Bilsthorpe as the pilot W/O P/780164 S Mierwiczek PAF was unable to find any aerodrome in bad visibility.

FRIDAY 14th JANUARY 1944

2045 hrs | Training

Oxford I NM307 of 16 (P)SFTS from Newton on take off run collided with Oxford HM608 which was still taxiing off the runway. The pilot was LAC P/784936 J Gesicki PAF.

2045 hrs | Taxiing

Oxford I HM608 of 16 (P)SFTS from Newton was taxiing off the runway when it was struck by Oxford NM307 which was taking off. The 1st pilot was F/L P/1402 M Wolandski and 2nd pilot Lt P/781237 E Polkowski.

2145 hrs | Training

Master III DL941 of 16 (P)SFTS from Newton landed at Tollerton, taxied to the runway intersection and stopped when it should have taxied clear. It was struck by Master EM385 which was taking off. The pilot, W/O P/778474 Mieczyslaw Edmund Popek PAF age 27, was killed and his body was taken to Newton Mortuary. He is buried in Newark-upon-Trent Cemetery. W/O Popek held the Cross of Valour and 2 Bars and was posthumously appointed to the Order Virtuti Militari V.

Master II EM385 of 16 (P)SFTS from Newton ran into Master DL941 on take-off (see above) from Tollerton and landed on one wheel at Newton The pilot was P/O Malinowski PAF and passenger Sgt P/781327 S Drazek PAF.

THURSDAY 20th JANUARY 1944

2050 hrs | Training

Wellington III BK273 of 18 OTU took off from Worksop and was on normal overshoot procedure at approximately 400 feet when the pilot lost control due to excessive vibration. The subsequent loss of a propeller blade caused the aircraft to crash in line with the runway 3½ miles from the aerodrome, at Worksop College, and caught fire. The crew of five were killed:

F/O 118399 Richard Harvey Brooke Jennings age 30 RAFVR (Pilot) buried Southend-on-Sea Cemetery, P/O 152946 Robert Frederick Wade age 21 RAFVR (Nav) buried Islington Cemetery, P/O 152995 Colin William Owen Sears RAFVR cremated at Beckenham Crematorium, Sgt 1671293 Patrick Downes age 20 RAFVR (W.Op/Air Gnr) buried Great

Crosby Roman Catholic Churchyard and Sgt 1216021 Kenneth Ernest Dudley Sillatoe age 22 RAFVR buried Harrogate (Stonefall) Cemetery.

FRIDAY 21st JANUARY 1944

0630 hrs — Training

Stirling III EF151 of 1661 HCU from Winthorpe was on its landing approach after a 3½ hour training flight when the port outer engine failed. With the undercarriage only partially down the aircraft became tail heavy, hit some trees, crashed and burst into flames at Glebe Farm, Brough, with the following casualties:

Sgt 1550988 J Docherty, (Pilot), admitted to Station Sick Headquarters and transferred to RAF Hospital, Rauceby.

Sgt 1814362 William Geoffrey Alexander Venables, age 19 RAFVR (F/Eng), admitted to Newark hospital and died the same day and is buried at Brymbo Churchyard, W/O R/150829 Gordon Chapman Munro, age 30 RCAF (Nav) buried Oxford (Botley) Cemetery.

Sgt R/145437 F C Biddle RCAF (Bomb Aimer) admitted to Newark Hospital.

Sgt 1586233 Alfred Frank Cooper, age 20 RAFVR (W.Op/Air Gnr) buried East London Cemetery Plaistow, Sgt 1875088 R Southey, MUAG) admitted to Newark hospital and A/428712 Sgt Alfred Samuel Humphreys age 20 RAAF (Rear Air Gunner) was admitted to the Station Sick Quarters.

Sgt Humphreys was killed in a mid-air collision near Lincoln, between a 463 Sqn Lancaster ED606 JO-E of which he was a crew member and Lancaster ND637 CF-L of 625 Sqn both returning from operations on 16th March 1944. He is buried in Cambridge City Cemetery. The 463 Squadron ORB reads: 'Aircraft collided with aircraft "L" of 625 Squadron, 1 Group (Captain, F/S Bulger) while circling the aerodrome preparatory to landing. All crew killed.'

1145 hrs — Training

Wellington III Z1733 of 18 OTU took off from Worksop for a combined navigation/bombing sortie. The aircraft lost power from one engine and as a result of making too fast an approach to land, crashed into a transformer hut, just off the airfield and burst into flames.

P/O 157529 Robert Thomas Harold Ellis age 21 RAFVR (W.Op) was killed and is buried in Neston Cemetery.

F/S 422097 R Bluett RNZAF (Pilot), F/S R B Turvey, Sgt J Alcock and Sgt C A McFarlane were injured.

SUNDAY 23rd JANUARY 1944

2300 hrs — Training

Wellington X LN169 of 18 OTU from Worksop starboard engine failed on take off and the aircraft was unable to maintain height and force landed straight ahead 1½ miles west of Worksop. The pilot was P/O 156653 G M G Harris.

THURSDAY 27th JANUARY 1944

2002 hrs — Training

Wellington X LN168 –O of 18 OTU took off from Gamston for a night exercise on high level bombing. Due to early loss of power from the port engine over Retford Bombing range the aircraft returned to base and crash landed wheels up caught fire but with no injuries to the crew. The pilot F/L J/6708 Davis Hamilton Perry age 26 RCAF subsequently lost his life on 12th May 1944 when piloting Halifax LW114 ZL-S of 427 Sqn for a raid on Boulogne. He lies in Calais Canadian War Cemetery.

2217 hrs **Training**

Wellington X HE983 of 18 OTU took off from Worksop and was carrying out night practice bombing at Clayworth Bombing Range when it dived vertically into the ground at high speed from 9,000 feet and was destroyed. The crash occurred near Hayton, one mile east south east of Lound, with the loss of five crew members. The cause was thought to be reduction gear failure.

Sgt 1600129 Michael Mullins age 21 RAFVR (Pilot) is buried in Salisbury Cemetery, Sgt R/153445 John Alan Jefferson age 28 RCAF buried Harrogate (Stonefall) Cemetery, Sgt 1456668 William Roy age 29 RAFVR buried Dinsdale Churchyard, Sgt 1321023 Robert Joseph King age 22 RAFVR (W.Op/Air Gnr) buried Barking Cemetery, Sgt 1594326 George Prentice age 19 RAFVR (Air Gnr) buried Sharlston Churchyard.

FRIDAY 28th JANUARY 1944

1125 hrs **Training**

Wellington X HE461 of 18 OTU from Worksop landed off the runway and the pilot, Sgt 1338028 R W Jenkins, carried out the overshoot procedure and hit logs at the end of runway.

MONDAY 31st JANUARY 1944

2035 hrs **Training**

Lancaster I R5854 of 5 LFS from Syerston made a heavy landing. The aircraft was undamaged but one of the crew received a fractured ankle. The pilot P/O 162951 Patrick Eric Norman Nice RAFVR had misjudged his height on levelling out.

P/O Nice was killed just 3 weeks later on 21st February. He was the pilot of Lancaster LM447 of 9 Sqn which took off from Bardney for a raid on Stuttgart and was lost without trace. He was age 23 and is commemorated on the Runnymede Memorial.

2132 hrs **Training**

Stirling III EF232 -J of 1660 HCU from Swinderby crashed near Bassingham bombing range, Carlton-le-Moorland shortly after taking off on a night bombing exercise and all the crew were killed. The cause was thought to be an engine fire whilst in flight. Its crew were:

F/O J/17624 James Hubert Mason DFC RCAF (Pilot) buried Aberdeen Cemetery, F/S 1390977 Stanley Edward Martin RAFVR (Pilot) admitted to RAF hospital and died 1.2.44 and is buried in Harrow Cemetery, Sgt 1573789 George Brown Lamb age 20 RAFVR (F/Eng) admitted to RAF hospital and later died and buried Aberdeen Cemetery Extension, Sgt 1724254 Roy Henry Appleton age 21 RAFVR (F/Eng) buried St Peter-in-Thanet Churchyard Kent, W/O 755362 James Bernard McKnight age 25 RAFVR (Nav) buried Newark-upon-Trent Cemetery, F/O J25122 Harry George Trueman age 24 RCAF (Air Bomber) buried Thurlby (St Germain) Churchyard, Sgt 1383442 Ronald Edward Duke age 23 RAFVR (W.Op/ Air Gnr) buried Thurlby Churchyard, Sgt 1896358 Harold Nelson age 20 RAFVR (MUAG) buried Easington Cemetery Durham.

F/O Mason was awarded the DFC on 10th December 1943 when serving with 50 Sqn. On 3rd April 1959 Mount Mason, situated on the east side of Douglas Creek, north of head of Harrison Lake, New Westminster Land District, Canada was named in his memory.

WEDNESDAY 2nd FEBRUARY 1944

1200 hrs **Training**

Oxford I MP452 of 16 (P)SFTS from Tollerton touched down with port and tail wheels, the aircraft swung to the left, the pilot LAC P/794876 J Gesicki PAF, opened the port throttles and used the starboard brake but the aircraft hit the third sodium flare due to the strong wind blowing at the time.

THURSDAY 3rd FEBRUARY 1944

1600 hrs Training

Wellington X HE749 of 84 OTU from Desborough took off on a solo cross country flight with a live bomb load. The aircraft had been in the air for 4 hours 50 minutes and on running short of fuel the pilot tried to make a landing at Scofton but overshot at his first landing attempt. The pilot opened up to go round again but the port engine failed, probably due to the shortage of petrol and the aircraft stalled and flicked over to port, crashed and caught fire at Crofton village. The bomb load exploded some time later and all 7 crew members on board were killed. On investigation the sump valve on the near port tank was found to be closed.

The pilot F/S 42189 Colin Arthur Harrison age 22 RNZAF is buried in Harrogate (Stonefall) Cemetery, F/O 148749 Clifford Craven Lumby age 29 RAFVR (Nav) buried Eccleshill Congregational Chapelyard, Sgt R/159216 Howard Leighton Mein age 32 RCAF buried Harrogate (Stonefall) Cemetery, F/O 151745 John Waring age 22 RAFVR (Air Bomber) buried Mount St Mary's Colledge Churchyard, Eckington, Sgt 1082323 John Robinson Ballantyne age 24 RAFVR (W.Op/Air Gnr) buried Mickley Churchyard, Sgt 1869643 Kenneth Buckler Lewis RAFVR buried Aspenden Churchyard, Sgt 1869819 Aubrey Ernest Walter Budden RAFVR buried Northfleet Cemetery.

Two members of the RAFVR, F/L 89044 Alfred George Spencer and F/O 145518 Albert Arthur attempted to rescue the crew from the burning aircraft and for their heroism were awarded the George Medal, gazetted on 1st September 1944.

The citation read: 'One day in February, 1944, an aircraft carrying a 500 lb bomb and incediaries, crashed near a Royal Air Force Station, and immediately caught fire. Flying Officer Arthur, a gunnery instructor, was soon on the scene and despite the great heat and exploding ammunition, he attempted to rescue the crew. Shortly afterwards he was joined by Flight Lieutenant Spencer, the station medical officer. The wreckage was blazing from end to end and several times these officers were compelled to break off their rescue attempts. Flying Officer Arthur entered the burning aircraft no less than four times, with a handkerchief tied round his nose and mouth. At the fourth attempt, he was driven back by the heat and flames, his eyebrows being burnt off and his right trouser leg and pocket burnt. Flight Lieutenant Spencer stayed close at hand and searched in the wreckage for possible survivors. It was not until the bombs were red hot and Flight Lieutenant Spencer was certain that the crew must be dead from the heat that these officers abandoned their efforts. They then warned the fire party to withdraw and cleared the area of spectators just before the 500 lb bomb exploded. Although the attempts of these officers to rescue the crew were in vain, they displayed high courage and a complete disregard for their own safety.'

1742 hrs Training

Wellington IC Z1114 of 28 OTU from Wymeswold had been in the air for 5 hours 40 minutes and on returning to base from cross country training the port engine began to fail and the aircraft overshot the runway, caught fire and was wrecked. 5 of the crew died:

Sgt R/160280 John Melville Stephens RCAF age 26 (Pilot), Sgt R/151184 Eric Edmond Cowie RCAF age 20 (Nav), Sgt John Halifax Casselman RCAF (Air Bomber), Sgt R/205766 William Reginald Stone RCAF age 19 (Air Gnr) all buried in Oxford (Botley) Cemetery, Sgt James Albert Webb RAFVR age 20 (W.Op/Air Gnr) buried Blackpool (Carleton) Cemetery, Sgt J/93274 John Richard Patterson RCAF age 21 (Air Gnr) was injured and on his recovery he joined 12 Sqn. He was promoted to P/O and was killed on 12th December 1944 when a member of the crew of Lancaster ND342 from Wickenby. He was lost on a raid on Essen and is buried in Reichswald Forest War Cemetery.

2220 hrs — Training

Wellington IC N2764 of 28 OTU from Wymeswold took off sluggishly on a solo cross country training flight so the undercarriage was raised immediately to lessen drag as height was being lost and trees were ahead. The pilot F/O 150146 Joseph Raymond Wilson RAFVR age 24 crash landed the aircraft in open space at Hoton and the port engine caught fire. The crew of seven were un-injured.

F/O Wilson who was by now a member of 166 Sqn was lost on a raid on Bochum on 5th November. He took off from Kirmington at 1725 hrs in Lancaster ME835 AS-T and was lost without trace. He and the rest of his crew are commemorated on the Runnymede Memorial.

Lancaster ME835 AS-T

—

Ossington

The Belgian authorities approved the award of the Croix de Guerre 1940 to F/S R/771168 (J/18746) John Henry Patrick Higgins RCAF who is based with 82 OTU at RAF Ossington. The citation stated 'this courageos and tenacious Non-Commissioned Officer has participated in 16 offensive sorties with Captain Pilot Zeger van Riel and has contributed to the success of experimental enterprises with the Belgians'. F/S Higgins was an Air Gunner with No.1369 Special Duties Unit at the time.

FRIDAY 4th FEBRUARY 1944

0026 hrs — Training

Wellington III X3409 of 82 OTU from Gamston was returning from a Bullseye and cross-country exercise to Gamston and at 2332 hrs was given a QDM. At 0026 hrs the aircraft was seen in a high speed vertical dive, hitting the ground and catching fire in Whisker Hills Woods, Babworth, with the loss of all five crew members. The cause of the crash was unknown.

The crew were: Sgt 1322490 Alick Charles Fisher age 21 RAFVR (Pilot) buried in Crystal Palace District Cemetery, F/S 424281 Clifford Desmond Jones RAAF aged 20 buried Ollerton Cemetery, Sgt R/180634 Joseph Louis Barber RCAF age 21 (W.Op/Air Gnr) buried Ollerton Cemetery, Sgt R/216087 Weston Ross Waldron RCAF age 20 (Air Gunner) buried Ollerton Cemetery, Sgt R/148733 Edmund Henry Duggan Maguire (Air Bomber) buried Ollerton Cemetery.

2310 hrs Training

Master II DM333 of 16 (P)SFTS from Tollerton was on night flying training with instructor and pupil and the pupil landed high and at low speed. The instructor, F/S P/793718 H Noga PAF opened the throttles but too late and the aircraft hit the ground breaking the starboard oleo leg. The pupil pilot was ? Gradzski PAF.

MONDAY 7th FEBRUARY 1944

1515 hrs

Auster NX592 of Army Co-Operation Unit from Barnby Moor crashed in a field east of Green Mile Lane, Babworth. The aircraft belonged to an Army Co-operation Unit which was thought to be operating from a field at Lee's Farm, Barnby Moor, where a detachment of the unit was temporary based. The Auster had been carrying out practice landings and when at about 150 feet the engine failed and it crashed into the field killing the crew of two.

The pilot was Capt 176674 Edgar Alan Gee, Air Observation Post Pilot Royal Artillery attached to 271 AOP Sqn RAF (7420 Army Co-operation) age 23 and is buried in Great Crosby Roman Catholic Churchyard. Sgt 571353 Thomas Henry Padmore (Fitter) aged 22, 271 Sqn RAF is buried in Hoo Churchyard Kent.

SATURDAY 12th FEBRUARY 1944

1100 hrs Training

Wellington III BK277 of CGS was on a day flying training flight from base to Newton when the pilot landed at the wrong aerodrome. The aircraft landed at Tollerton overshot, ran down the runway incline, the brakes failed to grip and the aircraft struck a drainage ditch and barbed wire and swung to starboard. The 1st pilot was F/O P/2147 Z K Jedrzejczyk PAF and 2nd pilot P/793958 W S Fedzinski PAF. There were no injuries.

SUNDAY 13th FEBRUARY 1944

Dominie I X7338 of 11 FP crashed in a forced landing at Mattersley Hill, near Mattersley.

A Dominie I aircraft

THURSDAY 17th FEBRUARY 1944

0025 hrs **Training**

Wellington X HE741 of 82 OTU from Ossington took off for night flying training and approaching to land at Gamston after a 3 hours 15 minutes flight the Air Bomber was instructed to turn on the fuel reserve tanks but the engines cut out and because they could not reach the airfield they landed straight ahead and the aircraft caught fire. The pilot, Sgt R/161767 J A Phillis RCAF, and his crew of 5 were un-injured.

WEDNESDAY 23rd FEBRUARY 1944

2116 hrs **Training**

Lancaster I W4113 of 5 LFS from Syerston landed and whilst taxiing hurried off the runway to avoid another aircraft landing, swung sharply and the undercarriage collapsed. Flying control was informed that the doors on the rear turret had to be forced open. The accident was due to wrong information being given to the pilot F/O A/409343 Tillatson RAAF by the rear gunner. The 2nd pilot was P/O A/414660 John Henry Dechastel RAAF who completed 32 operations and received the DFC with 463 Sqn.

THURSDAY 24th FEBRUARY 1944

2337 hrs **Training**

Wellington IC R1269 of 28 OTU took off from Castle Donington for night bombing practice. On return to base the port engine failed and while trying to go round again crashed near the airfield. The pilot was Sgt 1338622 J F Ross-Myring.

FRIDAY 25th FEBRUARY 1944

1847 hrs **Training**

Wellington X HE918 of 82 OTU from Gamston port engine failed after take off due to technical failure. The pilot F/O J/25868 L D Dickie lowered the undercarriage but approached landing too high, overshot and lost the undercarriage beyond the boundary.

2235 hrs **Training**

Master II DM283 of 16 (P)SFTS from Newton was on a circuits and landings exercise and had made 3 landings but got lost on the next take off. RT contact could not be made with the pilot. The aircraft hit high tension cables while flying low and crashed at Gregory's Rose Gardens at Stapleford. The pilot LAC P/704460 Marian Sierzega PAF, age 24 was seriously injured and died at 0430 hrs in Nottingham General Hospital on the 26th February. He is buried in Newark-upon-Trent Cemetery.

SATURDAY 26th FEBRUARY 1944

0130 hrs **Training**

Stirling III EF127 of 1661 HCU from Winthorpe was returning to base after a seven hour long night training flight when it hit some trees and crashed at Alby's Farm, Edwinstowe, scattering wreckage over three fields. The suspected cause was fuel shortage. A witness stated that the engines had stopped prior to the crash. Five members of the crew were killed and two seriously injured. The aircraft sent out a 'mayday' call which was heard by RAF Syerston but could not contact the aircraft.

F/S 401986 William Victor Manuel age 27 RAAF (Pilot) is buried in Oxford (Botley) Cemetery, Sgt 1677871 George Davison age 19 RAFVR (F/Eng) buried Tanfield St Margaret Cemetery, Co. Durham, F/S 418048 Campbell David Bird age 30 RAAF (Nav) buried Oxford (Botley) Cemetery, F/S 426127 George Macoun age 21 RAAF (Bomb Aimer) buried Oxford (Botley) Cemetery, F/S 423650 Sidney Edward Christie age 27 RAAF (W.Op/Air Gnr) also buried Oxford (Botley) Cemetery, F/S A/429483 R J Plath (MUAG) was injured and admitted to Mansfield General hospital and Sgt 434558 William Irving Taylor, RAAF (Rear Air Gunner) also injured and detained in Winthorpe Station Sick Headquarters.

F/S Taylor was killed on 23rd May when a member of the crew of Lancaster ND655 from 630 Sqn on a raid on Braunschweig. The aircraft was lost without trace and the crew are commemorated on the Runnymede Memorial.

WEDNESDAY 1st MARCH 1944

1207 hrs — Air Test

Stirling III EF518 GP-E of 1661 HCU from Winthorpe took off but as the throttles were advanced the aircraft veered sharply to port and ran into a bank of frozen snow losing its undercarriage. The pilots were S/L 124256 Malcolm Crocker RAFVR DFC and Bar and W/C B R Hallows.

Malcolm Crocker, now W/C, was killed on 22nd June 1944 piloting Lancaster LL900 of 49 Sqn on their 8th operation for a raid on Wesseling when the aircraft was shot down by a night fighter and crashed near Julich-Merach. He and his crew are buried in Rheinberg War Cemetery.

He was awarded the DFC on 15th October 1943. The citation read: 'For gallantry and devotion to duty in the execution of air operations.'

The following is courtesy of www.49squadron.co.uk: 'There was nothing unusual about Wednesday 21st June 1944; the weather, as with previous days remained dull and the slight northerly wind kept temperatures a little chilly. There had been no operations for the past five days but a Battle Order was posted detailing 20 aircraft and a briefing at 2000 hrs. A force of over 130 Lancasters from 5 Group was to attack the synthetic-oil plant at Wesseling, near Cologne, the target being marked by 5 Group Mosquitoes. One by one, the various specialists gave their talks, with W/C Malcolm Crocker concluding the briefing by stating that he too would be operating, and would be taking along Mr Stevenson, a War Correspondent from the BBC. Also flying would be both of 49's two Squadron Leaders. At 0332 hrs combat exhausted 49 Squadron crews began landing back at Fiskerton. Their opening remarks gave the first hints of the disaster that had befallen the aircrew of 5 Group. Written on the operations board in large chalk white capital letters...against the names of SIX aircraft captains were those three impassive words... "MISSING WITHOUT TRACE". Six aircraft equated to 42 good men, including its Commanding Officer, and a Squadron Leader.'

FRIDAY 3rd MARCH 1944

1435 hrs — Training

Stirling III EE956 from 1661 HCU from Winthorpe swung on landing due to port outer engine trouble and the aircraft ran into snow banks causing damage to the tail wheel unit. Harry Le-Marchant was radar navigator instructor aboard the aircraft and the pilot was F/L 130222 G Hildred. EE956 crashed at Rothwell, Northants on 17th May 1944 killing all the crew.

0135 hrs — Taxiing

Stirling III EF125 from 1661 HCU from Winthorpe was taxiing in preparation for take off on a training flight when it struck a snow bank on the edge of the runway and damaged the underside of the rear turret. The pilot was Sgt 742719 W Grantham.

SATURDAY 4th MARCH 1944

1605 hrs — Ferrying

Wellington X LP240 from 18 OTU was being ferried from Ossington to Finningley and on landing the aircraft bounced and drifted in the cross wind, hit the ground and was wrecked. No-one was injured. The pilot was Sgt 521103 W A Stewart.

MONDAY 6th MARCH 1944

0300 hrs — Training

Lancaster I W4122 of 5 LFS from Syerston landed high, bounced, hit a snow bank on the edge of the runway, and the starboard undercarriage collapsed. The aircraft ground looped at side of the runway. The instructor pilot was F/O 146323 W R P Perry and the pupil F/O 421134 Eric Walter Young RNZAF.

F/O Young was killed on 13th August 1944 flying with 83 Sqn age 23. He was the pilot of Lancaster PB240 -J which took off from Coningsby for a raid on Braunschweig with 17 other aircraft from 83 Sqn and a total of 242 Lancasters and 137 Halifaxes, and exploded in the air over the target area. All the crew are buried in Hanover War Cemetery. At the time of his death he had completed 669 flying hours and was on his 23rd Operation. He was on his 5th Operation with 83 Sqn having previously flown with 9 Sqn.

TUESDAY 7th MARCH 1944

2035 hrs — Training

Wellington X HE818 of 18 OTU took off from Worksop on an operational training flight and after an overshoot exercise climbed to 600 feet but was unable to maintain height and crashed out of control with smoke coming from both engines. The crash occurred 6 miles north of Worksop, at Blyth, and 4 crew members were killed: P/O 169914 Frank Reginald Bedford age 33 RAFVR (Pilot) buried Harrogate (Stonefall) Cemetery, Sgt 1549110 Charles Robson Peter Whisk age 21 RAFVR buried South Shields Cemetery, Sgt 1611612 Derek William Tindell age 21 RAFVR (Air Bomber) buried Camberwell New Cemetery, Sgt 1621263 Ralph Wallace Tunnicliffe age 22 REFVR (W.Op) buried Hasland Cemetery, Derbys.

Sgt 611721 Charles Cletheroe was injured but was killed, aged 24, on 16th August 1944 when a crew member of Lancaster LM674 of 625 Sqn on a raid on Stettin. He is commemorated on the Runnymede Memorial.

2350 hrs — Training

Halifax II HR657 of 1662 HCU from Blyton took off for a night navigation exercise, the crew having been attached from 300 Sqn of the Polish Air Force. The aircraft collided head-on with Halifax EB184 over the Misson Bombing range, broke up in the air, crashed and burnt on the ground between Graizelound and Haxey 11 miles south west of Scunthorpe.

The 7 crew were all killed: F/O P/0983 Zdzislaw Ingling age 26 buried Solihull Cemetery, Sgt P/794211 Boleslaw Kot age 27, F/O P/2280 Kazimierz Lenartowicz age 27, F/O P/2250 Henryk Juliusz Jarnicki age 24, Sgt P/782035 Gustaw Liskiewicz age 22, Sgt P/703437 Aleksander Loksza age 23 and Sgt P/703158 Boleslaw Machulak age 29, all buried in the Polish Plot of the Newark-upon-Trent Cemetery.

2350 hrs — Training

Halifax V EB184 GG-D of 1667 HCU from Sandtoft took off for night flying training and collided with Halifax HR657 (as above). The crew of 8 were all killed: Sgt 1320514 Peter Alfred Street age 27 RAFVR (Pilot) buried Bromley Hill Cemetery, Sgt 1591403 Harold Russon age

19 RAFVR (F/Eng) buried Rotherham (Moorgate) Cemetery, F/S 1542113 Alfred Fox RAFVR (Nav) buried Edgeside (St Anne) Churchyard, F/O J/27270 Edward Granville Bayer RCAF (Air Bomber) buried Harrogate (Stonefall) Cemetery, Sgt 1576896 Herbert Wilfred Green age 30 RAFVR (W.Op) buried Boston Cemetery, Sgt 591869 Leonard Frank Woods age 21 RAF (Nav) cremated Leeds (Cottingley Hall) Crematorium, Sgt 1825541 James Williamson Henderson age 19 RAFVR (Air Gnr) buried Walls Parish Churchyard, Sgt 1138457 Wilson Noel Farrell age 36 RAFVR (Air Gnr) buried Stretford Cemetery.

FRIDAY 10th MARCH 1944

2035 hrs — Taxiing

Wellington III X3407 of 18 OTU from Worksop was being marshalled to dispersal when an airman walked into the starboard propeller and was injured.

The pilot F/O 141768 Eliot John Welchman RAFVR age 26 was killed on 13th July. He was the pilot of Lancaster PD202 of 166 Sqn which took off from Kirmington to bomb rail facilities at Revigny and was believed shot down in an engagement with a 103 Sqn Lancaster. He and his crew are buried Prez-sur-Marne Churchyard.

MONDAY 13th MARCH 1944

0200 hrs — Training

Stirling III EF463 TV-D of 1660 HCU from Swinderby returned after a 3hour 25 minute flight with port outer engine failure, bounced on the starboard wheel on landing and tore off the undercarriage. The crew were F/O 422697 B K Purday RAAF (Pilot), F/O Hornsby (F/Eng), Sgt Frost (F/Eng), F/S Hind (Nav), F/O Papworth (Bomb Aimer), W/O Needham (W.Op), F/S Schmerl (MUAG) and Sgt Dever (Rear Gnr). There were no injuries.

1805 hrs — Training

Lancaster I R5851 RC-A of 5 LFS from Syerston was on a dual training flight on a 3 engine overshoot when, with F/L Ruskell at the controls, it banked to port to avoid a building and the starboard wing came up and the aircraft crashed. 5 of the crew were un-injured and 3 were slightly injured.

The pilot instructor F/L 131595 K Rustell and the pupil pilot F/S 421858 Edward Frank Champness RAAF were both injured. The other crew members were Sgt 1822545 John Peacock Craig Johnstone RAFVR, Sgt V S J Zucker RAAF injured, Sgt N C Scullard seriously injured, Sgt E Adair, Sgt L Jones and Sgt 1623919 Alan Leslie Pickering RAFVR.

On 22nd May 1944 a crew from 630 Sqn consisting of all but F/L Ruskell and Sgt Scullard of the above crew were tasked to attack Braunschweig in Lancaster JB546 from East Kirkby.

During that operation E Champness, now a P/O, Sgt Johnstone and Sgt Pickering all lost their lives when their aircraft was shot down by a night fighter and they are buried Rheinberg War Cemetery. F/S Zucker, Sgt E Adair and Sgt L Jones were taken prisoner.

TUESDAY 14th MARCH 1944

1615 hrs — Training

Stirling III EF120 of 1660 HCU from Swinderby was on conversion training and with starboard outer engine feathered at 11,000 feet, the pilot opened up for overshoot but swung and crash landed off the aerodrome, wheels up at Norton Disney. The crew were: F/S 418170 Lloyd Lewis Pemberton RAAF (Pilot), Sgt 524666 Leslie Peace RAF (F/Eng), Sgt 1823946 J Orr, Sgt 1321649 L W Bryan, F/O 151846 Andrew Clarkson RAFVR (Air Bomber), Sgt 1543162 Joshua Hebden Morrison RAFVR (W.Op), Sgt 1893193 L Hilder (MUAG) and Sgt 1592827

Irvin Bowley RAFVR (Air Gnr). There was only 1 injury to the crew of 8, Sgt Pemberton being admitted to the SSQ.

However F/S Pemberton, Sgt Peace, F/O Clarkson, Sgt Morrison, and Sgt I Bowley were all killed on 29th July 1944 whilst flying with 106 Sqn. They took off from Metheringham in Lancaster ME778 ZN-O for a raid on Stuttgart and were shot down by Major Heinz-Wolfgang Schnaufer of IV./NJG1, his 89th victory. The aircraft crashed at Durmersheim and all the crew are buried in Durnbach Cemetery, Bayern, Germany.

THURSDAY 16th MARCH 1944

1200 hrs

Lightning P-38J 42-68019 from 20 Group crashed into a house occupied by Mr and Mrs Dannett of Thorpe, near Newark. The house was made un-habitable. The pilot Robert L Wells was taken to hospital. 3 civilians were injured.

The following report is from the Newark Advertiser: 'The Lightning crashed into a house injuring its occupants and causing the death of Mr George Stansall a well known bricklayer age 62 who died from his injuries. At the time of the crash Mr Kirk was putting in new windows to the cottage which was now a charred and burnt out wreck.

Shortly after noon the plane piloted by an American airman who baled out, crashed into "Jasmine Cottage" at Thorpe and burst into flames. Partially demolished, the building took fire and all the four occupants received burns and suffered from shock. They were taken to Newark Hospital. Mr George Dannett 34 after being treated for slight burns was allowed to leave but his wife, Mrs Annie Dannett, Mr George Stansall and a workman, Mr George Kirk 38 of Flintham were detained. Mr Stansall died early on Friday morning and Mrs Dannett and Mr Kirk were "quite comfortable". At the inquest of Mr Stansall, Capt George Wemyss said the pilot of the plane had been seriously injured and was now at a military hospital.'

2320 hrs — Training

Wellington IC R1183 of 28 OTU from Castle Donington crashed near the aerodrome on take-off for a training flight and caught fire. After take off, at about 200 feet, the pilot noticed low air speed and slow rate of ascent, on cockpit check the flaps were found to be fully down. Of the 5 crew, 2 were killed and 3 injured.

Those injured were F/S 418454 A J Mosley RAAF (Pilot), Sgt W J Foxley and F/S J N Gunnis RAAF. F/S Mosley received the DFC serving with 103 Sqn.

Those who died were Sgt 1332442 Anthony William Herbert Rowley age 20 RAFVR buried in Kingsbury Churchyard, Middlesex and Sgt 1697611 Ernest Small age 20 RAFVR who died the next day buried in Gateshead Cemetery.

MONDAY 20th MARCH 1944

2200 hrs — Stationary

Wellington I X9603 of 28 OTU from Wymeswold bomb aimer left the aircraft due to ill health without telling the pilot and walked into a propeller. The pilots were F/O 156220 G Coleman and F/O 124176 P E Morris.

2342 hrs — Training

Wellington III DF638 of 82 OTU from Gamston had only been in the air for 5 minutes when the starboard engine began running rough. The pilot, F/O J/27647 W P Saye RCAF, opened the throttles and the engine caught fire and he force landed the aircraft in soft ground at the side of the runway and nose tipped up at Gamston. Two of the five crew members were injured.

TUESDAY 21st MARCH 1944

1524 hrs — Training

Stirling III LJ533 of 1661HCU from Winthorpe was totally destroyed whilst carrying out an overshoot at Winthorpe on day flying training. The port outer engine failed and would not feather and the pilot carried out a forced landing in a field near Syerston airfield. The aircraft hit some trees and 3 of the 7 crew were injured.

F/O 157097 Leslie Norman Simpkin RAFVR (Pilot) was killed on 22nd June 1944 whilst flying with 49 Sqn. He took off from Fiskerton piloting Lancaster NE128 EA-J for a raid on Wesseling and crashed in Germany. 5 of his crew were taken prisoner and he is buried in Rheinberg War Cemetery. This was a very sad day for 49 Sqn as 6 aircraft and 42 men failed to return from this operation.

2055 hrs — Taxiing

Wellington III X3541 of 18 OTU from Bircotes was stationary at its taxiing post when it was struck by Wellington BJ712 which was taxiing. The pilot of X3541 was F/S P/794535 M Wasilczuk PAF and F/S 415600 P Aldred RAAF of BJ712.

WEDNESDAY 22nd MARCH 1944

0050 hrs — Training

Halifax V LK930 of 1664 HCU from Dishforth took off for a night navigation exercise and after nearly six hours flight the port inner engine failed and would not feather. The pilot was unable to maintain height and he gave the order for the crew to bale out. F/O Pilkington, Sgt Peel and W/O Loucks ejected through the nose flap and by that time the aircraft was on fire and too low for anyone else to jump. The aircraft crash landed on Scarcliffe Lane, half way between Scarcliffe and Polterton, just over the Nottinghamshire border in Derbyshire. The aircraft finished up with its main fuselage straddled across the road.

Two of the crew were injured and three killed. One of the crewmen was trapped in the rear of the aircraft and died; another was taken to Chesterfield Royal Hospital but also died there.

The pilot Sgt H Ray Collver RCAF who was injured and taken to Mansfield Hospital was very experienced with 900 flying hours.

Sgt 1045627 Russell Irvine Pym RAFVR age 21 (F/Eng) was killed and is buried in Morecombe and Heysham (Hale Carr) Cemetery, F/O Ralph Pilkinton Navigator, Sgt Russell Peel (Bomb Aimer) and W/O Wally Loucks (Wireless Operator) were not injured.

Sgt R/201503 William (Bill) Arthur Roland Andrew RCAF age 20 (Air Gnr) and Sgt R/198952 Arley Carlisle Starnes RCAF age 22 (Air Gnr) are buried side by side in Harrogate (Stonefall) Cemetery.

Two brothers, Albert and Rolston Calow, attempted to rescue the crewmen still trapped in the burning aircraft and managed to release one of them, Sgt Starnes, who had been trapped in the rear of the aircraft, but he later died from his injuries at Chesterfield Royal Hospital. For their gallantry both brothers were awarded the BEM and they were both decorated by King George VI at a Buckingham Palace Investiture on 23rd October 1945.

The award was gazetted on 27th June 1944: 'Awarded the British Empire Medal (Civil Division): Albert Groves Calow, Process Worker, Palterton, Nr. Chesterfield. George Rolston Calow, Colliery Fitter, Palterton, Nr. Chesterfield.

When an aircraft crashed and caught fire George Calow immediately went to the scene. Hearing cries for help coming from inside the nose end of the machine which was burning furiously, he tried to enter the plane by breaking a hole through the fuselage but failed. He then found an opening about 18 inches high underneath the centre gun turret. Removing the wreckage which was in his way he reached a man whose clothes were on fire. Calow endeavoured

to lift him but was unable to do so. Albert Calow then arrived and came to his brother's aid. Together they smothered the flames which enveloped the man and dragged him towards the hole. By this time ammunition was exploding inside the machine and the fire was becoming fiercer. They removed exploding ammunition belts and other debris from their path and were then able to drag the man head first through the hole underneath the 'plane and carried him to safety.

Albert and George Calow, who were badly burned during the rescue work, showed courage and determination without regard for their own safety.'

A local man erected a stone post with a brass plaque attached in recognition of the 7 man crew. The location of the memorial is OS sheet 120 485684

1140 hrs — Training

Wellington III BK207 of 18 OTU from Worksop was on day flying training when the pupil pilot landed heavily and damaged the tail wheel. The Instructor took over and did another circuit and did a wheel landing but the tail wheel collapsed when the aircraft stopped and the tail lowered. The pilots were P/O 411961 M J Wells RNZAF and Sgt 1105172 D A Kelsall. Sgt Kelsall was involved in another incident on 31st March.

THURSDAY 23rd MARCH 1944

0235 hrs — Training

Wellington III BJ839 of 18 OTU from Bircotes touched down and when the brakes were applied they failed to hold, further application failed until the perimeter was reached when the wheels locked, the aircraft hit rough ground and the nose tipped.

The pilot, F/S 418380 Raymond Leslie Francis RAAF age 25, was killed on 8th June when, as pilot of Halifax LL459 of 1667 CU on a training flight, his aircraft stalled and crashed near Howden Dyke Island, Yorkshire. He is buried in Harrogate (Stonefall) Cemetery and he had enlisted in Melbourne on 22th May 1942.

FRIDAY 24th MARCH 1944

1000 hrs — Air Test

Martinet I MS904 of 82 OTU from Ossington crashed just after becoming airborne when engine cutting occurred and the pilot retracted the undercarriage due to imminent overshooting of the aerodrome. The pilots were F/O J/11145 W N Brown RCAF and F/L J/10506 W R Thompson RCAF. There were no injuries.

SATURDAY 25th MARCH 1944

1130 hrs — Air Test

Master III DL938 of 16 (P)SFTS from Newton took off for an air test with P/O P/2353 Tadeusz Szwede PAF at the controls. He took off in a semi-stalled condition and to remedy this probably intended to select flaps at 25 degrees, but accidentally selected full flaps. At 50 feet the aircraft banked to starboard and dived into the ground, out of control, killing both P/O T Szwede and his passenger Sgt 629871 Leslie William Henry Brown, Fitter II (Engines). P/O Szwede lies in Newark-upon-Trent Cemetery and Sgt Brown Leicester Cemetery.

Op; Nickel

Wellington IC T2922 of 28 OTU from Wymeswold took off for operations. During the flight the aircraft was shot up by a night fighter, returned to base, and landed with undercarriage retracted.

1457 hrs Training

Wellington IC X9644 of 28 OTU from Castle Donington attempted to take off but failed to become airborne and as the aircraft was nearing the end of the runway the pilot throttled back and raised the undercarriage and the aircraft stopped off the runway. The pilot was W/O R/133784 J F Winters RCAF.

SUNDAY 26th MARCH 1944

0955 hrs Ground

Wellington IC N2737 of 28 OTU from Wymeswold was having engine tests when the port throttle was closed by Cpl 1289403 P Barker and as he did so a sheet of flame erupted from the exhaust and set light to the fabric surfaces beneath the wing and engulfed the aircraft.

2010 hrs Training

Wellington III X3996 of 18 OTU from Bircotes had its engines run up by the pilot, F/S P/783102 L Dunayewski PAF, and in order to attract the attention of the ground crew he waved his left hand out of the front of the aircraft where upon it was hit by the port propeller.

THURSDAY 30th MARCH 1944

C-47A 42-100923 from 440 Group crashed and was destroyed by fire at Bottesford. The pilot was H E Locke.

1620 hrs Training

Oxford I HN598 of HGCU overshot the runway at Tollerton and struck a hedge after a previous attempt to land which also overshot. The 1st pilot was P/O 416610 N Pfeiffer RAAF and 2nd pilot F/O 150171 R Wilcox.

The photograph seen here was taken at Brize Norton on 7th October 1943 outside the Sergeant's mess where a heavy glider conversion unit was based.

The personnel illustrated are: F/L 411342 H C Long (Liaison Officer), F/S 416610 N Pfeiffer, Sgt 420128 R V Baker, F/S 413154 F L Conn and Sgt 413075 L J Colgan (Instructors)

It was at this unit that the army glider pilots who guided the first gliders to land in Sicily were trained.

MONDAY 31st MARCH 1944

0717 hrs — Op; Nurnberg

Lancaster III DV227 VN-L of 50 Sqn from Skellingthorpe returned from a raid on Nurnberg after a flight of 8 hours 40 minutes and overshot on landing at Winthorpe and the aircraft tipped up in a ploughed field. The pilot, Sgt 983718 A Hanley, was exonerated from any blame.

1335 hrs — Training

Wellington X LP290 of 18 OTU from Worksop overshot landing, the brakes failed to respond, the undercarriage was raised but only the port side retracted. The pilot Sgt 405172 D A Kelsall was involved in a previous incident on 22nd March.

2120 hrs — Training

Stirling III EF444 of 1661 HCU from Winthorpe returned from a cross country flying exercise, after 1 hour 50 minutes, with suspected engine trouble and on landing overshot, ran into soft ground and the aircraft tipped up onto its nose. The pilot was F/L 61974 Arthur Llewelyn Williams RAFVR. The aircraft was repaired on site by No.58 MU and returned to 1661 HCU on 6th June but crashed 2 weeks later. F/L Williams was promoted to S/L but was killed on 26th August age 30. He was the pilot of Lancaster PB345 -Q of 83 Sqn which took off from Coningsby with 6 other 83 Sqn aircraft for a raid on Darmstadt and crashed near Neckarburken. Three of the crew died and 4 were made POWs. F/L Williams is buried in Durnbach War Cemetery, he was awarded the DFC posthumously, on 29th June 1945.

SATURDAY 1st APRIL 1944

1210 hrs — Ground

Tomahawk I AH764 of 1685 Flt from Ossington was taxiing prior to take off for a fighter affiliation exercise, and collided with a motor transport vehicle. The pilot was W/O F Bidewell.

1310 hrs — Training

Wellington IC DV444 –D of 28 OTU from Castle Donington took off for bombing practice and while cruising at 9,000 feet the port engine failed and the aircraft returned to base. The pilot, Sgt 1247333 A R Harris, endeavoured to make a wheels up forced landing on the airfield but was unable to pump the flaps down and the aircraft overshot and belly landed in a field 200 yards beyond the end of the runway.

1600 hrs — Training

Lancaster I W4940 of 5 LFS from Syerston landed and the port wheel axle sheared. The instructor pilot, F/O 413192 Harvey RAAF, was demonstrating 3 engine landings with drift. The pupil pilot was F/O J/21880 Harold James Young RCAF.

F/O Young was killed 20 days later age 26 flying with 57 Sqn. He was the pilot of Lancaster ND582 which took off from East Kirkby for a raid on La Chapelle to bomb railway yards. On return the crew attempted to land at Croydon but overshot the runway and crashed at 0220 hrs into houses bordering the airport. He is buried in Brookwood Military Cemetery.

TUESDAY 4th APRIL 1944

1545 hrs — Training

Lancaster I R5726 VN-B of 5 LFS from Syerston was on a training flight when it dived out of low cloud at an angle of 45 degrees at great speed and broke up shredding pieces, fins, elevators and wing tips ½ mile from Brenston. The Air Accident Branch suggested that the crash could have been due to icing. All of the 7 crew were killed.

F/O 413640 John David Murray RAAF age 34 (Pilot) is buried in Oxford (Botley) Cemetery, Sgt 1890699 Sidney Chappell age 19 RAFVR (F/Eng) buried South Kelsey (St Nicholas) Churchyard, F/S 424190 William Henry Keeble age 24 RAAF, F/O 421105 William Leopold Towers age 33 RAAF, F/O 419308 Frank Lockyer Grimwood age 25 RAAF, F/S 417548 Raymond George Williams age 20 RAAF all buried in Oxford (Botley) Cemetery, Sgt 1895505 Robert Edward James Sisley age 19 RAFVR (Air Gnr) buried in Dover (Charlton) Cemetery.

F/O Towers's brother Sapper John Charles Towers was killed at El Alamein on 31st October 1942.

FRIDAY 7th APRIL 1944

1127 hrs — Training

Martinet I MS644 of 82 OTU from Gamston failed to get off the ground on take-off, the throttle was closed, undercarriage retracted but the aircraft went over the embankment at the end of the runway and finished up in the river Idle. The cockpit drill of the pilot P/O J/14101 J S McLeod RCAF was at fault.

2030 hrs — Training

Stirling III LK485 of 1661HCU was carrying out a training flight when it started to develop problems. First, the port inner engine failed and was feathered, later there was an oil leak in the port outer engine which failed and was also feathered. The aircraft then started to lose height and the pilot, Sgt 1322055 W North, could not un-feather the engines. A wheel down landing was attempted, but, as the undercarriage was not locked down, it collapsed on landing in some small pine trees in Clipstone Forest, near Ollerton. There were no injuries to the crew and Sgt North was recommended for a Green Endorsement in his Log Book.

It seemed that metal was found in the induction pipe of No.7 cylinder of the port outer and the big end bearing in the port inner had broken up. There was also an oil leak to the CSU accounting for the inability to un-feather. Sgt North was also involved in an incident on 20th March.

SATURDAY 8th APRIL 1944

1700 hrs — Training

Wellington X JA502 of 18 OTU from Bircotes took off and at 200 feet the port engine failed. The pilot, F/S 417454 Ronald William Brown RAAF, made a forced landing straight ahead as he was unable to maintain height on the starboard engine. The 2nd pilot was Sgt 614027 G A Price.

F/S Brown age 21 was killed 16 weeks later when he took off from Elsham Wolds on 28th July in Lancaster LL799 of 576 Sqn on a raid on Stuttgart. His aircraft crashed at 0230 hrs and he and 4 members of his crew are buried in Cronenbourg French National Cemetery.

—

An airman based at Syerston was brought into SSQ in a collapsed condition and died later in hospital from a cerebral haemorrhage.

1747 hrs — Training

Wellington III X3648 of 18 OTU from Bircotes landed and then fire broke out due to a wire shorting above the bomb aimer's panel. This was put out by the crash tender while the aircraft was taxiing. The instructor pilot was W/C 39295 Thomas William La Basse Bamford and the pupil F/S 417195 J McGuire RAAF.

MONDAY 10th APRIL 1944

1645 hrs Ground

Wellington VI HE424 of 82 OTU from Gamston piloted by W/C J/7456 W C Cameron RCAF was sitting at dispersal after a 1 hour 45 minutes training flight when the rear gunner left the aircraft and was struck by a propeller whilst walking to the front of the aircraft. The accident was caused by the rear gunner disobeying instructions by leaving the aircraft by the turret without the captain's permission then walking into a propeller. He had been told to get out of the aircraft through the front hatch.

TUESDAY 11th APRIL 1944

1629 hrs Training

Stirling III LK456 GP-T of 1661 HCU from Winthorpe was on a training flight, carrying practice bombs, when the aircraft caught fire in the air and crashed out of control at Winthorpe, causing the death of all nine crew members.

P/O J/85717 (R156160) John D'Arcy Langlois age 22 RCAF (Pilot) is buried in Harrogate (Stonefall) Cemetery, Sgt 1824300 Thomas Dunn age 19 RAFVR (F/Eng) buried Newton Parish Church Midlothian, Sgt 1817031 Leonard Frisby age 24 RAFVR (F/Eng) buried Dudley, Sgt 1862913 William John Clifford Lowin age 19 RAFVR (F/Eng) buried Cheshunt, F/O J/25023 Gilbert Alan Charlesworth age 27 RCAF (Nav) buried Harrogate (Stonefall) Cemetery, Sgt 1396829 Edgar William Buckley age 20 RAFVR (Bomb Aimer) buried Orpington Churchyard, Sgt 657943 James Miller Robertson age 28 RAFVR (W.O/Air Gnr), Sgt 1821022 Robert Nicholl age 19 RAFVR (MUG) and Sgt 1565415 William Baird Thomson RAFVR (Rear Gnr) are all buried in Oxford (Botley) Cemetery.

—

A WAAF based at Syerston was knocked off her bicycle by a passing lorry and died from a fractured skull soon after being picked up.

WEDNESDAY 12th APRIL 1944

0030 hrs Training

Stirling III EF447 of 1661HCU from Winthorpe landed off the runway and collided with the windsock pole. The pilot, Sgt 1391259 J Steven, and his 7 man crew were un-injured.

THURSDAY 13th APRIL 1944

1230 hrs Training

Wellington III BJ712 of 18 OTU from Bircotes landed on the rough grass airfield and the tail wheel unit collapsed and was forced up into the fuselage. The pilot, F/O 141352 George Nevill Conyngham Smyth RAFVR age 33, was not injured but was killed on 26th June. He was the pilot of Halifax DG395 which took off from Sandtoft for an exercise in night bombing and crashed 10 minutes later near Thorne, Yorkshire.

1845 hrs Training

Lancaster I L7580 of 5 LFS from Syerston carried out a 3 engine overshoot exercise on landing, but to avoid a 200 foot drop at the end of the runway the instructor pilot, P/O 169008 R J Hughes, swung the aircraft to stop. A section of the tail was damaged and also the port main undercarriage. The pupil pilot, P/O 172749 R C Lake, made an error of judgement and tried to land the aircraft after too high an approach speed to land.

FRIDAY 14th APRIL 1944

1630 hrs — Training

Lancaster I W4103 RC-E of 5 LFS from Syerston collided with Oxford LB415 at 1,000 feet and crashed 1½ miles south of Syerston aerodrome. The crew were on a dual training exercise and the crash could have occurred because of the failure of both crews to keep a good lookout. All crew were killed, they were: F/O J/17320 Henry Holmes Richardson DFM RCAF age 28 (Pilot), P/O 415800 Patrick William Laidler (Pupil Pilot) and Sgt 1822275 Henry Ernest Herbert age 19 RAFVR (F/Eng) all buried in Oxford (Botley) Cemetery, F/O 140864 Peter William Raymond Holes age 22 RAFVR (Nav) buried Colwyn Bay (Bronynant) Cemetery, F/O 151768 David Winchester McRuer age 22 RAFVR (Air Bomber) buried Newark-upon-Trent Cemetery, Sgt 1800248 Glyn Robert (Bob) Aspinall age 20 RAFVR (W. Op) buried Laxfield Cemetery, Sgt 1869475 Frederick William Edwards age 22 RAFVR (Air Gnr) buried Birmingham (lodge Hill) Cemetery, AC2 1677803 Sidney Stokoe age 19 RAFVR (Pilot U/T) buried Newcastle-upon-Tyne (West Road) Cemetery, Sgt 1892933 Victor Charles William Arras Gouldstone RAFVR age 27 (Air Gnr) buried Aylesford Cemetery.

F/O Richardson was awarded the DFM effective from 6th August 1943 when flying with 50 Sqn. He enlisted in his home town of Winnipeg, graduated from initial training on 18th August 1941, No.18 EFTS on 7th October 1941 and No.11 SFTS on 30th December 1941. He was invested with his award by King George VI on 25th March 1944. His citation read: 'By his excellent example this airman has helped to maintain a high standard of efficiency among the pilots of his squadron. Many of the sorties undertaken by him were raids on strongly defended targets in Germany. On several of these he avoided encounters with night fighters by skilful manoeuvring and flew his aircraft safely to base. Flight Sergeant Richardson also took some good shots. His courage and skill in pressing home his attack have invariably been worthy of high praise.'

1630 hrs — Training

Oxford I LB415 of 1521 BAT Flt from Wymeswold had been in the air for 40 minutes on beam approach training when it collided with Lancaster W4103, 1½ miles south of Syerston aerodrome and crashed and burnt out killing both crew members. One of the crew managed to get out of the Oxford and parachuted down but was injured and died soon after reaching hospital.

F/L 120119 James Addison Hawkins age 22 RAFVR (Pilot) is buried in Burton-on-the-Wolds Cemetery and P/O 160921 Bryan Hedley Dennis age 21 RAFVR (Pupil Pilot) is buried in St Albans Cemetery.

A memorial service was held at Screveton on Sunday 13th November 2005 to commemorate the 11 airmen killed in the above collision. A 7 ton granite memorial was also unveiled in Flintham Road, Screveton, between the 2 crash sites. (See chapter on memorials.)

SATURDAY 15th APRIL 1944

1515 hrs — Training

Wellington X HE804 of 1481 Flt from Ingham took off for a cine camera gun exercise and the starboard engine cut at 1,500 feet. The aircraft lost height and crashed into woods near Ollerton, 200 yards east of the Worksop to Ollerton Road. The pilot was faced with a difficult situation with 9 crew and a failed engine but there were few clear spaces in which to land. All crew members were injured: F/S 1147370 P Holt DFM (Pilot), F/O D A Black RCAF, F/O G Mann RCAF, Sgt F H Rout, Sgt E R Matthews RCAF, Sgt R L Holmgren RCAF, Sgt W R Field, Sgt R/210602 Eric Smith RCAF and F/S F A Sparks.

Eric Smith aged 20, now F/S, was an air gunner on his 27th sortie when he was killed on 4th November 1944 when a member of the crew of Lancaster LM290 UM-W2 of 626 Sqn. The aircraft took off from Wickenby for a raid on Bochum and crashed near Menen, Belgium. He is buried in St-Jean Communal Cemetery at Courtrai.

MONDAY 17th APRIL 1944

1605 hrs — Training

Lancaster I W4232 RC-Y of 5 LFS from Syerston took off on a training flight when 4 minutes later, at 1,000 feet, part of the port wing broke off and the aircraft crashed adjacent to Syerston airfield. All 7 of the crew were killed but only five bodies could be positively identified.

The crew were: Sgt 418120 Bruce Lettington Humphreys age 20 RAAF (Pilot) buried in Oxford (Botley) Cemetery, Sgt 2202697 Alan Townsley age 19 RAFVR an Australian and Sgt 2204830 John Albert Davies age 19 RAFVR are both commemorated on the Runnymede Memorial, F/S 1238840 Arthur Harkness Farrell age 26 RAFVR (Nav) was cremated Blackpool (Carleton) Crematorium, Poulton-le-Fylde, Sgt 1459698 Nelson Harcourt Cutler age 29 RAFVR (Bomb Aimer) buried Castleford (Whitwood) Cemetery, Sgt 1650995 Reginald John Brown age 20 RAFVR (W.Op) buried Newport (St Woollos) Cemetery, and Sgt 1894597 Alan Dennis Bale age 19 RAFVR (Air Gnr) buried Darlington West Cemetery.

Lancaster I W4232

WEDNESDAY 19th APRIL 1944

0305 hrs — Training

Wellington X MF200 of 28 OTU from Wymeswold made a normal take off in the dark and poor visibility but crashed 15 minutes later whilst on solo circuits and landings at Normanton-on-Soar. It was not possible to establish the cause of the crash. All the crew of 4 were killed.

F/O 145501 Donald Hugh King age 24 RAFVR is buried in Burton-on-the-Wolds Church Cemetery, P/O 154086 Douglas Robert Doyle RAFVR (Nav) buried in Greystones Cemetery, Ireland, Sgt 2207037 Desmond Fretwell age 19 RAFVR (W.Op/Air Gnr) buried Bradfield (St Nicholas) Churchyard and Sgt 1565479 Lawrence Emmerson Garrod age 22 RAFVR (Air Gnr) buried Blyth (Cowpen) Cemetery.

FRIDAY 21st APRIL 1944

0943 hrs — Training

Tiger Moth II T6268 of 25 (P)EFTS from Hucknall was piloted by AC2 P/705622 Wladyslaw Karol Michon PAF on day landing exercises. The aircraft crashed on the road, near the Rolls-Royce buildings and caught fire, after AC2 Michon had attempted to go round again to recover from a bad landing. He was killed and was buried in Hucknall Cemetery on 24th April. The Court of Enquiry concluded that the cause of the accident was due to the inexperience of the pilot and a certain amount of tenseness whilst flying solo.

SATURDAY 22nd APRIL 1944

0358 hrs | Training

Stirling III EF498 -P of 1660 HCU from Swinderby took off at 2205 hrs on a night navigation training flight and 5 hours 53 minutes later collided with Stirling III EH926 in the air on approach to Swinderby, after being given permission to land, and both aircraft crashed near Eagle and caught fire.

All of the crew were killed, they were: P/O 174542 Archibald Macpherson Lees age 22 RAFVR (Pilot) is buried in Ayr Cemetery, Sgt 1690176 Thomas Mitchell age 23 RAFVR (F/Eng) buried Thurlby (St Germain) Churchyard, Sgt 1247821 John Edward Rowley age 32 RAFVR (F/Eng) buried Wednesfield (St Thomas) Churchyard Extension, F/O 143498 Michael Patrick O'Keefe age 20 RAFVR (Air Bomber) buried Rhondda (Trealaw) Cemetery, Sgt 1387549 Peter Bartley Illingworth age RAFVR (Nav) buried Romford Cemetery, Sgt 1215321 Leslie Burman age 23 RAFVR (W.Op Air Gnr) buried Leeds (Harehills) Cemetery, Sgt R/194178 Neville Hugh Banning Garrity age 19 RCAF (Air Gnr) and Sgt R/180231 Albert Louis Stoneham age 29 RCAF (Air Gnr) both buried in Harrogate (Stonefall) Cemetery.

0358 hrs | Training

Stirling III EH926 -T of 1654 HCU from Wigsley took off at 2123 hrs, also on a night navigation exercise, and when preparing to land after a 6 hours 35 minute flight and circling, collided with Stirling III EF498 (see above) caught fire and crashed near Eagle village.

All 7 of the crew were killed: P/O 174615 George Rex Jeans RAFVR (Pilot) buried Yorktown (St Michael) Churchyard, Sgt 1853236 Reginald Victor Searle age 20 RAFVR (F/Eng) buried Long Crendon (St Mary) Churchyard, Sgt 1541433 James Godfrey Case RAFVR (Nav) buried Prescot Cemetery, Sgt 1431809 Joseph William Willies age 22 RAFVR buried Whitwell (St Lawrence) Churchyard, Sgt 1801474 Arthur James George (Jimmy) King age 20 RAFVR (W.Op/Air Gnr) buried Reading Cemetery, Sgt 1310572 Lawrence Allen age 30 RAFVR (Air Gnr) buried Manchester Southern Cemetery, Sgt 1590650 Alan Douglas Short age 19 RAFVR (Air Gnr) buried Sunderland (Bishopwearmouth) Cemetery.

Sgt Short's brother Cpl 4457476 Albert Edward Short also died on service with the Durham Light Infantry on 26.7.40.

SUNDAY 23rd APRIL 1944

0010 hrs | Ground

Wellington X HE866 of 82 OTU from Ossington was waiting at its take off post when it was struck by Wellington HE528 which was taxiing. The pilot was F/S R/161722 D D Conner RCAF.

1844 hrs | Training

Wellington III Z1621 of 28 OTU from Wymeswold took off for circuits and landings training but the boost pressure on the starboard engine fell off and the pilot closed the throttles. The aircraft sank rapidly and force-landed straight ahead. The pilot was F/O 413103 Murray David Muggeridge DFM RNZAF and the pupil pilot F/S 417081 P J McVerry RNZAF.

P J McVerry, now F/O, was a Pathfinder pilot of Lancaster NE130 of 582 Sqn on 17th January 1945 during a raid on Zeitz when it was abandoned over allied territory. Only one of his crew died.

F/O Muggeridge was awarded the DFM on 28th May 1943 while flying in the Middle East. The citation read: 'For gallantry and devotion to duty in the execution of air operations'.

MONDAY 24th APRIL 1944

2310 hrs Training

Stirling III LK460 -O of 1661 HCU from Winthorpe was on a training flight when the aircraft overshot landing after engine failure and ended up in a ditch on the Fosse Way.

The crew were: P/O A41773 J Bowen RAAF (Pilot), Sgt Cambell (F/Eng), F/S Hodgson (Nav), W/O Bradbury (Bomb Aimer), F/S Davies (W/Op), Sgt Simpson, (MUAG) and Sgt Laveney (F/Eng).

TUESDAY 25th APRIL 1944

0110 hrs Training

Stirling III LK552 JF-C of 1654 HCU from Wigsley was on a night navigational exercise and after a 3 hour 50 minute flight the aircraft began flying on 3 engines at 11,000 feet. The pilot complained of sluggish aileron control and the port inner engine gave sign of icing. Due to excessive vibration the pilot was unable to maintain flight on 3 engines and the aircraft went into a diving turn to port and control was lost and the aircraft was abandoned and crashed at Cheese House, 9 miles east of Bircotes, at West Burton. 2 of the crew were injured. The pilot was P/O 172975 G Lee.

2036 hrs Training

Stirling III EF132 of 1654 HCU from Wigsley was on training flight when during landing and trying to lower the undercarriage a loud bang was heard by the crew and the port leg failed to lower. On selecting up the starboard leg failed to retract but was finally lowered by diving the aircraft but the dinghy restraining straps broke.

The pilot, Sgt 1600735 W Fulstone, landed the aircraft safely and there were no injuries. The aircraft accident report states that the aircraft was saved by the skill and resourcefulness of S/L 44357 George Godfrey Petty DSO DFC who controlled the aircraft by communication with the pilot from the ground.

WEDNESDAY 26th APRIL 1944

1715 hrs Training

Stirling III BK651 of 1654 HCU from Wigsley had completed a training flight when on landing the starboard tyre burst and the aircraft veered to starboard and collapsed and a wing fell off. There were no injuries. The instructor pilot was F/O 159067 J Brown and the pupil F/O J/25975 A F Kemp RCAF.

THURSDAY 27th APRIL 1944

1652 hrs Training

Martinet I JM296 of 82 OTU from Ossington undershot on landing from fighter affiliation with a Wellington and made a heavy landing and the aircraft nosed over causing the collapse of the undercarriage.

The pilot, F/O 150048 Gordon Smith RAFVR age 22, was killed on 7th June. He was the pilot of Martinet MS870 of 82 OTU which took off from Ossington to practice interceptions and flew beneath a line of high-tension cables and crashed into a river bank near Burton-upon-Stather. He is buried in Selby Cemetery.

FRIDAY 28th APRIL 1944

0945 hrs Training

Whitley V Z9164 GM-I of 42 OTU from Ashbourne had been in the air on an operational training flight across country when the port engine failed at 1,700 feet due to a glycol leak. The pilot, F/S 657870 M Norbury, was unable to maintain height on the starboard engine and made a forced landing in field 3 miles north east of Hucknall. The crew of 5 escaped injury.

SATURDAY 29th APRIL 1944

An airman based at Syerston fell off a fire tender onto the perimeter track and died the next day from a fractured skull and lacerated brain.

MONDAY 8th MAY 1944

0437 hrs Training

Wellington X HE847 of 82 OTU from Ossington after a flight of one hour 50 minutes landed and another aircraft appeared ahead so the pilot, W/O R/122292 James Malcolm Murie RCAF, swung the aircraft off the runway, hit a ditch and the nose tipped violently. There were no injuries to the 6 man crew.

He was killed 2 months later on 14th July when as pilot of Halifax LW115 of 433 Sqn his aircraft took off from Leeming on a cross country training exercise to Douglas, IOM, then change course. By 1605 hrs the aircraft was already in trouble and approaching Douglas and at 1620 hrs there were explosions from the aircraft which then crashed in flames onto a house at Grawe Farm, which caught fire killing 3½ year old Alan Charles McCulloch. W/O Murie is buried in Andreas (St Andrew) Churchyard.

A memorial commemorating the crew and Alan McCulloch has been mounted on a wall in the All Saints Church grounds in Lonan.

TUESDAY 9th MAY 1944

0430 hrs Training

Wellington X JA131 of 82 OTU from Ossington on landing the pilot, W/O R/122292 J M Murie RCAF, swerved to starboard to avoid an aircraft in front and ran into a ditch. A similar incident had occurred just the previous day (see previous entry).

THURSDAY 11th MAY 1944

0035 hrs Training

Wellington X HE265 of 18 OTU from Worksop had only been in the air for 20 minutes when there was failure of the port engine at 1,500 feet and the pilot P/O 161612 R C Brady carried out an emergency landing. The aircraft over ran the airfield and tipped on its nose in a field adjoining the airfield after the main wheels sank into soft ground. The 2nd pilot was Sgt 1395967 R Bambehough.

0253 hrs Training

Stirling III LJ524 –H of 1654 HCU from Wigsley took off for a long cross country night training exercise. At 0253 hrs the pilot, P/O Dunn, reported that the port inner engine had cut out on the circuit but was instructed to carry out a normal circuit and landing. The aircraft flew over the end of the runway and appeared to be handling quite normally. The engines were opened up for overshoot procedure from about 20 to 50 feet and the aircraft climbed away over the watch office, went into a climbing turn to port which increased until the port wing dropped and the aircraft crashed from 150 to 200 feet about 200 yards from the hangar nearest the watch office. Apparently loss of control may have been aggrevated by a crew member winding an incorrect rudder. 5 of the crew of 8 were killed and the other 3 were injured.

P/O 422460 Robert Wyndham Dunn age 20 RAAF (Pilot), W/O 26382 Harold Eric Hughes age 23 RAAF, F/S 418963 William Joseph Lea age 21 RAAF, F/S 26355 Ronald Walter Ely age 28 RAAF, all buried in Oxford (Botley) Cemetery.

Sgt 941200 Ernest Arthur Wilmshurst age 23 RAFVR (F/Eng) buried Bottesford (St Peter Ad Vincula) Churchyard, F/S 434299 Geoffrey Roy Whimpey RAAF (Air Gnr), F/S 429881George Edward Dowling RAAF (Air Gnr) and Sgt E J Wild were injured.

F/S Whimpey was thrown clear but despite being badly shocked he was one of the first to enter the burning fuselage and began pulling bodies from the wreckage. For his courage, on 22nd August, he was awarded the British Empire Medal the citation reading 'After crashing, rendering service in releasing crew'.

The insignia was presented to his father on 10th July 1947 because on 5th July 1944 F/S Whimpey age 20 and F/S Dowling age 20 were killed flying with the crew of Lancaster HK536 of 463 Sqn on a raid on the V1 supply depot at St Leu Desserent, France. The aircraft crashed at Ellecourt (Seine-Maritime) and all the crew are buried in Ellecourt Communal Cemetery.

W/O Hughes and F/S Ely had both joined up on the same day, 27th April 1940 in Adelaide, Australia.

1140 hrs Taxiing

Wellington X HF514 of 82 OTU from Gamston was taxiing slowly downhill to take off for circuits and landings training when the brakes failed to hold and the aircraft swung of the perimeter track, hit trees and a blast wall. The brakes had overheated with no blame to the pilot Sgt R/153818 E F Baillie RCAF.

FRIDAY 12th MAY 1944

0930 hrs Training

Oxford I LW915 of 16 (P)SFTS from Newton climbed after take-off and was carrying out overshoot when it collided with Oxford LW965 with no blame to the pilot. The starboard engine failed but the pilot AC2 P/704928 Miernik PAF throttled back and landed safely.

0930 hrs Training

Oxford I LW965 of 16 (P)SFTS from Newton took off at 30 degrees out of wind, without permission, and was hit by Oxford LW915 also of 16(P)SFTS and crashed near the Relief Landing Ground at Orston. The pilot, F/L P/76725 Wladzimierz Peski PAF, was killed and his body was taken to Newton Mortuary. He is buried in the Polish plot at Newark-upon-Trent Cemetery.

1235 hrs Training

Wellington X LM584 of 18 OTU from Worksop was on an instructional training flight at 8,000 feet when the aircraft developed apparent engine trouble. The starboard propeller was feathered by the pilot, F/O 415047 G S White RNZAF, and the aircraft did a wheels up landing down wind on the aerodrome due to difficulty finding the aerodrome in bad visibility. F/O White had doubted the ability of the aircraft to maintain height on one engine. There were no injuries.

SATURDAY 13th MAY 1944

1140 hrs Training

Wellington X HE198 of 82 OTU from Castle Donington took off for a cross country exercise but aborted after the crew heard two loud bangs from the port engine. The pilot, F/L J/9485 J H Woods RCAF, could not get the aircraft to stop in time so retracted the undercarriage and the aircraft skidded through a hedge and caught fire after coming to a stop.

MONDAY 15th MAY 1944

0333 hrs Op; Rennes

Wellington X HE739 -H of 82 OTU from Gamston took off with seven other aircraft from 82 OTU on a Nickel Operation on Rennes. Seven completed the mission and six showed good ground detail from photographs. HE739, the eight aircraft, had a 5 hour 15 minute flight and on return the pilot was circling Gamston when the port engine failed followed shortly after by the starboard engine. The aircraft hit the tops of some trees then crashed and burst into flames after hitting a second lot of trees in Thoresby Park, near Ollerton. Five of the crew were killed and are buried in Harrogate (Stonefall) Cemetery, and one was injured: F/O J/17450 Kenneth Scott Johnson age 21RCAF (Pilot), F/O J/36316 George Scott Oliphant age 28 RCAF (Nav), W/O R/106362 Jack Tass age 29 RCAF (W.Op/Air Gnr), Sgt R/200655 Gordon Keith McLellan age 33 RCAF (Air Gnr), Sgt R/168038 Joseph Andre Lanouette RCAF age 31 (Air Bomber). The rear gunner survived but his name has not been ascertained.

This is a photograph of the crew of Wellington HE739 taken outside the Robin Hood Public House in Elkesley. Left to right; F/O Johnson, ? , ? , W/O Tass, ? , F/O Oliphant. Courtesy of W Taylor

Grave of F/O Johnson

Grave of F/O Oliphant

Grave of W/O Tass

Grave of Sgt McLellan

Grave of Sgt Lanouette

Harrogate (Stonefall) Cemetery

THURSDAY 18th MAY 1944

1022 hrs — Training

Wellington X LP149 of 28 OTU from Castle Donington was taking off when the pilot's escape hatch flew open. The pilot, F/O 152631 G C Kennedy decided to throttle back, overshot the runway, swung to avoid trees and the undercarriage collapsed.

FRIDAY 19th MAY 1944

1750 hrs — Training

Lancaster I DV368 of 5 LFS from Syerston swung on take off for circuits and landings training after the port tyre burst. The pilot closed the throttles and attempted to correct but it became uncontrollable, the undercarriage collapsed and the aircraft caught fire. The instructor was A F/Lt 49688 W H Kellaway and the pupil F/S 1602443 J H G Smith. There were no injuries.

SATURDAY 20th MAY 1944

0233 hrs — Op; Nickel

Wellington X LP381 of 18 OTU from Worksop took off with 5 other aircraft on a nickel operation on Roubaix and Tourgoing. When the aircraft had been in the flight for 4 hours 35 minutes and approaching to land the aircraft flew into a wood, about 1,000 yards outside of the airfield outer circle lights, and crashed and burnt out 2 miles north of Worksop at Carlton in Lindrick.

Of the crew, LAC P/780953 Josef Pawlik PAF age 23 (Pilot) and LAC P/705430 Piotr Pawlowski PAF age 29 were both killed and are buried in Newark-upon-Trent Cemetery. F/O Z Norski, Sgt W Sledziewski and Sgt Z Bukalo all PAF were injured.

1825 hrs Training

Tiger Moth II N9375 of 25 (P)EFTS piloted by pupil AC2 P/705616 S Boreejszo-Wysocki PAF crashed 2 miles north north east of Papplewick, at Kighill. The aircraft completed 4 loops and then flew downwards and crashed out of control. It was considered that the pilot may have blacked out and lost control of the aircraft. He was slightly injured.

MONDAY 22nd MAY 1944

1608 hrs Training

Wellington III BJ819 of 82 OTU crash landed with undercarriage retracted in a field between Cottam and Leverton after Spitfire P7820 collided with it whilst carrying out cine camera gun training. The weather conditions were very bad due to thick industrial haze. The crew escaped injury with the exception of the front air gunner who was trapped by his legs and cut free by rescuers. The pilot, F/O J/18416 J P Lee, was recommended for a green endorsement for making a successful forced landing in a badly damaged aircraft. A Corporal being carried as a passenger was mentioned in despatches for his calmness and efficiency. It is possible that this aircraft crashed at Sturton in Lincolnshire.

Spitfire II P7820 of 53 OTU collided with Wellington BJ819 whilst carrying out cine camera gun training. The aircraft crashed on railway wagons at Lea Road Railway Station, Gainsborough, killing the pilot F/O 151811 John Smith age 21 RAFVR who is buried in Embsay Churchyard Yorkshire. The Spitfire was one of the 'Presentation' Spitfires named 'PAGANAS'.

A 'Presentation' aircraft was one where an individual organisation or community could donate the cost of an aircraft to the government and an aircraft would be allocated to bear the name of the donor. The donor could select the type of aircraft.

TUESDAY 23rd MAY 1944

2330 hrs Training

Halifax II JD299 of 1658 HCU from Riccall was on a night training navigational exercise when for some reason the starboard outer engine feathered when the port outer engine failed. The port airscrew wouldn't feather and this, along with the loss of the starboard outer caused the aircraft to lose altitude and the pilot carried out a forced landing in a field, crashing into Dukes Wood between Kirklington and Eakring. The crash killed two of the crew and seriously injured five. The crew were F/O A/422766 P A Tuck RAAF, Sgt R G Middleton, Sgt C R Mudee RAAF, Sgt M P H Macdonnell and Sgt S J Kirk all injured. F/O 423789 Henry Horace Hackney age 25 RAAF died 4 days later on 27th May and is buried in Harrogate (Stonefall) Cemetery and F/O 422504 Marshall Hall age 28 died and is also buried in Harrogate (Stonefall) Cemetery.

Graves of F/O Hackney (right) **and F/O Hall** (far fright)

FRIDAY 26th MAY 1944

2009 hrs — Training

Stirling III LJ558 of 1661 HCU from Winthorpe took off for flying practice and after a 2 hour flight touched down, swung out of control and clipped Stirling III BK766 before crashing into a workshop at the edge of the airfield. The pilot Sgt 1516971 J S Laws was detained in the Station Sick Quarters suffering from shock.

2215 hrs — Training

Lancaster I L7578 RC-L of 5 LFS from Syerston was to be flown by Sgt Sanderson and crew on a practice cross country and bombing exercise. He and his crew were completing their course on Lancasters, before being posted to an operational squadron of No.5 Group. The aircraft took off normally in the evening and circled to the west of the airfield in order to gain height, before setting course for their objective. After being in the air for 3 hours 25 minutes, and presumably returning to base, the aircraft banked to port and dived out of control and, before control could be regained, crashed into the ground from 8,000 feet and exploded near Wood Barn, ½ mile north of Gonalston. The official crash log could not ascertain the reason for the accident but a likely explanation seemed to lie in the discovery of part of a parachute harness entangled in the 2nd pilots flying controls. All LFS Lancasters were fitted with dual controls, and it is feasible that the bomb aimers parachute harness could have caught in the right hand set of pedals as he crawled forward into the nose from his take off position in the fuselage. No.58 MU from Newark recovered the wreckage, but owing to the depth of the crater, it is thought possible that the engines and heavier pieces of the aircraft remain in situ.

The site of the crash is still visible in the centre of the field where it occurred, as a depression, now shallow and almost smoothed out by years of ploughing and harrowing. However, each year, when the land is re-ploughed, many small pieces of wreckage still emerge.

All the crew of 7 were killed: P/O J/86545 (R/175470) George Benjamin Sanderson RCAF (Pilot), Sgt 1450090 Bernard Broe RAFVR age 22 (W.Op/Air Gnr), Sgt 1822037 James Graham Middlemas age 19 RAFVR (F/Eng), Sgt 1473146 Albert Dennis Clark age 28 RAFVR (Nav), Sgt 1852333 Dereck Nicholl s age 19 RAFVR (Air Gnr), P/O J/87968 Archibald Thomas Noble age 28 RCAF (Air Bomber) and F/S R/203453 Dennis Wright age 20 RCAF (Air Gnr). All are buried in Newark-upon-Trent Cemetery.

L7578 was one of six aircraft from 44 Squadron which took part in the famous daylight raid to Augsburg to bomb M.A.N. diesel engine factory 1,000 miles across France and Germany.

A memorial stone was erected by the parents of Sgt Middlemas at the site of the crash, comprising a rough-hewn stone surrounded by a chain fence and engraved with the names of the crew. This memorial was originally placed 30 metres east of the crash site and in 1996 was restored and rededicated and now maintained by 1803 (Hucknall) Sqn ATC

This photo, released after the famous daylight raid on Augsburg on 17th April 1942, possibly for publicity purposes, shows Lancaster L7578 in the markings of S/L John Nettleton of 44 Sqn, who was awarded the VC for the operation. L7578 had service with 207 Sqn, 83 Sqn CF, 1654 CU and 1668 CU before its final flight with 5 LFS with the identification letters RC-L.

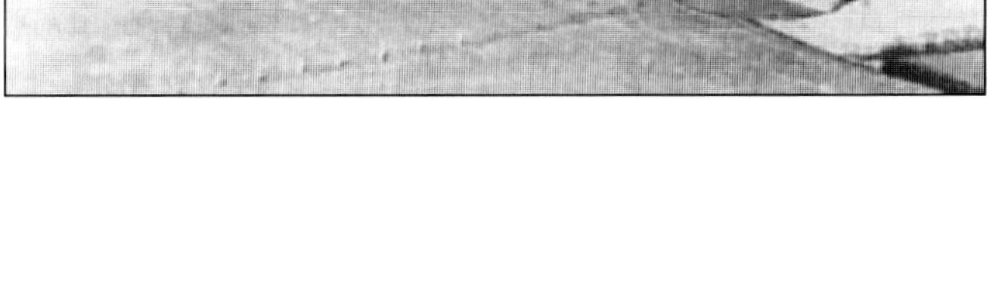

Graves of the crew in Newark-upon-Trent Cemetery

In the foreground is the crash site with the memorial in the hedgerow

Memorial to the crew

SATURDAY 27th MAY 1944

0139 hrs

Training

Lancaster I W4383 of 5 LFS from Syerston took off for dual circuit practice and was given permission to land, saw no other aircraft on the runway and landed on top of Lancaster W4258 GP-U. Both aircraft were on night training circuits and landings. W4258 was waiting on the runway running engines attempting to clear warning lights in the cockpit. Mitigating circumstances was thought to be the amount of interference on the RT.

The instructing pilot of W4383 was F/O J/17550 Ken W Brown CGM, RCAF and the other pilot was Sgt 1600735 W C Freestone. The rest of the crew were: Sgt Post, Sgt D A Cage, injured, F/O Woolam, Sgt Taylor, Sgt Bullivant and Sgt E E Henders injured.

F/O Brown

F/S Brown was awarded the CGM (Flying) effective from 23rd May 1943 when flying with 617 Sqn on a raid on the Sorpe Dam, which became known as the Dambusters Raid. His aircraft was Lancaster ED918.

He enlisted in Regina on 20th February 1941and graduated from training at No.6 EFTS on 21st July 1941 and No.4 SFTS on 5th December 1941. He first flew overseas in No.44 Sqn.

His citation, along with other crew members read: 'On the night of the 16th May 1943, a force of Lancaster bombers was detailed to attack the Moehne, Eder and Sorpe dams in Germany. The operation was one of great difficulty and hazard demanding a high degree of skill and courage and close co-operation between the crews of the aircraft engaged. Nevertheless, a telling blow was struck at the enemy by the successful breaching of the Moehne and Eder dams. This outstanding success reflects the greatest credit on the efforts of the above mentioned personnel who participated in the operation in various capacities, as members of aircraft crew.'

0139 hrs Ground

Lancaster I W4258 GP-U of 5 LFS, see above. The instructing pilot F/O A/405352 J Forsyth DFC RAAF and the pilot W/O R/125847 W M Blaine RCAF were both injured.

F/O J/28687 William Douglas Lewis age 22 RCAF (Air Bomber) from Trenton, Nova Scotia, is buried in Harrogate (Stonefall) Cemetery, Sgt R/212959 Robert Russell Lynch age 26 RCAF (Air Gnr) is buried in Harrogate (Stonefall) Cemetery.

Sgt 1543965 Walter Coldwell RAFVR (W. Op) also died and is buried in Barnsley Cemetery.

The rest of the crew were Sgt Jordan, Sgt J F Reid RCAF injured, and Sgt D E Reesor RCAF who was also injured.

MONDAY 29th MAY 1944 Ops; Nantes

Wellington X HE199 -J of 82 OTU from Ossington took off for a nickel operation along with 8 other aircraft, 7 completing their task and 6 of them landing back at base and 1 aircraft landing at Wittering. HE199 was presumed to have completed the task and was then shot down by a Mosquito in the Shaftesbury area on return. All the crew were members of the RCAF and 3 were killed and 2 injured: W/O2 R/153082 Donald Blair Machum MID age 20 (Pilot), Sgt R/213862 William Henry McGuigan age 19 and W/O1 R118243 Leonard Frank Davey (W.Op/Air Gnr) all buried in Brookwood Military Cemetery. P/O C McFarlane and Sgt J A Bugley were injured.

Wellington X LN443 –C of 82 OTU from Ossington took off with the above aircraft on the same raid and on return had the same fate, shot down by a Mosquito in the Shaftesbury area. All 6 RCAF crew members were killed: F/O J/26386 Donald Galloway Watt McKie age 24 (Pilot), F/O J/36399 Charles Allen Blackmore age 23 (Nav), F/O J/35016 Leonard Joseph Smith age 21 (Air Bomber), Sgt R/210945 Albert Howard Spinks age 18, P/O J/39029 William Howard Geddes age 21(W.Op/Air Gnr) and Sgt R/152957Bruce Gordon age 21 all buried in Brookwood Military Cemetery.

The above information is recorded in the 82 OTU ORB just a day after the incident. However the report in W R Chorley's 'Bomber Command Losses' states that the aircraft were shot down by anti-aircraft fire.

1705 hrs Training

Wellington X MF587 of 18 OTU from Finningley swung on take off which was corrected but the aircraft then swung again. The undercarriage was retracted but did not come up before the aircraft overshot the airfield boundary and crashed on the roadway midway between the camp and Finningley village. There were no injuries. The pilot was Sgt 1585650 E Allen.

—

AC2 1811657 Barratt of 93 MU was sitting on some bombs on the back of a lorry at Swinderby when it rounded a bend causing a bomb to slip. In attempting to prevent its fall he was pushed off the lorry by another bomb getting dislodged. He and the two bombs fell between the lorry and the trailer which passed over him and he was killed. The inquest was held on 31st May.

THURSDAY 1st JUNE 1944

1800 hrs — Training

Wellington III Z1719 of 18 OTU of 'B' Flight from Worksop swung on take off and the instructor pilot, F/O 161797 J M Costello, throttled back but the port throttle stuck at one boost so the undercarriage was retracted to avoid a collision with trees. The port engine throttle control rod eye end had fractured through jamming of the throttle control rack in the rack guide by a piece of circlip.

The pupil pilot, P/O J/37006 James Anthony Sherry RCAF age 22, was killed on 31st December flying with 166 Sqn. He was the pilot of Lancaster ME647 which took off from Kirmington for a raid on Osterfeld and was lost. He and his crew are buried Nederweert War Cemetery.

FRIDAY 2nd JUNE 1944

1500 hrs — Air Test

Wellington X LN610 of 28 OTU from Wymeswold crash landed after failure of the port engines at 300 feet when the pilot F/L 87436 E C Stewart could not maintain height on one engine. There were no injuries to the pilot and his 6 man crew.

SATURDAY 3rd JUNE 1944

0230 hrs

A 500 lb bomb believed to be British was dropped and exploded in a grass field 100 yards west of the junction of Carlton by-pass and the Old North Road, Cromwell.

TUESDAY 6th JUNE 1944

0630 hrs Operation Overlord. The 'D-Day' landings begin.

Aircraft ready to support the D Day landings

1620 hrs — Training

Oxford II BG396 of 16 (P)SFTS from Newton landed after a cross country exercise, and due to bad weather and rain struck stationary aircraft Oxford EB951. The pilot was AC2 P/704928 C Miernik PAF.

Training

Oxford I EB951 of 16 (P)SFTS from Newton was stationary after landing from a training flight when it was struck by Oxford BG396. The pilot was W/O P/780466 W Koczwarski PAF.

WEDNESDAY 7th JUNE 1944

0415 hrs Training

Halifax LL231 of 1667 HCU from Sandtoft made an emergency landing at Gamston as the the port inner engine failed due to a coolant leak and swung off the runway, colliding with Wellington X LN535-V in dispersal, in poor visibilty. P/O 416487 C H Henry RNZAF and the crew of the Halifax were un-injured. Both aircraft were write-offs.

0334 hrs Ground

Wellington X LN535-V of 82 OTU from Gamston was hit while parked in dispersal at Gamston by Halifax LL231 from Sandtoft making an emergency landing, and piloted by P/O C H Henry.

0440 hrs Training

Stirling III EE907 of 1661 HCU from Winthorpe swung on landing and collided with Stirling IV LK562. The pilot F/S 985073 G James, who was on his first night solo flight, had trouble with the starboard undercarriage and had to use the emergency system. This aircraft crashed near Swinderby on 28th October with the loss of 3 crew members.

0440 hrs Stationary

Stirling IV LK562 of 1661 HCU was hit by Stirling III EE907 at Winthorpe (see above) while parked in dispersals and was later salvaged and rebuilt as TS265.

1500 hrs Training

Hurricane LP345 of 1685 BDT Flt was on an affiliation exercise and on landing at Worksop the undercarriage collapsed. The pilot was W/O R/102774 A E J Flannagan.

FRIDAY 9th JUNE 1944

1730 hrs Training

Master III DL890 of 16 (P)FTS from Tollerton was on a training flight when the aircraft was seen to be performing aerobatic manoevres, it then performed a number of rolls which brought it close to the ground. The pilot then took the aircraft into a steep climb using full power but the engine stalled and it spun into the ground at the junction of Nuthall Road and Whitemoor Avenue in Bobbers Mill, Nottingham. The force of the crash embedded the aircraft up to 10 feet into the ground and it caught fire. A few civilians received minor injuries. The crew were both killed and are buried in Newark-upon-Trent Cemetery. LAC P/704883 Boleslaw Grejcium PAF age 20 was piloting the aircraft and AC2 P/704945 Zbigniew Pulnarowicz PAF age 22 was the safety pilot.

The crash of Master DL890.
Courtesy of the Nottingham Evening Post

SATURDAY 10th JUNE 1944

0330 hrs Training

Oxford I NM706 of 16 (P)FTS from Newton was taking off on a training flight when the port engine cut at 50 feet and the aircraft lost height and came into contact with the airfield bomb dump netting post. The crew who were both un-injured were, 1st pilot P/O P/740123 L Peczek PAF and 2nd pilot F/L P/0388 J Krysiak PAF.

2315 hrs Training

Lancaster I ME791 KM-K of 44(B) Sqn from Dunholme Lodge was on a high level bombing exercise when it was struck by a flash bomb from another aircraft which destroyed one of the Lancaster's ailerons and started a fire. An immediate crash landing was made under very difficult conditions near Hucknall and the aircraft caught fire.

F/S A/41037 Charles Ernest Binion DFC RAAF (Pilot), F/O 137168 Francis Dalglish Richardson Hildrew age 33 RAFVR (Nav), Sgt 1147248 William Burke age 23 RAFVR, Sgt 710203 Clive Hore age 20 RAFVR and Sgt 710275 John Graham Phillipson Payne RAFVR were all killed.

F/O Hildrew was cremated at Newcastle-upon-Tyne (West Road) Crematorium. The others are commemorated on the Runnymede Memorial. Because of inconclusive reporting by the Duty Clerk reporting the Squadron records, it is not absolutely certain that the deceased airmen were aboard this aircraft.

F/S Binion was awarded the DFC on 17th November and the citation read: 'Skill and fortitude in Operations against the enemy.' Crash location: OS sheet 129 506483

SUNDAY 11th JUNE 1944

1050 hrs Training

Master II DK861 of 16 (P)FTS hit a 14 foot high flagpole during air-to-ground camera gun practice at Owthorpe Bombing range when the pilot dived too low, and crashed in flames. The pilot, LAC P/704973 S Zochowski PAF, was injured, suffering from multiple abrasions and shock and taken to Newark EMS.

SATURDAY 17th JUNE 1944

0110 hrs Training

MosquitoVI HJ767 of 60 OTU fromNewton spun into the ground at Keyworth, presumably after control was lost in cloud at night and burnt out. Both crew members were killed and the pilot, F/L 126151 Joseph Kevin De Roeck RAFVR age 24, is buried in Nottingham Southern Cemetery.

0345 hrs Training

Stirling III EF209 TV-H of 1660 HCU from Swinderby took off to practice dual circuits and landings. The instructor feathered the starboard outer engine for a 3 engine practice landing but an aircraft was reported by one of the crew as approaching so he took violent evasive action to avoid a mid-air collision and crashed near Stapleford Woods on the Notts/ Lincs border. 7 of the crew were killed and 3 were injured:

F/O 414734 Milton Frederick Smith age 23 RAAF DFC (Instructor Pilot) is buried in Cambridge City Cemetery, F/S 919965 Francis Arnold Martin age 23 RAFVR (Pupil Pilot) buried Lanreath (St Marnarch) Churchyard, Sgt 1593642 Jim Stabler age 19 RAFVR (F/Eng) buried Shildon Cemetery, Sgt 1796569 John Totten age 24 RAFVR buried Lisburn Cemetery, F/S 1299326 Ronald Howard Turrell age 22 RAFVR DFM (F/Eng) buried Paignton Cemetery, F/S 573758 Raymond Lister Wade age 21 RAFVR (Nav) buried Warley Congregational

Cemetery, F/S R/155964 Harry William Robert Tufts age 23 RCAF (Air Bomber) buried Harrogate (Stonefall) Cemetery. Sgt E E Allen, Sgt 1807509 David Frederick Cook RAFVR (Air Gnr) and Sgt D G Smith were injured.

D F Cook, by now a F/S, age 21 was killed on 4th March 1945 flying in Lancaster PA197 CA-B of 189 Sqn on a raid on Ladbergen crashing at Bevergern. He is buried in Reichswald Forest War Cemetery.

F/O Smith was awarded the DFC on 30th June and the citation read: 'Skill and fortitude in operations against the enemy'.

Recovery of Stirling III EF209

SUNDAY 18th JUNE 1944

1645 hrs — Training

Tiger Moth II N6721 of 25 (P)EFTS from Hucknall was on flying training and approaching to land when at 50 feet the pilot saw another aircraft coming in to land. He opened the throttles and tried to land at the side of the aircraft but did not open the throttle enough and the aircraft stalled and hit the ground with damage to the undercarriage. The pilot Cpl P/705734 G Albrecht PAF who was on his 3rd solo flight was un-injured

WEDNESDAY 21st JUNE 1944

1738 hrs — Training

Stirling III EH940 of 1661HCU from Winthorpe took off for the pilot's first solo flight on this type of aircraft and while flying at 1,800 feet an engine caught fire and was feathered but got worse. The pilot lost control and the aircraft went into a diving starboard turn and crashed and burst into flames at Park Farm, Kettlethorpe on the Notts/Lincs border. 5 of the 8 man crew were killed: F/O 143735 Frederick Shaw Bradbury age 23 RAFVR (Pilot), Sgt 1892881 Joseph Albert Micallef age 19 RAFVR (Air Gnr), Sgt 1880698 William Henry Miller age 27 RAFVR (Air Gnr), all are buried in Oxford (Botley) Cemetery, P/O 171432 William Robert Clayton age 30 RAFVR (Nav) buried Ashton-under-Lyne (Hurst) Cemetery, F/O 153309 George Wallace Rankin RAFVR (Air Bomber) buried Cathcart Cemetery.

Sgts F Dauble, T W Farrell, A M McCune were all injured.

Memorial to the crew of EH940 in Laughterton village

FRIDAY 23rd JUNE 1944

0930 hrs Training

Tiger Moth II T5788 of 25 (P)EFTS from Hucknall was on a training flight when the pilot entered cloud against orders, lost control and went into a spin and baled out. The aircraft crashed ½ mile south east of Hucknall. The pilot under training, LAC K Loma PAF, was injured. Crash location grid ref: OS sheet 129 546488.

SATURDAY 24th JUNE 1944

0347 hrs Training

Wellington X LN698 of 28 OTU was on a training flight when the pilot, Sgt 1810917 D G Stuart, approached too high and overshot the runway on landing at Bircotes. 5 of the crew were injured.

2210 hrs Ground

Wellington X JA452 of 82 OTU from Ossington burnt out at dispersal when an oxygen bottle exploded during recharging of the oxygen system.

MONDAY 26th JUNE 1944

Wellington X MF528 of 29 OTU from Bruntingthorpe took off for high level bombing training, encountered adverse weather and when the port engine failed at 4,300 feet the pilot, Sgt 778948 T Spencer, was unable to maintain height. After ordering his crew to bale out he began a controlled descent with the intention of force-landing. At around 0115 hrs the starboard engine stopped at 800 feet and he took to his parachute. The aircraft crashed 4 miles north of Thorney near Saxilby and burnt out.

FRIDAY 30th JUNE 1944

2300 hrs Training

Stirling III BK803 of 1654 HCU from Wigsley was on a cross country exercise when the port inner engine failed in flight and caught fire. The crew baled out and the aircraft crashed on waste ground at Rufford Colliery, near Ollerton. The pilot, F/O 55086 Walter George Frederick Filby RAF,was commended for his behaviour. None of the crew members were injured.

F/O Filby age 21 was subsequently killed flying with 630 Sqn on 17th August 1944. He was a member of the crew of Lancaster LL972 which took off from East Kirkby for a raid on Stettin. All the crew are buried Poznan Old Garrison Cemetery, Poland.

SUNDAY 2nd JULY 1944

1201 hrs Training

Stirling III EE899 JF-B of 1654 HCU from Wigsley took off for bombing practice and landed at Winthorpe on three engines but bounced, stalled and crashed injuring both air gunners.

The pilot was P/O A/413232 J McKern DFC RAAF. The injured air gunners were F/O A M Harrison RAAF and Sgt K J N Williams RAAF.

THURSDAY 6th JULY 1944

2225 hrs Op; Croixdalle

Halifax III MZ519 LK-U of 578 Sqn from Burn took off just after 1900 hrs for a raid on the V1 launch site at Croixdalle with P/O Reginald Parfitt at the controls with 4 members of his regular crew and 2 substitutes, F/S J J Godin and Sgt R A Rolph. This was barely 13 hours after returning from another raid on a flying bomb site at St Martin L'Hortier, also in Halifax MZ519.

The daylight attack was successful and on the return journey eyewitnesses reported seeing one of the aircraft engines engulfed in flames, part of a wing broke away from the fuselage and the aircraft dived into the ground south of the village of Farnsfield with the loss of all seven crew members.

On the 50th anniversary of the crash a memorial was erected and a small copse of trees planted, followed by a dedication service to the fallen airmen which was organised by the Farnsfield British Legion.

The crew members were: P/O177439 Reginald Parfitt (Pilot) age 22 RAFVR who is buried in Cardiff (Cathays) Cemetery, F/S R/151252 John Joseph Godin (Air Bomber) age 19 RCAF buried in Harrogate (Stonefall) Cemetery, F/O 152501 Brian Grahame Turnidge (Nav) age 24 RAFVR buried in Bristol (Canford) Cemetery, Sgt 1621271 Thomas Frederick Pitts age 21 RAFVR (W.Op/Air Gnr) buried in Altrincham Bowdon and Hale (Altrincham) Cemetery, Sgt 1535267 Thomas Arthur Hill (Air Gunner) RAFVR buried at Bilston Cemetery, Sgt 2220239 Leonard Granville Leatham (Air Gunner) age 20 RAFVR buried in Tipton Cemetery. Sgt 1645930 Raymond Albert Rolph (F/Eng) age 23 RAFVR, buried in Hawkwell (St Mary) Churchyard.

John Godin was the sole Canadian amongst the crew and it was his first mission with 578 Sqn as he was filling in for the usual Bomb Aimer, F/L Alan Miles, who was away on training.

The memorial is sited at OS SK644553. Further to the memorial being erected, Alan Knight whose cousin was the late F/O Turnidge, commissioned the renowned aviation artist Keith Woodcock to paint an interpretation of MZ519. This was duly produced with the poignant title 'Slipping Earth's Surly Bonds'. A commemorative sign has been erected on a road in Farnsfield named after the pilot. His memory and that of his crew has been permanently commemorated with a unique sign erected on Parfitt Drive which was unveiled in February 2001.

Top left and above: **P/O Parfitt.** Both photographs courtesy of Ann and Ken Harris

Left: **A Halifax aircraft similar to that piloted by P/O Parfitt**

FRIDAY 7th JULY 1944

1620 hrs Training

Tiger Moth II DE259 of 25 (P)EFTS from Hucknall had been in the air for one hour and failed to recover from a deliberate spin at 4,000 feet and crashed at Annesley Hall. The pilot, AC2 P/706520 W Tymczak PAF, was un-injured. This aircraft also crashed on 23rd June 1942 near Blidworth RLG but was not written off.

SATURDAY 8th JULY 1944

1630 hrs Training

Wellington X LN611 of 17 OTU from Finningley at 2,000 feet the port engine failed but picked up again and on approach to land the throttles were closed slightly and on re-opening again both engines failed to respond. The aircraft overshot the aerodrome and ran into a ditch and the starboard undercarriage collapsed. The pilot was F/S 1390960 N C Blacker.

TUESDAY 11th JULY 1944

1620 hrs Training

Master III EM400 of 16 (P)SFTS was on training for glide approach and landing when the undercarriage collapsed in a heavy landing at Orston RLG. The instructor pilot, F/S P/794480 Palul PAF, and the pupil pilot, W/O P/780565 G Gorny PAF, were both un-injured.

—

Wellington III X3548 of 82 OTU from Ossington caught fire at dispersal whilst re-fuelling.

WEDNESDAY 12th JULY 1944

0330 hrs Ground

Wellington X ME984 of 82 OTU from Ossington stopped at the tyre checking point to be topped up with compressed air when LAC 1356581 Charles Leslie Ingram age 31 RAFVR walked or stumbled into a propeller and was killed instantly. He is buried in Thorne Cemetery. The pilot was F/O C/26068 J E Anderson RCAF.

1210 hrs Training

Master II DM437 of 16 (P)SFTS from Tollerton collided with Master W9021 whilst in the air during final approach to land and landed heavily causing the undercarriage to collapse. The pilot, AC2 P/704854 Adamowicz PAF, failed to see the other aircraft.

Master II W9021 of 16 (P)SFTS from Tollerton was hit in the air by by Master DM437 but landed safely at Tollerton. The pilot was AC2 W Flieszer PAF.

THURSDAY 13th JULY 1944

0230 hrs Training

Wellington III Z1696 of 18 OTU from Finningley took off for night training and on return crashed in the circuit and burnt out about one mile south south west of the airfield. The cause was not known owing to the divergence of eyewitness statements; one said that the aircraft exploded in the air and another that it exploded after crashing.

All the crew died and are buried in the Polish plot of Newark-upon-Trent Cemetery: W/O P/784745 Leon Gawlowski, Sgt P/704065 Andrzej Chmielowiec, Sgt P/704258 Stanislaw T Hryniewiecki, Sgt P/704993 Wladyslaw Doda, Sgt P/706635 Lucjan Klepacki and Sgt P/706290 Marian Lewicki.

SATURDAY 15th JULY 1944

1500 hrs — Ground

Wellington X LN226 of 86 OTU from Gamston was sitting on the airfield ready to take off when the 2nd pilot P/O 175580 P Maxwell in the left hand seat waved for chocks away and a propeller struck his finger. The 1st pilot was P/O J/85054 Vernon John Bouchard DFC, RCAF.

His recommendation for the DFC dated 17th March 1944 read: 'In the course of his present tour of operations, in which he has flown 18 sorties comprising 132 flying hours, this officer has displayed outstanding qualities of courage, determination and efficiency, bringing to successful completion attacks against some of the most important targets in Germany. He has on ten occasions attacked targets in Berlin and has returned with invaluable photographic evidence. For his continual devotion to duty and determination to carry through successfully his operational missions, I consider he fully merits the award of the Distinguished Flying Cross.'

F/O Bouchard was killed on 22nd December age 25 and is buried in Brookwood Military Cemetery. He was the pilot of a two man crew aboard Albemarle V1823 of 22 HGCU, RAF Keevil, which took off at 1350 hrs on a glider training flight. At 600 feet Horsa Glider I DP280 got out of position and pulled the Albemarle's tail around to one side, F/O Bouchard cast off the glider but his aircraft stalled and dived into the ground at 1400 hrs at South Horsecroft Farm, Bratton, Wiltshire. Both personnel aboard the Albemarle aircraft lost their lives in the accident but the Instructor, Pupil Pilot and the three other personnel aboard the Horsa survived the incident, despite it force-landing in a field and sustaining sufficient damage for it to be repaired at a Maintenance Unit.

Horsa heavy glider

SUNDAY 16th JULY 1944

1105 hrs — Training

Master II DM428 of 16 (P)FTS was landing from a training flight when the aircraft stalled and landed heavily damaging a wing at Tollerton. The pilot's vision was impaired due to an oiled windscreen. The pilot was AC2 P/705851 A Fabisiak PAF.

1415 hrs — Training

Tiger Moth II T6262 of 25 (P)EFTS from Hucknall on dual instruction training collided with Tiger Moth DF150 on take off. DF150 had taxied onto the take off path to allow another aircraft, a Dakota, to land. However it was considered that the Instructor pilot P/O P/0909 T Hajdutczek PAF had not kept a good lookout. The pupil pilot was AC2 Czech PAF. No-one was injured.

1415 hrs — Ground

Tiger Moth II DF150 was hit by Tiger Moth II T6262 at Hucknall (see previous entry for details).

TUESDAY 17th JULY 1944

Training

Stirling I BF533 of 1654 HCU was on a cross country exercise when the port outer engine failed and a 3 engine landing was made at Wigsley and the aircraft overshot the runway and the starboard undercarriage collapsed. The pilot was F/S A/427077 T Ayre.

WEDNESDAY 18th JULY 1944

0233 hrs — Training

Wellington X LP296 of 28 OTU from Bircotes took off from Bircotes for night circuit training during which the wind changed direction. The aircraft touched down out of the wind and as a result ran beyond the runway and the undercarriage collapsed. The pilot and co-pilot were F/O 161798 J E Burton and W/O 1311784 O R Herbert.

1120 hrs — Training

Stirling III EJ114 of 1654 HCU from Wigsley was practicing 3 engine overshoots when the pilot was unable to maintain height and the aircraft crash landed and caught fire at Girton near Wigsley. The pilot F/O 53221 John Sidney Ludford and the pupil pilot F/O 419511 Richard Allan Jones RAAF escaped injury.

F/O Jones age 20 was lost on a raid on Calais on 24/25th September 1944 piloting Lancaster DV171PO-Y of 463 Sqn. His aircraft crashed in the target area and he is commemorated on the Runnymede memorial. F/O Ludford was involved in another incident on 20th September.

WEDNESDAY 19th JULY 1944

Night — Training

Oxford I PG994 of 16 (P)SFTS was on a training flight when the pilot under training lost control and before it could be regained the aircraft struck the ground and burnt out. The aircraft crashed between Normanton-on-Trent and Skegby killing all 3 crew members. Loss of control may have been caused by the slip stream of another aircraft.

The crew were Plt P/794710 Bogdan Koper PAF age 21, W/O P/780164 Stanislaw Mierniczek DFC,DFM, PAF age 29 (Pilot) and Pchor P/704806 Ignacy Tomaszewski PAF age 24 (Pilot under training). They are all buried in the Polish plot at Newark-upon-Trent Cemetery.

1310 hrs — Training

Stirling III LJ539 of 1654 HCU from Wigsley took off, but on the climb out the wheels braked and the aircraft began to vibrate. The pilot, F/S 959241 C Bausch, throttled back, overshot the runway and landed in a ditch which broke the undercarriage, 800 yards from the airfield.

2355 hrs — Training

Wellington X HE420 of 18 OTU from Finningley was at 18,000 feet when a loud explosion was heard and a hole was seen in the starboard wing. The pilot, Sgt P/794946 A Niemiec PAF, landed the aircraft but was unaware that a tyre had burst and it swung to starboard and the undercarriage collapsed.

THURSDAY 20th JULY 1944

0145 hrs Training

Stirling III EH951 of 1654 HCU from Wigsley was on a training flight when at 11,000 feet the port inner engine failed and then at 8,000 feet the starboard inner engine failed. The pilot ordered the crew to bale out and the aircraft crashed at Glebe Farm, Clipstone near Ollerton. The cause of the crash was fuel starvation caused by a faulty fuel tank change. The pilot was F/S A/419583 Leslie Christie Peart RAAF. There were no injuries.

SUNDAY 23rd JULY 1944

2320 hrs Training

Wellington X MF696 of 18 OTU of 'B' Flight from Finningley took off and at 100 feet the starboard propeller became unserviceable. The pilot, F/S P/1324633 R J E Bastick PAF, was unable to feather the engine and maintain so force landed in a field 3 miles north of Worksop.

MONDAY 24th JULY 1944

0230 hrs Training

Mitchell II FV986 of 13 OTU from Bicester had been in the air for 65 minutes on a cross country training flight when the aircraft crashed vertically into the ground at Hallams Lane, Chilwell. It was not known if the aircraft was out of control and there was no evidence of stalling or spinning. It was possible that the pilot, F/O 430040 Alan Martin Montgomery RAAF age 23, was taken ill as he was suffering from grumbling appendix and he may have fallen forward on the control column. It was also possible that there was structural failure although no aircraft parts were found away from the crash wreckage. Hucknall aerodrome were informed of the accident and F/O Morris, Sgt Sutherland and LAC Boyden arrived at the scene in the ambulance at 0320 hrs by which time the fire was under control. Despite an extensive search no bodies were found.

F/O Montgomery was identified by wrist watch, which was engraved with his initials and service number, and he is buried in Botley Cemetery together with F/O 423264 Ronald Frederick Stephens age 25 RAAF (Nav). W/O 414907 Allan Alfred Cook age 22 RAAF (W.Op) could not be identified and is commemorated on the Runnymede Memorial. Sgt 224413 Norman Angus Hartrick age 20 RCAF (Air Gnr) was identified by his identity disc and is buried in Harrogate (Stonefall) Cemetery.

Mitchell aircraft

0043 hrs

Training

Stirling III EH978 of 1660 HCU from Swinderby took off shortly before 0040 hrs and failed to gain sufficient height, lost its port tail plane and elevator on hitting a oak tree. The now extremely unstable aircraft attempted to make an emergency landing straight ahead at nearby Winthorpe airfield but crashed and burnt out on the perimeter when thwarted by an aircraft already on the runway, with the loss of all nine crew members.

F/O 149633 John Basil Josling DFC RAFVR age 21 (Staff Pilot) buried Brentwood Cemetery, F/L 414677 Arthur Lyall Ray age 25 RNZAF (Pilot U/T) buried Cambridge City Cemetery, Sgt 1685014 Herbert Samuel Buckley, age 21 RAFVR (W.Op) buried Oldham Ccemetery, Sgt 1593043 Norman Fox age 19 RAFVR (F/Eng) buried Hemsworth Cemetery Yorks, Sgt 1897760 Adolphus Sylvanus Akinpelu Johnston age 20 (F/Eng) buried Cambridge City Cemetery, F/O 153741 Harry James Bennett RAFVR (Air Bomber) buried Cambridge City Cemetery, Sgt 1585928 George William Holford age 20 RAFVR (Nav) buried Heston and Isleworth Cemetery, Sgt 1851671 Raymond William Parker age 19 RAFVR (Rear Gnr) buried Andover Cemetery, Sgt 1595302 John Mitchison age 20 RAFVR (MUG) buried Penshaw Churchyard.

F/L Ray's brother Dudley Thomas Ray was also killed, flying with 14 Sqn. He took off in a Marauder 1A FF375 from Libya on 3.1.43 for an attack against enemy shipping and was shot down by enemy fighters and ditched in the sea.

WEDNESDAY 26th JULY 1944

0930 hrs

Training

Stirling III LK483 -V of 1660 HCU from Swinderby swung on take off due to a cross wind the pilot throttled back and corrected but had to raise the undercarriage to stop. There were 5 injuries. The crew were the pilot F/O 152545 T Bain, Sgt 1602131 Derrick William Dunthorne (Nav) RAFVR, Sgt 1578595 R J Harris, Sgt 1330466 C J Western (W.Op/Air Gnr) all three injured, Sgt 1853898 Cryer (Nav), Sgt Melody, Sgt Hardy and Sgt Oberneck.

Sgt Dunthorne was killed on 25th February 1945 and is buried in Romford Cemetery (see entry for 25th February 1945).

FRIDAY 28th JULY 1944

What was thought to be three American P-47 Thunderbolt fighter planes flew low over Lambley when a black object fell from one of them. It crashed into soft farmland and bounced along for about 300 yards then burst showering aviation fuel towards a house on Catfoot Lane called Chelville, the home of Mrs Thelma Tagg. Also in and around the house were her mother Mrs Clara Helen Pearman, her brother Melville and sister Mrs Bernice McLaughlin. In a pram outside the farmhouse was Bernice's baby, 6 months old Anne. The fuel showered through a window, broken by the impact of the fuel tank and splashed over a fire in the open hearth soon setting the house on fire. Melville, who was in the house had no chance to escape and, outside, baby Anne's pram was engulfed by the blaze. Both died later in Nottingham General Hospital. The death toll might well have been higher but for the bravery of a young man, Cyril Sneath, working nearby for nursery firm W C Wicks, who raced to the scene on his bike. He climbed up the sloping roof to reach an upstairs room, smashed a window, cutting his arm in the process, and searched through the choking smoke. He found two year old Patrick Dineen who was on holiday at the cottage and handed him to Mrs Pearman. He then dragged Melville outside. Cyril Sneath was commended for his bravery. (This was extracted from the Nottingham Evening Post.)

The following was published in the 'Supplement to the London Gazette on 21st November 1944' under the section CENTRAL CHANCERY OF THE ORDERS OF KNIGHTHOOD: 'The KING has been graciously pleased to give orders for the publication in the London Gazette of the name of the person specially shown below as having received an expression of Commendation for his brave conduct; When rescuing people from a burning house; Cyril Sneath, Market Gardener, Lambley, Nottinghamshire.'

SATURDAY 29th JULY 1944

1840 hrs Training

Stirling III LJ585 of 1654 HCU from Wigsley had been in the air for 2 hours 35 minutes on a training flight when the starboard outer engine caught fire. This was extinguished momentarily but then caught fire again and spread to the mainplane which then caused the aircraft to crash at Normanton-on-Trent. 5 crew members were able to bale out of the aircraft but the other 4 crew crashed with it and were killed. The rear gunner reported seeing pieces of the aircraft flying past him during the flight.

F/S 1338808 Peter Alan Jacobs age 21 RAFVR (Pilot) is buried in Croydon Cemetery, Sgt 1821527 Stuart Alexander Findlater age 19 RAFVR (F/Eng) buried Edinburgh Eastern Cemetery, F/S 1869815 Jack Jones age 27 RAFVR (F/Eng) buried Leicester (Belgrave) Cemetery, P/O 172355 Norman Harold Brian Lucas age 20 DFC RAFVR (Nav) cremated at Hull Crematorium.

Sgt Harding, F/S Mackenzie, Sgt Morgan, Sgt Sasey, and Sgt Hodgkins were un-injured. P/O Lucas had been awarded the DFC three days before on 26th July 1944. Crash location: OS sheet 121 787693.

1220 hrs Training

Magister I N3941 of 418 Sqn from Hurn overshot a forced landing while short of fuel during bad weather and made an emergency landing on Ilkeston Recreation ground. A propeller and one wheel were damaged but the pilot F/O J/22036 S P Seid? RCAF escaped injury.

WEDNESDAY 2nd AUGUST 1944

1855 hrs Training

Halifax III NA581 KW-U of 425 Sqn from Tholthorpe took off on a navex training flight and had been in the air for 3 hours 18 minutes when it went into a dive at 4,000 feet, did not recover, and crashed bursting into flames roughly one mile south west of Blyth, 5 miles north north east of Worksop. The cause was not known but it was thought that the pilot might have lost control following possible loss of power.

All 7 members of the crew were killed and as members of the RCAF were buried in Harrogate (Stonefall) Cemetery: F/L J/85641 George Douglas Stark DFC age 21 (Pilot), P/O C/90376 (R70189) Mervin Hugh Waters age 24 (F/Eng), P/O J/86151 Edmund Francis Pitkin age 20 (Nav), P/O J/89298 (R155052) John Jerome Pigeon age 22 (Air Bomber), P/O J/87366 Paul Patrick Davies age 25 (W.Op/Air Gnr), Sgt J/89073 (R192720) Lloyd Snider (Air Gnr), P/O J/89332 John Edward Code age 21 (Air Gnr).

F/L Stark was awarded the Distinguished Flying Cross effective from 2nd October 1944 whilst flying with 425 Sqn. He enlisted in his home town of Vancouver on 16th February

This memorial at Blyth commemorating the crew was dedicated on 14th September 1997.

1942. He graduated from initial training on 14th August 1942, No.6 EFTS on 20th November 1942 and No.7 SFTS 19th March 1943. He was commissioned in 1944.

The award was presented to his next of kin on 27th June 1945. His citation read: 'completed numerous operations against the enemy in the course of which he has invariably displayed the utmost fortitude, courage and devoted to duty'.

The following recommendation was published after his 31st sortie totalling 136 hours 30 minutes: 'An outstanding pilot F/L Stark has consistently displayed superb captaincy and airmanship throughout an operational career that comprises 31 sorties against enemy targets. These operations include two attacks on Berlin, as well as others on such strongly defended targets as Essen, Stuttgart and Frankfurt.

On one occasion, this officer was pilot of a Halifax bomber detailed to attack Hamburg. The aircraft was badly off track both on proceeding to and on returning from the target. F/L Stark's skill and coolness under these trying conditions made possible the successful completion of the mission and the safe return of the aircraft. This officer's determination, cheerful courage and fine offensive spirit are an example and an inspiration to the other members of his crew.'

THURSDAY 3rd AUGUST 1944

1110 hrs — Air Test

Wellington III X3937 of 82 OTU from Ossington took off and on returning to land the pilot, F/O 133259 P J Helyar, failed to lower undercarriage and crashed, a fire breaking out soon afterwards. There were no injuries.

1558 hrs — Training

Stirling III EE967 KB-Q of 1661 HCU from Winthorpe began to swing to starboard on take off but was corrected by the pilot, F/O 143283 Matthew William Bell RAFVR (Pupil pilot), but to avoid a collision with another aircraft he deliberately swung the aircraft again resulting in the undercarriage collapsing and the aircraft breaking in two at about the mid-upper position. Harry Le-Marchant (Nav) was in the aircraft as an instructor.

M W Bell, now a F/L, was killed on 15th March 1945 when he took off from Balderton piloting Lancaster PA214 of 227 Sqn on a raid on Lutzkendorf, a synthetic oil plant. He is buried in Durnbach War Cemetery.

This day was the biggest slaughter of manned aircraft by a single night fighter in one sortie. Martin 'Tino' Becker shot down 16 aircraft.

SATURDAY 5th AUGUST 1944

2010 hrs — Training

Wellington X HE821 BZ- of 86 OTU from Gamston crashed with the loss of all crew at Hennymoor Farm near Creswell after a 6 hour cross country training flight. The pilot was making a forced landing after starboard engine failure due to fuel starvation, when he lost control at 800 feet, the aircraft stalled and spun into the ground. Six parachutes were found in the wreckage but only five crew men were found. Later it was found that the sixth parachute belonged to a crew member who had gone sick just before take-off and stayed at base.

W/O I R/116943 Willis Don Murdie (Pilot), P/O J/41540 Lowell Milton Brehaut age 21 (Nav), F/O J/40083 Walter William Cooper age 32 (Air Bomber), Sgt R/207295 James Robert Clarke (W.Op/Air Gnr), Sgt R/259992 John Joseph Lee age 19. All the crew were members of the RACF and are buried in Harrogate (Stonefall) Cemetery.

P/O Brehaut joined the RCAF in June 1941, completed his navigation course and received a commission as Pilot Officer. He took his Officer Graduate course and then transferred to the UK. He left a wife and daughter in Canada.

MONDAY 7th AUGUST 1944

1630 hrs Training

Wellington X LN571 of 86 OTU from Gamston took off for a general training flight and immediately had engine failure due to faulty plugs. The pilot, P/O J/37968 W V Warner RCAF, retracted the undercarriage and landed the aircraft straight ahead without injuries.

WEDNESDAY 9th AUGUST 1944

1615 hrs Training

Wellington X HE787 TD-P of 82 OTU from Gamston landed after a training flight and the brake pressure fell. The pilot, P/O J/39627 K K Beych RCAF, informed flying control but then the pressure returned then failed again and as the aircraft was on a slope with another aircraft in front and obstructions either side he retracted the undercarriage to stop. The pressure loss was due to a punctured rubber hose supplying air to the port brake drum. There were no injuries. This aircraft was also involved in an incident on 8th November.

SATURDAY 12th AUGUST 1944

0153 hrs Training

Halifax V EB192 of 1667 HCU from Sandtoft was on a bombing exercise during very low cloud and rain when it struck high ground whilst in a starboard turn and crashed on the Wiseton cricket field with the loss of all 7 crew.

The Halifax was starting a practice bombing run at Clayworth Bombing range near Retford. The aircraft was loaded with practice bombs and on the first impact with the ground and engines on full power it carved out a long furrow and lost one engine. On the second impact another large furrow was carved and another engine ripped off and on the third and final impact it collided with a large beech tree in front of Wiseton Hall breaking the port wing off, disintegrating and bursting into a ball of flames. The cricket pitch and Farm Orchard nearby was like a scrap yard. Fuel tanks were thrown into Grange Farm Orchard setting it on fire. The main landing wheels were found lying in front of the Hall. Foliage and surrounding trees were on fire and ammunition exploding with the intense heat.

P/O 177936 William Wells age 22 RAFVR (Pilot) is buried in Doncaster Old Cemetery, F/S 432081 Kevin Kenny Abrams RAAF aged 24 buried Harrogate (Stonefall) Cemetery, F/S 417674 Allan Benjamin Talbot RAAF age 24 buried Moorthorpe Cemetery, F/S 436136 Wallace Thompson RAAF aged 22 buried Harrogate (Stonefall) Cemetery, Sgt 1590875 Ernest Heath age 20 RAFVR (F/Eng) buried Owston Churchyard, Sgt 1667930 Alfred Gordon Monnington RAFVR Aged 19, buried Harrogate (Stonefall) Cemetery, Sgt 1824374 Alexander Steedman Watt age 22 (Air Gnr) buried in his home town of Cupar in the New Cemetery, Fife.

0235 hrs Training

Wellington III BK562 -R of 30 OTU from Seighford was on a night cross-country flight and 4 hours 6 minutes into the flight the aircraft's artificial horizon indicator failed. Whilst descending through 10/10ths cloud from 9,500 feet the gyros began to spin and control was lost and the instructor pilot, F/O 155502 P J Clifton, ordered the crew to abandon the aircraft. He had to bail out to allow other members of the crew to use the front escape hatch. The aircraft crashed at Wilford near Coronation Avenue and blew up. It had approached from over the old Wilford Power Station, went behind the Ferry Inn, just cleared the houses on the road to the left of the Inn, knocking off a chimney pot of an outhouse behind the house and into a tennis court scattering pieces into two fields alongside the railway line. The pilot, W/O 1282513 James William Jesse Butler RAFVR age 28, was killed and is buried in the City of London Cemetery.

Two others did not bale out and were killed, they were Sgt 1573888 William Struthers Owens age 21 RAFVR (Air Gnr) buried St Ninians (Bannockburn) Parish Burial Ground, and Sgt 1740042 Denys Edward Townsend age 20 RAFVR (Air Gnr) buried Bockleton (St Michael) Churchyard. Four crew men escaped, two of which were injured and one with a badly lacerated leg.

2247 hrs — Training

Wellington X LN446 of 12 OTU took off from Chipping Warden for a night bullseye training flight and undershot Worksop airfield whilst making a south east approach after starboard engine failure. Of the crew Sgt 1851711Alexander Arthur Jolly age 22 RAFVR was killed and is buried in Dowsby Churchyard. The following were injured, F/S 427415 J D Forbes RNZAF (Pupil Pilot), P/O L S R Smith RCAF, Sgts W R Malvern, R Fuller and R Johnson.

SUNDAY 13th AUGUST 1944

0115 hrs — Training

Halifax XX MZ560 LK- of 578 Sqn from Burn undercarriage collapsed on a 3 engine landing at Finningley, a strange aerodrome to the pilot, F/O 128866 R D Davies. The port inner engine was feathered following failure at 17,500 feet but became un-feathered necessitating an early landing.

1150 hrs — Training

Wellington X LN987 of 28 OTU from Wymeswold took off for circuit and landings training and on touch down the brakes failed so the pilot, P/O J/37099 Merlin Leigh Matkin RCAF, raised the undercarriage to avoid running off the runway, turned slightly and ran into a ditch. No-one was injured. P/O Matkin was killed on 17th January 1945 when flying with 514 Sqn. He was a member of the crew of Lancaster PB906 which was lost on a raid on Wanne-Eickel and is commemorated on the Runnymede memorial.

MONDAY 14th AUGUST 1944

1525 hrs — Training

Wellington X HE428 of 82 OTU from Ossington was returning from a 5 hour cross country flight with P/O 175815 R H Wintle, Instructor Pilot and F/L 10986 (R104047) James Frederick Hadley RCAF pupil Pilot when it force landed in a field, wheels up, near Egmanton village. Both engines had cut due to the Mid-Upper Gunner turning off the fuel cocks. The seven man crew were un-injured.

F/L Hadley was killed on 22nd March 1945 when piloting Lancaster KB777 NA-V of 428 'Ghost' Sqn on a raid on Hildesheim. His aircraft was last seen on the return flight, flying below 5,000 feet with flames streaming from an engine. The aircraft was abandoned and 3 crewmen died and 4 were taken prisoner. The crew were F/L Hadley and F/O J/45349 Daniel Frame age 30 (Air Gnr) both buried in Rheinberg War Cemetery and F/S J/95385 John MacKenzie age 20 commemorated on the Runnymede Memorial. Sgt R R Duke, F/O W J Spence, F/O C A Goodier and F/S J W Bellamy were taken prisoner. All were members of the RCAF.

F/L Hadley and his crew at Ossington in 1944 in front of a Wellington. Back row; Jimmy (Hadley), Mac (probably MacKenzie), Bill (probably Spence), Goody (probably Goodier). Front row; Jack, Davy

THURSDAY 17th AUGUST 1944

1615 hrs Ferrying

Stirling III EH929 –F of 1661 HCU took off from Swinderby to be ferried to Winthorpe and swung from side to side as it went down the runway, the throttle was cut and the the undercarriage collapsed. The pilots were S/L 67707 S Cockbain DFC RAFVR and F/L A/413349 Jim Cowans DFC RAAF and P/O Faraday was the 2nd Engineer. The engines were presumed ok as the aircraft had just finished a major overhaul and inspection.

S/L Cockbain was awarded the DFC on 9th June 1944 when flying with 44 Sqn. The citation read: 'In March, 1944, this officer was the pilot of an aircraft detailed for a mine-laying mission. On the outward flight the aircraft was attacked by a fighter and sustained much damage. One engine was rendered useless, the cupola of the mid-upper turret was shattered and the hydraulic gear was damaged. Despite this, Squadron Leader Cockbain succeeded in evading a second attack and went on to the target to complete his task. This officer has completed a large number of sorties and has displayed great skill, leadership and devotion to duty.'

The following is an extract from the log book of one of the crew: 'On 17 Aug we went to Swinderby from Winthorpe to collect the Stirling after its major overhaul. We went bounding down the runway but the a/c wouldn't take off and was swinging from side to side. Finally the port u/c gave way and collapsed as it swung into the grass, did a semi-circle and came to a halt one wing down. No injuries.'

Previous to the incident reported above, Stirling EH929 had taken off from Winthorpe for Swinderby, climbed to about 300 feet and then the aircraft took over the controls despite the efforts of both pilots. Fortunately the main runway at Winthorpe was in line with the main runway at Swinderby where it landed safely. The aircraft then had the major overhaul mentioned above.

MONDAY 21st AUGUST 1944

1135 hrs Training

Oxford I BG624 of 16 (P)SFTS from Newton undershot landing, after a gliding descent, at Orston relief landing ground and the aircraft struck a hedge. It was considered that the pilot under training, 2nd Lt J Bielecki, should have opened up the throttles to maintain the engine temperature.

1802 hrs Training

Mosquito IV DZ433 of 1655 MTU from Wyton had been on a cross country training flight for 45 minutes when it spun into the ground out of cloud 5 miles south of Finningley airfield and crashed at Barrow Hills between Scaftworth and Everton.

The aircraft was seen breaking cloud at 400-500 feet out of control in a stable flat spin. The enquiry found it impossible to diagnose the primary cause of the accident but stated that the pilot had been warned that the aircraft would be slightly tail heavy as it was carrying a 500 lb bomb. Both crew members were killed: W/O 655586 Matthew Crowe aged 28 (Nav) is buried in Paisley Cemetery and F/O 52508 Robert Byron Bingham aged 24 (Pilot) buried Finningley Churchyard Extension.

SUNDAY 27th AUGUST 1944

0155 hrs Training

Stirling III LK616 GP-G of 1661HCU from Winthorpe took off at about 2100 hrs on a cross country training flight when on returning to base at 0140 hrs was instructed to enter the circuit. The aircraft was last seen over the airfield at about 1,000 feet and apart from a routine position report nothing further was heard until 15 minutes later when it crashed and caught fire near Hawton AA camp, 4 miles south west of the airfield. 6 of the 7 crew died. The injured survivor could not recall anything of the accident and the subsequent investigation failed to establish the cause.

P/O 415496 Heathcote George Round age 25 RNZAF (Pilot) is buried in Oxford (Botley) Cemetery, Sgt 1125712 Frank Beeby age 22 (F/Eng) buried Stanwix Cemetery, Carlisle, F/S R/194133 William Clyde Brown RCAF age 29 (Nav) buried Harrogate (Stonefall) Cemetery, F/S R/159249 Donald James McAllister age 29 (Air Bomber) RCAF buried Harrogate (Stonefall) Cemetery, F/S 1314595 Leonard Hanford, age 21 RAFVR (W.Op/Air Gnr) buried Blaenavon Cemetery, Sgt 1429615 D Solly (Air Gnr) was slightly injured with burns to his face and hands.

Sgt 1506086 Eric Sanderson (Air Gnr) age 24 RAFVR, was admitted to RAF hospital, Rauceby with a fractured skull and died from his injuries at 1230 hrs on 1.9.44. He was cremated at Nottingham Crematorium.

P/O Round's brother F/O Arthur Knuhan Round was also killed flying with the RAF. He died on 26.5.41 while flying with 98 Sqn piloting Battle P2330 on transit from Melgerdi to Kaldadarnes when he crashed into a cloud covered mountain.

WEDNESDAY 30th AUGUST 1944

0449 hrs — Training

Wellington X HE485 BZ- of 86 OTU from Gamston took off for circuit and landings practice and 2 minutes later suffered engine trouble, caught fire and exploded. The aircraft crashed into Haughton Hall near Bothamsall with the loss of all five Canadian crew members. Luckily the Hall was empty as the occupant, a Mr R Bedford, had moved out the previous week.

It was possible that the pilot lost control whilst trying to remedy the engine trouble. The crew were: F/O J/37961 (R182940) Lloyd Edwin Chapman age 24 (Pilot), F/O J/40881 George Walker Davidson age 22 (Nav), F/O J/40029 William Stewart Ross age 28 (Air Bomber), P/O J/43740 Meryn Kram (W.Op/Air Gnr), F/O J/41054 Peter Paul Loszchuk age 20 (Air Gnr). All the crew were members of the RCAF and are buried in Harrogate (Stonefall) Cemetery.

Graves of P/O Kram, F/O Loszchuk, F/O Davidson, F/O Ross and F/O Chapman

1532 hrs **Training**

Stirling III EF200 of 1660 HCU from Swinderby was on aircraft conversion training and flying at 12,000 feet when the port outer engine failed and was feathered so an emergency landing was attempted at Gamston. It was given permission to land but by this time it had two engines feathered and because the aircraft was not lined up with the runway the pilot attempted an overshoot but did not have enough height. The airspeed dropped, control was lost and the Stirling crashed into large trees at Double Clump, near Hardwick village, Clumber Park, with an engine already on fire which then spread to the fuselage. Five crew members were killed and taken to RAF Gamston and three injured.

P/O 427632 John Leslie Bairstow age 25 RAAF (Pilot) is buried in Oxford (Botley) Cemetery, Sgt 1800885 Frederick John Ward age 24 RAFVR (F/Eng) buried Ilford Cemetery, F/S 429230 Ivor Hawkins Jones age 24 RAAF (Nav) buried Oxford (Botley) Cemetery, F/S 1684698 Edgar Smith age 21 RAFVR (F/Eng) buried Halifax Cemetery, F/S 427861 Walter Douglas Fawcett age 21 RAAF (W.Op) buried Oxford (Botley) Cemetery.

F/S A D O'Hara RAAF (Air Gnr), Sgt W Toole (MUAG) and Sgt W P Mills (Rear Gnr) were injured.

THURSDAY 31st AUGUST 1944

0215 hrs **Training**

Stirling III LJ637 -H of 1660 HCU from Swinderby was on a training flight when the starboard outer engine failed and this was feathered. The aircraft was brought into land by the pilot, F/O 143736 W A Verrals, but while landing was still gently turning and bounced laterally wheel to wheel which caused the undercarriage to collapse.

2250 hrs **Training**

Wellington III Z1661 of 82 OTU from Ossington took off for a night cross country exercise but made an early return when the port engine failed as the aircraft flew at 10,000 feet. The pilot used the emergency system which did not lower the undercarriage sufficiently to lock in place and so the aircraft crashed on landing. Friction occurring between the aircraft and the runway caused it to catch fire. There were 6 crew members, the pilot P/O J19098 H M Wilton RCAF and the pilot under training F/L J/9554 R W Andres RCAF with only one injury.

2350 hrs **Training**

Stirling III LJ630 of 1654 HCU from Wigsley took off with a raw crew making their first cross country navigation flight together. 25 minutes after take-off the aircraft was seen to have a starboard engine on fire. It crashed close to Grove Farm, Stanton-by-Dale and exploded with a huge flash, killing all the crew. The blast just missed the farmhouse itself. One engine was hurled into the yard of a farm now covered by Stanton tip, and blazing fuel set fire to the stooks of corn in the field behind Grove Farm. The generally accepted reason for the crash was that the aircraft had been struck by lightning as a heavy storm was in progress at the time. There is a plaque on the war memorial in St Michael's churchyard in memory of the 7 crew who were killed.

P/O 30829 Bruce Gordon Wilkinson RAAF age 28 (Pilot) is buried in Oxford (Botley) Cemetery, Sgt 1607283 Raymond George Alexander RAFVR age 27 (Nav) buried in Thorney (St Helen) Cemetery, F/S 422093 Paul Druce Arthur RAAF age 22 (W/Op) buried Oxford (Botley) Cemetery, F/S 1607195 William Edwin John Cox RAFVR age 21 (F/Eng) buried in Thorney (St Helen) Cemetery, Sgt 1622403 Aereon Hughes age 20 RAFVR (Air Bomber) buried in Thorney (St Helen) Cemetery, Sgt 1594880 James Lambell RAFVR age 36 (F/Eng) buried in Thorney (St Helen) Cemetery, Sgt 650407 Thomas Henry Westhead RAF age 25 (Rear Gnr) buried Brierley (Grimethorpe) Cemetery. The following is an extract from the Ilkeston Church magazine:

'In 1943 groups of about a hundred new RAF aircrew were brought together in a large room when they had finished their initial training. Over a cup of tea and biscuits they chatted to each other and formed themselves into bomber crews. One such crew of seven young men, aged 20/21, included Sgt H C Rogers (Pilot), and Sgt W J Cox (F/Eng). When they had completed their training they were posted to 630 Squadron (code LE), flying Lancaster bombers from East Kirkby, Lincs.

Between 20th December 1943 and 31st March 1944 they made 17 raids on Germany, including seven on Berlin, then in April and May made twelve raids on occupied France, plus two minelaying attacks to Danzig and Keuil. After 31 operational flights, having flown together for some 360 hours (including the later stages of their training), the crew was disbanded in early June 1944.

Following established custom, such veterans were sent to training squadrons, to recuperate and teach others. In July 1944 Sgt W "Bill" Cox DFM was transferred to RAF Wigsley, to 1654 Heavy Conversion Unit. Here newly formed crews learned to work together and to handle four-engine aircraft.

Heavy Conversion Units often used obsolescent Stirling bombers for training, thus releasing the better Halifax and Lancaster bombers for operations. Crews then attended a Halifax (or Lancaster) Finishing school for a brief period before posting to a front line squadron. As the Stirling had some troublesome features, an experienced flight engineer was carried to resolve any problems beyond the experience of the trainee crew.

On the evening of 31st August 1944, Sgt Cox took off from Wigsley, with a raw crew making their first cross country navigation flight together. They were flying Stirling LJ630 (coincidentally the same as Cox's previous squadron number), which had been built by Short Brothers at Rochester, and delivered to RAF Syerston on 1st May 1944.

Some 25 minutes after take-off, having flown about 25 miles in a direct line, the aircraft was seen to have a starboard engine on fire. It crashed close to Grove Farm at 11 pm and exploded with a huge flash, killing all the crew. The blast just missed the farmhouse itself. One engine was hurled into a yard now covered by Stanton tip, and blazing fuel set fire to the stooks of corn in the field behind Grove Farm. However, the "worst storm in memory" was raging at the time and extinguished these flames, but the wreckage of the aircraft itself burnt for some time. The generally accepted reason for the crash was that the aircraft had been struck by lightning (the Air Ministry records of the crash no longer survive).

Despite the storm a number of people from both village and works hurried to the scene, but there was nothing they could do except watch the masses of white and gold flame.

The Stanton-by-Dale War Memorial is unusual. Not only does the bronze tablet for WWII commemorate the men from the village who gave their lives during the war, but it continues: "AND OF THE CREW OF THE AIRCRAFT WHICH CRASHED WITHIN THE PARISH ON 31st AUGUST", and then lists the crew.

Men from RAF Hucknall cleared the site of the wreck, but one propeller blade and a cigarette case survive in private hands, and the farmer still ploughs up fragments of metal. The site is clearly visible. About 150 yards on the Stanton side of Grove Farm is a long narrow field running from Dale Road north towards the Works. In the eastern edge of this field is a 20 yard length of wire fencing, replacing the hedge which was destroyed in the crash. In the western hedge opposite is an oak tree, which for years bore no leaves down one side where it had been burnt.

Rumours that W Cox had been killed in a crash reached other members of his former crew, but the times did not encourage investigation. In post war years they attempted to discover his whereabouts, but to no avail.

S/Ldr Cliff Rogers OBE, DFC went on to become Chief Test Pilot at Rolls-Royce, Hucknall living at Morley. For some reason early in 1992 he visited Stanton-by-Dale and saw Cox's name on the War Memorial. Subsequently he brought anothet member of his crew (who died a short time afterwards) to see the War Memorial. Their search lasting over 40 years was over.'

Crash location: Cassini grid 1942 sheet 54 918587; OS sheet 129 457387.

The crash site of Stirling LJ630

FRIDAY 1st SEPTEMBER 1944

2327 hrs

An enemy aircraft crashed at Warsop, east of Cottage Lane with no sign of the crew. There is a report in the Public Records Office on repairs to houses. The following is a report made by Police Sgt W Hancockt dated 2nd September:

'I have to report that at 11.25 pm on Friday 1st September 1944 I was on High Street, Warsop, when I saw the sky illuminated with a vivid flash from the direction of Clipstone, and then heard a heavy explosion and falling glass from shop windows. Just previously I had seen what appeared to be two British aircraft, with lights on, both travelling at right angles with High Street, one East-South East and the other East, and several miles apart. The flash came between these two aircraft, but I had heard the sound of an aeroplane between the two mentioned above.

In company with Sgt Nixon I immediately went in the direction where the explosion occurred and later saw two fires, in the direction of Clipstone, which were rapidly dying down.

In company with Sgt Nixon, PC171 Adams and SC663 Wood, I made a search and found the main wreckage of an unidentified enemy aircraft in a field at Warsop, approximately one mile North West of Parliament Oak, Peatfield Lane, Warsop.

In the next field, about 50 yards from the main wreckage, was a crater approximately 20 feet wide by 6 feet deep and close by was a large piece of metal bearing a large swastika. Wreckage from the aeroplane was found in nine fields, covering an approximate area of half a mile. The boss of an aeroplane three blade propellor was found in a corn field ¼ mile away, and another boss and an engine were found in a turnip field ¼ mile away. A second engine was found in the same field as the main wreckage about 250 yards away. Large quantities of rubber were found over the area.

Flight Sergeant Wills of RAF Gamston came on the scene and stated that he was unable to identify and could only say that it was an enemy wreckage. Divisional Headquarters and the Report Centre were notified. Inspector Levers of Mansfield Woodhouse, with other officers, also Sergeant Reddish, from DHQ were also on the scene. Search was made by the Police, Special Constables, Home Guards, and Wardens, but there was no trace of any bodies or clothing.

Shop windows and windows of houses on High Street, Dawney Hill, Mansfield Road, Spion Kop, King Road, Wood Street, Sherwood Street and Forest Road, Warsop, Church Warsop, and Warsop Vale were damaged by blast.

Shop windows on Central Drive, Market Place, King Edward Street, Shirebrook were damaged by blast. Houses in various parts of Shirebrook and on Station Road, Langwith, were also damaged. There were no casualties.

An RAF guard was placed on the wreckage and attention given by Police and Special Constables to prevent damage to crops by souvenir hunters. The wreckage of the plane appears to be that of the lower component of a German composite aircraft.'

WEDNESDAY 6th SEPTEMBER 1944

1147 hrs | Training

Wellington X LN861 of 28 OTU from Wymeswold port engine failed in flight due to spark plug failure and when coming into land the undercarriage failed to lower when the emergency air bottle was operated and the aircraft belly landed on the airfield. The instructor pilot was F/L 118556 B A Kitson and the pupil P/O 164629 J C Aitchison.

1315 hrs | Training

Wellington III BK124 of 18 OTU from Worksop suffered an engine failure whilst at 3,000 feet and, unable to maintain height, the pilot carried out a wheels-up landing in a field at Rampton, four and a half miles east of Retford. There were no injuries to the crew of six. It was later established that the cause of the engine failure was a sleeve seizing in 1,3 and 7 cylinders. The pilot was a Canadian P/O 41168 L K Laurin.

FRIDAY 8th SEPTEMBER 1944

2300 hrs | Ground

Wellington X LN863 of 86 OTU from Gamston was stationary on the airfield when the air gunner left the aircraft by the rear turret, which was against orders, and was struck by a propeller. The instructor pilot P/O J/85759 A J Headland RCAF had ordered the crew to leave the aircraft.

The pupil pilot aboard the aircraft, P/O J/38360 Gilbert Paul Haliburton RCAF, was killed on 31st March 1945 age 27. He was the pilot of Lancaster KB911 of 434 Sqn which took off from Croft to bomb shipyards at Hamburg when it crashed near Bergedorf. He has no known grave and is commemorated on the Runnymede memorial.

SATURDAY 9th SEPTEMBER 1944

0045 hrs | Training

Wellington X LP613 of 28 OTU from Castle Donington during overshoot the pilot Sgt 1393195 E G Parsons retracted the undercarriage too soon, the aircraft sank and the propeller struck the ground so he closed the throttles and belly landed.

MONDAY 11th SEPTEMBER 1944

1550 hrs | Training

Master II W9033 of 17 SFTS from Cranwell was struck in flight by Hurricane IIC LF382 of 1690 Flt from Fiskerton when it made a mock attack and crashed at Carlton-le-Moreland.
Lt F Koroglu (Pilot), who was a Turkish Air Force student, baled out and received a broken leg.

Training

Hurricane IIC LF382 of 1690 Flt from Scampton took off with the intention of carrying out a training sortie with a Lancaster. On arriving in the practice area, the pilot sighted a Master trainer, W9033, which seemed reluctant to depart. The Hurricane dived towards the Master in a mock attack in an attempt to drive the aircraft out of range of the fighter affiliation exercise but a collision occurred and both aircraft spun into the ground at Carlton-le-Moreland. The pilot, Sgt 571776 Howard William Ramsay age 23 RAF, tried to control the aircraft and as a consequence did not bale out until at 200 feet but at that height his parachute would not fully open and he was killed. He was cremated in Bristol (Arnos Vale) Crematorium. (see above).

TUESDAY 12th SEPTEMBER 1944

1345 hrs — Training

Martinet I HP321 of 1690 Flt from Syerston encountered engine failure and force landed at Hucknall aerodrome causing the death of both crewmen. The crew were, W/O 1391860 Ambrose Alexander Graham age 24 RAFVR (Pilot) nicknamed 'Sonny' died instantaneously and is buried in Hucknall Cemetery. LAC 1454475 Victor Ernest Lewis age 22 RAFVR was taken to SSQ with a fractured skull and right leg and after treatment was transferred to hospital where he died 2½ hours after the crash and is buried in Ilford (Barking side) Cemetery.

MONDAY 18th SEPTEMBER 1944

1230 hrs — Training

Master II DM244 of 7 (P)AFU from Peterborough took off at 1140 hrs detailed to carry out stalling, steep turns, aerobatics above 6000 feet, precautionary landings and forced landings. The flight was to take approximately 90 minutes, the weather being suitable at the time. The aircraft was seen by the Newark ROC post 'beating up' the district area just south of Newark at Hawton at a low altitude. It then made a steeply banked turn to the left at very low level when the nose suddenly dropped and the aircraft dived vertically into a bungalow, immediately bursting into flames. The bungalow, 'Elgon', of Hawton Road, was the residence of Mr and Mrs H Mackender. Mrs Mackender, who was indoors at the time of the accident had a remarkable escape, but was badly shaken. The back of the bungalow was seriously damaged and floorboards and furniture caught fire and the flames were put out by the Newark Fire Service.

Apparently the pilot, Sgt 1583327 William Herbert Maynard RAFVR age 21,was 'beating up' the house of his parents. He was killed and is buried in Oxford (Botley) Cemetery.

Sgt Maynard was the son of of Mr and Mrs S T W Maynard of 87 Boundary Road, Newark. He was educated at Bridlington where he was senior boy and senior server at Trinity Church until his parents moved to Grantham. There he continued his education and joined the Home Guard and when his father was transferred to Newark County Court office 3½ years ago he became a student at the County Technical College and joined the ATC and the Newark Home Guard. Prior to joining the RAF in October 1942 he worked at Worthington Simpson's. He did his flying training in Canada where he won his wings as a pilot. He was to have proceeded shortly to a flying instructors' school to which he had been posted.

2105 hrs — Training

Stirling III BF481 of 1654 CU from Wigsley took off for night circuits but after landing the undercarriage collapsed which was probably damaged on take off, the aircraft swung to starboard. The pilots were staff pilot F/O 156319 J G Barker and F/O J/35848 Edward Roy Newland RCAF.

F/O Newland was killed on 17th December when serving with 61 Sqn. He was the pilot of Lancaster LM729 which crashed after being hit by flak on a raid on Munchen. He is buried in Durnbach War Cemetery.

WEDNESDAY 20th SEPTEMBER 1944

1645 hrs Training

Stirling III EF115 of 1654 HCU from Wigsley was practicing 3 engine landings and on approach the aircraft swung to port just before touchdown and the pupil pilot tried to overshoot below 50 feet on 3 engines. The instructor pilot took over and landed straight ahead in rough ground to the side of the runway. The undercarriage was ripped off by a tree trunk and also the ground the aircraft was crossing made damage inevitable.

The crew were: F/O 53221 John Sidney Ludford DFC (Pilot Instructor) who was injured, F/S 434058 Jocelyn King Waring RAAF (Pupil Pilot), Sgt H W Parkins also injured, Sgt 1556800 John Smith RAFVR (F/Eng), F/S 428396 John Lane Brosnan RAAF (Nav), F/S 428642 George Caleb Groves RAAF (Bomb Aimer), F/S 430207 Robert Magnay Howell RAAF (W.Op), Sgt 431591 Robert Park Templeton RAAF (Tail Gnr), Sgt L H J Cheesman RAAF (MUG).

F/O Ludford was awarded the DFC on 12th May 1944 whilst flying with 57 Sqn and the citation read: 'In February1944, this was the pilot of an aircraft detailed to attack Leipzig. When some 100 miles from the target the aircraft was attacked by a fighter. The hydraulic gear and the starboard inner propeller were damaged; the electrical circuits were also damaged, causing a failure of the lighting and heating systems. In no way deterred, Flight Lieutenant Ludford flew on to the target and made a successful attack, afterwards flying safely to base with bomb doors open. This officer displayed praiseworthy courage and determination. He has completed many sorties, including 8 attacks on Berlin.'

F/O Waring age 21, Sgt Smith age 23, F/S Brosnan age 20, F/S Groves age 29, F/S Howell age 20 and F/S Templeton age 19 were all lost on a raid on Heilbronn on 4th December 1944. They were members of the crew of Lancaster PB792 JO-O of 463 Sqn from Waddington when they flew into the side of a hill near Le Hohwald (Bas Rhin) about 20km north west of Selestat, when homeward bound. They are buried in Choloy War Cemetery.

Sgt Cheesman was also a member of the crew but he survived the crash. F/O Waring had only been posted to 463 Sqn on 15.11.44 and this was only his 2nd Operation.

The following compiled from information provided by F/S Cheesman is recorded in the Squadron Operational Record Book:

'Sortie completed hear B/A direct Captain on to markers. Attack successful. Having bombed we set course for "D" 48.25N 08.15E, descending in steps as briefed, and when we arrived at approx 48.30N 07.45E the Nav told Captain we were below' safety height', and the Captain replied that he wanted to get out of cloud. "I, Sgt Cheesman, declare that this was the last speech heard over the intercom". Also I have no idea of the height of A/c, and that immediately after this remark the A/c hit the hillside. The A/c crashed at 48.27N 07.22E approx. I was thrown out of my turret and landed up under the mid upper turret. I eventually regained consciousness, and after calling out the names of the other members for 15 minutes, decided to sit in the A/c until daylight out of the inclement weather. Daylight arrived with a heavy fall of snow and I found my missing boot which with great difficulty I put on with my right arm and left hand being broken, and jumped out of the A/c. The A/c had broken in half behind the wings. The hillside was covered with trees 20/30ft high. The Mid Upper was dead in his turret and the others were 15/20 yards from the A/c all dead. I set course SW with aid of compass, walking all day on 5th, spent that night in an uninhabited tower, walked again on the 6th and that afternoon contacted a vacant house. Sat on the veranda for two hours and eventually a man came and directed me to Hohwald with 6 F.F.I. men who took me to St Blaise. The next day an ambulance took me to American hospital at Mulheim. The Americans arranged for the burial of the six crew at Hochfeden. Arrived in UK 20/1/45.'

Oxford II AB705 of 12 (P)AFU crash landed near Oxton.

THURSDAY 21st SEPTEMBER 1944

1425 hrs | Training

Wellington X HE528 of 82 OTU from Ossington had been in the air for 1 hour 40 minutes on a training exercise when at 16,000 feet the port engine failed and was unfeathered by the pilot F/O J/24766 E C McDonald RCAF. The aircraft returned to base, jettisoned its petrol and 4 of the crew baled out. The approach was made in bad visibility and the undercarriage was lowered by the emergency system but would not fully lower due to excessive air speed and the aircraft overshot the runway and landed at the extreme end. There was one slight injury.

FRIDAY 22nd SEPTEMBER 1944

0100 hrs | Training

Oxford I LX475 of 6 (P)AFU flew into the ground 300 yards from Castle Donington airfield when descending through cloud in search of the airfield after becoming lost. The pilot, W/O A/416777 V T Mills RAAF, who was injured should have landed when he saw the flare path on an earlier attempt to land. Interference on radar made contact with base difficult.

MONDAY 25th SEPTEMBER 1944

0040 hrs | Stationary

Master II AZ598 of 16 (P)SFTS from Tollerton was hit at dispersal by Master III DL894 which had swung off the runway during landing. An investigation came to the conclusion that the Flying Control Officer had packed aircraft too close to the runway.

0040 hrs | Training

Master II DL894 of 16 (P)SFTS from Tollerton was training on circuits and landings and swung on landing in a 24mph cross wind, piloted by the pupil pilot, and hit two aircraft including Master AZ598. The instructor pilot was W/O P/780665 J Nudzinski PAF.

0255 hrs | Training

Stirling III LK547 of 1661 CU from Winthorpe landed 500 yards down the 1400 yard runway too fast in a light wind and overshot. The Stirling's brakes failed due to lack of air pressure during circuits and bumps exercise. The aircraft was having to be pumped up with air every alternate landing.

The pilot, F/L 114399 Marcus Sydney Francis Pritchard RAFVR age 30, crashed in his Lancaster NN726 of 106 Sqn from Metheringham on a raid on Gdynia on 18th December. He lies at rest in Malbork Commonwealth War Cemetery, Poland.

TUESDAY 26th SEPTEMBER 1944

0600 hrs | Taxiing

Lancaster III ED727 of 5 LFS from Syerston landed and after parking the aircraft in dispersal and stopping the engines the pilot, F/O 421344 John Graham Anderson RNZAF, released the brakes and left the cockpit. ED727 ran forward into another parked aircraft, Lancaster ED756. F/O Anderson was killed on 16th November 1944 age 32 piloting Lancaster NF979 EM-B on a raid on Duren. F/O Anderson left St Heliers Bay, New Zealand, in January 1943 to complete his training in Canada, and after being commissioned he was posted to Bomber Command. He and his crew are buried in Venray War Cemetery.

1235 hrs Training

Wellington X LP386 of 28 OTU from Castle Donington was on a training flight when the pilot, F/L 122975 T D Henderson, tried to overshoot after a south east approach at 300 feet. The aircraft continued to lose height and one propeller struck an inner marker beacon and the pilot decided to crash land ahead. There were no injuries to the five man crew.

WEDNESDAY 27th SEPTEMBER 1944

0110 hrs Training

Stirling III LK453 of 1654 HCU from Wigsley was on bombing practice when on return to base it circled waiting for cloud to clear and for some unknown reason dived into the ground and caught fire one mile north of Wigsley airfield. The crew of 7 were killed.

Sgt 185161 James Raymond Townley age 28 RAFVR (Pilot) is buried in Preston Cemetery, Sgt 1076061 Thomas William Lightley RAFVR F/Eng buried Seaton Hirst (St John) Churchyard, Sgt 1603327 Anthony Thomas Collins age 20 RAFVR (Nav) buried Winchester (Magdalen Hill) Cemetery, Sgt 1455924 George Peter Barber age 22 RAFVR (Air Bomber) buried Rotherham (Masbrough) Cemetery, Sgt 1862131 Norman Eric Mead age 19 RAFVR (W/Op) buried Great Sutton (All Saints) Churchyard, Sgt 1453876 Stanley Clifford Howard age 22 RAFVR (Air Gnr) buried Thurrock (West Thurrock) Cemetery, Sgt 1896425 Kenneth Clayton age 21 RAFVR (Air Gnr) buried Shirland (St Leonard) Churchyard.

THURSDAY 28th SEPTEMBER 1944

0150 hrs Training

Stirling III LJ474 TV-Q of 1660 HCU from Swinderby was on high level bombing training when the port and starboard outer engines were feathered in flight and on the first two attempts to land the pilot could not lower the undercarriage in time. He was instructed to belly land which was done successfully without any injuries.

The pilot, F/S 427019 Noel Somervell Culpan RNZAF was killed age 20 while flying as 2nd pilot in Lancaster LM626 from 57 Sqn on a raid on Munchen on 17th December 1944. It was his 1st operation. He is buried in St Sever Cemetery Extension, Rouen.

2035 hrs Training

Wellington X LP342 of 29 OTU from Bruntingthorpe took off for a cross country exercise and 70 minutes later broke up in the air due to diving at excessive speed, at Branton, near Finningley. The aircraft exploded and caught fire on impact. The crew of 6 were all killed:

F/S A429922 Anthony James Cantwell age 21 RAAF (Pilot), Sgt 2235489 James Edward Conchie RAFVR, F/S 432577 Jeffrey Noel Smith age 20 RAAF, Sgt 1566258 Cecil Ralph Gollop age 24 RAFVR (Nav). All buried in Harrogate (Stonefall) Cemetery, Sgt 1580619 Maxwell Woodhead age 21 RAFVR (Air Bomber) cremated Birmingham Municipal Crematorium, Sgt 1868113 Neil Graham age 21 RAFVR buried Gress Old Churchyard, Stornoway.

F/S Smith's cousin George Winter lost his life with 267 others when the Australian Hospital Ship *Centaur* was sunk on 14th May 1944 by a Japanese torpedo. F/S Cantwell was an electrician in civilian life.

FRIDAY 29th SEPTEMBER 1944

2110 hrs Training

Wellington X LN529 of 18 OTU from Gamston was conducting dual cross country training when it overshot the airfield on a single engine landing as the port engine caught fire in flight.

The pilot feathered the engine but it did not go out, the graviner was then operated but this did not extinguish the fire at once. The pilot, P/O 174406 J Littlewood, then tried to retract the undercarriage but the aircraft ran through a hedge into a ploughed field and the port undercarriage collapsed. The pilot under training was Sgt R/197749 R E Congdon RCAF.

SUNDAY 1st OCTOBER 1944

0838 hrs — Training

Lancaster I W4941 RC-M of 5 LFS from Syerston took off for night training but on landing 20 minutes later the wheels failed to lock down but the emergency system then operated and the aircraft landed safely. Eight hours later at 0838 hrs with the aircraft parked on its dispersal pan the undercarriage collapsed.

The pilot, F/L 419881 Edward McMaster Lawson, age 22 RAAF, was killed on 2nd March 1945 piloting Lancaster ME473 EM-H from 207 Sqn. His aircraft collided with Lancaster ND572 over Spilsby, Lincs. He is buried in Cambridge City Cemetery.

THURSDAY 5th OCTOBER 1944

0423 hrs — Training

Stirling III LJ624 TV-C of 1660 HCU from Swinderby landed in bad weather conditions to the right of the runway and collided with a stationary aircraft Stirling III LK389. The pilot was F/O J/35620 H R Hayward.

MONDAY 9th OCTOBER 1944

1625 hrs — Taxiing

Lancaster III EQ802 of 5 LFS from Syerston undercarriage collapsed while taxiing due to faulty manipulation of the gear. The pilot instructor was F/O 155774 P T Richards and the pupil P/O 174874 A Cuckworth.

TUESDAY 10th OCTOBER 1944

1500 hrs — Training

Master II DM333 of 16 (P)SFTS from Tollerton failed to get airborne on take off because the pilot, AC2 P/705508 J Witkow PAF, left the throttles in coarse pitch. He throttled back, overran the runway and the aircraft overturned. He escaped without injury.

THURSDAY 12th OCTOBER 1944

2015 hrs — Training

Master II DM424 of 16 (P)SFTS from Tollerton caught fire in the cockpit on overshoot and dived into the ground one mile north east of Plumtree and burnt out. The pilot, LAC P/704930 Zdziskaw Maciula PAF age 21, was killed and is buried in Newark-upon-Trent Cemetery.

The source of the fire was obscure but the condition of the pilot's goggles indicated that there were flames in the cockpit.

SUNDAY 15th OCTOBER 1944

1430 hrs — Training

Tiger Moth II EM815 of 25 (P)EFTS from Hucknall was on approach to Hucknall at 30 feet when it collided with Tiger Moth T7687, stalled and crashed. The pilot AC2 P/706163 J Jarocki PAF who was not injured, did not keep a good lookout.

THURSDAY 19th OCTOBER 1944

1245 hrs — Training

Oxford I HM905 of 16 (P)SFTS from Newton landed and the aircraft swung to port and the port undercarriage collapsed. The pilot was 2nd Lt W Blazejewicz.

SATURDAY 21st OCTOBER 1944

1625 hrs — Training

Tiger Moth II T6030 of 25 (P)EFTS from Hucknall was on circuits and landings training when it stalled in cloud. The aircraft spun out of control, failed to recover, hit the ground and caught fire at Starthwood Farm, north west of the runway and was a total wreck. The pilot AC2 P/706657 W Skoczek PAF had superficial injuries.

MONDAY 23rd OCTOBER 1944

0104 hrs — Ground

Wellington X HN544 of 82 OTU from Ossington was parked in dispersal when it was run into by Wellington LN602.

TUESDAY 24th OCTOBER 1944

1901 hrs — Weather Test

Wellington X LP844 of 18 OTU from Worksop took off on a weather test but crashed three minutes later, one mile north of Worksop airfield, after stalling at low altitude without adequate flying speed. 3 crew members were killed.

P/O J/86486 William Henry Wright DFC age 27 RCAF (Pilot) is buried in Harrogate (Stonefall) Cemetery, P/O 186745 Denis Nigel Phillips age 20 RAFVR buried Aberdare Cemetery, Sgt 2209824 John Norman Corlett age 20 RAFVR buried Liverpool (Allerton) Cemetery. Sgt K Hounslow and Sgt R J Winters were injured.

P/O Wright was awarded the Distinguished Flying Cross effective from 3rd October 1944 while flying with 433 Sqn. He enlisted in his home town of Toronto and graduated from initial training on 6th June 1942, 13 EFTS on 11th September 1942 and No.16SFTS on 30th December 1942. The award was presented to his next of kin on 8th April 1948.

The citation read: 'This officer has completed a large number of sorties including attacks against Berlin, Essen, Frankfurt, Stuttgart and Nuremburg. On one occasion he was captain of an aircraft detailed to attack Berlin. When in the target area the aircraft was attacked 4 times by a Focke-Wulf Fw190. P/O Wright, displaying great skill and coolness, successfully evaded the enemy and pressed home his attack. This officer has at all times shown exceptional qualities of leadership and skill and has set a fine example to his crew.'

FRIDAY 27th OCTOBER 1944

1125 hrs — Training

Mosquito II DZ256 HB- of 239 Sqn from West Raynham took off at 1105 hrs to carry out fighter affiliation with a Lancaster. Twenty minutes later it stalled and spun into the ground in Stapleford Woods, near Coddington, two miles east north east of Newark, as it was following the Lancaster in a slow (150mph) spiral, with the loss of both crew members.

The crew were F/L 128948 John Hubert Roberts age 21 RAFVR (Pilot) buried Herne Bay Cemetery and Sgt 1817180 Albert Henry Ashcroft age 19 RAFVR buried Wolverley Churchyard.

1810 hrs Ferrying

Wellington X HE427 of 17 OTU landed too fast at Gamston, the pilot F/S A/434732 B R Bartlett RAAF swung the aircraft to prevent overshooting the runway and the undercarriage collapsed. The pilot was landing on a strange airfield and the light wind were contributory factors.

SATURDAY 28th OCTOBER 1944

1700 hrs Training

Wellington X HZ480 of 18 OTU from Finningley on landing the starboard undercarriage collapsed shortly after touch down. The instructor pilot was F/O 171645 J C Smith and the pupil W/O R/120937 K Bates RCAF

2250 hrs Op; Bergen

Lancaster III LM746 PO- of 467 Sqn took off from Waddington at 2214 hrs to bomb U-boat pens and grazed Lancaster NN714 in the air at 2245 hours near Newark/Swinderby while losing time prior to forming up in the air for Operations. There were 74 aircraft wasting time in a confined space, NN714 landed safely but LM746 was badly damaged. The pilot, F/O Boxsell, jettisoned his load, 12 x 1000 lb bombs, over the sea and after returning inland 4 crew members baled out and F/O Boxsell, the navigator and flight engineer flew the Lancaster to Carnaby airfield landing at 0032 hours without any injuries. The crew were:

F/O A/427431Walter Kitchiner Boxsell DFC RAAF (Pilot), Sgt R J Bauchop, F/S A/432399 V E Aubourg RAAF, F/S A/437742 L Pegler RAAF, F/S A/417763H H Leach RAAF, F/S A/434271 J R Stokes RAAF and F/S A/428252 N C K Leonard.

2320 hrs Training

Stirling III EE907 -K of 1661 HCU from Winthorpe was on a solo training flight and due to bad weather the aircraft was diverted to Swinderby. Whilst on a three engine approach to land the aircraft crashed at Housham Woods, Morton near Swinderby, after control was lost when the landing flaps were lowered. The aircraft was a total wreck with the loss of three crew members and five injured. The injured crew were: F/L 49148 S H Martin (pilot), F/O R J Fairhead, (F/Eng), F/O 154954 Alfred William Gayford TAFVR age 29 (Air Bomber) was so severely injured he was admitted to Lincoln Military Hospital where he died on 31st October, being buried at Thurrocks Grays, Essex, 1899075 Sgt A W Coombes (Air Gnr) and Sgt J E Buckminster.

The crew who died were: Sgt 1590929 Robert Reed, age 20 RAFVR (W.Op/Air Gnr) buried in Hartlepool Cemetery, Sgt 1581293 John James Glasgow age 25 RAFVR (Nav) cremated at Coventry Crematorium, F/O 155090 James Robertson, DFC age 30 (Nav) buried Elgin New Cemetery.

F/O Robertson was awarded the DFC on 21st April 1944 flying with 467 Sqn. Crash location: Cassini grid 1940 sheet 47 352836; OS sheet 121 888641.

SUNDAY 29th OCTOBER 1944

1022 hrs

Blenheim IV Z6176 of RAF Film Servicing Unit was returning from trips to collect some kit and during low flight hit some overhead colliery cables and crashed at Coxmoor Golf club near Mansfield. The pilot, F/L 122761 Francis Wall Strover Mansfield RAFVR age 29, of RAF Catterick, was dead on arrival in the ambulance at RAF Hucknall and is buried in Herne Bay Cemetery. The pilot was told before take off that the weather would be bad as cloud was down to 300 feet.

1623 hrs Training

Tiger Moth II DE157 of 25 (P)EFTS from Hucknall was on a training flight for solo aerobatics and forced and precautionary landing practice. The aircraft was seen to dive into the ground after a slow roll to port and burst into flames at Barrack Farm, Papplewick. The pilot, W/O P/781660 Stanislaw Cieslik PAF age 26 was trapped and unable to get out of the cockpit and burnt to death. He is buried in Hucknall Cemetery.

MONDAY 30th OCTOBER 1944

2355 hrs Training

Stirling III EF212 TV-U of 1660 HCU from Swinderby took off for night conversion training and on landing both undercarriages collapsed when the pilot swung the aircraft to avoid a collision with a Halifax aircraft on the runway. The pupil pilot was F/O 157507 K Johnston.

THURSDAY 2nd NOVEMBER 1944

1150 hrs Training

Oxford I HM608 of 16 (P)SFTS from Newton was practicing forced landings when the aircraft overshot the Orston relief landing ground. The pilot AC2 P/705598 Szymanski PAF tried to go round again but ran into the boundary fence.

SATURDAY 4th NOVEMBER 1944

0925 hrs Training

Stirling III EF266 -M of 1661 HCU from Winthorpe had been in the air for 65 minutes on conversion and three engine landing training when on approach to land the pilot closed throttles at 800 feet and selected full flap. The aircraft was overshooting so the instructor took control, applied full power and the aircraft swung to starboard, but could not land at the side of the runway, so full power was again applied, the aircraft swung violently to starboard again and crashed in a field at Collingham, near Newark. All eight members of the crew were injured, with four taken to Newark General Hospital and four to Station Sick Headquarters.

F/L 55014 James Charles William Weller, DFC (Pilot Instructor), F/O 165207 A A Chapell, (Nav), F/S 1504087 Newby (Bomb Aimer), and P/O 1771290 W L Lund (MUAG), to Newark and F/L 115576 W A W Strachan (Pilot), Sgt 2210971 J H Harrison (F/Eng), F/S 1760919 Powell (Staff Sgt Engineer), and F/S A/430435 R T M Fuller (W.Op/ Air Gnr), to Station Sick Headquarters at Winthorpe.

F/L Weller was awarded the DFC on 11th April 1944 whilst flying with 630 Sqn. The citation read: 'One night in March, 1944, this officer piloted an aircraft detailed to attack Stuttgart. Shortly after the take-off several instruments, including the air speed indicator, became unserviceable. Flight Lieutenant Weller continued his mission, however, and successfully bombed the target. Whilst over the area the oxygen supply failed. Four members of the crew were badly affected but were given assistance by the flight engineer. Later, one of the engines became useless but Flight Lieutenant Weller flew back to an airfield in this country.'

SUNDAY 5th NOVEMBER 1944

1730 hrs Training

Lancaster I LL778 of 5LFS from Syerston was on flying training on 3 engine practice landings when the pupil pilot allowed the speed to drop. The instructor took overshoot procedure too late and had to crash land the aircraft at Syerston. The pilot F/L 417020 J G Claridge RNZAF, pupil pilot P/O 434058 J Daring RAAF and 6 other crew were not injured.

WEDNESDAY 8th NOVEMBER 1944

2150 hrs — Training

Wellington X HE787 TD–P of 82 OTU from Ossington took off for an exercise in dual flying and after a flight of 3 hours 34 minutes was wrecked in a landing accident at base. The aircraft was difficult to control due to the left wing being too low, bounced badly, swung to port, swung again on second touch down and the aircraft caught fire in the navigators and wireless operators position as the undercarriage collapsed. None of the 7 crew were injured.

The pilot was F/O J/85738 L Pappas RCAF and F/O J/36138 Arne Paul Jensen RCAF age 20 the 2nd pilot.

F/O Jensen was killed on 8th April 1945 whilst flying in Halifax NP769 of 408 Sqn for a raid on Hamburg. He is buried Becklingen War Cemetery, Soltau Niedersachsen Germany.

THURSDAY 9th NOVEMBER 1944

0405 hrs — Training

Stirling III LJ532 of 1661 CU from Winthorpe landed on the airfield after failure of the port engines at 3,000 feet due to fuel starvation because the fuel tanks had not been charged correctly. The pilot, F/O 424367 A C Campbell RAAF, did not have time to allow the undercarriage to lock down and the aircraft made a belly landing. There were no injuries.

The crew were F/O Campbell, Sgt 3022003 Hempseed (F/Eng), F/O 163967 Worswick (Bomb Aimer), F/O 162266 Thompson (Nav), F/S A/432178 Higgs (W.Op/Air Gnr), Sgt 3025361 Edwards (MUG), Sgt 1882308 Everett (Rear Gnr), F/S 1179903 Eyles (Staff F/Eng).

Another Stirling aircraft belly lands. Courtesy of Malcolm Vardy

FRIDAY 10th NOVEMBER 1944

2150 hrs — Training

Tiger Moth II T7689 of 25 (P)EFTS from Hucknall took off at 0930 hours on a 'going around again' practice flight with LAC P/706795 Leopold Janczewski PAF, a pupil pilot, at the controls, and while so doing the aircraft failed to climb sufficiently and collided at 400/500 feet with Tiger Moth T7741, also of 25 (P)EFTS, that was in front and piloted by Cpl E Wilkowski PAF which had been correctly signalled to take off on a Flying Training flight. T7689 crashed at Starthwood Farm killing LAC Janczewski instantly. He is buried in Hucknall Cemetery.

Tiger Moth II T7741 of 25 (P)EFTS from Hucknall was taking off and was hit at 400/500 feet by Tiger Moth T7689. The pilot, Cpl P/706083 E Wilkowski PAF, switched off the engine then regained part control and landed on the aerodrome just avoiding the boundary. The pilot was commended for his efforts and admitted to the SSQ suffering from shock. The following is a detailed report of the accident courtesy of W Taylor.

On the 10th November flying was in progress from RAF Hucknall. Cpl Janczewski, a pilot u/t, was carrying out over shoots, approach and landings in Tiger Moth T7689 and at the same time another pilot u/t, Cpl Wilkowski, was carrying out the same exercise in Tiger Moth T7741.Both aircraft were serviceable having been flown by instructors immediately prior to the solo flights by the pupils. Cpl Janczewski was seen to make two satisfactory landings and take-offs and as he was approaching for his third, he was seen to open up his engine and take overshoot action at a height of 2-300 feet, because there were some other aircraft on the landing strip.

Cpl Wilkowski was also seen to make two satisfactory landings and take-offs. He then was given a Green for his third take-off and took off in the normal manner starting to climb after take-off. Cpl Janczewski in T7689 was seen to come up from behind but above him. The two aircraft converged and collided, Cpl Janczewski's aircraft's starboard wings breaking off the rudder, port elevator and tail plane of Cpl Wilkowski's aircraft at a height of 4-500 feet. Cpl Janczewski's aircraft was seen to turn to the right and suddenly go into a steep dive from which it crashed in an inverted position killing the pilot on impact. Why Cpl Janczewski lost control of his aircraft must remain a mystery because the only apparent damage in the air, was slight damage to top and bottom starboard main planes. The ailerons, elevators and rudder were free and had only been damaged on impact with the ground.

Cpl Wilkowski's aircraft was seen to make a steep diving turn to the right. A recovery was made from the dive, and in order to avoid some houses the pilot pulled the control column back, the aircraft stalled onto Hucknall airfield after the pilot had switched off the engine, and the pilot got out un-injured. It was noted that Cpl Wilkowski exhibited a very high degree of skill, on this his second solo flight, in pulling his aircraft out of the dive immediately after the collision and again in avoiding the houses over the edge of the airfield. He also displayed great presence of mind in switching off his engine when he saw a crash was inevitable. It was recommended that he should be highly commended for his remarkable efforts.

Cpl Janczewski made his first solo flight of 15 minutes on the 6th November which was followed by two 30 minutes duration solo flights on the 8th November. He had received dual instruction on overshoots on four separate occasions since his first solo and on eight separate occasions before going solo. Instruction was given on spinning and recovery and had been carried out in a satisfactory manner on four occasions before going solo.

Cpl Wilkowski made his first solo of 15 minutes on the 8th November and was making his second solo on the 10th when the accident occurred. He had also carried out dual overshoots and spinning in a satisfactory manner before going solo.

These two views show the demise of Tiger Moth T7689 at Starthwood Farm. Courtesy of W Taylor

The remains of Tiger Moth T7741 on Hucknall aerodrome. Courtesy of W Taylor

MONDAY 13th NOVEMBER 1944

1000 hrs | Ground

Wellington X HE750 of 91GSU from Gamston caught fire and burnt out when an airman working in one of the hangars accidently slipped from some metal steps and a spark ignited some petrol that had dripped onto the concrete.

THURSDAY 23rd NOVEMBER 1944

A party of aircrew from RAF Swinderby were walking up the Fosseway on the left hand side of the road after dark when a car ran into them from behind. An officer sustained a fractured skull and died instantly and 3 others received injuries.

FRIDAY 24th NOVEMBER 1944

1155 hrs | Training

Halifax V LL132 of 1669 HCU from Langar took off for dual landing instruction and on landing again the aircraft bounced, swung, and due to an imminent collision, the pilot opened up the starboard engines which led to a crash into an aircraft stand. The instructor pilot was F/O 1388849 G C G Davies and the pupil Sgt P/784706 K Szynaski PAF.

SATURDAY 25th NOVEMBER 1944

2240 hrs | Training

Halifax II DT519 of 1669 HCU from Bottesford was on a training cross country flight making 3 engine approaches when the pilot lost control, failed to carry out overshoot procedure, struck some trees and a nissen hut before coming to rest. The pilot, F/S 427426 N V Dunsford RNZAF, and the 7 crew were un-injured.

Barracuda II MX709 of 7 FPP from was being ferried from 15 MU Wroughton to RNAS Dunino when it flew into the ground in bad weather at Annesley North railway junction. The pilot, Third Officer John Platt Murphy age 33, of Air Transport Auxiliary was killed. He was laid to rest in Cheadle and Gatley Cemetery.

THURSDAY 30th NOVEMBER 1944

1135 hrs Training

Wellington X LN167 -S of 82 OTU from Ossington took off on a practice bombing flight when the port engine failed. The exercise was aborted and when nearing base, which the pilot had difficulty in locating because of bad weather, control was lost at 80 feet and the aircraft crashed and burnt out near Crow Park Farm, Sutton on Trent with the loss of all five crew. It was later established that it was a big-end bearing which caused the failure of the port engine.

Mr J E Headland, a farmer, saw the aircraft crash and went to assist in the rescue of the crew. The Rear Gunner was taken from the wreckage but later died from his injuries.

Mr Headland later received a letter of appreciation from the Air Council for his brave attempt to rescue the crew from the burning Wellington.

All five crew died and are buried in Brookwood Military Cemetery: F/O J/41261 John George McCaffery Rowe age 29 RCAF (Pilot), F/O J/43567 Jack Alfred Smallwood age 20 RCAF (Nav), F/O J/45515 Joseph Rodolphe Gaston Farlette age 26 RCAF (Air Bomber), Sgt R/191097 Samuel Lorne Wilfred McCron age 34 RCAF (W.Op/Air Gnr), Sgt R/278665 Gladstone Clifford Morris age 19 RCAF.

SATURDAY 2nd DECEMBER 1944

1830 hrs Taxiing

Stirling III LK462 of 1661 CU from Winthorpe was taxiing in slight rain and swung to avoid a lorry, seen at the last moment, and collided with Stirling LK429. The pilot was F/O 161596 R H Lloyd and pilot under training P/O 185687 D L Boyle.

1830 hrs

Stirling III LK429 from Winthorpe was hit by Stirling LK462 on the aerodrome.

SUNDAY 3rd DECEMBER 1944

0045 hrs Training

Stirling III BK818 of 1661 HCU from Winthorpe landed on the short runway which was in use, with 3 engines, and the pilot suspected further problems, taxied into the overshoot area to clear the aircraft following and the tail wheel collapsed, probably due to the uneven ground. The pilot was F/O 429060 H R Andrews RAAF.

MONDAY 4th DECEMBER 1944

2218 hrs Training

Halifax V LL172 -Q of 1669 HCU from Langar took off for initial night circuit dual training and on landing the aircraft bounced, swung, corrected and then struck Halifax II JN917 which was parked on its pan 80 yards from the runway. The pilots were W/O P/783224 K Artymuik PAF and Sgt P/7046251 P A Wlowiczer PAF.

2218 hrs Stationary

Halifax II JN917 of 1669 HCU from Langar was hit by Halifax LL172 while stationary on its pan.

FRIDAY 8th DECEMBER 1944

2235 hrs Training

Lancaster III LM340 of 1668 CU from Bottesford was flying at 24,000 feet when the rear gunner's oxygen mask inlet valve froze. The Flight Engineer went to assist but lost his gloves and suffered frostbite. The Mid Upper Gunner then went to assist and was also frost bitten. When the aircraft got to 9,500 feet the first signs of oxygen came back. The pilot was F/S R/179395 M K Hart.

TUESDAY 12th DECEMBER 1944

1410 hrs Training

Wellington X LN934 of 17 OTU from Castle Donington had the starboard engine give trouble in flight so the pilot, Sgt 1605231 H B O'Neil, made an emergency belly landing on the airfield in bad visibility.

THURSDAY 14th DECEMBER 1944

2046 hrs Taxiing

Halifax V LB248 of 1669 CU from Langar was taxiing on the perimeter track and due to inadequate lighting, a tail wind and hot brakes the pilot F/O 143889 S A Humphreys failed to turn until too late, swerved and collided with stationary Halifax LV318. The 2nd pilot was F/O 16178 W A Steel RNZAF.

SATURDAY 16th DECEMBER 1944

2140 hrs Training

Halifax II HR691 of 1669 HCU from Bottesford took off from Langar for initial night dual instruction. Shortly after taking off for another circuit the port outer engine began to overspeed and the pilot was unable to bring it under control. With high ground ahead he made a turn to port and crash-landed on the aerodrome. All the crew were slightly injured. They were: F/O 157428 L J Morgan (Pilot), F/S A J Evans, P/O J Smith, F/S G Hopkins, W/O E H Clegg, P/O 186311 Eric Norman Bickley DFM and F/S F B J Burton.

SUNDAY 24th DECEMBER 1944

0545 hrs

A bomb was dropped in a field at Sturton Steeple and created a crater 18 feet diameter by 4 feet deep.

THURSDAY 28th DECEMBER 1944

1620 hrs Training

Wellington X LN585 of BCIS from Finningley landed and the port undercarriage collapsed and after running some distance the aircraft swung off the runway and the port wing and propeller became damaged. The pilot was S/L 85258 William Renshaw Dibb. He was awarded the AFC on 1st September 1944.

1945

THURSDAY 4th JANUARY 1945

1130 hrs Training

Spitfire V W3575 of 53 OTU was on a dive bombing exercise when engine lost power and the aircraft belly landed in a field five miles south of Wickenby, in Lincolnshire.

The pilot, Sgt 1424995 Maurice Hubert Paul Remy RAFVR, was not injured but died on 18th December and is buried in Hotton War Cemetery. He was serving with 349 (Belgium) Sqn.

FRIDAY 5th JANUARY 1945

1945 hrs Training

Wellington X LP841 of 82 OTU from Ossington took off for a night exercise but stalled and crashed just beyond the runway at Laxton and burnt out. It is believed that the flap lever was left slightly below neutral and the flap crept down causing the aircraft to sink.

Of the crew four were killed and are buried in Brookwood Military Cemetery, they are: F/O J/42059 (R205363) John Clair McLeod RCAF age 20 (Pilot), F/O J/43561 Edward Earl Fernandez age 28 (Nav) RCAF, F/O J/45658 (R180916) Lou Jean Robillard age 32 (Air Bomber) RCAF, Sgt R/202976 Edward Archibald Bishop age 21 (W.Op/Air Gnr) RCAF.

The only member of the crew to survive was Sgt R Eden RCAF who was seriously injured during the crash.

2152 hrs Training

Lancaster I SW243 of 1668 HCU from Bottesford after a training flight of 3 hour 5 minutes landed, undershot and struck a hedge on the airfield boundary. Mitigating circumstances were that the airfield runway lighting was unserviceable at the time and visibity was down to 1,700 yards. The pilot was W/O 958350 A C Hulme.

SATURDAY 6th JANUARY 1945

1126 hrs Training

Lancaster III LL636 of 1668 HCU from Bottesford returned from a training flight and on landing a starboard engine caught fire while taxiing but was extinguished before any other part of the aircraft was damaged. The pilot instructor was F/O A/413369 G D George RAAF and the pupil P/O A/422897 J K Watts RAAF.

TUESDAY 9th JANUARY 1945

1045 hrs Training

Master II DM437 of 16 (P)FTS from Newton took off for practice formation but engine cut at 15 feet and the pilot lowered the undercarriage, throttled back and the engine picked up but the aircraft crashed through the boundary fence and came to rest 50 yards further on. The pilot W/O 105627 McDowell was injured.

FRIDAY 12th JANUARY 1945

2150 hrs **Training**

Lancaster III JB125 of 5 LFS from Syerston was on night training exercise and after three hours returned to base and encountered low cloud down to 500/600 feet with rain and a dark night. While circling base and turning steeply three miles to the west, 150 feet below the level of the airfield, the aircraft flew into the ground ¾ mile north of the Elm Tree Hotel, Hoveringham caught fire and burnt out. All 7 crew members were killed. It was thought that the pilot was neglecting to use instruments after breaking cloud and was watching the airfield lights. Also even though the pilot had over 450 flying hours to his name he only had 4 hours night flying and should have been diverted to another airfield.

The Court of Inquiry said: 'At 2121 hrs, Lancaster JB125, flown by P/O Dunlop, was over Syerston, having returned from a cross country flight. On calling up on R/T, the pilot was told to rejoin the circuit. He had already obtained a QFE at 2105 hrs by W/T and had been given the cloud base as being 900 feet. At 2142 hrs P/O Dunlop called a second time and in reply, was given a turn to land, which he did not acknowledge. At 2142 hrs he called again. He was given a turn to land, but replied that he was at 1,000 feet and could not see the ground.

P/O Dunlop was instructed to descend to 700 feet to see if he could see the airfield lighting and it was then that the Airfield Controller saw him break cloud momentarily at about 700 feet. At 2150 hrs the pilot said on R/T that he could not see the "funnel". Two or three seconds later the Airfield Controller saw the aircraft which was in a steep turn to port over the "funnel", at a height which was only slightly above aerodrome level. The aircraft then disappeared below the edge of the aerodrome and crashed. At the western end of the aerodrome the ground falls away steeply to the River Trent, about 150 feet below. The position of the crash was on the opposite side of the river from the aerodrome, almost in line with the runway in use.

The marks on the ground indicate that the first part of the aircraft to strike the ground was the port outer airscrew. This, together with the fact that the starboard wing did not strike a post (12 feet in height) which was only five yards from the point of impact, indicates that the aircraft was banking to port as it struck the ground.'

The opinion as to the cause of the accident was the weather conditions. The cloud base at the time was 500 to 600 feet with slight to moderate rain below it. The night was dark.

The crew were: P/O 425241 Guy Rerenui Dunlop age 28 RNZAF (Pilot), F/S 425790 Peter John Hill age 22 RNZAF (Nav), Sgt 1422223 Albert John Evans age 26 RAFVR BEM (Air Bomber), F/S 4212868 Richard Ludgvan Staples age 23 RNZAF (W.Op/Air Gnr) all buried in Oxford (Botley) Cemetery, Sgt 1897240 Patrick Joseph Vincent Browne age 20 RAFVR (F/Eng) buried Barking (Rippleside) Cemetery, Sgt 1852400 Richard Henry Sedgley age 19 RAFVR (Air Gnr) buried Oddington (St Nicholsa) Churchyard, Sgt 1822619 William Fordyce Cairns age 19 RAFVR buried Glasgow (Cardonald) Cemetery.

Graves of P/O Dunlop, F/S Hill, Sgt Evans and F/S Staples

A memorial was dedicated in May 2010 near the crash site on the bank of the River Trent at Hoveringham.

F/S Hill's brother P/O Howard Perry Hill also died flying with the RAF, on 20th September 1940 with 92 Sqn. He took off in his Spitfire I X4417 with 9 others to patrol over Gravesend and was attacked by enemy fighters and shot down. He had been credited with destroying 3 enemy aircraft and damaging 2 others. He is buried at Hawkinge, near Folkstone.

SUNDAY 14th JANUARY 1945

1015 hrs — Ferrying

Stirling III EH988 of 1661 HCU from Winthorpe took off as part of an exercise ferrying Stirlings to Maghaberry and Longkesh, Northern Ireland, for scrapping which only necessitated 5 crew members. The exercise was for a number of Stirlings to be flown out and their crews brought back by a 'taxi' Stirling or Lancaster. Very early in the flight the aircraft suffered a loss of power, first from one engine and then from two and smoke was seen to be coming from one of the starboard engines. The pilot, S/L Cockbain, struggled to control the aircraft and attempted to reach Hucknall airfield. As the aircraft became increasingly unmanageable he had no option but to attempt a forced landing in fields. Unfortunately however the aircraft continued to lose height rapidly as it made a wide turn. It flew in an easterly direction and crashed into a ridge at Home Farm, Annesley Park, Mansfield. An Ambulance was sent from RAF Hucknall and easily located the burning aircraft where the ambulance crew were able to find and identify 4 members of the crew but Sgt Harris, who was found trapped under the nose of the aircraft, was not identified immediately. All the crew were taken to SSQ at Hucknall before being taken back to their base at Winthorpe.

S/L 67707 Stephen Legh Cockbain DFC RAFVR age 28 (Pilot Instructor), is buried in Oxford (Botley) Cemetery, F/S 1587047 Edwin Charles Barton, age 21 RAFVR (Nav) buried Bristol Arno's Vale Cemetery, F/S 1874899 Terence Arthur Balls age 20 RAFVR (F/Eng) buried Woolwich Cemetery, Sgt 2204311 John Littlemore, age 19 RAFVR (W.Op) buried Southern Cemetery, Manchester, Sgt 1651299 Kenneth Harris,age 22 RAFVR (Air Gnr) buried Whitchurch Cemetery, Glamorgan.

An inscribed stone memorial was placed near the site at the Ashfield Stirling roundabout, on 16th September 1998 (see entry for memorials).

S/L Cockbain was awarded the DFC on 9th June 1944 when a member of 44 Sqn. The citation read: 'In March, 1944, this officer was the pilot of an aircraft detailed for a mine laying mission. On the outward flight the aircraft was attacked by a fighter and sustained much damage. One engine was rendered useless, the cupola of the mid-upper turret was shattered and the hydraulic gear was damaged. Despite this, Squadron Leader Cockbain succeeded in evading a second attack and went on to the target to complete his task. This officer has completed a large number of sorties and has displayed great skill, leadership and devotion to duty.' Crash location: OS sheet 120 509527.

2305 hrs — Op; Sweepstake

Wellington III X3465 BB-H of 27 OTU from Church Broughton took off on a sweepstake exercise over the North Sea comprising one hundred and twenty six aircraft. During the exercise X3465 was attacked by a German night fighter and on its return most of England was fog bound and an emergency landing at Wymeswold was attempted due to an imagined petrol shortage. The aircraft stalled 3 times and crashed near RAF Wymeswold in a field between Swift's Close, Hoton Road and the end of Lower Brook Street. Several people rushed to the scene to see if help was needed, they included Mr L Daft, Mr C Mills and F/L Griffiths. They jumped a gate into the field where the aircraft had crashed and found it had burst into flames. Two members of the crew were on fire and running away from the wreckage to try and extinguish the flames. Another was caught up in the tail-plane which was suspended in one of the willow trees in the field boundary hedge. He was released and taken to the ambulance which had arrived. The crew were all members of the RAAF.

F/O 8309 Eric Ralph Peace age 25 was killed and is buried in Oxford (Botley) Cemetery. The other crew members who all survived were: F/O 434971 K E Cranley (Pilot) and F/O 429950 J H Hann (Bomb Aimer) who were rescued unconscious from the burning wreckage by F/S 434412 J F Reuter (W.Op/Air Gnr), F/O 432596 D G Thomson (Nav) and P/O 36889 E F Minns (Air Gnr). Crash location: OS sheet 129 601231.

The following personal account of the incident has been provided by Leslie Daft via Chris Wass: 'Around midnight on the day in question I was aroused out of my sleep upon hearing a terrific bang in the close proximity and I hurriedly dressed with shoes taken from a different pair, and sped along the gitty by the side of the churchyard from Church Street to Stockwell in mythological language "like one on a winged horse or as one wearing seven league boots" then along Lower Brook Street to the field on the left with an entrance opposite Clay Street. Arriving at the same time was F/L Griffiths (RAF-Admin) and both jumped the gate simultaneously immediately seeing the crashed plane enveloped in flames. Running left alongside the hedge I could see the front of the plane as one inferno with flesh as though melting away from a protruding limb (arm or leg) of a member of the crew. Moving swiftly across the starboard side of the wreck the ammunition exploding and the odd large burst of flame as though from a ruptured fuel tank I heard screams coming from the opposite side of the wreck and noticed two crew members in flames fleeing the wreckage in what appeared to be a dash for the open ground and maybe roll in the grass and so extinguish the flames or maybe use water from the nearby brook for the same purpose. I am not sure. It was then I noticed the tail of the plane suspended in a willow tree on the boundary hedge with a member of the crew trapped inside.

With patience and assistance to hand persistant strenuous efforts to release the crew member paid off and he was gradually eased out of the plane and carried to an ambulance which had now arrived on the scene. By coincidence I was able to put into practice a first aid carrying position using crossed wrists recently rehearsed on a first aid refresher course. At the same time I observed a fire tender had arrived and was spraying foam around the wreck to contain the fire. Some days later the RAF returned, via Cpl Phillips (Admin), my Swan fountain pen which had apparently fallen from my jacket when placing the airman in the ambulance. Cpl Phillips knew of my loss through having accommodation with my family'.

At the time of the above account Leslie Daft was stationed in the RAF at Leicester and cycled home when time permitted. This was one such occasion.

F/S Reuter, F/O Minns, F/O Hann, F/O Cranley, F/O Thompson and F/O Peace

—

Two other aircraft crashed in Nottinghamshire having taken part in this Sweepstake exercise, Wellington LP828 and Wellington LP830 (see entry for 15th January).

2325 hrs Training

Stirling III EF204 of 1654 HCU from Wigsley took off for a Bullseye exercise and after 5 hours when in low flight and descending in conditions of low cloud and poor visibility the aircraft flew into the ground at Barnby-in-the-Willows near Newark-on-Trent. It was thought that the pilot had failed to check his altimeter during the flight. The crew were:

P/O 189857 Robert William Holditch age 22 RAFVR (Pilot) was injured but subsequently died from his injuries on 17th January and is buried in Thorney (St Helen) Churchyard, Sgt 2210578 Norman Thompson RAFVR (F/Eng) buried Eccles (Peel Green) Cemetery, Sgt 1804542 Charles Henry Gilbert age 34 RAFVR (Nav) buried Southgate Cemetery, F/O 178378 Graham Douglas Wright age 19 RAFVR (Air Bomber) buried Carshalton (All Saints) Churchyard, Sgt 1586576 James William Humphrey age 23 RAFVR (Air Bomber) buried Thorney (St Helen) Churchyard, Sgt 1608602 Gerald Richard Best age 21 RAFVR (Air Gnr) buried Peterchurch (St Peter) Churchyard, Sgt O M Aldrich (Rear Gnr) was only slightly injured.

SUNDAY 15th JANUARY 1945

0046 hrs Op; Sweepstake

Wellington X LP828 of 30 OTU from Hixon took off on a sweepstake exercise and returned after seven hours in the air and due to poor visibility was diverted from its own airfield. The pilot, F/O 150788 P N Hickman, made several unsuccessful attempts to land at an airfield, but due to low cloud cover and eventually being short of fuel climbed to a safe height and all the crew baled out. RT distortions had made understanding difficult. The aircraft crashed at Wilford, Nottingham.

0030 hrs Op; Sweepstake Training

Wellington X LP830 -M OF 30 OTU from Hixon took off on a sweepstake exercise and returned after seven hours in the air and due to poor visibility, was diverted from its own airfield. The pilot F/S 1685569 D Hudson, made several unsuccessful attempts to land at an airfield and eventually being short of fuel climbed to a safe height and all the crew baled out. The aircraft apparently crashed in the Arnold area. The above account is an extract from the aircraft accident log which gives the pilot as F/O Hickman.

The Operation Record Book of RAF Station Hucknall states that they received a report that a aircraft had crashed at Woodthorpe Park, Nottingham. An ambulance was sent to the scene and searched the wreck of the aircraft for the crew and despite an extensive search of the area failed to find anyone. They were then informed by the NFS that 3 crew members had successfully parachuted from the aircraft and been taken to their HQ at Mapperley and then handed over to the civilian police at Nottingham. On arrival at the police station it was found that all 6 crew members were there, the 3 others having been taken by a F/L Ruse. All 6 crew members were then taken to RAF Hucknall and given a medical check up before being staying the night.

The crew were F/O Watts, Sgt Rettles, Sgt Miles, another Sgt Miles, Sgt Ashton and Sgt Revis. Note that there is no mention of F/O Hickman.

The following is a report produced by Brian Walker, courtesy of the Nottingham Evening Post: 'Residents in Arnold were startled to hear a mid-air collision between two aircraft shortly after midnight on the 14 th January 1945. A number of aircraft had overflown the district during the hours of darkness, so two or more occasioned little or no interest until the sound of a violent impact followed by screaming engines, heralded a major catastrophe. The noise was brought to a sudden halt by an explosion and flash of light as one of the aircraft struck the ground a short distance from one of the most northerly housing estates in Arnold. The other aircraft continued on a southerly course, its engines sounding hesitant and laboured, until it faded from airshot.

The two aircraft were from No.30 OTU RAF Hixon in Staffordshire and were operating on a scarecrow exercise. Both were Vickers Wellington Mk. X Bombers, serial numbers LP828 and LP830. The Wellington which had crashed at Arnold fell into an area of allotment gardens known locally as the "Hobbocks", an area sited on the northern edge of the Killisick estate. All members of the crew baled out successfully, one landing in Woodthorpe Drive and another in a tree a few hundred yards from the crash site. The aircraft struck the ground with terrific force, burying the engines deep in the earth. The remains were scattered over a wide area. A witness stated that the surface metal was carted away by a party from No.58 MU on the morning of the 16th of January on a low loader. He was of the opinion that the engines were left where they lay, the holes filled in with surface debris and earth. A surface search was carried out in 1985 yielding a large piece of of the Bristol Hercules cylinder and several pieces of of geodetic structure and a piece of fabric still bearing black dope was found to be in use as a notice board nailed to the allotment gate.

The second aircraft made a despairing effort to continue on its course, but it was finally abandoned over the southern suburbs of Nottingham, crashing in the vicinity of Ruddington-Clifton Lane after the crew had abandoned it successfully. Two crew members landed in West Bridgeford and one on the roof of No.3 Winster Close, Lenton Abbey Estate. The latter was assisted in his descent from his precarious position by the householder, who found a ladder somewhere locally and skilfully organised the airmans escape. Four airmen were treated in the Nottingham General Hospital.'

The pilot of Wellington LP828 was F/O 150788 P N Hickman and LP830, F/S 1685569 D Hudson. The crash report card which is held by the Royal Air Force Museum at Hendon states that neither aircraft could find the airfield they were looking for. As No.30 OTU was due to move into Gamston on February the 2nd it was thought the aircraft were being routed from Hixon to Gamston on familiarisation flights at the time. The relevant entry in the RAF's No.30 OTU's Operational Record book gives the list of aircraft which either came to grief or made emergency landings at other airfields that night. In the case of LP828 and LP830 the reason for abandonment is given as shortage of fuel. However, local residents who heard the crash of the Arnold aircraft were in no doubt of the cause. The noise of the collision was heard by many observers, and after the collision another aircraft was heard flying off in a southerly direction.

2030 hrs — Training

Lancaster III LM619 of 1668 HCU from Bottesford was engaged in a night bombing exercise when the aircraft overshot the airfield and crashed in a dive into a haze patch and burnt out at Westborough, about ½ mile from Long Bennington. 6 crew members were killed and only Sgt G F Ashby (Reat Gnr) survived but was injured. The pilot, F/O 429081 Ivan Lindsay Vinall Thompson RAAF age 23 was only on his 4th solo landing and is buried in Oxford (Botley) Cemetery, F/S 2218660 James Rawlinson age 19 RAFVR (F/Eng) buried Bootle Cemetery, Sgt 1623968 John Gordon Hazelden age 21 RAFVR (Nav) buried Rainford (All Saints) Churchyard, Sgt 1586368 Cyril Reuben Clifford Mann age 23 RAFVR (Air Bomber) buried Cheltenham Cemetery, F/S 429069 Allen Benjamin Thomas age 22 RAAF buried Oxford (Botley) Cemetery and Sgt 1251125 Dennis Gilbert Burn RAFVR (Air Gnr) buried Tottenham Cemetery. F/S Thomas was a telephonist in civilian life. Crash location: Cassini grid 1940 sheet 55 312641

FRIDAY 19th JANUARY 1945

1130 hrs — Training

Oxford I HN587 of 21 (P)AFU had been in the air on a training flight for 2 hours when the pilot attempted to ascertain his location in poor visibility, flew low and executed a steep turn, stalled and crashed in a snowstorm at Beeston Rylands. Both crew men were killed. The pilot instructor F/L 88254 Bernard Moores RAFVR age 33 was cremated at Sheffield Crematorium. The pupil pilot was F/O 160650 George Robert Oliver Langton, RAFVR age 29 is buried in Wakefield Cemetery.

MONDAY 22nd JANUARY 1945

1146 hrs Training

Oxford I EB951 of 16 (P)SFTS from Newton was on a training flight practicing circuits and landings when the pilot under training, 2nd Lt Stalony-Dobrzanski PAF, came in to land too high. He touched down, was too late to go round again and the aircraft overshot landing, crashed into boundary hedge and the undercarriage collapsed. He was not injured.

SUNDAY 28th JANUARY 1945

1730 hrs Training

Stirling III LK400 of 1660 HCU from Swinderby was on a conversion training in low flight at 1,400 feet when both inner engines cut and the aircraft lost height and belly landed in a field at Morton Hall near Swinderby. The pilot, F/S A/422862 F G M Khan RAAF, received a bruised forehead and F/S Shimmons (W.Op) a cut knee. Both inner engines cut out due to manipulation of the fuel cocks by the flight engineer.

MONDAY 29th JANUARY 1945

0216 hrs Training

Lancaster III LM308 RC-F of 5LFS from Syerston took off at 0001 hrs on a night navigation cross country exercise when it crashed at high speed near the Elm Tree Hotel, Hoveringham, and exploded on impact. The 7 crew were killed:

W/O II R/168095 Richard Barlow Rathbone age 28 RCAF (Pupil Pilot), with nearly 300 hrs flying time, F/S R/203166 Hugh Munro MacKenzie age 21 RCAF (Nav), F/S R/189328 John Alexander Emerson age 30 RCAF (Air Bomber), F/S R/190328 John Henry Reid age 20 RCAF (W.Op/Air Gnr), Sgt R/264756 Joseph Francis Fitzgibbon RCAF age 20 all buried in Harrogate (Stonefall) Cemetery, Sgt 2218573 Albert Mercer age 23 RAFVR (F/ Eng) buried Southport (Duke Street) Cemetery, Sgt 1595881 Jasper Martin age 20 RAFVR (Rear Gnr) buried Castleford (Whitwood) Cemetery.

Sgt Fitzgibbon and his neighbour and school friend Bill Halley joined up on the same day and in the course of training and operations were always together. On the day of the crash Bill Halley had asked to be grounded by the MD due to a bad head cold and he was replaced in the crew. However he went down to the plane to see his friend take off at 2030 hrs on the Sunday evening but was asleep when the crash occurred.

A Court of Inquiry was held at RAF Syerston on 31st January into the accident. Many witnesses were called, all RAF personnel. The location of the crash was given at the enquiry as '1½ miles north east direction from Hoveringham village Notts. 2½ miles in a south west direction from Syerston Aerodrome on the west side of R. Trent. Height of ground ASL 75 feet'.

The findings of the Court of Inquiry are reproduced overleaf.

The graves of F/S Reid, W/O Rathbone, F/S MacKenzie, F/S Emerson and Sgt Fitzgibbon

10. **CONCLUSIONS.** Under this Heading the following should always be included :

(a) Brief description of the accident and its attendant circumstances.
(b) Diagnosis of cause or causes including all contributory factors.
(c) Recommendations, if called for by the convening authority.

(a) F/Sgt Rathbone and crew took off in Lancaster LM.308 at 0001 on 29th January, 1945. for the purpose of completing Cross Country exercise and practice bombing exercise F/Sgt Rathbone (Pupil Pilot) completed his cross country and returned to base (R.A.F. Syerston) and called up on R/T for permission to carry out practise bombing. This was refused as the bombing range was covered by cloud and he was told to rejoin the curcuit. This was at 0214.hrs. About this time witnesses have stated they saw an aircraft diving at great speed and in flames at 02.15. hrs. the aircraft was seen to crash and an explosion followed which was witnessed by various witnesses, whose statements are recorded. The weather at the time was good vis --- Cloud base 3000' no icing in cloud. Surface wind N. by W. 3 m.p.h. Copies of weather report, photographs of crash, aerodrome lighting and sketch of locality of accident are included.

(b) On assessing the evidence given and examination of the wreckage (see Technical Officers report) it is presumed the aircraft got out of control, and the Pilot F/Sgt Rathbone was unable to regain control before hitting the ground. Owing to the fact F/Sgt Rathbone called up on R/T at 02.14 hrs and made no statement to the effect his aircraft LM.308 was unseriveable and at 02.16 hrs the aircraft crashed, and also the fact the wreckage is so widely dispersed after the explosion it is impossible to ascertain the cause of the crash.
(c) No recommendations.

FRIDAY 2nd FEBRUARY 1945

1100 hrs Training

Harvard IIB KF148 of 16 (P)SFTS from Tollerton was on a low flying exercise when it collided with a flock of birds owing to poor visibility but landed safely at Tollerton. The pilot was P/O P/2103 Wujastyk PAF.

SUNDAY 4th FEBRUARY 1945

2030 hrs Training

Lancaster III LM629 of 5LFS from Syerston had been in the air for three hours fifteen minutes on a training flight when coming in to land it overshot on 3 engines due to a too fast approach and the undercarriage was raised to stop. The pilot was P/O A408499 H Hudson RAAF.

MONDAY 5th FEBRUARY 1945

1850 hrs Training

Wellington X LP846 of 30 OTU was on cine gun training and stationary at Gamston. An aircrew change was taking place when Sgt 412086 V W K Bollero (Rear Gnr) was about to enter the aircraft but then moved forward under the wing into the port propeller. He broke both his arms and the propeller was damaged and needed replacing. Sgt Bollero was found guilty of carelessness. The instructor pilot was F/L 51535 John Millar Wyllie DFM and the pupil pilot F/O J/29402 A R Taylor RCAF.

WEDNESDAY 7th FEBRUARY 1945

2208 hrs Training

Lancaster III JA684 of 1668 HCU from Bottesford on circuit and landing training crashed just beyond the runway into straw stacks when the pupil pilot raised all the flaps when making a 3 engine overshoot, lost height, and the aircraft struck the ground and was burnt out. The crew

F/O J/38380 F G Wilkinson RCAF (Pupil Pilot), F/O 176914 J L Walker RAFVR (Instructor), and Sgt C M L Thomson were injured and Sgt Mullen, F/S McLean, Sgt Roper and Sgt Munro were un-injured.

FRIDAY 9th FEBRUARY 1945

1205 hrs Taxiing

Tiger Moth II DE315 of 25 (P)EFTS from Hucknall piloted by AC2 P/706848 M Dudzinski PAF was taxiing slowly when it was caught by a gust of wind and turned over.

1830 hrs Air Test

Lancaster I PD731 of 227 Sqn from Balderton was taking off for an air test but did not get airborne due to the failure to remove the pitot cover and the aircraft crashed through the airfield boundary. The air speed indicator did not function due to the failure to remove the cover and so flying speed was not attained.

The pilot, F/O 421372 Maurice Leonard Hunt RNZAF, was not injured but was killed five weeks later on 18th March flying with 227 Sqn. He was the pilot of Lancaster RA546 which took off from Balderton on 14th March for a raid on Lutzkendorf and crashed near Durbach injuring himself and one other, 2 crew members were killed and 4 taken prisoner. F/L Hunt died 3 days later and is buried in Durbach War Cemetery.

SATURDAY 10th FEBRUARY 1945

2050 hrs Training

Lancaster I HK739 of 1669 CU from Langar made a normal landing and the tail wheel collapsed. The pilot was F/S 427437 N A Donsford RNZAF.

WEDNESDAY 14th FEBRUARY 1945

1855 hrs Training

Wellington III BK439 -K of 30 OTU from Gamston landed with starboard engine out of action and touched down short of the runway and the tail wheel was damaged in a shallow ditch. The pilot was Sgt 1567282 T C Kirkwood.

SUNDAY 18th FEBRUARY 1945

1445 hrs Unauthorised Training

Harvard IIB FT395 of 16 (P)SFTS from Newton was carrying out unauthorised battle practice with Oxford I EB797 from 16 (P)SFTS, collided with it and crashed out of control, one mile south of Newton airfield. The pilot, F/L P0257 Zbigniew Staerz PAF age 33, was killed and is buried in Newark-upon-Trent Cemetery.

1445 hrs

Oxford I EB797 of 16 (P)SFTS from Newton as above. The pilot, P/1442 Kapitan Radomir Walczak PAF age 30 was also killed and buried Newark-upon-Trent Cemetery.

2040 hrs Training

Lancaster I PA228 of BCIS from Finningley made a normal landing and the tail wheel collapsed. The pilot was F/L 136701 Hing and the 2nd pilots S/L 409638 Woolley and S/L 144277 Wade.

MONDAY 19th FEBRUARY 1945

2358 hrs | Taxiing

Lancaster I SW247 of 227 Sqn from Balderton starboard wing collided with the tail of Lancaster PB644 whilst taxiing back up the runway after an abortive take off for a night bombing operation. The pilot was F/L 429919 R E R Robertshawe RNZAF.

2358 hrs | Taxiing

Lancaster I PB644 of 227 Sqn from Balderton was preparing to take off on a bombing operation when its tail was struck by the starboard wing of Lancaster SW247. The pilot was F/O 179695 R T Ward. This aircraft was lost on 6th March on a raid over Germany.

TUESDAY 20th FEBRUARY 1945

2120 hrs | Training

Lancaster I HK729 of 1669 HCU from Langar had been on fighter affiliation and bombing training when coming in to land in funnels at 750 feet there was an explosion in the bomb bay. All the engines cut, and the aircraft crashed in a field ½ mile south east of Barnstone railway station and burnt out. The Langar ambulance was called out to the crash near the cement works at Barnstone. On arrival at the scene of the crash the machine was found to be blazing furiously and valiant efforts were being made by neighbouring farmers to extricate one of the crew, Sgt Luck, who was trapped underneath the wreckage. Eventually he was got out alive but died shortly afterwards. The cause of the crash was a flash bomb sliding along the bomb bay and exploding on striking the front bulkhead and the fuselage catching fire.

Sgt 1814168 Robert Frank Luck age 19 RAFVR (W.Op/Air Gnr) is the only crew member who died and is buried in Northampton (Kingsthorpe) Cemetery. The other six crewmen were all injured: F/S A/428956 A N H Davis (Pilot), Sgt F L Dean, F/S W Jakubowski RCAF, Sgt A T Dunn, Sgt A Hawkes, Sgt D Llewelyn.

WEDNESDAY 21st FEBRUARY 1945

0412 hrs | Training

Lancaster III ND862 of 1661 HCU from Swinderby touched down on the right hand edge of the runway, and in an endeavour to get back to the centre of the runway, the untrained pilot over corrected twice. The instructor pilot was too late in taking over and the port leg collapsed. There were no injuries. The instructor pilot was F/O 158695 D Paul and the untrained pilot was F/O A/423409 J A Simmonds RAAF.

THURSDAY 22nd FEBRUARY 1945

1342 hrs | Familiarisation

Wellington X MF555 of BCIS from Finningley took off and a loud noise came from the port engine followed by excessive vibration. The 1st pilot, F/L 133480 J H Clark, used emergency feathering but failed and the aircraft landed without further damage. The aircraft would not maintain height on the good engine after failure of the port engine. The enquiry considered that 'the pilot put up a very good show'. The pupil pilot was F/O J/20188 K A Petch RCAF.

SUNDAY 25th FEBRUARY 1945

1515 hrs | Training

Lancaster I ME490 of 1660 HCU from Swinderby was practicing 3 engine landing and overshoot procedure. At 300 feet the aircraft was seen to turn to port, a wing dropped and the aircraft crashed out of control into the ground at Camp Road, Swinderby and burnt out. Six crew members were killed and one was injured. It was likely that the pilot let the air speed drop causing the crash.

F/O 415639 James Ernest Gibberd DFC RAAF age 27 (Pilot) is buried in Cambridge City Cemetery, S/L 131547 John Bertram Sayers AFC, MID RAFVR age 25 (Pupil Pilot) buried Sedgefield New Cemetery, Durham, F/S 572871 Harold Hayes age 23 RAF (F/Eng) buried Dinnington Church Cemetery, F/S 1602131 Derrick William Dunthorne (Nav) RAFVR buried in Romford Cemetery, W/O 1324221 Harold Bowen Jones age 29 RAFVR (Air Bomber) buried Llandingat (St Dingat) Churchyard, W/O 1025303 Harold Whitney Bennett age 23 RAFVR (W.Op/Air Bomber/ buried Bradford (Scholemoor) Cemetery.

F/S T V W Rigby (Rear Gnr) received a compound fracture of the right tibia and facial burns. F/O Gibberd was awarded the DFC on 22nd September 1944. The citation read: 'Courage and devotion to duty in numerous sorties'. The insignia was presented to his wife on 21st February 1946. S/L Sayers was awarded the AFC on 1st January 1943.

1900 hrs Training

Lancaster I NG382 of 1669 HCU from Langar swung on take-off and the pilot overcorrected and the aircraft swung violently to starboard, ran off the runway and came to rest between hangers 3 and 4 and caught fire. The aircraft was completely wrecked and considerable damage was done to the MT vehicles. The pilot and engineer had opened the throttles too quickly but the throttle friction nut was tightened far too soon so that the pilot was not able to throttle back. One member of the seven man crew was injured. The pilot was F/S 428149 D F E White RAAF.

1120 hrs Training

Mitchell II FL183 of 2GSU from Fersfield took off at 1002 hrs for a map reading cross country training flight briefed to keep below cloud at a safe height of 1,500 feet. After around one hour fifteen minutes, 2 miles south of Manton Colliery, the aircraft struck the tops of 80 feet high pine trees standing on the northern edge of a wood where ground rose to just over 200 feet. The aircraft shot up steeply to about 400 feet shedding pieces of airframe, stalled, dived and crashed in woods 300 yards south west of the first point of impact with the trees in Clumber Park. 3 of the crew members were killed: W/C 29236 Cyril Nelson Carpenter RAF (Pilot) is buried in Oborne Churchyard, F/L 130785 Frederick William Silvester age 32 RAFVR (Nav) buried in Tupsley Churchyard and W/O 1282820 Frank Albert Russell age 23 RAF (Air Gnr) buried in West Wickham Churchyard.

The crash was due to structural failure whilst the pilot was pulling out of a dive. The investigation concluded that the accident was due to error of judgement by the pilot who, in conditions of low cloud and poor visibility, flew into trees on rising ground. Crash location: Cassini grid 1940 075955; OS sheet 120 602757.

MONDAY 26th FEBRUARY 1945

0840 hrs Training

Lancaster II LL666 of 1668 HCU from Bottesford struck a flock of birds during take off damaging the forward cupola and starboard outer propeller. The pilot, F/O 153680 Petfield, landed the aircraft safely.

1420 hrs Taxiing

Lancaster II DS838 of 1668 HCU from Bottesford was taxiing to take-off position for the pilot's first solo on this type of aircraft and overshot the perimeter track. The aircraft became bogged down causing damage to the propeller. The pilot, F/O J/43777 K J MacKenzie RCAF, had used too much brake causing them to overheat and become inefficient.

FRIDAY 2nd MARCH 1945

0100 hrs Training

Lancaster I NG222 of 1654 HCU from Wigsley was on a training flight when it had a successful landing after failure of the port outer engine due to over speeding propeller and failure of the feathering mechanism. The pilot was P/O 187782 G W Everitt.

SATURDAY 3rd MARCH 1945

0030 hrs Training

Lancaster I NN809 of 1660 HCU from Swinderby took off for night conversion training and immediately after landing, fifteen minutes later the starboard tyre burst, a violent swing developed and the aircraft left the runway and the undercarriage collapsed. There were no injuries to the 7 crew. The pilot was F/S 4310175 S Goodall RNZAF.

SUNDAY 4th MARCH 1945

In the early hours of 4th March 1945, in Unternehmen (Operation) Gisela, some 200 Junkers Ju88 night fighters of the Luftwaffe Nachtjagdeschwader Gruppen (Night Fighter destroyer Group) had been deployed to intercept the allied bombers returning to base at their most vulnerable point, just before landing. The marauding aircraft crossed the North Sea at points stretching between the Thames Estuary and up the east coast to the North Yorkshire Moors.

The fact that these intruders were able to cross the North Sea coast without being picked up by English radar operators would seem to have been a result of a degree of complacency that had set in amongst Bomber Command, as the Luftwaffe appeared to be subdued.

The Bomber Command mission scheduled for that evening was a duel attack on the synthetic oil producing plant at Keman and a raid on the Dortmund Elms canal. 234 aircraft from the northern 4 and 6 Groups took on the first mission, with 222 bombers from 5 Group, Lincolnshire, tackling the canal, departing bases at around 2200 hrs on 3rd March.

The mission ran smoothly, until the return, when they ran into trouble in the form of Operation Gisela. On this clear night, some of the early returning aircraft had inexplicably switched on their navigation lights much earlier than usual, despite warnings of the dangers of possible predators, which was copied by those following. This gave the circling intruders a clear, enticing target.

In just a couple of hours Bomber Command had lost 19 aircraft to operation Gisela in addition to the 9 reported missing on the raids themselves. The Luftwaffe lost 25 fighters out of the 200 involved in the operation.

Observer J P Kelway, a member of the ROC, was motoring to duty early in the morning along the Welton to Hackthorn road, 2 miles from Scampton airfield. Feldwebel Heirich Conze and crew, who had minutes earlier shot down a 460 Squadron Lancaster and then strafed the crashed bomber, were looking for ground targets. Despite Observer Kelway's car headlight being hooded his car was seen by Conze and his Ju88 flew down to ground level aiming at the car when it struck telegraph wires, hit the ground before hitting the car instantly killing Observer Kelway and the 4 crew. Observer Kelway is buried in Newport Cemetery, Lincoln and the German crew in Scampton Churchyard. (Courtesy of Ian Richardson and theYorkshire Air Museum and Allied Forces Memorial)

0057 hrs Training

Lancaster III PB118 JF-Q of 1654 HCU from Wigsley was on a night exercise, bombing practice over the Brassingham ranges almost halfway between Lincoln and Newark, a few miles to the east of the A46 Fosse Way. The crew had seen one aircraft shot down in flames so were on the alert for enemy aircraft when the rear gunner saw a Ju88 over Brassingham and the pilot immediately headed in a westerly direction as instructed. A little time later, and over Worksop, PB118 was hit on the starboard engine inner and then strafed again making the Lancaster out of control. The pilot, F/S R H Pinkstone, gave the order to bale out in the vicinity of Warsop Windmill approximately one mile from where the blazing bomber crashed near Sookholme Lane, Warsop. 3 ambulances attended the scene and took 5 members of the crew who were suffering from burns and shock to Mansfield Hospital: F/S R H Pinkstone (Pilot), F/S H Evans (F/Eng), Sgt J Pringle (Bomb Aimer), Sgt J S Morgan (Rear Gunner), Sgt C G Rouse (Nav). Sgt 1820283 Roderick Campbell age 19 RAFVR (MUG) was killed and is buried in Gamerig Cemetery.

0105 hrs Op: Diversion

Lancaster III LM748 UG-H of 1654 HCU from Wigsley took off as part of a diversionary force supporting the main operations and on return was shot down at about 2,000 feet by an enemy aircraft with the loss of all crew at Stapleford near Newark, a victim of Operation Gisela.

P/O 429710 Alfred Edward Lutz RAAF age 32 buried Oxford (Botley) Cemetery, F/S 1583336 Henry Francis Cox (Pilot) RAFVR age 22 buried Birmingham Cemetery (Brandwood End), F/O 164041 John Austin Charles Chapman RAFVR age 31 commemorated on the Runnymede Memorial, Sgt 958767 Stanley Shaw RAFVR age 30 also commemorated on the Runnymede Memorial, Sgt 1853234 Arthur Frank Warbey age 20 RAFVR (W.Op/Air Gnr) buried Shilton (Holy Rood) Churchyard, Sgt 1647508 Harry Frost age 20 RAFVR buried Norton (St Andrew) Churchyard Suffolk, Sgt 1816775 Alan Churchill Davy RAFVR age 20 is commemorated on the Runnymede Memorial.

MONDAY 5th MARCH 1945

1450 hrs Training

Tiger Moth II N6774 of 25 (P)EFTS was on a training flight when the pilot became lost, attempted a precautionary landing in a small field, ran into a hedge and overturned at Pilsley Colliery. The pilot AC2 P/706665 J Marzec PAF was not injured.
Crash location: OS sheet 120 425632.

2341 hrs Training

Lancaster I PD437 of 1662 HCU from Blyton was returning to base after a five hour night navigational cross-country flight when it crashed into a field, on the west side of Rampton Hospital near Woodbeck Village, after striking a 25 foot high tree with the starboard wing. A witness said that the aircraft was on fire in the air. All 7 crew members were killed. The cause was not known.

F/S 427597 Alexander Wilson RAAF age 21 (Pilot) is buried in Cambridge City Cemetery, Sgt 1523986 Arthur Bligh RAFVR age 21 (Nav) also Cambridge City Cemetery, Sgt 1602672 Richard Henry Page RAFVR age 21 (Air Bomber) buried Eastleigh Cemetery, Sgt 1866600 Frederick William Ward RAFVR age 20 (W.Op) buried Lawford Churchyard, Sgt 1883315 Herbert Albert Warman RAFVR age 20 (MUG) also Cambridge City Cemetery, F/S R/264550 John Hedley Skinner RCAF age 21 (Rear Gnr) buried Harrogate (Stonefall) Cemetery, Sgt 1898052 Peter Edward William Moore RAFVR age 23 (F/Eng) buried Worthing Churchyard.

TUESDAY 6th MARCH 1945

1015 hrs Taxiing

Lancaster III JB181 of 5 LFS from Syerston was taxiing around the flying control building to take off for a training flight when the starboard wing tip hit a hanger door. The instructor pilot was F/O A/414986 E Berry RAAF DFC and the pupil pilot F/O 135724 Sievwright.

WEDNESDAY 7th MARCH 1945

0340 hrs — Taxiing

Lancaster I PB898 of 1654 HCU from Wigsley was taxiing when it ran off the perimeter track and was damaged. The pilot P/O J/41471 N B Babey RCAF was negotiating a sharp turn.

0346 hrs — Op; Sassnitz

Lancaster III PB610 9J-O of 227 Sqn from Balderton on return from Operations after a nine hour thirty minute flight the starboard tyre burst as the aircraft touched down which caused the bomber to swerve, leave the runway and the undercarriage collapsed. A fire broke out but the crew managed to get out of the aircraft without serious injury. The aircraft was burnt out with the result that action was taken to overcome the failings of the fire fighting equipment.

The crew were: F/L 143283 Matthew William Bell (Pilot), F/O 160198 Leonard Sidney Smith, F/O E Foster, F/O 153497 Gerald Francis Orry, F/O 161024 Henry Albert Thomas, Sgt 1805639 Raymond Cecil Stanley Wells and Sgt R O H Stephen.

F/L Bell, F/O Smith, F/O Orry, F/O Thomas and Sgt Wells were all killed one week later on 15th March when their aircraft, Lancaster PA214, was lost on a raid on Lutzkendorf. They are all buried in Durnbach War Cemetery.

THURSDAY 8th MARCH 1945

0955 hrs — Training

Tiger Moth II T6270 of 25 (P)EFTS from Hucknall undershot and hit a blister hanger on approach to land. The aircraft approached from the north side of the aerodrome, stalled and suddenly dropped with its wheels going through the corrugated roof of a hanger and stuck there. The untrained pupil pilot, AC2 P/706580 J Blasgyk PAF had been watching another aircraft landing ahead and had to descend the hangar by ladder.

SATURDAY 10th MARCH 1945

1100 hrs — Stationary

Lancaster I LL856 of 6 LFS from Ossington had just stopped on the perimeter track from being taxied by the pilot, F/L 51168 G E Dixon when a MT vehicle backed into the fuselage near the door.

SUNDAY 11th MARCH 1945

1510 hrs — Training

Tiger Moth II T6202 of 25 (P)EFTS from Hucknall returned from circuits and landings training piloted by pupil pilot AC2 P/706711 W Warhaftig PAF and hit the ground on landing and overturned. He was not injured.

FRIDAY 16th MARCH 1945

1330 hrs — Ground

Tiger Moth II L6932 of 25 (P)EFTS from Hucknall was being started up when the propeller struck the arm of an airman. This was considered negligence on the part of the pilot who did not understand the instructions given to him by the mechanic who was starting the engine, as he was adjusting his harness at the same time. He put the switches on 'contact' while the propeller was being turned in the 'sucking in' process. Some blame was attached to the mechanic who should have seen that the pilot was completely ready in the cockpit before he commenced the starting up procedure. The 1st pilot was W/O P784742 J Derma PAF and the pupil AC2 P706640 L Kafel PAF.

1717 hrs Training

Harvard IIB FX381 of 16 (P)SFTS from Newton was on a training flight with AC2 P/706450 Waclaw Dabrowski PAF as the pilot under training when the crew 'shot up' Harvard FT344. A collision occurred and FX381 crashed at Pummel Pit Farm near Wroot killing AC2 Dabrowski. He is buried in Newark-upon-Trent Cemetery.

The crew of Harvard FT344, AC2 P/705478 W Nakoneczny PAF and AC2 P/705756 R Zywicki PAF, both pilots under training, landed the badly damaged aircraft at Newton.

Harvard IIB FT344 of 16 (P)SFTS from Newton was flying straight and level when it was crashed into by Harvard FX381 and the badly damaged aircraft landed at Newton (see above). The pilots were highly commended for landing the aircraft safely.

No.16(P)SFTS Harvard IIB at Newton similar to FT344. Courtesy J B Cynk

2305 hrs Training

Oxford I NM420 of 16 (P)SFTS from Newton was making a right hand south east circle after having trouble with the port engine when the aircraft undershot and struck a building causing it to crash. The crew, Waclaw Piotrowski from the Polish Army, who was under training, and the pilot, F/L P/0121 Stanislaw Sadowski PAF age 30, were both killed and are buried in the Polish plot of Newark-on-Trent Cemetery. W/O J Ballard RAFVR (W.Op/Air Gnr) survived. The court of enquiry concluded that the crash was caused by a defective rocker bracket.

Crashed Oxford NM420. Courtesy of W Taylor

TUESDAY 20th MARCH 1945

A lone Junkers Ju 88 raided Bottesford Airfield, dropping several bombs in a low pass over the runways and buildings and attempting to fire cannon shells into a train standing at Bottesford station.

WEDNESDAY 21st MARCH 1945

1032 hrs — Training

Wellington X HF514 of BCIS from Finningley took off to practice single-engine landings but crash landed on Worksop airfield with the undercarriage retracted after failure of the starboard engine to restart after practice feathering. The crew who were un-injured were pilot S/L 125761 V Hughes, pupil pilot F/L 131084 W P Ervine DFC, F/S 1378505 A E Barford DFM.

F/L Ervine was awarded the DFC on 24th March 1944 whilst serving with 9 Sqn. The citation read: 'One night in December, 1943, this officer piloted an aircraft detailed to attack Berlin. It was his seventh sortie against this target. On the outward flight the aircraft was hit by anti-aircraft fire and shortly afterwards was attacked by a fighter. Much damage was sustained, making the bomber difficult to control. Nevertheless, Flight Lieutenant Ervine went on to make a successful attack and afterwards flew safely to base. This officer has invariably displayed great skill and determination, qualities which have enabled him to complete a large number of missions successfully.'

F/S Barford was awarded the DFM on 16th February 1945 when a member of 15 Squadron. The citation read: 'In recognition of gallantry and devotion to duty in the execution of Air operations.'

SATURDAY 24th MARCH 1945

2020 hrs — Training

Lancaster I HK738 KB-D of 1661 HCU from Winthorpe took off for what was to be a cross country exercise and completing the flight with some practice bombing at Wainfleet bombing range. It was usual practice on these exercises to give the pilot one or two practice overshoots on three engines before setting course. A four engine overshoot was completed and then the first three engine overshoot began with the intention of feathering one outboard engine with wheels down and full flap on then open up at 50 feet when over the runway. The pilot opened up the three engines when over the runway, selected wheels up but no height was gained. He then tried to retract the flaps but they would not retract. The instructor took over the aircraft which was skimming the tree tops and still losing height. He then saw a row of houses ahead and decided he couldn't clear them so belly landed the aircraft in a field at Langford one mile from the airfield. The impact caused the fuselage to break in half just forward of the mid-upper turret, burst a petrol tank which then caught fire and the red hot engines, ammunition and practice bombs then began exploding. The crew quickly escaped from the aircraft except for Sgt McArdle who was trapped in the rear turret. He was rescued from his position by the crew who cut away his clothing with a knife and pulled him clear of the wreckage.

The seven crew members were: F/O 170431 J J Lett (Instructor Pilot), F/O 164417 T M Rae (Pupil Pilot), F/O 164711 D Tracey (Air Bomber), F/S 1605056 M W Fauxheux (F/Eng), Sgt 1602607 C Haines (Nav), Sgt 1596225 J A Jaffrey (W.Op), Sgt 543066 W Williamson (MUAG) and Sgt 873055 P McArdle (Rear Gnr).

The Commander-in-Chief, Sir A T Harris, issued a statement commending the crews and highly commending F/O Lett.

TUESDAY 27th MARCH 1945

1720 hrs | Training

Wellington LP616 BT-M of 30 OTU from Gamston piloted by F/S 130070 T W Harper suffered a port engine failure shortly after take-off and owing to the emergency bottle failing he was unable to lower the undercarriage so landed wheels up with no injuries to the crew.

FRIDAY 30th MARCH 1945

2125 hrs | Training

Lancaster III ND808 of BCIS from Finningley took off for night circuit training then approached the airfield on three engines landed and swung to starboard and crashed into the petrol dump and burst into flames. Three of the crew were F/O 160771 G A Cooper who was seriously injured, F/L 55201 Ronald William Mathers DFC and F/S D W Cole, injured. F/L Mathers was 'Commended for valuable service in the air' by King George VI on 10th June 1948.

TUESDAY 3rd APRIL 1945

1230 hrs

Oxford PH406 of 12 Gp CF had an incident on Hucknall aerodrome. Hucknall Flying Control received a message that an aircraft had crashed on the aerodrome and an ambulance proceeded to the spot with a crash team and found the wreck of PH406. The crew F/L 517315 Covington (Pilot), F/S McTaggart, Cpl 529107 Nelson and LAC 1798489 Goult all escaping without injury.

WEDNESDAY 4th APRIL 1945

1240 hrs | Training

Tiger Moth II T7148 of 25 (P)EFTS from Hucknall with pilot AC2 P/706299 Pawlowicz PAF in the cockpit was carrying out forced landing practice and side slipping and struck the ground heavily with aircraft's wheel and turned over at Papplewick RLG.

SATURDAY 7th APRIL 1945

1415 hrs | Training

Oxford I EB866 of 16 (P)FTS from Newton began circuit and landings training and when the aircraft became airborne the pilot lost control due to the tail trim being too heavy and crashed. The pilot was AC2 P/706460 L Gorlewski PAF who was un-injured had failed to carry out cockpit drill prior to take off.

SUNDAY 8th APRIL 1945

0135 hrs | Training

Lancaster III PB758 of 1661 HCU from Winthorpe on landing after dual circuits and landings, overshot, the pilot swung the aircraft to avoid a totem pole, and ran into a four foot deep ditch and the port undercarriage was torn off. The 1st pilot was F/O 178521 F W Hubbard and the pupil pilot F/O 168650 Bernard Hall RAFVR. The aircraft had been landed at excessive speed and need not have swung on the runway.

F/O Hall was killed the next month on 17th May piloting Lancaster RF124 on a training flight when it crashed at Short Heath, near Wolverhampton. He is buried age 24 in Boulton (St Mary) Churchyard.

1600 hrs Training

Wellington I LN585 of BCIS from Finningley took off on dual practice overshooting on one engine and while circulating the airfield again crashed out of control off a slow turn to starboard and burst into flames killing three of the crew of four. The aircraft's air speed had fallen below the critical speed for an aircraft engine.

F/L 160772 Gerald Arthur Clark age 24 RAFVR (Pilot) cremated at Sheffield Crematorium, F/O 416549 William Gordon Craig DFC age 23 RAAF buried Darlington West Cemetery, F/S 1293225 Bertram Frederick Griggs age 25 RAFVR buried Plymouth (Weston Mill) Cemetery, F/O 172415 G Lofthouse DFC was injured.

F/O Craig was awarded the DFC on 13th October 1944 at Buckingham Palace the citation read: 'Numerous attacks on targets over Berlin, Essen etc.'

MONDAY 9th APRIL 1945

1415 hrs Training

Lancaster III ND808 of 1668 HCU from Bottesford on take off the port tyre burst and the aircraft swung, ground looped and damaged the undercarriage. The pilot was F/O 55279 J V Turner.

SATURDAY 14th APRIL 1945

0325 hrs Taxiing

Lancaster III JB309 of 1668 HCU from Bottesford taxied off the end of the runway, overshot and turned off 50 yards too far and struck a barbed wire fence. The pilot was F/L 50608 L G Gratton.

SUNDAY 15th APRIL 1945

0025 hrs Training

Lancaster III PB213 GP- of 1661 HCU from Winthorpe was on a training flight and at about 1,500 feet the pilot, F/S 1393077 F E Hearn, fell asleep and the aircraft flew level into the ground and burnt extensively in the crash.

A 15year old boy, Derek Fearn, of Private Road Southwell, was walking home from a dance in Oxton, when he was struck by the debris from a crashing bomber at the top of Oxton Hill. He ran to a nearby farm for help, and Dr Snell, of Southwell, was soon on the scene, followed by Inspector Arnold and PC Schofield of Southwell and PC Stirland from Oxton.

The aircraft was approaching Epperstone bombing range from the North. Flying very low it struck the brow of the hill just East of Hall Farm, at the top of Oxton Hill on the Southwell Road. The Lancaster skidded some distance across a field before coming to rest with its fuselage broken in two, the front part catching fire and burning out. Four members of the crew were injured and taken to Nottingham General Hospital and three killed. Those who died were:

F/S 647200 Edward Arthur Crutchfield age 23 RAF (Air Bomber) is buried in Queens Road Cemetery, Walthamstow, Sgt 1678403 Peter John Froggatt RAFVR age 20 (Nav) buried Oxford (Botley) Cemetery, Sgt 1899005 Philip Leslie Doggett RAFVR age 21 (W.Op/Air Gnr) buried at Wymering (SS. Peter and Paul) Churchyard, Sgt 1006035 George Martin, RAFVR age 27 died from injuries in Nottingham General Hospital on 28th April and is buried in Belfast City Cemetery.

Sgt 939102 S C Bowring (MUAG) suffered leg injuries, Pilot 1393077 F/S F E Hearn, suffered burns, and 1236970 Sgt Edwin Dash (Rear Gnr) suffered foot injuries.

The map shown opposite is from a 1940 OS Map with kind permission of the Ordnance Survey. The map uses the Cassini grid system. Crash location grid ref: 54/ 112719 (marked as ◉).

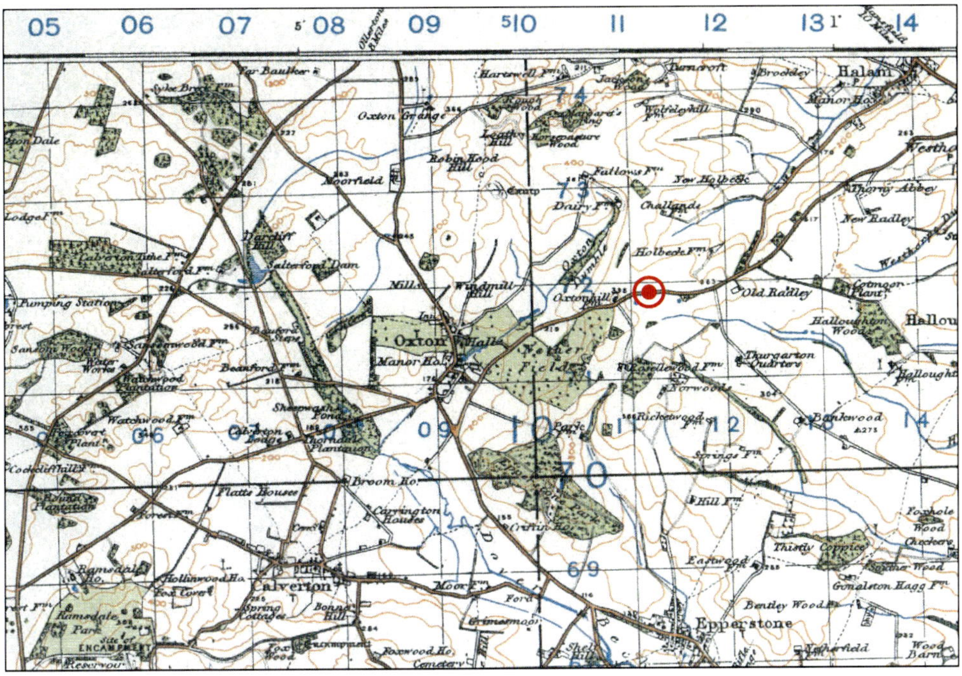

1525 hrs Training

Lancaster III PB565 of 1667 HCU from Sandtoft took off at 1505 hrs for a solo cross country flight and after 30 minutes the aircraft was seen to be in level flight at 3,000 feet then go into a steep dive breaking up and crashing out of control one mile south west of Owston Ferry on the bank of Wasping Drain. An eyewitness stated the aircraft was flying level at 1500 feet, seconds later went into a steep almost vertical dive. At 400 to 500 feet the wing tips folded backwards and came off, followed by the outer wings, tail unit and rear portion of the fuselage. The aircraft was spinning to starboard as it hit the ground and burst into flames. Another eye witness stated that the aircraft broke up in the air and shed pieces of structure over a wreckage trail of about 1¼ miles. It was considered that the accident was due to the pilot losing control at a considerable height followed by a high speed dive resulting in structural failure.

All eight members of the crew were killed: P/O 188176 Howard Percy Speed RAFVR age 23 (Pilot) is buried in Bromsgrove Cemetery, F/S 1523074 Raymond Ollerton RAFVR age 21 buried Bolton (Heaton) Cemetery, F/S 25661 John William Hamilton RAAF age 29 buried Harrogate (Stonefall) Cemetery, who had enlisted 4 years previously on 29th April 1941, F/O 153755 Bertram Arthur Savage RAFVR age 28 also buried Harrogate (Stonefall) Cemetery, F/O 165049 Edward Boon Carss RAFVR age 25 buried Blyth (Cowpen) Cemetery, Sgt 1097768 Sidney James Kingdon RAFVR (Nav) buried South Molton Cemetery, Sgt 1893896 Robert Bertram Roy Cook RAFVR age 19 (Air Gnr) buried Wadhurst (SS. Peter and Paul) Churchyard and Sgt 1813197 Edwin Horace John Martin RAFVR age 20 buried Harrogate (Stonefall) Cemetery. Crash location: Cassini grid 1940 sheet 38 265185; OS sheet 112 795986.

WEDNESDAY 16th APRIL 1945

1135 hrs Training

Wellington X JA345 of 30 OTU from Gamston was taking off but the starboard engine revs fluctuated as low as 1800 rpm so the pilot, F/O 132739 A P S Cloke, throttled back and then retracted the undercarriage to prevent overshooting.

TUESDAY 17th APRIL 1945

2105 hrs — Training

Wellington X HE858 BT-L of 30 OTU from Gamston piloted by F/S 125889 R Thwaites suffered starboard engine failure while taking off when almost airborne. A violent swing developed which was controlled by the pilot who then belly landed the aircraft. No injuries were reported of the four man crew.

WEDNESDAY 18th APRIL 1945

1536 hrs — Air Test

Lancaster I NG196 of 467 Sqn from Swinderby port outer engine was on fire in the air and would not feather so the pilot F/O Pilkington decided to come straight in but could not get the undercarriage to fully lock down in time and belly landed on the airfield. As the fire subsided at 200 feet the pilot should have reversed his decision to force land and taken overshoot action.

THURSDAY 19th APRIL 1945

1505 hrs — Training

Hurricane IIC MW347 TN-A of 30 OTU from Gamston was taking off on a fighter affiliation exercise when the engine cut and a wheels up landing was made straight ahead in a field near the airfield. F/O 158106 C Koder (Screened Pilot) was slightly injured.

FRIDAY 20th APRIL 1945

1025 hrs — Training

Lancaster III JA962 of 1668 HCU from Bottesford made a normal landing and normal cockpit checks and then towards the end of his run the undercarriage collapsed. The pilot was W/O 1210631 K R Jones.

1650 hrs — Training

Lancaster I HK598 of 1660 HCU from Swinderby was on practice bombing training when control was lost while low flying on two engines and the aircraft crashed at Claypole and caught fire. Three of the crew were killed and their bodies taken to Swinderby mortuary and four injured.

The crew comprised P/O J/93938 J B Kram RCAF (Pilot), Sgt R221951 C E Brenton (F/Eng), F/S R252680 F T Thompson (Nav), W/O R195917 R C Fleming (W.Op) all injured.

F/S R/252616 Roger Thomas Bridger RCAF age 24 (Air Bomber), F/S R/290092 Francis Clesphas Martial Robitaille age 28 RCAF (MUAG) and F/S R/274376 Gordon Phillip Charlebois age 29 RCAF (Rear Gnr) are all buried in Harrogate (Stonefall) Cemetery.

SATURDAY 21st APRIL 1945

1120 hrs — Training

Harvard IIB KF366 of 16 (P)SFTS collided with Harvard FT375 of 16(P)SFTS during formation flying practice and crashed at Cotgrave. The leader broke away and KF 366 followed across the path of FT375. The pilot, LAC P/706585 Tadeusz Kazimierz Czarniecki PAF age 21, was killed and is buried in Newark-upon-Trent Cemetery. No-one was killed in FT375. Crash location grid ref: OS sheet 129 656355.

1120 hrs Training

Harvard IIB FT375 of 16 (P)SFTS was hit by Harvard KF366 during formation flying practice but landed safely at Cotgrave. Crash location grid ref: OS sheet 129 648353.

TUESDAY 24th APRIL 1945

1455 hrs Training

Tiger Moth II DE920 of 25 (P)EFTS from Hucknall had been in the air for ten minutes on AC2 P/707227 F Skrzepecki's, first solo and on landing he allowed the control column to go forward and the aircraft turned onto its nose.

THURSDAY 26th APRIL 1945

0040 hrs

Tiger Moth DE376 of 25 (P)EFTS from Hucknall piloted by pilot under training Lt Olesinski turned on its nose when landing due to error of judgement.

SATURDAY 28th APRIL 1945

One of the first airborne V-bombs, carried pick-a-back, crashed in the Warsop area, in a potato field off Sherwood Street with only superficial damage to 380 houses. There were no injuries. A twin engine plane, parts of which were scattered over the field when it crashed, fell on the west side of the high embarkment which carries the railway from Warsop station to Welbeck Colliery.

WEDNESDAY 2nd MAY 1945

2308 hrs Training

Lancaster III PB733 KB-Q of 1661 HCU from Winthorpe took off for night circuit practice and coming in to land the pilot misjudged his height and levelled off too high. The aircraft hit the runway heavily and the undercarriage collapsed. The 1st pilot F/O 178521 F D Hubbard received minor injuries and was detained in the SSQ and the 2nd pilot F/S 436376 A J Kalms RAAF was un-injured.

THURSDAY 3rd MAY 1945

1500 hrs Air Test

SpitfireVB BM474 of BCIS from Finningley took off to test the flaps and on landing ¾ down the runway the aircraft swung sharply and lost its undercarriage. The pilot was F/L J/23043 Saunderson RCAF.

FRIDAY 4th MAY 1945

2255 hrs Training

Lancaster III ME309 of 1654 HCU from Wigsley took off for night circuits and landings practice but as the aircraft returned to land it swung to port and its starboard undercarriage collapsed. The instructor pilot was F/O 179596 J Vasey and the pupil pilot F/O 185286 J R Leadon.

TUESDAY 8th MAY 1945

VE-Day. The war in Europe ends. The Prime Minister Winston Churchill announced the German surrender in the House of Commons.

FRIDAY 18th MAY 1945

1054 hrs Training

Lancaster I HK739 J9-K of 1668 HCU from Bottesford began take-off but failed to become airborne and was wrecked having swung off the runway and crashed through the hedge bordering the airfield. The pilots were F/O 171014 G S Sanders and P/O 177153 H H Pickett. There were no injuries to the seven man crew.

1140 hrs Air Test

Wellington X NA718 BT-O of 30 OTU from Gamston took-off for an air test with F/O 174908 Robert Fraser Thompson (Screened Pilot) RAFVR age 22 at the controls and LAC 1353162 Douglas Fletcher Dryden, a member of the ground crew, as a passenger. Immediately after take-off, for some reason unknown, the pilot decided that he needed to make an emergency landing and the aircraft stalled in an endeavour to reach a field and crashed at Haughton Warren Farm, near Bothamsall. On hitting the ground the aircraft cart-wheeled and burst into flames. Both pilot and passenger died in Worksop, Victoria Hospital from injuries received.

F/O Thompson is buried in Newcastle-upon-Tyne Cemetery and LAC Dryden age 24 RAFVR in Paisley (Hawkhead) Cemetery. Due to the excessive burning of the aircraft in the crash no technical failure could be proved.

FRIDAY 25th MAY 1945

2353 hrs Training

Lancaster III PB227 of 1661 HCU from Winthorpe was landing when it swung violently to port and both undercarriages collapsed. The instructor pilot S/L 413349 J V Cowans RAAF, the pupil pilot F/S 1587194 T E Stubbs and the 6 other crew were not injured.

THURSDAY 31st MAY 1945

1020 hrs Training

Tiger Moth II T6234 of 25 (P)EFTS from Hucknall piloted by AC2 P707310 J Firko PAF, on his first solo flight, landed heavily on the starboard leg, went round again and the undercarriage collapsed on the subsequent landing.

MONDAY 4th JUNE 1945

1619 hrs Training

Lancaster III JA909 of 1661 HCU from Waddington had been on a dual training instructional flight for two hours fourteen minutes when the pupil pilot made a three engine approach to land with the port outer engine feathered. He allowed the aircraft, in bumpy conditions, to creep to the port side of the runway and the instructor realised the error too late, took over, realised they were too low for overshoot but opened up to clear the control tower and hangar and belly landed in a field at Langford, near Winthorpe. No injuries were sustained by any of the 10 members of the crew who were treated in Station Sick Quarters for shock.

The instructor pilot was F/L 143736 W A Verrals and the pupil pilot was W/O 658829 B J Manning.

WEDNESDAY 6th JUNE 1945

0115 hrs — Training

Lancaster I PA228 of BCIS from Finningley had been on a two hour twenty minute flight, training on three engine circuits and overshoots, when it landed with the port outer engine feathered as both pilots F/O J/85330 H D F Frith RCAF and F/O 176948 A G Frish had forgotten to lower the undercarriage.

FRIDAY 8th JUNE 1945

1205 hrs — Training

Hurricane IIC PG605 of 1654 HCU from Swinderby took off for a fighter affiliation sortie but on reaching 300 feet the engine cut so the pilot F/O 182711 J R Hendry turned downwind and crash-landed wheels up on the airfield. He was not injured.

SUNDAY 10th JUNE 1945

1420 hrs — Training

Tiger Moth II N9322 of 25 (P)EFTS from Hucknall bounced on landing but the pilot, AC2 P/707684 L Kowalski PAF, failed to carry out the correct action to recover from the bad landing and the result was a heavy landing on one wheel which damaged the aircraft.

THURSDAY 14th JUNE 1945

1833 hrs — Training

Oxford I NM419 of 16 (P)SFTS collided with HN378 of 16(P)SFTS whilst in formation one mile west south west of Kinoulton. The pilot, AC2 706454 J Dabrawski PAF, was flying No.3 and told by the leader to throttle back and come lower. He opened the throttles and the aircraft dived and turned towards the leader who took evasive action to avoid a collision, passed below the leader and hit HN378 and baled out and was un-injured.

1833 hrs

Oxford I HN378 of 16 (P)SFTS was hit in flight by NM419 whilst flying in formation and was abandoned one mile west south west of Kinoulton. The pilot, HN378 M Krwawicz of the Polish Army, was killed and is buried in Newark-upon-Trent Cemetery. He was flying No.2 and was hit by No.3 of the formation who passed below the leader and across the path of this aircraft.

SATURDAY 16th JUNE 1945

1700 hrs — Training

Tiger Moth II T8179 of 25 (P)EFTS from Hucknall was stationary and was struck by Tiger Moth DE978 which was being started without chocks and ran forward. The pilot was Lt A Kozlowski PAF. The pilot of DE978 was AC2 P/704355 Z Grodzicki PAF.

1710 hrs — Taxiing

Tiger Moth II DE978 of 25 (P)EFTS from Hucknall was having a hot engine turned with switches off and chocks not in position when it fired and the aircraft ran forward and collided with Tiger Moth T8179. The pilot was AC2 P/704355 Z Grodzicki PAF.

TUESDAY 19th JUNE 1945

0055 hrs Training

Hurricane IIC LF374 of 1690 Flt from Syerston was on fighter affiliation when the aircraft had engine failure at 4,500 feet in the vicinity of the aerodrome. The aircraft struck bad ground, and undershot, when trying to force land at Syerston. The pilot was F/O 170762 F H A Watts.

WEDNESDAY 20th JUNE 1945

1711 hrs Training

Lancaster I NN808 of 1660 HCU from Swinderby had been in flight for three hours on conversion training practice when the pupil pilot made a three engine approach to land at 50 feet with the port outer engine feathered. The port inner engine was then seen to feather and the port wing dropped until the aircraft became vertical. The nose dropped and the aircraft crashed, burst into flames and disintegrated. Six of the nine men aboard were killed instantly and the mid-upper gunner, who was trapped in his turret and then rescued, died from extensive burns at 2323 hrs. It was considered possible that the pilot feathered the port inner engine instead of un-feathering the port outer.

S/L 44404 Henry Richard Pooley, age 28 DFC RAFVR (Pilot Instructor) is buried in Cambridge City Cemetery, F/L 129345 Thomas Clay age 24 RAFVR (Pupil Pilot) buried Kirk Hallam (All Saints) Churchyard, Ilkeston, Sgt 1823486 Kenneth Edward Terry age 28 RAFVR buried Oban (Pennyfuir) Cemetery, F/L 135922 Leslie Green age 22 RAFVR (Nav) buried Audenshaw Cemetery, F/O 165408 Henry Signey age 27 RAFVR (Air Bomber) buried Newcastle-upon-tyne (Byker and Heaton) Cemetery, F/O 178511 George Mason Eden age 26 RAFVR (W.Op) buried Marthall (All Saints) Churchyard, Sgt 1853258 John Bryan Russell Brazier age 19 RAFVR (Air Gnr) buried Manor Park Cemetery.

F/O B W Alford and Sgt E Such were injured. S/L Pooley was awarded the DFC on 16th February 1945 when flying with 9 Sqn.

FRIDAY 22nd JUNE 1945

1542 hrs Air Test

Beaufighter VIF MM883 of 1668 HCU from Bottesford took off for a night flying test and on return the starboard tyre blew out on landing causing the aircraft to swing violently and the undercarriage to collapse. The pilot F/O 176566 D F Gillman and one other were injured.

1615 hrs Taxiing

Tiger Moth II T6024 of 25 (P)EFTS from Hucknall piloted by AC2 P/707243 W Potempski PAF was struck from behind while waiting to take off by Tiger Moth T7294. T7294 was piloted by Lt A Kozlowski who was also involved in a similar incident on 16th June.

1615 hrs Taxiing

Tiger Moth II T7294 of 25 (P)EFTS from Hucknall piloted by Lt A Kozlowski collided with Tiger Moth T6024 which was stationary prior to taking off.

SUNDAY 24th JUNE 1945

1330 hrs Training

Tiger Moth II T6237 of 25 (P)EFTS from Hucknall was carrying out forced landing practice when the pilot, AC1 P/707235 S Smigielski PAF, came in too low and the aircraft wheels caught in the long grass and tipped onto its nose at the Papplewick RLG. Crash location: Cassini grid sheet 54 042728; OS sheet 129 580530

TUESDAY 26th JUNE 1945

1602 hrs — Training

Master II W9015 of BCIS from Finningley landed and bounced, drifted off the runway and stalled from 10 feet on to the starboard wing. The pilot was W/O 1209184 W K Bale.

TUESDAY 3rd JULY 1945

0235 hrs — Training

Lancaster III PD381 of 1661 CU from Winthorpe was taking off when the port tyre burst while the aircraft was travelling fast and it swung to port and the port undercarriage collapsed. Fire broke out in an engine and was extinguished. The instructor pilot was F/O 425796 J S Morris RNZAF and the pupil P/O 191311 J L Walker. There were no serious injuries.

THURSDAY 5th JULY 1945

2350 hrs — Training

Lancaster I W4950 of 6 LFS from Ossington was on solo practice when a tyre burst on landing and undercarriage collapsed. The pilot was P/O 170209 E C Gregory.

TUESDAY 10th JULY 1945

0835 hrs — Training

Lancaster III ND928 of 1654 HCU from Wigsley was taking off when the port tyre burst, the throttles were closed and the aircraft kept straight. Unfortunately the wheel came off which caused the aircraft to swing and the undercarriage collapsed. The pilots were F/L A/424153 R C Davie RAAF and P/O A/423530 F W Hargraves RAAF.

WEDNESDAY 11th JULY 1945

0125 hrs — Training

Tiger Moth II N9322 of 25 (P)EFTS from Hucknall was on circuits and bumps practice at night when the pilot undershot on landing and touched down in a corn field and ran into a hedge on the Hucknall airfield boundary. The pilot AC2 P/707206 R Bobrowicz PAF was un-injured.

FRIDAY 13th JULY 1945

0025 hrs — Training

Wellington X LN844 –G of 11 OTU from Westcott took off on a cross country exercise suffered starboard engine failure and was diverted to Bottesford. The aircraft would not maintain height so petrol was jettisoned but the port engine failed on approach to the runway and the aircraft crash landed in a field with wheels and flaps up and caught fire.

The pilot was F/O 172619 J W Heames and the pupil pilot F/O 172382 P Smith who was injured.

The rest of the crew were F/O S E Jones, P/O R G Nelson, F/O C W Tiplady, W/O L Wild all injured and Sgt H R Grant.

1230 hrs Training

Tiger Moth II R4769 of 25 (P)EFTS from Hucknall on approach to land flew into the ground, bounced, the pilot AC2 P/704950 Z Romecki pushed the stick forward and the aircraft tipped on its nose.

SATURDAY 14th JULY 1945

W/O 591321 John Campbell RAF age 24 was employed as a pilot and serving at No.6 Lancaster Finishing School, RAF Ossington, No.4 Group, Transport Command. He was killed in a motor accident at 0600 hrs on the Nottingham to Grantham Road near Ratcliffe-on-Trent. He is buried in Kettle Cemetery.

TUESDAY 17th JULY 1945

1130 hrs Taxiing

Tiger Moth II DF204 of 25 (P)EFTS from Hucknall collided with stationary Tiger Moth DF150 piloted by AC2 P707693 Unczur. The pilot of DF204 was AC2 P/704536 W Gorgynski PAF.

1300 hrs Taxiing

Tiger Moth II DF150 of 25 (P)EFTS from Hucknall was taxiing and the pilot AC2 P/707693 Z Uncgar PAF saw another aircraft taxiing in the opposite direction, stopped, saw that aircraft turn to port towards him but did not turn himself, saw it was too late, switched off his engine and there was a collision.

THURSDAY 19th JULY 1945

0025 hrs Training

Lancaster I HK746 of 1654 HCU from Wigsley took off for a night training exercise climbed to 150 feet then turned to port with its port wing down, a port engine failed and before any recovery action was taken it swung through 180 degrees and dived into the stations bomb dump. 6 of the crew were injured and one died. The injured crew were: F/L 150327 G A May (Pilot), F/S T Howe, Sgts A W McMaster, W B Smart, J H Dawson, A E Driver. The crewman who died was Sgt 1593519 James William Roberts age 29 RAFVR (Air Gnr) who is buried in Newcastle-upon-Tyne (St John's Westgate) Cemetery.

TUESDAY 24th JULY 1945

1055 hrs Training

Oxford I V4228 of 16 (P)SFTS was on a training flight and after one hour twenty five minutes the port engine cut on overshoot and the pilot under training 2nd Lt Timler was unable to maintain height to get round and land on the airfield. He force landed undercarriage up near Bingham Station. Crash location grid ref: OS sheet 129 705402.

THURSDAY 9th AUGUST 1945

0215 hrs Training

Tiger Moth II DE956 of 25 (P)EFTS from Hucknall was conducting night circuit and landings in low flight looking for the airfield in mist and the pilot made a quick turn onto the airfield lost control and crashed two miles south east of Hucknall and burnt out. A bank of fog and with the cloud base down to 50 feet developed suddenly and caused the pilot to lose the airfield lights.

RAF Hucknall Flying Control had received a call that a fire could be seen on the Watnall Road and that an aircraft had crashed due to the bad weather. An ambulance was sent to the scene but saw the pupil pilot walking towards them and he was taken to the SSQ at Hucknall with severe burns. A second ambulance was sent to the crash and brought back the body of the pilot instructor. The pupil pilot was transferred to the hospital where he died at 0600 hrs on 10th August.

F/L P/1082 Ryszard S Ronowicz PAF age 29 (Instructor Pilot) is buried in Bexley (St Mary) Church Cemetery and AC2 P/707269 R Szoplik PAF age 19 (Pupil Pilot) is buried in Hucknall Cemetery. Crash location grid ref: OS sheet 129 504470.

0226 hrs Training

Hurricane IIC LF161 of 1690 Flt from Syerston landed in bad weather at night without flaps and touched down well up the runway and overshot into rough ground and overturned. The pilot was F/O 168674 John Alfred Sanders DFC and Bar.

F/O Sanders was awarded the DFC on 25th April 1944 when flying with 49 Sqn. The citation read: 'In February, 1944, this officer piloted an aircraft detailed to attack Augsburg. When approaching the target the aircraft was attacked by a fighter and sustained severe damage. Large holes were torn in the fuselage, while the starboard rudder and elevator were almost shot away. The aircraft dived steeply out of control. At this stage, the rear gunner reported that the bomber was on fire near the turret. Nevertheless, Pilot Officer Sanders, with the assistance of the flight engineer, managed to regain control. Meanwhile, other members of the crew fought the fire and, although bullets were exploding in the fuselage they succeeded in putting out the flames. The inter-communication system was now out of action as the wiring had been burned through. The rear gunner lay unconscious through lack of oxygen, in spite of these trying circumstances perfect discipline prevailed. Course was set for home and, displaying great skill, Pilot Officer Sanders, succeeded in flying the badly damaged aircraft to base. He displayed courage, coolness and determination of a high order'.

F/O Sanders was then awarded the Bar to the DFC on 5th December 1944 now flying with 617 Sqn. The citation read: 'In October, 1944, this officer piloted one of a formation of aircraft detailed to bomb the sluice gates of the Kembs Barrage. In the face of much light anti-aircraft fire, Flying Officer Sanders, pressed home his attack with great determination. His heavy bomb fell very close to the required position. This officer has completed many sorties since being awarded the Distinguished Flying Cross and has displayed the highest standard of skill and captaincy'.

THURSDAY 6th SEPTEMBER 1945

0940 hrs

Oxford I HM862 of 16 (P)SFTS was in flight at 3,000 feet when the aircraft went into a spin while performing steep turns and crashed at Kinoulton Gorse. The pupil pilot AC2 P/706713 S Wojtecki PAF baled out and was un-injured.

The instructor pilot Kapitan P/0650 Jan Winiarek PAF age 31 was killed in the crash and is buried in Newark-upon-Trent Cemetery. It is thought that the port airscrew had managed to come adrift in flight and may have caused the accident. Crash location grid ref: OS sheet 129 660309.

1545 hrs Training

Wellington X HE284 of BCIS from Finningley was on single engine landing practice and coming in to land the pilot, F/L 137204 J E Peatfield, forgot to lower the undercarriage. Flying Control notified the crew and the emergency air bottle was used but the port undercarriage failed to lock in time and collapsed after landing. The 2nd pilot was F/O 176031 R H Catlow.

Lancaster III PB596 J9-0 of 1668 CU from Bottesford tyre burst on landing causing the aircraft to swing to port and the undercarriage to collapse. The pilot was W/O 4214113 W H Upton RNZAF.

WEDNESDAY 26th SEPTEMBER 1945

1530 hrs Local Flying

Magister I N3774 of 16 (P)SFTS engine cut and overshot forced landing into a ditch ½ mile north of Bingham. The pilot S/L 39244 E J C Richardson and co-pilot F/O 191478 R Barker were un-injured.

MONDAY 1st OCTOBER 1945

1535 hrs Ferrying

Mosquito XVIB RV352 of 3 FP undercarriage selector jammed in the neutral position in flight and the undercarriage could not be lowered so the pilot F/O P J Frisby bellylanded the aircraft on grass at Wymeswold.

THURSDAY 29th NOVEMBER 1945

0945 hrs Training

Airspeed Horsa I RJ161 of 1333 TSCU force landed in a field at Mole Farm, Caunton near Newark after tug aircraft engine failure. The glider was cast off at 500 feet. The pilots were S/C 277060 C L King and Sgt 1483641 G F Burton. There were no injuries.

FRIDAY 30th NOVEMBER 1945

1050 hrs Training

Lancaster I NN814 of 1660 HCU from Swinderby took off for circuits and landings then landed normally, ran straight ahead but starboard tyre burst causing aircraft to swing to starboard. The port wheel and axle then sheared. The pilot was F/L 52029 G Gregory.

WEDNESDAY 5th DECEMBER 1945

1205 hrs Training

Wellington X LN590 of BCIS from Finningley starboard undercarriage collapsed after landing by a pupil crew due to technical failure. The pilot was F/O 150585 A F H Pearson and 2nd pilot F/L 51739 H L Mellor.

Nottinghamshire Airfields

Balderton
OS sheet 120/SK816498. Three miles south south east of Newark, west of the A1 road.

This airfield opened in June 1941 as a satellite for No.25 OTU, Finningley, as a bomber airfield. During September 1942 work started on constructing runways for four engine bombers and this was completed in August 1943. The airfield closed in 1954 and was totally destroyed in the mid-60s during construction of the Newark A1 bypass.

Bircotes (Bawtry)
OS sheet 111/SK642940. One mile west of Bawtry on the A631 road.

This airfield is sometimes known as Bawtry because the headquarters were based at Bawtry Hall. The airfield opened in November 1941 as a grass surfaced airfield and during 1942 was upgraded as a satellite for Finningley but retaining grass runways.

The station was used as the base for the Communications Flight by Officers of the HQ due to its proximity to the RAF Bomber Command 1 Group HQ. The airfield closed to flying in 1944.

Blidworth
OS sheet 120/SK575532. South east of Mansfield between the A614 and A60 roads.

The airfield is located to the west of Blidworth Lodge and was established as a Satellite Landing Ground and identified by SLG No.35. The airfield opened on 1st August 1941 as a grass strip of approximately 1,000 yards and was used mainly for the temporary storage of fighter aircraft.

It was abandoned by the RAF in 1945. The guardroom, at what was the main gate, has been converted into a bungalow. There are two hard standings to the south of the landing strip, parallel with Longdale Lane, with aircraft securing rings still in position.

Farnsfield
The Air Ministry raised warning notices indicating that an airfield was to be built at Farnsfield to be used for RAF flying training. This notice was cancelled in December 1942.

Gamston
OS sheet 120/SK693762. Three miles south of Retford, north of the A1 road at Elkesley. Gamston airfield is situated just north of the main road at the village of Elkesley and was constructed to the wartime pattern of three runways with the main runway parallel to the B6387 road.

The airfield opened in December 1942 as a satellite of No.14 (P) AFU, Ossington. At its peak the station had 30 heavy bomber hard standings and 1300 RAF personnel.

The station closed at the end of 1945 then in May 1953 it re-opened as a satellite to Workshop. It finally closed down in 1957.

Gamston Control Tower. Courtesy of W Taylor

Grove Park
OS sheet 120/SK734796. East of East Retford No.38 Satellite Landing Ground opened in August 1942 by No.51 MU from Lichfield. No aircraft were received for storage and by September it was decided to close the landing ground for the winter. It opened again in the spring of 1943 but it is not known if the airfield was used. In April 1944 the SLG was passed to No.27 MU based at Shawbury who used it as a dispersed aircraft storage facility. The SLG closed down in June 1945.

Hardwick Park
OS sheet 120/SK465645. Midway between Mansfield and Chesterfield.

Hardwick Park was opened in May 1941 as a Satellite Landing Ground with a grass runway of around 1000 yards. This airfield was located within the grounds of Hardwick Hall and was used for aircraft storage, the first aircraft arriving on 27th September 1941. The ground suffered from water-logging in winter which restricted its use. Late September 1942 the HQ of the 1st Parachute Brigade took over use of the Hall and the RAF eventually gave up the landing ground during September 1943. At the end of the war the Hall was returned to its owners.

Hucknall
OS sheet 129/SK525470. South of the B6009 road on the outskirts of Hucknall.

Hucknall opened during the First World War as a training ground and remained such throughout the war. After the 1914-18 war it was thought that the site would be made into a permanent aerodrome for Hucknall but it was not taken up and the buildings were offered for sale by the Ministry. One of the hangars was occupied and some of the buildings were made into houses. The rest of the land was sold to a Hucknall farmer.

With the birth of the Nottingham Aero Club the Ministry decided to buy the land back plus some additional land from the County Council and Bulwell Wood Hall.

On 26th March 1928, No.504 (County of Nottingham) Squadron was formed here as a Cadre unit of the Special Reserve. It converted to an auxiliary squadron on 18th May 1936 and had a day bomber role, and then on 31st October 1938 changed to a fighter role. Meanwhile, in December 1934, Rolls-Royce moved into the aerodrome and set up an engine test-flying facility.

At the outbreak of WWII the airfield was in Fighter Command, no Fighter Command units appeared but during the war the airfield was used by various units of the RAF.

In 1957 RAF involvement was terminated at Hucknall and Rolls-Royce Flight Development continued.

Langar
OS sheet 129/SK740335. Fifteen miles south east of Nottingham, south east of Bingham.
Work started in early 1940 on the bomber station and was first used as a satellite for Bottesford. A V Roe opened workshops during September 1942 and carried out major repairs and reconditioning on Lancasters. The only operational squadron to use the station was No.207 which arrived in September 1942 from Bottesford. The airfield then became an American base in October 1943 as Station 490, Station code LA.

The airfield closed down completely on 18th December 1946.

In 1951 the airfield re-opened as RCAF Langar, part of Canada's contribution to NATO and continued to operate until 1963. In September 1968 A V Roe also closed down and today the airfield is used by the British Parachute School. In 1994 a memorial was laid down in memory of the 251 aircrew whose lives were lost during WWII. It is located at the north east corner of the airfield at the side of the Langar to Harby road.

Newton
OS sheet 129/SK680415. Seven miles east of Nottingham between the A52 and A6097 roads and east of the A46(T) road.

Newton was established as an airfield in 1936 and became operational in July 1940 with sorties being flown by Fairey Battles and then Wellingtons. In July 1941 the station was transferred from Bomber to Flying Training Command and No.16 (Polish) SFTS moved from Hucknall. The airfield finally closed in March 2001.

Orston
OS sheet 129/SK780413. East of Nottingham and Orston village, north of the main A52 road.

Orston airfield opened during 1941 as a satellite for 16(Polish) Service Flying Training School, based at Newton.

It was a grass strip with a maximum length of just over 1200 yards. The airfield was used only by Newton and had very primitive facilities with around 120 RAF personnel. It closed in 1945 and reverted to farmland.

Ossington
OS sheet 120/SK745645. Situated west of the village of Ossington in the grounds of Ossington Hall (now demolished), with the Hall forming part of the accommodation, eight miles north west of Newark, west of the A1(T) road at the Carlton-on-Trent junction and just west of Ossington village.

Construction work started in 1941 and the airfield was originally selected as a bomber station with a decoy airfield at Upton.

Soon after opening in January 1942 it was transferred to Flying Training Command.

In May 1946 the airfield completed its flying commitment and closed in August 1946. By 1979 all the runways had been broken up and disposed of for hardcore.

Right: **Ossington Control Tower 1959.** Courtesy W Taylor

Above: **Ossington Hall previously used as the Officers Quarters Demolished in 1962.** Courtesy of W Taylor

Below: **The map of Ossington Airfield during WWII**

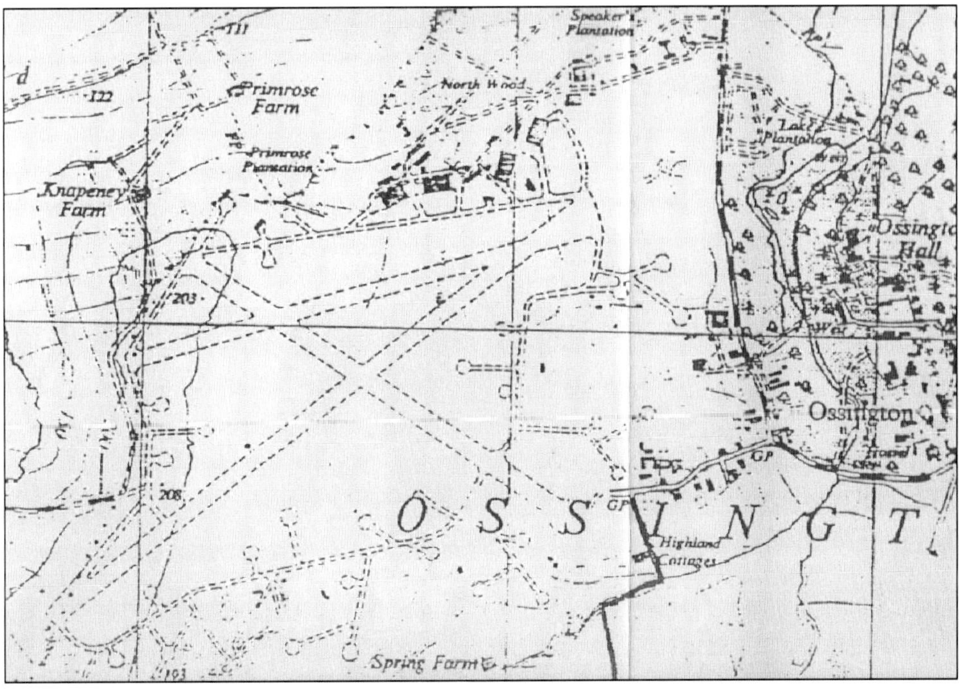

Papplewick Moor

OS sheet 120/SK550510. Approximately seven miles north of Nottingham at Papplewick crossroads, south of the B6011 and west of the B683 roads.

Papplewick was first established as a relief landing ground for Hucknall. This formed on 1st April 1918 but disbanded the following year. During the Second World War the field was again brought into service and the site was used as a relief landing ground for the Tiger Moths of 25 EFTS based at Hucknall.

Syerston

OS sheet 129/SK730480. Six miles south west of Newark-on-Trent and west of the A46 road.

The airfield was positioned between the main A46 road and the river Trent and opened on 1st December 1940 as an Operational bomber command station. It had a satellite airfield at Balderton and a decoy airfield at Kneeton about 2 miles south west of the station.

The station closed to flying in December 1941 while the runways were constructed in preparation for the four-engined bombers then coming into service.

Accommodation was dispersed with many of the aircrew Nissen huts built in the grounds of Flintham Hall. In May 1942, Syerston re-opened as a heavy bomber station.

Wing Commander Guy Gibson, then of 106 Squadron piloted an aircraft from Syerston on the Schneider Armament works at Le Creusot.

Flight Lieutenant Reid while serving at Syerston was awarded the Victoria Cross for bringing home his crippled bomber, Lancaster LM360, from a raid on Dusseldorf despite being severely wounded.

When 61 and 106 Squadrons left in November 1943 Syerston ceased to become operational and became a training station.

In April 1945 No.49 Squadron moved from Fulbeck and the station again became operational until the end of the war.

Tollerton

OS sheet 129/SK620360. Three miles south east of Nottingham.

The airfield, which was owned by Nottingham Corporation, officially opened in 1930 and was leased to National Flying Services who erected a club house and hangar.

Further development took place over the following years with the formation of the Civil Air Guard and a RAF Volunteer Reserve Training School. Field Aircraft Services Ltd erected a large factory hangar for repair and servicing.

The airfield was taken over by the Air Ministry for use by the RAF at the beginning of the war and became a satellite to Newton for training purposes. In early 1941 three runways were laid and more buildings and hangars were built.

The airfield was used until 1946 and throughout this period Field Aircraft Services used the airfield for major overall and repair of a wide variety of aircraft, and this was the main role of the airfield.

Today the airfield is still in use for private aviation.

There is a plaque mounted on a pillbox on the airfield commemorating the crew of Wellington bomber W5365 which crashed on Cotgrave Golf club killing all aboard when coming in to land.

Wigsley

OS sheet 121/SK855695. West of Lincoln, between the villages of Wigsley and Spalford.

Wigsley opened in February 1942 as a satellite for Swinderby and remained open as a satellite for Swinderby until July 1958 when it was de-requisitioned.

Today the airfield has resumed its agricultural role and the control tower and a few huts are the only reminders that this was once an active airfield.

Wigsley Control Tower 1994

Winthorpe
OS sheet 121/SK825565. North east of Newark between the villages of Winthorpe and Coddington.

Winthorpe officially opened as a satellite for Swinderby in September 1940 and Polish Squadrons, Nos 300 and 301 arrived in October 1940.

During 1941 the airfield continued to be used for training, in November 1941 control of the airfield passed to RAF Ossington and it became a 2nd satellite for RAF Syerston in February 1942. During early 1942 the airfield was closed for runway construction and there was no further activity there that year.

The airfield eventually closed down in 1959 and is now the location of the Newark and Nottinghamshire Show Ground.

Worksop (Scofton)
OS sheet 120/SK625815. Four and a half miles west of East Retford.

Workshop airfield was built in a wooded area near the village of Scofton, and it is sometimes known by that name.

The land was requisitioned in July 1942 and the airfield opened in November 1943. Throughout its life Workshop was used as a training station. The airfield finally closed in December 1960.

The airfield has returned to agricultural use with no buildings in existance.

Airfields on the Border

Bottesford
OS sheet 130/SK820415. Sited 2 miles north of Bottesford village.

Construction work started on the airfield in late 1940 which was sited almost on the boundaries of Nottinghamshire, Leicestershire and Lincolnshire, and opened in September 1941. Due to its location the airfield was also known as Normanton to the local people.

To the south lay Bottesford and the church which had a red light fixed to the spire because it was in line with the main runway.

Flying ceased at the airfield in 1945 but was used after the war for storage of bombs before disposal. The control tower and a large number of other structures remain and the airfield is now used for storage purposes.

Castle Donington
OS sheet 129/SK450260 South east of Nottingham between the villages of Castle Donington and Diseworth.

The airfield was opened on 1st January 1943 with 3 concrete runways, as a satellite for Wymeswold and used as an OTU. In October 1944 the OTU was replaced by a transport unit equipped with Dakotas. The airfield was abandoned as an RAF airfield in September 1946.

After major structural changes it re-opened as the East Midlands Airport on 1st April 1965.

Finningley
OS sheet 111/SK665980. 5 miles south east of Doncaster.

Construction work started in 1935 and the airfield officially opened in September 1936. The airfield was being equipped with various squadrons and aircraft until the outbreak of war and its main role was training aircrews for operational squadrons. From the end of 1942 until March 1943 urgent repairs were conducted on the airfield and dispersals and concrete perimeter tracks were laid. It re-opened in March 1943 but in November 1943 Finningley again closed for hard runway construction and re-opened in May 1944. After the war Finningley was continuously used by the RAF for various roles until its decommissioned in 1996.The airfield re-opened in 2005 as a civil airport under the name of Robin Hood Airport Doncaster Sheffield.

Loughborough
OS sheet 129/SK525215. One mile north west of Loughborough.

This airfield was a grass field and was the second airfield to be opened by Brush Coachworks Ltd as a direct response to the war effort, pooling resources towards the test flying of built and repaired aircraft. The company produced 300+ Dominie aircraft and test flew them from the airstrip from 1943. The airfield closed when the war was over.

Netherthorpe
OS sheet 111/SK538804. Situated to the west of Worksop just south of the A57 road.

The site became an airfield on 12th April 1935 and was used by the Sheffield Aero club.

The airfield was only used during the war for a few months in 1940 by the Lysanders of No.613 Squadron. Today the airfield is still in use for club flying.

On 1st September 1993 a plaque was unveiled in memory of P/O Grosvenor Edmonds who died when his plane crashed whilst landing at the airfield.

Swinderby
O/S sheet 121/SK880620. On the A46 road between Lincoln and Newark.

The airfield opened in August 1940 when Polish Sqns Nos 300 and 301 arrived with Fairy Battles and Ansons. Concrete runways were built early 1942 and the airfield ceased to be a front line station after November 1942. It became a training airfield until the end of the war and closed in 1993 as part of the Ministry of Defence spending cuts.

Wymeswold
OS sheet 129/SK585225. Situated to the east of Loughborough between Hoton and Wymeswold.

The airfield opened on 16th May 1942 with the standard 3 concrete runways and was used for the training of bomber crews. During October 1944 the emphasis changed to training bomber crews for a transport role. The airfield closed down on 10th December 1947. In February 1949 the airfield re-opened and on 3rd May No.504 (Nottingham) Auxiliary Squadron arrived with Spitfires and then subsequently Meteors. The airfield closed to flying in 1957.

Wymeswold Control Tower 1994

Support Installations

Anti-aircraft artillery defences
Ack-Ack Command was formed on 1st April 1939 and consisted of 7 anti-aircraft divisions and was responsible for the use of heavy and light ack-ack guns, rockets and searchlights.

Listed here are some of the locations of the heavy anti-aircraft batteries in Nottinghamshire during World War Two using the British National Grid as published by Ordnance Survey.

The locations recorded in official documents are by grid references, taken to 6 figures and accurate to 100 metres. Wartime Ordnance Survey maps for England, Scotland and Wales used a different projection and grid from the present day called the 'Cassini' grid and so had to be converted. The grid references shown here relate to Ordnance Survey sheet 129.

REF	GRID REF	LOCATION	REF	GRID REF	LOCATION
DNH14	SK534412	Robins Wood	DNH19	SK584426	Mapperley (Hospital)
		(nr Beechdale Rd, Bilborough)	–	SK565449	Sunrise Hill, Bestwood
DNH15	SK549353	Clifton	DNH20	SK562447	Sunrise Hill, Bestwood
		(nr Clifton College)	DNH21	SK549452	Bulwell Forest Golf Course
DNH16	SK573355	Wilford Cemetery	DNH18	SK601298	Bunny Park
–	SK604383	Adbolton	DNH23	SK600298	Bunny Park
DNH17	SK605380	Adbolton	DNH26	SK663409	Near Shelford
	SK601394	Colwick Wood	DNH28	SK605471	Bank Hill Arnold

Budby/Cuckney

Cuckney was the site of 66 GED (Ground Equipment Depot) or 61 MU (Universal Equipment Depot, stores). The A616 now runs through the site between Cuckney and Budby.

Formed on 2nd March 1942 as Equipment Dispersal Depot; became Equipment Distribution Depot on 7th May 1942 later Ground Equipment Depot 6.

Above: **Budby installations in 1993**

Below: **Loacation map**

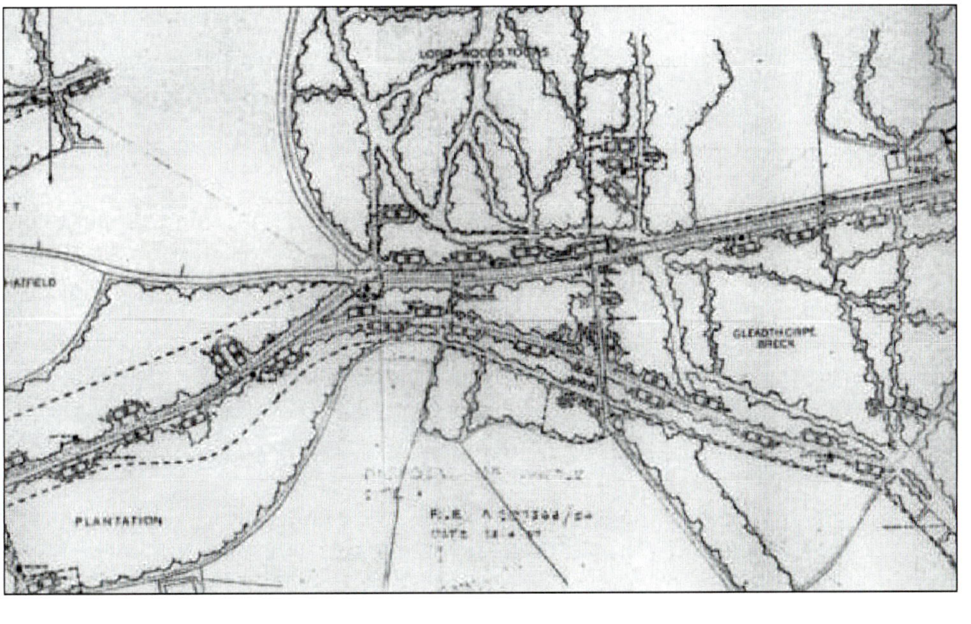

Clayworth (Lincs)
Bombing range. Mentioned in Wellington crash 27th January 1944.

Clifton Pastures
Practice bombing range, opened in August 1940. Mentioned in forced landing on 31st October 1940.

Cotgrave
Firing range at location OS sheet 129 645 343.

Epperstone
Bombing range. Mentioned in Lancaster crash 16th April 1945.

Misson
Bombing range parented by RAF Finningley. Became wartime Q site.

RAF Misson was first used as a bombing range and its first use was in 1939. The 850 acre range was used by aircraft predominately based at 25 and 18 OTU at nearby RAF Finningley during WWII for night bombing practice. The base later became a Bristol Bloodhound Surface to Air Missile battery location and was installed to protect the V Bomber location at Finningley. Today the area is a nature reserve.

Morton Hall
OS sheet 121/SK878643. Morton Hall was No.5 Group HQ from November 1943 to 1947.

The Hall was also used as an Aircrew Commando School training aircrew in survival and evasion techniques which would be put into action if they were forced to bale out over enemy territory.

Opened 1943 and closed 1st March 1955. Now HM Prison

Newark
OS sheet 121/SK796543. No.58 Maintenance Unit (58 MU) was a non-flying unit of the RAF which recovered crashed aircraft. It moved to Newark in September 1939 from RAF Henlow and occupied the LMS Railway Station (Castle Station) yard where a large hangar was built. In 1940 the unit moved to Lincoln Road where the York Drive estate now stands.

The unit crash gangs usually included an engine fitter, airframe fitter, armourer, electrician and crane driver.

Norton Disney
OS sheet 121/SK865645. The site opened in August 1939 as No.3 Air Ammunition Park, Swinderby and was positioned immediately north west of Swinderby railway station occupying part of Eagle Wood.

In November it was renamed No.93 MU and when Swinderby airfield opened in August 1940 the ammunition site was re-designated Norton Disney.

Bombs for No.5 Group Bomber Command arrived by rail from factories around the country to be stored before being delivered to local airfields. Deliveries were often made at night and a hidden railway line was used to transport the bombs from the main line.

The intended capacity of the unit was 1250 tons of bombs. By 1942 satellite depots to store high explosives and incendiary bombs were found to be necessary. These were found at Fox Covert, Long Plantation, Sands Lane, Besthorpe and North Scarle. Country lanes at Eagle Wood and Spalford were used for additional explosive storage.

Chemical weapons were also stored at the site and as stocks mounted a separate remote site was found at Spalford, south west of Wigsley airfield. A site in Eagle Wood was opened in January 1944 to store chemical weapons. The site comprised 2 underground concrete lead lined tanks each of 250 tons capacity. Norton Disney was closed in 1957.

Owthorpe
Bombing range. Mentioned in Master crash 11th June 1944.

Rauceby
RAF Rauceby was a wartime RAF Hospital open from 1940 to 1947 situated near Spilsby. The site is now known as Greylees and has been developed for housing.

Rauceby Hospital just prior to demolition

Torksey
OS sheet 121/SK837794. Torksey was a fuel depot supplying most of Lincolnshire's aviation fuel and fuel for other airfield vehicles during WWII. Ammunition and oxygen were supplied by RAF Norton Disney, RAF Market Stainton and RAF South Witham.

Watnall
OS sheet 129/SK500460 about 6 miles north west of Nottingham on the A613.

Watnall was not an airfield but was a very important RAF station. It was a secret site and work started on the underground section in 1938 but it was not ready at outbreak of war and No.12 group HQ did not move in from nearby Hucknall until late 1940.

RAF Watnall was sited on both sides of the main road just south of Watnall Chaworth.

On the east side the Underground Operations Block was situated which was some 60 feet below ground. From this underground base there was a direct link into the main defence telephone and teleprinter network with direct lines to all operational Headquarters.

In 1941 work started on a 2nd Operations block just to the south of the main site, close to Watnall Wharf railway siding. This was known as the Filter Block which housed top secret equipment. It became operational in 1943 and through the Filter block passed all information received from all the Radar and Ground Control Interception Stations.

After the war No.12 Group HQ moved to RAF Newton in December 1946 and the Operations Block closed but the Filter Block remained in use. In early 1950 the buildings were updated by 5002 Airfield Construction Squadron and the site was used during the top secret 'ROTOR' programme throughout the 1950s. RAF Watnall closed in 1961.

Filter block entrance

Dummy and Decoy Airfields

The principle of the decoy airfield was to draw German bombers away from a genuine airfield onto a dummy site five or six miles away.

The grid references shown are National Grid References as used by the Ordnance Survey in Britain. Wartime grid references were quoted on a system known as the 'Cassini grid'.

K-sites for daytime deception
K-sites were daytime airfields equipped with dummy aircraft but were not very successful and most were closed down in 1942/43.

Q-sites for night-time deception
The night time equivalent of the 'K' site was the 'Q' site, which intended to represent the working lights of an airfield after dark. This decoy made use of electric 'runway' lighting laid out to genuine operational patterns and controlled by cable leading from a generator and switchgear housed in a bunker, and usually had a night time staff of two. The following decoys were 'Q' type:

Armthorpe – a decoy for Finningley.
OS sheet 111/SE645040.

Bassingham – a decoy for Swinderby.
OS sheet 120/SK943612.

Brant Broughton – a decoy for Swinderby.
OS sheet 120/SK905552.

Belvoir – a decoy for Bottesford.
OS sheet 120/SK805342.

Cotgrave – a decoy for Newton. OS sheet 120/SK659358.

Foston – a decoy for Bottesford. OS sheet 120/SK872408.

Kneeton – a decoy for Syerston. OS sheet 120/SK717457.

Owston Ferry – a decoy for Finningley. OS sheet 112/SE792012.

Tythby – a decoy airfield for Bottesford and Newton. OS sheet 120/SK709347.

Upton – a decoy airfield for Ossington. OS sheet 120/SK738564.

SF sites for cities and industrial locations. These sites were based on fire for deception. SF or Starfish sites as they were known were based on the idea of lighting huge fires outside cities and towns, up to eight miles away, once it was known a bombing raid would be under way. The 'Starfish' sites for Nottingham were:

Barton in Fabis (near Clifton) OS sheet 120/SK535314.

Clipston (near Cotgrave) OS sheet 120/SK643337.

Cropwell Butler – OS sheet 120/SK653364.

Lowdham – OS sheet 120/SK650455.

Royal Observer Corps

An aircraft observation system was organised during World War One around London due to the number of successful air attacks made on the south coast and London.

Before World War Two this was expanded to cover most of the country and all the groups were in place by 1938.

Observer posts were provided with a basic instrument which gave a bearing and angle to the target. By comparing readings from 2 or more posts it was possible to fix the position of the aircraft which was then passed to central control in London.

The posts were provided with a wooden hut, beds, cooking facilities and a stove. The Corps had a strength of over 3200 men and manned in excess of 1400 command posts around Britain.

The Corps were stood down from 1945-47 and resumed on a limited basis in 1948.

During 1954 it was decided that the ROC should act as the national nuclear warning and monitoring organisation and that the posts should be constructed from concrete and re-sited below ground. The Observer Corps were given the prefix 'Royal' in 1941.

Listed below are the warning posts sited in Nottinghamshire, it should be noted that some have been re-designated over the years.

The locations have been extracted from the book on the history of the Royal Observer Corps, 'Attack Warning Red', written by Derek Wood.

The key to references are: 129/SK548969, 6/P1; 129 is the Ordnance Survey sheet number, SK is the area reference, 548969 is the map reference, 6 is the group number and P1 is the post cluster reference.

Above ground post World War Two

Blyth
Opened December 1937 120/SK548969, 6/P.1. Resited to 120/SK626863 in November 1941.

Resited to 120/SK635862 in Nov 1963. Resited to 120/SK635861 in 1991.

Above: **The entrance hatch and shaft leading down to the 1960s Underground ROC Post at Burton Joyce.**

Burton Joyce/Lowdham
Opened Dec 1937 129/SK.675468, 6/V.2. Resited to 129/SK643448 in March 1954.

The site was visited in 1995 when access to the underground chamber was possible. The entrance to the chamber has subsequently been padlocked.

Clifton
Location 129/SK540336. When the site was visited in 2002 the post had been demolished.

Collingham
Opened November 1949 121/SK837628, 11/A.3.

Cotgrave
Opened January 1938 129/SK652345, 6/V.3. In January 1997 the entrance was seen to be capped with concrete but has subsequently been demolished.

Dunham-on-Trent
Opened November 1936 121/SK804747, 11/A.2. Resited to 121/SK822738 in January 1961.

East Markham
Opened February 1943 120/SK729737, 11/A.4.

East Retford
Opened July 1938 120/SK678070, 6/P.2. Resited to 120/SK704816 in March 1942.

Edwinstowe/Ollerton
Opened July 1938 120/SK648676, 6/K. Resited to 120/SK656673 Nov 1942.

Farnsfield
Opened December 1937 120/SK640577, 6/K.2. Resited to 120/SK635586, 1943; the post was demolished in 1992 and placed nearby at the side of the road is a brass plaque set on a concrete base containing the following words: '*In this field stood the Royal Observer Corps Post of Group (Coventry) 22 Post Farnsfield sited here in 1943 for reporting aircraft and as a granite post to aid friendly a/c. Built underground Sept 1961 for nuclear reporting role. Corps stood down 30-9-91 post demolished 1992. 14 loyal volunteers manned the post led by C/Obs P K J Robinson B.E.M.*

Harby
Opened March 1948 129/SK754306, 5/J.2.

Hucknall
Opened December 1937 129/SK518492, 6/V.4.

Newark
Opened January 1936 121/SK788523, 6/V.1. Resited to 121/SK75357 2nd October 1959.

Newton
Location 129/SK679421. An underground building, similar in construction to an ROC shelter, exists in the north east corner of Newton airfield but as this is not recorded in the ROC records it was probably an observation post.

Walkeringham/Wiseton
Opened July 1941 SK770929, 10/B.4. Resited to 112/SK756917, 18/H.2, November 1963.

Brass Plaque at Farnsfield

Newark ROC Post

Monuments and Memorials

Runnymede Memorial
This Memorial overlooks the River Thames on Cooper's Hill at Englefield Green between Windsor and Egham on the A308, 4 miles from Windsor.

The Memorial commemorates by name over 20,000 airmen who were lost in the Second World War during operations from bases in the United Kingdom and north and Western Europe, and who have no known graves. They served in Bomber, Fighter, Coastal, Transport, Flying Training and Maintenance Commands, and came from all parts of the Commonwealth.

Oxford (Botley) Cemetery
The Cemetery is situated adjacent to the Oxford Western bypass (A34) near the Botley Interchange (A34-A420 junction).

The cemetery was designated a Royal Air Force regional cemetery during the Second World War and was used by RAF stations in Berkshire and neighbouring counties. Practically all of the 516 Second World War burials (one of them unidentified) are in the war graves plot, which was extended from the section used during the First World War. In addition to the Commonwealth war graves, Oxford (Botley) Cemetery contains almost 70 war graves of other nationalities.

Harrogate (Stonefall) Cemetery

The Cemetery is located south east of Harrogate just off the A661 on Forest Lane. Nearly all of the 998 Second World War burials are of airmen, two thirds of them Canadian.

Annesley

OS sheet 120/SK507528 at the junction of the A608 and A611.

An engraved memorial stone was unveiled on 16th September 1998 by Group Captain R Cook Btech RAF Waddington in memory of the crew of Stirling Bomber EH988 which crashed near this site on 14th January 1945. The aircraft was flying from Winthorpe to Northern Ireland to be scrapped.

The crew were: S/L 67707 Stephen Legh Cockbain DFC RAFVR age 28 (Pilot Instructor), F/S 1587047 Edwin Charles Barton, age 21 RAFVR (Nav) buried Bristol Arno's Vale Cemetery, F/S 1874899 Terence Arthur Balls age 20 RAFVR (F/Eng) buried Woolwich Cemetery, Sgt 2204311 John Littlemore, age 19 RAFVR (W.Op) buried Southern Cemetery, Manchester, Sgt 1651299 Kenneth Harris,age 22 RAFVR (Air Gnr) buried Whitchurch Cemetery, Glamorgan.

Runnymede Memorial

Oxford (Botley) Cemetery

Harrogate (Stonefall) Cemetery

Below: **The Memorial Stone and Plaque at Annesley**

Arnold

There is a plaque mounted in the Scout hut in Calverton Road commemorating Harold Edwin Burton RAF Bomb Disposal who was a member of the 2nd Arnold St Marys Scout troop from 1932, a Rover Scout, Scribe, and Assistant Scout Master. He is also listed in a book of remembrance in St Marys Church, Arnold.

Cpl Burton enlisted into the RAF and after training was posted to the RAF Bomb Disposal Unit. He lost his life at RAF Aldergrove, Northern Ireland, together with an RAF sergeant, Arthur Boulden who was trying to save him. It was decided to re-open a shaft to establish whether some fragments were a German bomb or just a tail fin. Cpl Burton was working in the shaft when the soil collapsed around him and he disappeared into the cavity created when a bomb explodes beneath the ground but doesn't break the surface, known as a camouflet. Cpl Burton tried to climb out but was overcome by the residual fumes and carbon monoxide from the explosion of the bomb and fell back into the cavity. Sgt Boulden climbed down to attempt a rescue but he was overcome as well and could not be pulled out in time to save him.

Following these deaths a modified parachute harness was developed to be worn by men in the shaft where a camouflet is suspected.

There is a framed plaque hanging in the Robert Mellors Infants School, Arnold, commemorating all those pupils who attended the school and lost their lives during the Second World War. 3 of those lost were members of the RAF.

Sgt 1212563 Joseph Peck (W.Op/Air Gnr) was brought up at 4, Hardstaffs Yard, Arnold. He was employed by the Raleigh

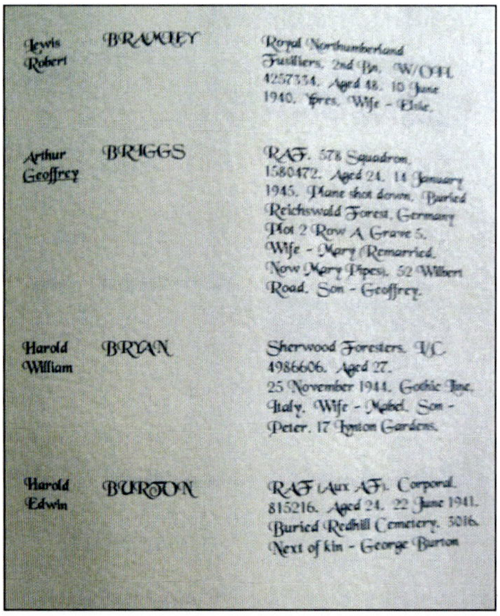

Left: **Book of Remembrance**

Above: **Robert Mellor's plaque**

Below: **2nd Arnold Marys Scout Group plaque**

Cycle Company and was married to Audrey Peck about six weeks prior to his death. He enlisted in the RAF at the outbreak of the war when aged 17 years and at the time of his death was flying with 102 Sqn. He took off with his crew from Pocklington in Halifax BB428 on 3rd July 1943 for a raid on Koln. His aircraft is believed to have crashed near Winterscheid and he is buried in Rheinberg War Cemetery.

Sgt 1198507 Keith Edward Savage was also born in Arnold in 1922 and enlisted in the RAF and was eventually posted to 58 Sqn. In April 1942 they were transferred to Coastal Command and stationed at St Eval, Cornwall. On 6th May, flying in Whitley Z9426 on patrol in the Bay of Biscay they were reported missing and never returned. He was only 20 years old and is commemorated on the Runnymede Memorial.

P/O 154513 George Williams (Air Bomber) was also born in Arnold and lived at 6 Wellington Street. On leaving school he worked at the Henry Mellish school, Bulwell, as a laboratory assistant and was also a member of the 2nd Arnold St Marys Scout Troop. He enlisted in the RAF when only 17½ years old and 8 months later was sent to Canada where he obtained his commission. He joined 2 (Observers) AFU and on 25th April 1944, age 20, was aboard Anson AX583 on a night navigational cross-country exercise flown by Sgt 1585333 Reginald William Thomas Smith when due to pilot error in not checking the flight plan and navigator error in giving a heading on the wrong course, the aircraft flew into a mountainside at 2300 feet at 0050 hrs, near Dolgarrog, North Wales. All five crew were killed.

Blyth

There is a memorial sited on Blyth village green commemorating two separate crashes. Halifax III NA581 KW-U of 425 Sqn took off from Tholthorpe on a navex training flight on 2nd August 1944 during flight it went into a dive at 4,000 feet, did not recover, and crashed bursting into flames roughly one mile south west of Blyth.

All 7 members of the crew were killed and as members of the RCAF were buried in Harrogate (Stonefall) Cemetery. The memorial plaque reads: RCAF 475 (Alouette) Squadron, Halifax NA581 RAF Tholthorpe in memory of F/L G D Stark DFC, P/O E F Pitkin, P/O J Pigeon, P/O M H Waters, P/O P P Davies, Sgt L Snider, P/O J E Code died 7th August 1944 Hodsock.

Wellington X HE818 of 18 OTU took off from Worksop on 7th March 1944 on an operational training flight and after an overshoot exercise climbed to 600 feet but was unable to maintain height and crashed out of control with smoke coming from both engines. The crash occurred at Blyth, and 4 crew members were killed. The memorial plaque reads: RAF 18 OTU RAF Worksop WellingtonHE818 in memory of P/O F R Bedford, Sgt C R P Whisk, Sgt R W Tunnicliffe, Sgt W Tindell died 7th March 1944 Blyth. Sgt C Cletheroe was injured.

Above: **Memorial to the crew of Wellington HE818**

Below: **Memorial to the crew of Halifax NA581**

Bottesford

OS sheet 130/SK807391. St Mary the Virgin Church has the tallest spire in the Vale of Belvoir and attracted WWII's last Luftwaffe raid. Some of 207 Sqn's casualties lie buried in the churchyard. A Memorial Tablet to the 138 who were killed or made POW whilst 207 Squadron served at Bottesford from 18th November 1941 to 21st November 1942 was dedicated on Sunday 17th September 1995. The unveiling was done by W/C Russell Jeffs AFC, one of 207's C/O's at Bottesford, escorted by Bill Hamilton DFC AE and W/C Goldie Goldshaw DFC, who also served there. A Book of Remembrance was also placed in the church during the service. The tablet is inscribed 'Between 18th November 1941 and 21st September 1942 No.207 Royal Air Force was based at Bottesford Aerodrome near this church of St Mary the Virgin. Flying mainly at night in Avro Manchester Bombers until March 1942, and thereafter in Avro Lancasters each with seven crewmen. They defended their country and fought for freedom. During this period 122 men of No.207 Squadron were killed, of whom 41 have no known grave. They included one of the ground staff and aircrew from Great Britain, Canada, Australia and New Zealand. 16 more did not return from operations and became Prisoners Of War until May 1945. 'Lest we Forget'.

Also a plaque was dedicated on 25th April 1993 in the renovated Bottesford Airfield Control Tower, now used as offices, commemorating the units which served there: 207 Sqn, 463 Sqn, 467 Sqn, 90 Sqn, 9th Air Force USAAF and 1668 HCU.

The plaque is inscribed 'Dedicated to the memory of the men and women of all nationalities who served with the units based on this airfield during World War Two and of those who gave their lives that freedom might prevail'.

The brass plaque placed below a eucalyptus tree is inscribed with the following words: 'This eucalyptus gunnii tree was planted by surviving comrades in 1995 to remember our allies especially the Australian and Kiwi members of 467 Squadron RAAF based at Bottesford airfield (Normanton) during World War II'.

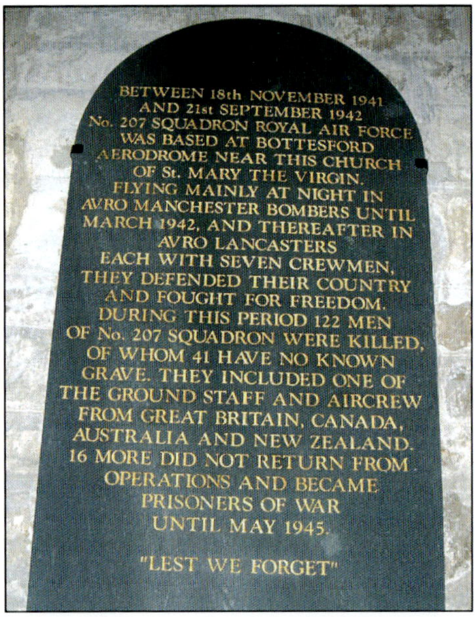

Left: **Memorial tablet**

Below left: **Book of remembrance**

Below right: **Brass plaque placed in 1995 in the churcyard**

Opposite page, top: **Memorial to the crew of Lancaster LM311**

There is a memorial located north of Bottesford and central between Long Bennington and Staunton in the Vale commemorating the crew of Lancaster LM311.

The memorial in Yorkshire stone was laid and a tree planted to commemorate the crew of Lancaster LM311 of 467 Squadron which crashed on 13th July 1943 by the family of Jack Greenwood, a member of the crew, and the 467 RAAF Squadron Association, in 1999. It is located on the edge of the field where the crash occurred.

Location OS sheet 130; 825 442. For more information on the incident refer to the diary entry for 13th July 1943.

Calverton

OS sheet 120/SK606516 off the A614.

In Watchwood Plantation, 50 metres north of the crash site is a memorial to the crew of Fairy Battle L5499 of No.300 Squadron, which crashed on 13th October 1940, owing to loss of control in fog whilst returning to base after a night raid on Boulogne. It was the Polish Air Force's first operation from Britain, and the crew were: F/O J Gebicki (Pilot), Sgt E Morawa (Observer), and Sgt Tegierski (Air Gunner). They are all buried at Southern Churchyard, West Bridgford.

The original memorial, which consisted of a tubular steel cross with a plaque welded to it bearing the crews names and the further inscription: 'Perished for our and your freedom- 300 Polish Squadron 13th October 1940'. has now been replaced by a stone monument surrounded by a chain link fence. The stone has the inscription 'In memory of the Polish Aircrew of the Fairy Battle killed 13th October 1940 F/O Jan Gebicki, Sgt Edward Morawa, Sgt Tadeusz Egierski'.

Above: **Watchwood plantation memorial 1992**

Below: **Watchwood plantation memorial 1995**

Watchwood plantation memorial in 2010

Cotgrave

OS sheet 129/SK632371. There is a plaque adjacent to the clubhouse at Cotgrave Golf Course which commemorates the crew of Wellington W5365 who died when the aircraft hit a tree on the course on 8th February 1941.

The crew were: S/L 32228 Phillip Cutliffe Lawrence RAF age 27 (Pilot), P/O 46325 Robert Atkinson age 29 (Pilot), Sgt 525889 James John Castleman Batty 26, Sgt 550950 Robert Tod Tomlinson DFM age 22, Sgt 636137 Arthur Crooks (W.Op/ Air Gnr) age 20, Sgt 650974 Edward Frederick Ted Carter (W.Op/Air Gnr), Sgt 903054 Neil Colin Jim Boyle RNZAF (Air Gnr).

Plaque next to Cotgrave Golf Club clubhouse

The two surviving crew members were Sgt William Cecil Percy Watkins who was seriously injured and Sgt Henry William James Gill who was slightly injured.

Farnsfield

OS sheet 120/SK644553. On the 6th July 1994, a memorial was unveiled to seven airmen who died when their bomber crashed outside the Nottinghamshire village of Farnsfield exactly 50 years previously. The Halifax bomber, MZ519 LK-U of 578 Squadron from RAF Burn in South Yorkshire, was returning from attacking V-1 launch sites in the Palais de Calais area of France. Suffering from battle damage, an engine caught fire and the right wing collapsed and the aircraft crashed in Farnsfield, just fifteen minutes from its Yorkshire base, killing all seven members of its crew.

Air Marshall Sir John Curtiss, who flew with 578 Squadron during the war, unveiled the memorial, which is located on the site of the crash, with a flypast by a Dakota of the Battle of Britain Memorial Flight.

The two tonne monument is made from dolomite limestone and there is a copse of trees planted, two Canadian Red Maple, and, in a curve, seven English Oaks, one for each of the crew who died.

An oak case of photos, text and pieces of the wreck are displayed in St Michaels church.

The members of the crew were: P/O Reginald Parfitt, pilot, 22 of Cardiff, F/O Brian Turnidge, Navigator, 24 of Bristol, F/S John Joseph Godin, Bomb Aimer, 22 of North Bay, Ontario, Canada, Sgt Raymond Rolph, Engineer, 23 of Rochford,Essex, Sgt Thomas Pitts, Wireless Operator/Air Gunner of Hale, Cheshire, Sgt Leonard Leatham, Air Gunner, 20 of Tipton, Staffordshire and Sgt Thomas Hill, Air Gunner, of Bilston, Staffordshire.

All are buried in their home towns with the exception of John Godin who is buried Harrogate (Stonefall) Cemetery, Yorkshire.

Two of the men, F/S John Godin and Sgt Raymond Rolph were not usually part of the crew, they were replacements for one man who was ill and for Allan Miles who was on a course. Allan Miles attended the ceremony.

A commemorative sign has also been erected on a road named after the pilot P/O Reginald Parfitt. His memory and that of his crew is now being permanently commemorated with a unique sign erected on Parfitt Drive at Farnsfield.

Memorial at Farnsfield to the crew of MZ519

Gonalston

There is a memorial at the crash site of Lancaster L7578. The aircraft took off on a practice bombing operation and dived out of control near Wood Barn, ½ mile north of Gonalston and crashed on 26th May 1944.

The memorial was originally placed 30 yards east of the crash site by the family of Sgt Middlemas and in 1996 it was restored and re-dedicated and now maintained by 1803 (Hucknall) Sqn ATC. The memorial consists of a rough hewn stone surrounded by a chain fence and engraved with the names of the crew.

The crew were: P/O George Sanderson, pilot; Sgt Bernard Broe, W.Op/Air Gnr age 22; Sgt James Middlemas, F/Eng age 19; Sgt Albert Clark, Nav. age 28; Sgt Dereck Nicholls, Air Gnr age 19; P/O Archibald Noble, Air Bomber age 28; F/S Dennis Wright, Air Gnr age 20.

Hucknall

There is a plaque mounted in a wall in West Lane, Hucknall, dedicated to LAC P780509 Edmund Rozmiarek age 25 of No.18 Operational Training Unit (18 OTU).

LAC Rozmiarek was the pilot of Battle I K9480 which took off from RAF Hucknall on 23rd September 1940 for a circuits and landings exercise and having attained a height of 500 feet the aircraft went into a right hand turn against the circuit, lost height and crashed into two houses at the corner of Ruffs Drive and Laughton Crescent, Hucknall.

All the family in the house were also killed. They were Albert Evans, age 28, his wife Alice, age 30, and their children Ronald age 8, Alice (jnr) age 6 and John age 2 who are all buried in Hucknall Urban District Cemetery.

The memorial in West Lane, Hucknall. The translated inscription reads: 'Sleep friend within your dark grave and let Poland be in your dreams' or 'may you dream of Poland'.

Kimberley

There is a plaque to the memory of Sgt 1211045 Richard Bolitho, Royal Air Force Voluntary Reserve, located adjacent to the war memorial in Main Street, Kimberley.

Sgt Bolitho was a rear gunner in the attack by Lancaster bombers of 617 Squadron on Germany's Ruhr Valley dams known as Operation Chastise on 17th May 1943, led by W/C Guy Gibson. He was a member of the crew of Lancaster ED864 AJ-B piloted by F/L W Astell DFC which took off from RAF Scampton at 2159 hrs on 16th May and was shot down when the aircraft flew through 2 lines of tracer intersecting in a criss-cross. The gunners returned fire but the aircraft crashed near Dorsten. He is buried in Reichswald Forest War Cemetery.

Richard Bolitho was born in 1920, in Portrush, Co. Antrim, Northern Ireland, the only child of William and Jane Bolitho. When Jane's father died in 1927, the family moved to England and bought a hotel on Castle Boulevard in Kimberley. When Richard was 7 or 8 years old it was decided that he should live with his aunt Emily Bolitho at 11 James Street, Kimberley, and he attended the Church Hill School.

Richard joined the RAF in 1940 and on 25th March 1943 he was posted to the newly formed and highly secretive 617 Squadron at Scampton in Lincolnshire where all the crew were hand picked from the best bomber command crews. 617 Squadron had been formed with one aim in mind, to breach the dams of the Rhur valley and disrupt Germany's arms manufacruring capability. The dams were to be destroyed using Barnes Wallis's bouncing bomb.

Langar

OS sheet 129/SK734333. During the time that Langar airfield was the home of 207 Sqn between September 1942 and October 1943, 251 aircrew lost their lives flying 149 operations over enemy territory in Lancaster bombers.

The Langar airfield memorial was originally erected by the local community and dedicated on Thursday 12th May 1994. It is located at the entrance to the airfield from the Harby Road/Langar Lane, not far from the Control Tower.

It was unveiled by Mrs Dorothy Ware and AVM David Dick, President of the Association. The inscription on the memorial reads: 'Always prepared. In memory of those who gave their lives with 207 Squadron RAF Langar. This Memorial was erected by the local community in tribute to the 251 members of 207 Squadron who gave their lives whilst serving at this airfield 21st September 1942 to 13th October 1943. Dedicated 12th May 1994'.

A Memorial Book has also been placed in St Andrew's Church, Langar.

A wooden seat situated beside the airfield memorial has also been donated. An inscription reads: 'This seat was donated by Mrs Dorothy Ware in loving memory of her husband Sergeant Thomas Skelton- age 19 years who flew from Langar airfield on the night of 13th May 1943 on a raid to Duisburg- never to return. Also to his crew, always remembered. The Roll of Honour book for 207 Squadron RAF Langar is on view in St Andrew's Church, Langar.

The memorial was re-dedicated on 8th May 2004.

Netherthorpe

OS sheet 120/SK563803. On 1st September 1993 1325 Sqn ATC unveiled a plaque at Netherthorpe airfield in memory of P/O Grosvenor Louis Edmonds. There was flypast of four Bulldog aircraft from RAF Finningley.

P/O Edmonds was the pilot of Lysander P1692 which crashed at Netherthorpe on 6th September 1940.

Newark

OS sheet 121/SK805526 on the A6065. In the cemetery, to the south of the town, is the Polish Air Force memorial.

It consists of a tall cross with Polish Air Force flying badges and the inscription, in Polish and English:

'1940-1945. To the memory of Polish airmen. I have fought a good fight, I have finished my course, I have kept the faith. (II Timothy. IV7)'.

Engraved on the base are the words: 'Za Wolnosc – For Freedom'. The cross stands within the Polish Forces Cemetery and was unveiled on 15th July 1941 by President Raczkiewicz, President of the Republic of Poland. At the foot of the cross are the graves of several Presidents of the Government in Exile, Raczkiewicz, Zaleski and Ostrowski, and General Sikorski, Commander-in-chief, Polish Armed Forces.

Immediately adjacent is the Warsaw Air Bridge Memorial depicting the badge of the RAF and those of the Royal Australian, Royal Canadian, South African and Polish Air Forces, and the Polish National Eagle.

On the front of the stone is a symbolic bridge linking the letters 'RAF' and 'AK' (Armia Krajowa, the Polish Home Army). Beneath is the inscription: 'Warsaw Air Bridge Memorial. In tribute to 250 airmen of Britain, the Commonwealth and Poland who sacrificed their young lives in desperate attempts to fly from distant RAF bases in Italy with essential supplies for the front line City of Warsaw during the 1944 uprising'.

The memorial was dedicated on 3rd October 1989.

In 1992 a plaque was unveiled in memory of those who died in the Ransome and Marles' raid of 7th March 1941. The graves of some of those killed can be seen to the rear of the Polish War Cemetery on Elm Avenue, Newark.

A memorial plaque was unveiled by the mayor, Mr Harry Furness, on the outside of the National Westminster Bank, Stodman Street, in the centre of Newark on 4th June 1993 as a tribute to all those airman who served on the airfields surrounding Newark and also in remembrance of the airmen who died at night over Europe.

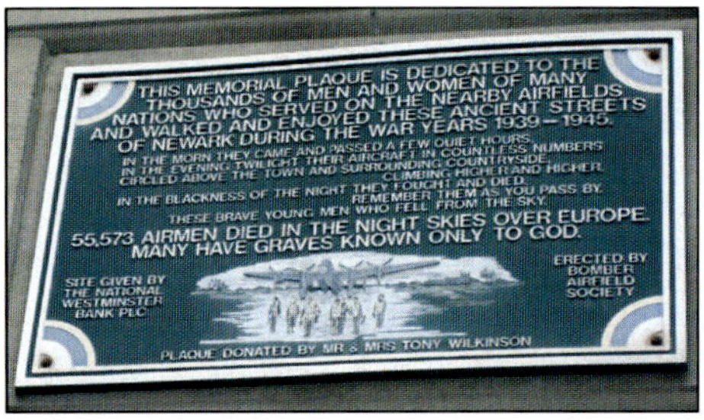

The plaque carries the following words: 'This memorial plaque is dedicated to the thousands of men and women of many nations who served on the nearby airfields and walked and enjoyed these ancient streets of Newark during the War years 1939-1945. In the morn they came and passed a few quiet hours in the evening twilight their aircraft in countless numbers circled above the town and surrounding countryside climbing higher and higher in the blackness of the night they fought and died these brave young men who fell from the sky 55,573 airmen died in the night skies over Europe may have graves known only to God site given by the National Westminster Bank Plc erected by bomber airfield society plaque donated by Mr and Mrs Tony Wilkinson.'

Located in St Mary Magdalene church is a wooden panel with the following inscription: 'The 21st Independent Parachute Company left Newark in September 1944 to lead the 1st Airborne Division to Arnhem. Those who survived the battle attended a service in this church and caused this panel to be inscribed in memory of their comrades who did not return'. There is an Airborne Crest above the text.

Newark Air Museum

OS sheet 121/SK830560. For the year 2000 the museum decided to erect a memorial in the grounds of the museum dedicated to honour Bomber Command and those who served at 1661 HCU RAF Winthorpe. The stone memorial is inscribed: 'RAF WINTHORPE 1661 HCU. To commemorate those of Bomber Command those who made the supreme sacrifice and all who served here. PER ARDUA AD ASTRA'.

One of the exhibits at the museum is the propeller boss and reduction gear from Stirling EF186 which had crashed on 4th December 1944 killing all 9 crew members. The propeller boss was the property of the Stirling Project who had excavated the site much earlier who gave permission to mount the boss on top of the memorial. 9 trees were planted around the memorial each one dedicated to one of the crew. The crew were: F/O G R Campbell RAAF, F/S D J Standring, Sgt L G Diggins, Sgt W L Howarth, Sgt E W Heaton, Sgt A L Terry, Sgt A Winn, Sgt B Stowe, Sgt K C Glinz RCAF.

One other tree was planted around the memorial dedicated to all Polish Air Force personnel who served at RAF Winthorpe.

There is also a plaque in memory of Sgt Kevin Cyril Glinz (RCAF) who died on 4th December 1944. He is buried in Harrogate (Stonefall) Cemetery.

Norton Disney
OS sheet 120/SK890590. There is a memorial plaque on the south side of the Church of St Peter commemorating 300 Sqn and 301 Sqn's operations from RAF Swinderby.

Next to it is a second plaque in memory of F/O Michel Liniewski of 301 Sqn.

F/O Liniewski took off from Hemswell in Wellington T6265 for a raid on Hamburg and was shot down by a night fighter and crashed near at Schans near Winschoten, Holland. 3 other crew members were killed an all are buried in Hannover War Cemetery. 2 crew members were made POWs.

Nottingham
OS sheet 129/SK580350. A commemorative plaque was unveiled at the Co-Operative Wholesale Society's bakery in Meadow lane in May 1966 in memory of 48 bakery employees who died during an air raid on 9th May 1941.

The plaque has since been re-located to Nottingham Crematorium

Ossington
OS sheet 120/SK759652. There is a tablet mounted on the south side of the nave, close to the Altar of Holy Rood Church, Ossington in memory of all who served in the RAF at Ossington airfield.

The inscription reads: 'This tablet was presented by the officers, senior NCO's, airmen and airwomen of the RAF and WAAF as a token of gratitude for the hospitality of this Church and to commemorate the men and women who worshipped here during the period of their service at RAF Ossington 1941-46.'

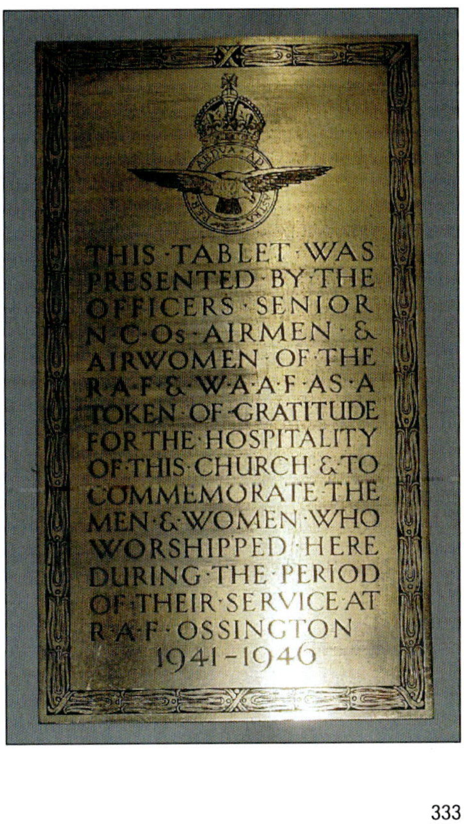

Screveton

OS sheet 129/732438.A seven-tonne granite memorial was erected on Remembrance Sunday 2005 in memory of the deaths of 11 airmen killed when two planes collided over the village on 14th April 1944. The memorial was unveiled in Flintham Road, between the two crash sites.

The mid-air collision between an Avro Lancaster and Airspeed Oxford could have killed many people on the ground but for the brave actions of the pilots. Witnesses watched as the pilots manoeuvred the falling planes away from the village and into nearby fields.

The Lancaster, on a training flight from RAF Syerston was carrying nine airmen, and the Oxford, on a training flight from RAF Wymeswold was carrying two pilots. The aircraft crashed into fields just outside Screveton. The Lancaster landed in what was known as Clarke's field, off Flintham Lane.

The crew were: F/O D W McRuer, AC1 S Stoke, Sgt G R Aspinall, F/O P W R Holes, Sgt F W Edward, Sgt V C W Gouldstone, Sgt H E Herbert, P/O P W Laidler and F/O H H Richardson DFM.

The Oxford came down off Lodge Lane. On board wereF/O B H Dennis and F/L J A Hawkins. There is also a brass plaque commemorating the same airmen located in St Wilfrid's Church.

Stanton-by-Dale

OS sheet 129/SK464381. There is a plaque on a war memorial in St Michaels Churchyard in memory of seven aircrew who were killed when Stirling Bomber LJ630 crashed on 31st August 1944.

The crew were: P/O B G Wilkinson, pilot age 28, Sgt R G Alexander, nav. age 27, F/S P D Arthur, W/Op age 22, F/S W E J Cox F/Eng age 21, Sgt A Hughes Air bomber age 20, Sgt J Lambell F/Eng age 36 and Sgt T H Westhead Rear Gnr age 25. There is also a street lamp mounted on the walkway to the church in memorial to the flight engineer, Bill Cox.

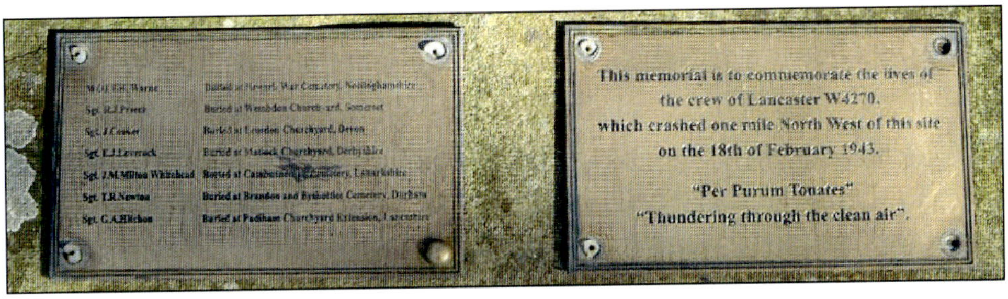

Staunton

There is a memorial (pictured above) to the crew of Lancaster W4270 of 61 Sqn from Syerston which crashed at Staunton whilst on a training flight on 18th February 1943 during a circuit of Bottesford airfield. All 7 members of the crew were killed.

W/O R/102085 Thomas Herbert Warne age 23 RCAF pilot is buried in Newark-upon-Trent Cemetery, Sgt 576765 George Arthur Hitchon age 19 F/Eng buried in Padiham Churchyard, Sgt 1174086 Robert John Preece age 22 RAFVR buried Wembdon Churchyard, Sgt 1119116 Thomas Raine Newton age 21 W.Op/Air Gnr RAFVR buried Brandon and Byshottles Cemetery, Sgt 975551 James Milton Whitehead age 22 W.Op./Air Gnr RAFVR, age 22 buried Cambusnethan Cemetery, Sgt 950159 Edward John Loverock age 21 RAFVR buried Matlock Churchyard, Sgt 1276786 John Coaker age 22 RAFVR buried Leusdeon Churchyard Devon.

The Farndon Archaeological Research Institute have researched the crash and crash site and many pieces of debris was found.

The memorial with a Lancaster propeller blade stands near St Mary's church.

Syerston

OS sheet 129/SK737479. On the north perimeter of the airfield at the side of the road, adjacent to Syerston Hall, there is a small plaque placed in memory of Cpl Audrey Mee WAAF.

The plaque is inscribed 'In loving memory of Cpl Audrey Mee WAAF later Mrs Donald Henderson who served at SHQ RAF Scampton 1943-1944 RAF Conningsby 1944, RAF Syerston 1944-1947'.

Tythby

OS sheet 129/698369. There is a wooden plaque above the door of Holy Trinity Church commemorating F/O Clyde Euan Miles Graham MID. He was the son of Major-General Sir Miles William Arthur Peel Graham, KBE, CB, MC. and of Lady Evelyn Cathryn Graham (nee King) who lived at Wiverton Hall, Bingham. He was the Navigator in the crew of Lancaster NF923 KC-M of the famous 617 Squadron which took off at 1918 hrs from Woodhall Spa for an attack on Ladbergen to breach the Dortmund-Ems Kanal. For some reason they did not release their Tallboy bomb and on their return they were intercepted by a night-fighter who shot out 3 of the Lancaster's engines. The aircraft was abandoned over Holland and of the 7 man crew one was injured, two evaded capture, two were made POWs and two were killed of which one was F/O Graham. He was interred at the Arnhem Oosterbeek War Cemetery.

Tollerton

OS sheet 129/616361. The Tollertom memorial consists of a hexagonal pillbox constructed of red bricks. Nine plaques are positioned on the six walls and commemorate aspects of the airfield's history.

One plaque commemoraes the crash of Wellington W5365, on 8th February 1941, into a tree on what is now Cotgrave Golf Course, taking the lives of 7 crew members.

S/L 32228 Phillip Cutliffe Lawrence RAF age 27 pilot and P/O 46325 Robert Atkinson age 29 pilot both cremated at Nottingham Crematorium; Sgt 525889 James John Castleman Batty 26 buried Garston (St Michael) Churchyard Lancashire, Sgt 550950 Robert Tod Tomlinson DFM age 22 buried Mount Jerome Cemetery County Dublin, Sgt 636137 Arthur Crooks W.Op/ Air Gnr age 20 buried Barnstable Cemetery, Sgt 650974 Edward Frederick Ted Carter, W.Op/Air Gnr RAF age 20 and Sgt 903054 Neil Colin Jim Boyle,Air Gnr, RNZAF age 25 both buried in Cotgrave (All Saints) Churchyard Extension. The two surviving crew were Sgt William Cecil Percy Watkins (seriously injured) and Sgt Henry William James Gill (slightly injured).

Three plaques read: '12 Squadron ROYAL AIR FORCE', '44 SQUADRON ROYAL AIR FORCE' and '50 SQUADRON ROYAL AIR FORCE'. Two further plaques relate to the station's former status as 'SATELLITE OF RAF SYERSTON' and 'SATELLITE RAF NEWTON'. In 1991, the 50th anniversary of the Air Training Corps, a plaque was dedicated by 2425 Squadron, ATC, to all who served at Tollerton during World War Two. Also remembered are No.27 E & RFTS Royal Air Force Volunteer Reserves 1937-1945. A roll of honour lists all the crew who were killed and injured in the crash of Wellington W5365 (see above) 8th February 1941.